# CICS Debugging; Dump Reading; Problem Determination

# CICS Debugging; Dump Reading; Problem Determination

Phyllis Donofrio

**Intertext Publications**
**McGraw-Hill Book Company**

New York  St. Louis  San Francisco  Auckland  Bogotá
Hamburg  London  Madrid  Mexico  Milan  Montreal
New Delhi  Panama  Paris  São Paulo
Singapore  Sidney  Tokyo  Toronto

Library of Congress Catalog Card Number 89-83760

10 9 8 7 6 5 4 3 2 1

ISBN 0-07-017606-X

Intertext Publications/Multiscience Press, Inc.
One Lincoln Plaza
New York, NY 10023

McGraw-Hill Book Company
1221 Avenue of the Americas
New York, NY 10020

*This book is dedicated to my parents,*
*David and Marion Donofrio, to whom I owe everything.*

# Contents

# Acknowledgements

If someone told be ten years ago that I would be writing a book on CICS debugging, I would have thought them mad. I have been fortunate, however, to have had people who believed in me, and encouraged me through my career. The first was John Jackson, who got me into my first system programming position. Thank you for taking that chance on me. Mike Geiger and Jon Bebeau took me in and threw me to the wolves. These two brilliant system programmers taught me so much, and pushed me when I was ready to give up on many occasions.

I am indebted to Al Stephan, Senior Vice President of Customer Information Services at Dun & Bradstreet Plan Services. He encourages technical excellence, mainly because he's so technical himself, and constantly tells me to "go for it." Al, along with Cliff Bateman, Senior Vice President at Dun & Bradstreet Plan Services, graciously gave permission to use the installation's computer facilities to produce various dumps and listings. The application programmers at Plan Services gave me a great deal of material to work with; their systems are especially sophisticated and push CICS to its limits. Steve Sutherland helped me construct most of the examples in Chapter Four. Plan Services has a very special IBM account team, Ellen Shannahan and Bob Thomas. Our account poses special CICS challenges; they deserve combat pay for their accomplishments. A special debt is due to Jack Murray, President and COO of Dun & Bradstreet Plan Services. His commitment to technology has kept the installation on the leading edge, and provided an environment that reflects the most current architecture available in the industry.

This book would not have happened without the help and encouragement of my friends in the Share CICS Project, especially Nils Ekberg and Barry Brooks. They watched me stumble during my first presentation, and keep encouraging me to be "fearless."

The entire IBM group that supports CICS needs to be recognized, for they are truly talented people. In Dallas (actually Irving), Bob Yelavich and the entire staff of CICS folks have helped me throughout my CICS career. The CICS service staff, Level 2, in Raleigh help so much, and get so little credit. They've saved me from many jams. A special thanks to Lee Thompson for being a special friend and giving me a special gift. A great deal of credit for this book needs to go to Jim Grauel, "IBM CICS Wizard Extraordinaire." He knows more about CICS problem determination than I would ever be able to learn in a lifetime. He's taught me a great deal, especially during our endless phone conversations in the CICS/VS 1.7 install. I value his wisdom immensely.

A special thanks to the CICS development, test and change team staff in Hursley. They provide the challenges and opportunities that make system programmer's lives worthwhile. Tom Baldwin and Andy Krasun deserve special thanks for being so supportive, and listening to all the war stories from us in the trenches.

A special debt is due to my editor and friend, Jay Ranade. His writing experience and advice helped me in every phase of production. These and many more people helped to build the experiences that produced this book. I value their friendship and support and know that part of their thoughts are in many of the chapters. In closing, my most sincere thanks to Jon Bebeau for reading and editing many of the chapters. He started my career in CICS support, and continues to teach and encourage. His depth of technical knowledge is incredible, and his contribution to this book is significant.

# Preface

CICS is THE transaction processor of the 1980s and will continue to be so into the 1990s. The number of licenses continues to grow, and businesses are finding new and novel ways to gain competitive edge with CICS applications. The product continues to evolve, provide new functions and take advantage of new technologies. For those of us who have seen this evolution, the CICS of the 1990s will look nothing like the early releases of the product. Application and system programmers who possess skills in CICS will become more valuable to their installations, especially since the applications provide the financial lifeline of the organization. Educational institutions that do not provide instruction in CICS concepts, and command level COBOL will be doing a disservice to their students. Of course, once a programmer can develop an application in CICS, the first hurdle is to diagnose the problem when it fails. One of the most intimidating situations to anyone is a program abend, and the corresponding dump. Many experienced application and system programmers still hesitate to analyze hexadecimal output, and attempt to locate the problem. IBM may change some of that in the next version, but for now the only solution is to develop sound techniques for CICS problem determination with existing formatted and unformatted dumps.

## AUDIENCE FOR THE BOOK

This book can be used by both application and system programmers responsible for development and support of CICS systems. Even DBAs (data base administrators) may find sections relevant, since installations using DB2 with the CICS attach facility will need to investigate some of their failures in the CICS system. Although the materials are divided into two sections, applications and systems, each group of technicians may find both sections of interest. I have found that many CICS application programmers become very successful system programmers. If you feel this career path is of interest, the section covering system programming issues and failures may help prepare you for the environment. Many CICS system programmers are called upon to assist the application staff in diagnosing transaction failures. The application section may provide techniques that can be used in various situations.

I have attempted to structure this book so that even inexperienced CICS programmers can use it. If you have never looked at a dump before, the chapters on dump content and format should be very informative. I have included discussion of several facilities, or "tools" that are available in the CICS or MVS products. Some programmers were previously unaware of these facilities, even if they have been using CICS for years. Hopefully, even experienced CICS programmers may find this book helpful, and will see new techniques, or alternative methods that may not have been thought of before. Of course, in no way can these materials cover all issues, and all types of failures. Hopefully the numerous abends, and examples will serve as guidelines for any additional failures that you experience. I am always interested in other techniques that can be used to solve similar problems. There is certainly no ONE way to analyze an abend. If you would like to comment on these techniques, or share some that you have developed yourself, please let me know. You can always find me at Share, with the CICS Project. If you would like additional information, or want to comment on CICS problem determination, you can contact me at: P. O. Box 1521, Lutz, FL 33549.

## OPERATING SYSTEM ENVIRONMENT

This book has been written primarily for CICS/VS 1.7 and CICS/MVS 2.1, and includes examples from both versions. Of course, many of the concepts are similar to situations that could be experienced in previous releases of CICS, or even CICS/VM and CICS/VSE. I have also attempted to include issues that could be experienced in an MVS/ESA environment. These issues are primarily system-related, and will change the way technical support personnel process unformatted dumps.

## PREVIOUS KNOWLEDGE OF CICS

Although there are really no prerequisites, I have assumed that the reader understands the concepts of COBOL, especially CICS command level COBOL. Knowledge of, and the use of, the CICS APRM (Application Programmer's Reference Manual) is a must, since the basics of CICS COBOL are covered there. Knowledge of CICS concepts and facilities would be helpful, but not necessary. Once you have diagnosed several CICS abends, CICS facilities become much clearer. I have assumed no previous dump reading skills, and tried to provide a simple, step-by-step approach. The multiple examples, with highlighted references of each noted item relevant to the dump, should lead you through the process of analyzing the problem.

## BENEFITS TO THE PROGRAMMER, AND THE INSTALLATION

I have found that few installations have any procedures in place to assist application or system programmers in problem determination methodologies. Any failures at the installation are dealt with as they arise, and this contributes to additional down time and outages. Use of specific techniques can solve problems more quickly, and save thousands of dollars in outages. Availability and reliability will improve, and service levels can be met on a more regular basis.

## BOOK CONTENT

Part One discusses basic concepts and methodologies of problem determination and lays the foundation for the rest of the book. It includes discussion of tools available in both CICS and MVS to assist in developing a basic technique. It covers formatted transaction dumps at great length, including most important components within typical dumps.

Part Two is designed for applications programmers, and explains many issues that programmers should be aware of when developing applications in CICS. An entire chapter is dedicated to ASRA abends, the most common failure in CICS programs. Typical file abends, and terminal abends are included since they are also important to CICS processing. Interactive tools for debugging are discussed, including two non-IBM products that may be considered in addition to EDF.

Part Three is designed for system programmers and, like Part Two, begins with issues that should be considered when supporting CICS systems. Many current topics are covered, including terminal autoinstall, service strategies, and the new dump formatting routine, DFHPDX. In addition to typical system abends, extensive coverage is given to storage violations. These seem to be the most difficult failures for many technicians to diagnose. An entire chapter is dedicated to new procedures for dump processing, including the print dump exit and IPCS.

## SUMMARY

After finishing this book, you will be a problem determination wizard, and the envy of your peers. Problems that had previously frustrated you will now become much simpler to solve, and the intimidating subject of dump analysis will become a second language. You will understand the contents of CICS trace entries, the sections of formatted dumps that produce answers to failures, and techniques that you can take into most CICS abends to resolve the problem. After completing the materials in this book, I believe that you will be able to resolve most of the CICS failures that occur in your installation, and even take necessary steps to avoid the problem before it happens.

One word about CICS futures. IBM's Statement of Direction for CICS was significant in many ways, especially in the function that will cease to be supported. Unstated, however, were the underlying changes that we will see in the CICS product. These changes may substantially alter the way that problem determination will be done in CICS. If the code base changes, customers' external view of the product will change. I think problem determination will evolve significantly in future offerings of CICS, and the view of the internals (formatted dumps) will not remain as we know it today. The techniques, however, and the understanding of the facilities will continue to be important skills. Look at the internals now, and understand how the product functions. It will continue to enhance your ability to analyze problems in all future releases.

# Problem Determination Concepts and Methodologies

# What is Problem Determination?

For many programmers, problem determination poses the greatest challenge they ever face. Many classify problem determination along with other favorite activities, such as paying taxes or being audited. Most of the time, however, we dislike analyzing problems because it cuts into our "creative" projects of developing new programs and systems. Now granted, poring over hexadecimal dumps of our programs may not be on the top of our list of things that we enjoy. It can be, however, not only a very keen mental challenge, but also a fantastic learning experience. When faced with a difficult problem to solve, many of us dig in our heels and push ourselves harder than we would otherwise to find the solution. When we dig deep into our own abilities and knowledge, start to ask questions and research the possibilities, we begin to truly learn. Most true understanding of customer information control systems (CICS) comes from struggling with problems, diagnosing failures (IBM's and ours), and finally realizing what was **REALLY** happening in the code. We can write programs, install systems, read manuals. Until we have to diagnose problems and **FIX** them, we are only spectators, not participants in the process of supporting CICS systems.

## 1.1  CICS-UNIQUE PROBLEMS

Many problems arise in CICS that are unique to a programming environment. Many programmers spend a great deal of their career in a batch environment, designing systems, writing programs, and otherwise developing important skills. As companies move toward more interactive environments, with transaction processors such as CICS driving their business, they move resources, including people, into CICS groups. Programmers, therefore, take skills learned from previous projects into this new environment. Some skills are transferable. COBOL, for instance, is COBOL. High-level languages have national standards, and rules of syntax apply across environments.

But also consider some major differences. Batch programs read input records. Some are still 80-byte records, a holdover from the old punched card input. The input is now recorded on magnetic media, tape or disk, and is usually fixed, stable, standard. Consider a CICS program and the source of input that it usually accommodates. CICS input normally comes from a terminal keyboard, dynamically keyed by a terminal operator. The operator is prompted by fields, or constants, on the screen and responds by entering some, or all, of the information requested. The input is entered "on the fly," can be whatever the operator thinks is appropriate, and many times is invalid or incomplete. The programmer, therefore, must edit the input, attempt to validate possible alternatives, and only accept the input when correct and complete. A significant difference from a fixed length record previously recorded on magnetic media!

Consider some other CICS-unique problems with output. Batch programs are typically printing reports, or writing output to magnetic media, or both. Once the format of the output file and the report is designed and accepted, the programmer codes the appropriate COBOL statements. Granted, these can be very sophisticated reports and not a simple task. The CICS programmer writes back to the terminal screen, and may display additional information on the original screen, display a different screen, or **branch to a different application altogether.** Since **all output in a transaction processor is interactive and is displayed on a terminal,** additional problems arise. Batch reports go to printers, 132-position devices. CRT (cathode-ray tube) devices are quickly becoming very sophisticated. Only a few years ago, a CRT was a "dumb terminal." They were 3270-type devices, 80 columns with 24 rows. Many CICS devices are now "intelligent workstations," possibly a personal computer (PC) or a Personal System/2 (PS/2). Even if they are only a terminal, the screen size may be any number of alternatives. The CICS programmer, therefore, must accommodate all possible devices in the installation. What size is the screen? Does it support extended data streams: highlighting, underlining, reverse-video? In addition, interactive processing is enhanced by the networking possibilities of modern technology. Is the terminal operator at the local site? Will the operator enter data at the local site and want to have it transmitted to another location in another city, another state, or even another country?

These are just a few of the issues that CICS programmers have to face daily. As new technologies are announced, CICS programmers are challenged to take advantage of these new technologies. CICS-unique programming problems will continue to require increased skills in problem determination and diagnosis.

## 1.2   TOOLS AVAILABLE FOR PROBLEM DETERMINATION

The process of problem determination can be a very complicated one, and may require utilization of various tools. Some of these tools are readily available, and you may already be using them. Some of them may be available, and you are not even aware that they exist. IBM provides many tools, such as monitors, CICS transactions, and facilities called "Service Aids." Some are provided free of charge with the product. Some must be purchased or leased as additional products. Many of these are documented, some are not, or are difficult to locate. If you are serious about analyzing the problem, you may need to use any and all resources available. Locating and familiarizing yourself with these tools can make a big difference in the time spent, and the frustration experienced during the process. Some resources available are:

CICS Service Aids
MVS Service Aids
CICS Supplied Transactions
CICS Monitors (IBM and non-IBM)
Non-IBM Products

### 1.2.1   CICS Service Aids

Many CICS services are operational during normal execution of a CICS region. Some have to be invoked, or turned on. All are part of the product and are, therefore, provided with the CICS license. Customers should use all of them during analysis, since each contains valuable information pertaining to different CICS functions. Familiarity with CICS service aids prior to a failure can also be important, since information concerning the normal messages would be relevant before determining which are caused by the problem. Several CICS service aids to become familiar with are:

CICS trace entries or AUX trace
Transaction dumps
CICS initialization messages
CSMT or CSSL log
CICS shutdown statistics

**CICS Auxiliary Trace.** CICS trace facilities can be turned on and off dynamically, but are normally set in the system initialization table (SIT). This table is used not only to turn trace on, but to specify how many entries to place in the table for region execution. These trace entries are recorded and can be found in all formatted CICS dumps, both transaction and system types. The trace shows all activity during execution of a transaction. To track the logical progression of the program through various situations, simply request a trace and then view specific instructions. The auxiliary trace function of CICS can turn this external trace on, trap a specific interval of CICS activity, and then report the trace entries via a batch program. This can be valuable in analyzing a transaction that is not abending, therefore not producing a dump. An auxiliary trace is produced via the following steps:

1. Add a DFHAUXT DD statement to the CICS startup, for example:

   ```
   //DFHAUXT DD DSN=CICS.AUXTRACE,DISP=SHR
   ```

   where the dataset CICS.AUXTRACE has been previously allocated

2. Start auxiliary trace with the master terminal CEMT command:

   ```
   CEMT SET AUXTRACE OPEN ON
   ```

3. Perform the CICS transaction or function to trace

| Action | Message |
|---|---|
| Acquire address space storage | CICS STARTUP IN PROGRESS |
| SITxx loaded with SYSIN overrides | |
| Build CICS nucleus from macro tables | LOADING CICS NUCLEUS |
| Build trace table | |
| Establish type of startup | |
| Build user exit control blocks and table | |
| Open transient dataset | DFHINTRA BEING OPENED |
| Warm/cold start FCT | |
| Build LSR pools | |
| GRPLIST parameter processed | INSTALLING GROUP LIST xxx |
| Build PPT and PCT | |
| Allocate storage for programs | PROCESSING RESIDENT PROGRAMS |
| Initiate task control | |
| Attach CICS tasks | |
| Open journal datasets | OPENING JOURNAL FILES |
| Execute PLT programs | |
| Open files specified or mark enabled | |
| | DFH1500 - CICSPROD : CONTROL IS BEING GIVEN TO CICS |

Figure 1-1    CICS initialization sequence example.

4. Quiesce the auxiliary trace with the CEMT command:

```
CEMT SET AUXTRACE CLOSE OFF
```

5. Process the trace records with the CICS trace utility:

```
//TRACE EXEC PGM=DFHTUP
//STEPLIB DD DSN=CICS.LOADLIB,DISP=SHR
parms
```

The complete documentation on using the trace utility would be found in the CICS Installation and Operation Guide in CICS 1.7 or CICS Operations Guide in 2.1.

**CICS Transaction Dumps.** Output from a transaction failure is written to a dump dataset, identified to the CICS region through DFHDMPx dataset DDs in the startup job control language (JCL). There can be two of these datasets, as noted by the "A" or "B" suffix. To locate a specific dump, the dump dataset currently being utilized must be processed by the batch utility. Once processed, locate the failure within the listing that pertains to your particular transaction. A complete chapter has been allocated to formatted dump processing. This process is a function of normal CICS execution, and is definitely a service that will be utilized in problem determination.

**CICS Initialization Messages.** It is amazing that so many CICS application and system programmers do not view the CICS startup as a valuable tool in analyzing problems. Many do not even review the messages on a regular basis, and therefore cannot tell whether a message is normal or related to a problem. The CICS developers have created and documented CICS initialization. In doing so, they have given us information pertaining to initialization sequence. By viewing these messages and being aware of proper initialization sequence, problems can be detected that appear during a startup of a region. Although many programmers feel that startup is a system, not an application function, there are a number of things that can happen to delay or abort CICS initialization. Figure 1-1 is an abbreviated list of CICS initialization sequences, and the messages generated. A complete sequence of events is documented in CICS Problem Determination Guide.

Note that CICS provides messages throughout initialization, and identifies the place within sequence of its status. Locating the last message during initialization of a failed startup helps determine at which stage CICS successfully completed before the failure. Many times, trace has not activated yet, or contains so little information that the startup messages may be one of the few sources available. Note also that the Program List Table, DFHPLTPI, is executed in a specific sequence within initialization. Any problems with PLT programs will cause initialization to fail. These could very well be application programs executed during PLT processing. An abend message is produced, initialization terminates, and the last message is usually "Opening Journal Files." This can sometimes be extremely frustrating and difficult to diagnose. A good rule is to monitor startup from time to time, and get to know which normal messages appear. In this way, different messages can be recognized and identified as potential problems.

**CICS CSMT or CSSL Log.** During a normal day, CICS writes a great deal of information to an output destination. These entries are printed at termination, along with the shutdown statistics. They can also be viewed at any time while the region is up. Most installations have products such as the Spool Display and Search Facility (SDSF), or editors that can "attach" an address space's log file. In this log are many entries, some merely sign-on and sign-off messages. Other entries may be very valuable and log a failure of a transaction to perform some important function. With CICS 1.7 and later, autoinstall of terminals became widely used. This facility gave installations the ability to dynamically accept VTAM terminals into their CICS regions, and the TCT macro table generation became unnecessary. Most of the functions of autoinstall are routed to CSSL, and people began to scan this log whenever terminal problems were reported. Dynamic allocation of files also became standard in CICS 1.7. Files may not open, as a result of allocation problems. These failures and the corresponding VSAM return codes are written to CSMT. The output becomes a very important resource in resolving many problems. Application programmers also are beginning to use the CICS log to record information for problem determination. With the inability to see, many times, what is happening in a remote system, or a remote terminal, the log becomes an excellent place to send alerts, or warnings. A programmer has the ability to handle conditions, as will be covered in a later chapter. If a condition arises that can be recovered from, or perhaps not, an alert can be sent to the log to record that condition. The programmer can then monitor the output to detect the frequency of these conditions and perhaps take some action. Figure 1-2 shows a portion of a typical output, and the potential entries that might be found. As mentioned, terminal autoinstall messages are written to this destination if specified in the Destination Control Table (DCT). Entries appear such as the install items in Figure 1-2 (1). In this example, terminal C102 is requesting to be installed, followed by message DFH5935I. This second message contains the VTAM netname, model name chosen to build the proper terminal control

blocks, and result of the request, "SUCCESSFUL." If the installation was not successful, this message would contain additional information to assist in determining what it will not autoinstall. If the dynamic allocation feature of file control is used, available starting in release 1.7, messages appear (2) for file allocation. Remember, in CICS 1.7 file data definitions (DDs) may be omitted in the CICS startup JCL, and specified in the File Control Table (FCT) instead. When the request is made to open, therefore, allocate the file to this CICS region, a message appears in the CICS log. This example indicates the file or DD name, plus the operating system (fully qualified) dataset name that was allocated. If, for some reason, this allocation failed, the message would indicate the failure and a reason code associated with the failure. This procedure will be fully described later in the chapter dealing with application problems in file control, Chapter 5. Several other messages from this CICS output destination will be described later, in chapters dealing with the specific problem that caused the message. At this point, be aware of the log, and the volume of messages that can be found within it.

**CICS Shutdown Statistics.** CICS reports many conditions at shutdown, and provides a great deal of information compiled during the execution of the region. Many programmers never look at the shutdown statistics, and have no idea what normal or typical activity their regions have experienced. Many times the shutdown statistics can warn of resources that are becoming dangerously close to running out. Of course, they can be reported, or dumped, at any time. The transaction CSTT, can be used to write the statistics dynamically to the CICS log. These statistics, then, can be reviewed and analyzed anytime during problem determination. What are some potential entries in the shutdown statistics that could be of value? Figure 1-3 contains several entries that could be found in a typical shutdown report. A complete listing would be extensive; a small section is included at this time for potential importance.

Task control statistics (1) are primarily for monitoring the activity in the region. Storage statistics (2), however, reflect acquisition and releases of storage requests, and also reflect any storage violations that occurred (3). Storage violations can be recovered by CICS recovery, and therefore could go unnoticed. A review of this item can relate potential problems that did not yet cause a failure. Another area in the shutdown related to problem analysis is the dump statistics. This is depicted in Figure 1-4 (1). Of course, this number should be zero, but that is not always possible. By monitoring this number on a daily basis, failures that CICS has detected

```
DFH3464I CA21 CSSF  5:53:58 NODE CA21 RELEASED BY MT OPERATOR
DFH3437I CA21 CSSF  5:53:58 NODE CA21 ACTION TAKEN : CLSDST
DFH3462I CA21 CSNE  5:53:59 NODE CA21 SESSION TERMINATED
05/09/88  00554005 DELETE TERMINAL(CA21);
DFH5966I DELETE FOR TERMINAL: CA21, SUCCESSFUL
05/09/88  00554019 INSTALL TERMINAL(C102);           ①
DFH5935I INSTALL FOR TERMINAL: C102, NETNAME: PSI1C102, MODEL_NAME: PSI1    , SUCCESSFUL
DFH3461I C102 CSNE  5:54:02 NODE PSI1C102 SESSION STARTED
05/09/88  00554032 INSTALL TERMINAL(CA21);
DFH5935I INSTALL FOR TERMINAL: CA21, NETNAME: CA21    , MODEL_NAME: PSI1    , SUCCESSFUL
DFH3461I CA21 CSNE  5:54:03 NODE CA21 SESSION STARTED
DFH0984I  05/09/88   05:54:12    FILE TURBDATA ALLOCATED TO 'PSIPD.TB000000.TURBO.FILE'
DFH0984I  05/09/88   05:54:20    FILE NAXALTN  ALLOCATED TO 'PSIOL.NA100000.XREF.ALTN.PATH'
DFH0984I  05/09/88   05:54:21    FILE NAFILE   ALLOCATED TO 'PSIOL.NA100000.NAME.ADDR.MASTER'
05/09/88  00621195 INSTALL TERMINAL(CJ10);
DFH5935I INSTALL FOR TERMINAL: CJ10, NETNAME: PSI1CJ10, MODEL_NAME: PSI1    , SUCCESSFUL
DFH3461I CJ10 CSNE  6:21:19 NODE PSI1CJ10 SESSION STARTED
05/09/88  00622371 INSTALL TERMINAL(C901);
DFH5935I INSTALL FOR TERMINAL: C901, NETNAME: PSI1C901, MODEL_NAME: PSI1    , SUCCESSFUL
DFH3461I C901 CSNE  6:22:37 NODE PSI1C901 SESSION STARTED
DFH0984I  05/09/88   06:22:54    FILE LRMSTR   ALLOCATED TO 'PSIOL.LR000000.LETTER.MASTER'
05/09/88  00624450 INSTALL TERMINAL(C903);
DFH5935I INSTALL FOR TERMINAL: C903, NETNAME: C903    , MODEL_NAME: PSI1    , SUCCESSFUL
DFH3461I C903 CSNE  6:24:45 NODE C903 SESSION STARTED
DFH0984I  05/09/88   06:27:04    FILE MSTRCHNG ALLOCATED TO 'PSIPD.IS000000.MASTER.CHANGES' ②
DFH0984I  05/09/88   06:27:05    FILE MSTRHIST ALLOCATED TO 'PSIOL.IS000000.MASTER.HISTORY'
DFH0984I  05/09/88   06:27:23    FILE BILLREG  ALLOCATED TO 'PSIOL.BC130000.REGMSTR'
DFH0984I  05/09/88   06:27:41    FILE BROKER   ALLOCATED TO 'PSIOL.IS000000.MASTER.BROKER'
DFH0984I  05/09/88   06:27:42    FILE NAXREF   ALLOCATED TO 'PSIOL.NA100000.XREF.MASTER'
DFH0984I  05/09/88   06:29:07    FILE NEWRATE  ALLOCATED TO 'PSIOL.IS110000.RATE.FILE'
05/09/88  00633556 INSTALL TERMINAL(C906);
DFH5935I INSTALL FOR TERMINAL: C906, NETNAME: PSI1C906, MODEL_NAME: PSI1    , SUCCESSFUL
DFH3461I C906 CSNE  6:33:55 NODE PSI1C906 SESSION STARTED
DFH0984I  05/09/88   06:38:27    FILE BC50001  ALLOCATED TO 'PSIOL.BC50001.TRANS'
05/09/88  00640262 INSTALL TERMINAL(CK18);
DFH5935I INSTALL FOR TERMINAL: CK18, NETNAME: CK18    , MODEL_NAME: PSI1    , SUCCESSFUL
DFH3461I CK18 CSNE  6:40:26 NODE CK18 SESSION STARTED
DFH0984I  05/09/88   06:49:05    FILE NAALTN2  ALLOCATED TO 'PSIOL.NA100000.ALPHPTH2.NAME.ADDR'
05/09/88  00651317 INSTALL TERMINAL(C803);
DFH5935I INSTALL FOR TERMINAL: C803, NETNAME: PSI1C803, MODEL_NAME: PSI1    , SUCCESSFUL
DFH3461I C803 CSNE  6:51:31 NODE PSI1C803 SESSION STARTED
05/09/88  00651526 INSTALL TERMINAL(CI07);
DFH5935I INSTALL FOR TERMINAL: CI07, NETNAME: PSI1CI07, MODEL_NAME: PSI1    , SUCCESSFUL
DFH3461I CI07 CSNE  6:51:52 NODE PSI1CI07 SESSION STARTED
05/09/88  00653372 INSTALL TERMINAL(CK16);
DFH5935I INSTALL FOR TERMINAL: CK16, NETNAME: CK16    , MODEL_NAME: PSI1    , SUCCESSFUL
DFH3461I CK16 CSNE  6:53:37 NODE CK16 SESSION STARTED
05/09/88  00654084 INSTALL TERMINAL(CH02);
DFH5935I INSTALL FOR TERMINAL: CH02, NETNAME: PSI1CH02, MODEL_NAME: PSI1    , SUCCESSFUL
DFH3461I CH02 CSNE  6:54:08 NODE PSI1CH02 SESSION STARTED
05/09/88  00654573 INSTALL TERMINAL(CF15);
DFH5935I INSTALL FOR TERMINAL: CF15, NETNAME: PSI1CF15, MODEL_NAME: PSI1    , SUCCESSFUL
DFH3461I CF15 CSNE  6:54:57 NODE PSI1CF15 SESSION STARTED
05/09/88  00658002 INSTALL TERMINAL(FA02);
DFH5935I INSTALL FOR TERMINAL: FA02, NETNAME: TP12FA02, MODEL_NAME: PSI1    , SUCCESSFUL
DFH3461I FA02 CSNE  6:58:01 NODE TP12FA02 SESSION STARTED
05/09/88  00658297 INSTALL TERMINAL(C004);
DFH5935I INSTALL FOR TERMINAL: C004, NETNAME: C004    , MODEL_NAME: PSI1    , SUCCESSFUL
DFH3461I C004 CSNE  6:58:30 NODE C004 SESSION STARTED
DFH0984I  05/09/88   06:58:43    FILE TP00V01  ALLOCATED TO 'PSIOL.TP000000.EXT.ATTR'
```

Figure 1-2  Typical output in the CICS CSMT or CSSL log.

can be reviewed. Follow the instructions in the next chapter to format the transaction dumps. VTAM statistics and autoinstall activity [Figure 1-5 (1,2)] could be of significant value if you are experiencing problems within the network. Keep track of these numbers, and become aware of what the normal values are. Shortages of VTAM resources or failures in autoinstall can be detected here. File statistics (3) are mostly used in performance monitoring, but could be a significant factor if failures are data-related. Transient data and temporary storage statistics can be useful not only in tuning, but in moni-

toring the consumption of these resources. Refer to Figure 1-6 for these items. The number of times that a peak value is reached (1), or if auxiliary storage ever logs "No. of Times Aux Storage Exhausted" (2), could create significant problems in the region, or even a system failure. These are just a few of the items in the shutdown statistics that could assist in diagnosing problems. Monitor this resource to become familiar with the normal conditions of the installation.

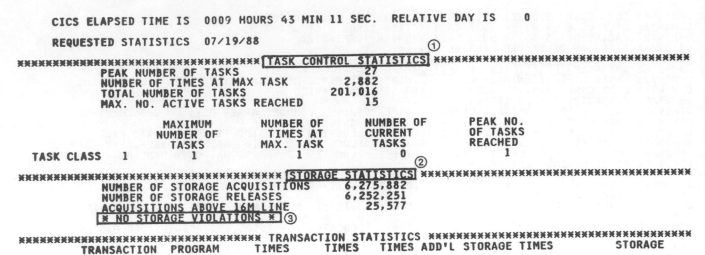

```
CICS ELAPSED TIME IS  0009 HOURS 43 MIN 11 SEC.  RELATIVE DAY IS   0

REQUESTED STATISTICS  07/19/88
                                                              ①
*****************************TASK CONTROL STATISTICS*****************************
           PEAK NUMBER OF TASKS                27
           NUMBER OF TIMES AT MAX TASK      2,882
           TOTAL NUMBER OF TASKS          201,016
           MAX. NO. ACTIVE TASKS REACHED      15

                   MAXIMUM      NUMBER OF    NUMBER OF    PEAK NO.
                   NUMBER OF    TIMES AT     CURRENT      OF TASKS
                   TASKS        MAX. TASK    TASKS        REACHED
     TASK CLASS  1    1            1            0            1
                                                        ②
**************************** STORAGE STATISTICS ****************************
           NUMBER OF STORAGE ACQUISITIONS    6,275,882
           NUMBER OF STORAGE RELEASES        6,252,251
           ACQUISITIONS ABOVE 16M LINE          25,577
      * NO STORAGE VIOLATIONS *  ③

**************************** TRANSACTION STATISTICS ****************************
    TRANSACTION  PROGRAM    TIMES     TIMES    TIMES ADD'L STORAGE TIMES      STORAGE
```

Figure 1-3  CICS shutdown statistics: task and storage.

### 1.2.2  MVS Service Aids

There are several facilities available in MVS, whether running MVS/XA or not, that can be used to help in CICS problem determination. These facilities may be slightly different, or enhanced in the newer releases of the operating system, but will all be documented within the release. An attempt will be made to identify to the appropriate manual, but with so many versions of MVS currently supported, the publication numbers could be difficult to identify. IBM is also announcing and shipping new releases of MVS so often, these facilities will change. The functions are so basic to operating systems, however, the function will remain, and will be located in the appropriate manual. Several MVS service aids that may be helpful at various times are:

AMDPRDMP (print dump facility)
IPCS (interactive problem control system)
GTF (generalized trace facility)
OS DUMP console command
SYS1.LOGREC

**AMDPRDMP.**  The batch facility to format and print unformatted dumps prior to MVS/ESA is AMDPRDMP. With the announcement of MVS/ESA, AMDPRDMP is replaced entirely with IPCS facilities. IPCS will be covered later, but be aware that AMDPRDMP can only be used in MVS operating systems up to and including MVS/XA 2.2.

It's documented in the publication *MVS Service Aids*, GC28-1159. This manual documents how to run the program and ask for MVS control blocks and data areas. Of course, the facility was originally designed for formatting of MVS system dumps. It has been enhanced to format many other subsystems of MVS. There are verbs and commands to format system dumps of VTAM, DB2, and other subsystems. These other facilities are documented in the appropriate product manuals, such as the DB2 Diagnostic References. IBM has finally provided the facility to format CICS dumps via AMDPRDMP. It was announced as available in CICS/MVS 2.1, and is documented in 2.1 publications. IBM has also graciously agreed to make the facility available in CICS/OS 1.7. It is not, however, documented in any 1.7 manuals and is being shipped via service as a PTF. Since the availability is hidden in CICS 1.7, and so new in CICS 2.1 that many customers may not realize the significance of this facility, an entire chapter has been dedicated to its use. The utilization of the AMDPRDMP function in CICS can be a substantial benefit to a CICS system programmer, and adequate understanding can save numerous hours in analyzing a problem. Chapter 14 covers the entire process from installation to customization.

**IPCS.**  It is surprising that many CICS installations are still unaware of IPCS. IPCS is a facility of MVS, and is therefore part of the license. In fact,

```
****************************** DUMP STATISTICS ******************************
           NUMBER OF STORAGE DUMPS        5
```

Figure 1-4  CICS shutdown statistics: transaction dumps.

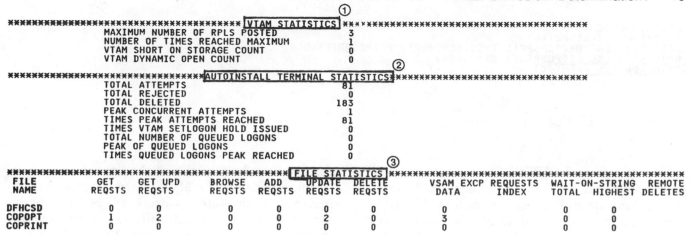

```
*********************************** VTAM STATISTICS ****************************************
                    MAXIMUM NUMBER OF RPLS POSTED        3
                    NUMBER OF TIMES REACHED MAXIMUM      1
                    VTAM SHORT ON STORAGE COUNT          0
                    VTAM DYNAMIC OPEN COUNT              0
*************************** AUTOINSTALL TERMINAL STATISTICS *******************************
                    TOTAL ATTEMPTS                      81
                    TOTAL REJECTED                       0
                    TOTAL DELETED                      183
                    PEAK CONCURRENT ATTEMPTS             1
                    TIMES PEAK ATTEMPTS REACHED         81
                    TIMES VTAM SETLOGON HOLD ISSUED      0
                    TOTAL NUMBER OF QUEUED LOGONS        0
                    PEAK OF QUEUED LOGONS                0
                    TIMES QUEUED LOGONS PEAK REACHED     0
*****************************************  FILE STATISTICS ********************************
FILE      GET      GET UPD    BROWSE   ADD     UPDATE  DELETE          VSAM EXCP REQUESTS   WAIT-ON-STRING   REMOTE
NAME      REQSTS   REQSTS     REQSTS   REQSTS  REQSTS  REQSTS          DATA      INDEX      TOTAL  HIGHEST   DELETES

DFHCSD    0        0          0        0       0       0               0                    0      0
COPOPT    1        2          0        0       2       0               3                    0      0
COPRINT   0        0          0        0       0       0               0                    0      0
```

Figure 1-5   CICS shutdown statistics: terminal autoinstall and files.

IPCS is IBM's strategic product for MVS problem determination, was enhanced in MVS/XA 2.2, and will continue to provide new functions in future releases. It is the only dump formatting facility in MVS/ESA, both in batch and online. This product takes minimal time to implement and is fairly well documented. The publication prior to MVS/XA 2.2, GC28-1297, IPCS User's Guide, contains most of the information required for setup and usage. Since IPCS was enhanced in MVS/XA 2.2, new publications are available. Listed below are the IBM publications that contain IPCS documentation for MVS/XA 2.2 support:

GC28-1406 IPCS Planning and Customization
GC28-1407 IPCS User Guide
GC28-1408 IPCS Command Reference
GC28-1182 IPCS Messages and Codes

IPCS can be used with CICS unformatted dumps to go beyond the information provided in AMDPRDMP (prior to MVS/ESA). The batch utility formats many CICS control blocks, and gives excellent representation of both the active and suspend chains. A great deal of information about the environment at the time of the failure can be reviewed from the print dump report. Many times, however, further analysis is required. After analyzing the failure, for example, a customer may need to call IBM service for assistance. In many cases, IBM would ask a great deal of questions pertaining to contents of the dump. There are two choices: print the entire contents of the dump, or use IPCS to view the dump on-line. Being partial to the preservation of trees, IPCS should be the best alternative. IPCS provides the facilities to browse through the dump and locate any address or block of storage required.

```
********************* TEMPORARY STORAGE STATISTICS *****************************************
                NUMBER OF PUT/PUTQ REQUESTS (MAIN)       2,381
                NUMBER OF GET/GETQ REQUESTS (MAIN)       3,354

                PEAK STORAGE USED FOR TS MAIN           73,040

                NUMBER OF PUT/PUTQ REQUESTS (AUX)        4,602
                NUMBER OF GET/GETQ REQUESTS (AUX)        6,582

                PEAK NUMBER OF TS NAMES IN USE              87
                NUMBER OF ENTRIES IN LONGEST QUEUE         149

                QUEUE EXTENSION THRESHOLD (TSMGSET)          4
                   NUMBER OF TIMES QUEUE CREATED         1,260
                   NUMBER OF QUEUE EXTENSIONS CREATED      402

                CONTROL INTERVAL SIZE                    4,096
                   NO. OF WRITES GREATER THAN CISIZE         0

                NUMBER OF CIS IN TS DATASET              1,050
                   PEAK NUMBER OF CIS IN USE                51
                   NO. OF TIMES AUX STORAGE EXHAUSTED         0
```

Figure 1-6   CICS shutdown statistics: temporary storage.

```
00000000PROC 0
00000100CONTROL NOFLUSH
00000201ALLOC DA('DPSPPID.IPCS.DUMPDIR') F(IPCSDDIR) OLD
00000300ALLOC F(IPCSPRNT) SYSOUT(A)
00000400IPCS PARM(50)  ①
```

Figure 1-7  Typical IPCS CLIST contents.

How to set up for IPCS? The process is actually as simple as allocating a few datasets and adding a few statements to the logon procedure (PROC) of a TSO session. The new dataset allocation is fairly well documented in the IPCS User's Guide or IPCS Planning and Customization; use their examples and standard space allocation. The command list (CLIST) to execute IPCS is shown in Figure 1-7. The main variable in the CLIST is the IPCS parm, line 00004 in the example. The parameter references the member in a system library that contains default IPCS specifications. In the example, the parameter PARM(50), means that the CLIST will utilize the system library SYS1.PARMLIB, member IPCSPR50. Installations may use different suffixes of IPCSPRxx for default IPCS parameters. The best bet would be to contact the MVS system programmers to find out where the IPCS parameters are stored.

What type of dumps can be viewed with IPCS? Remember, unformatted dumps are the only type used. These dumps can be produced in CICS releases back to 1.6, but the technique is slightly different. In CICS 1.6, an SYSMDUMP is available. These datasets should be pre-allocated using DCBs (data control block) similar to the system dump datasets. To discover these values, simply view the DCBs of any system dump dataset, they always have the format of SYS1.DUMPxx. After allocating the SYSMDUMP dataset, identify it to the CICS region with a data definition in the startup JCL. It will probably look like this:

```
//SYSMDUMP  DD  DSN=CICS.SYSMDUMP,DISP=SHR
```

Not all system CICS failures will be directed to the SYSMDUMP dataset, but many will, especially if the address space has to be canceled after a "hang," "wait," or "loop." Once the dump is created, IPCS can be used to view the contents.

In CICS 1.7 and beyond, an unformatted dump can be requested with the new SIT parameter. If you specify, in the SIT,

```
DUMP=(PARTN,SDUMP)
```

most CICS failures will be directed to a SYS1.DUMPxx dataset. An empty system dump dataset must be available at the time of the failure. Again, check with the MVS system programmers to insure that adequate resources will be available to accommodate the CICS failures. These system dump datasets can then be viewed via IPCS during the course of analysis.

How to use IPCS? After a few simple commands to initialize the dump, most commands are documented in the user's guide. The initialization process is started with the SETDEF command. Look for the complete syntax in the manual; however, a typical example would be

```
SETDEF DSNAME('SYS1.DUMP00') NOPRINT TERMINAL
```

Of course, when running CICS 1.6, the dataset name will reference the SYSMDUMP dataset created. During initialization, IPCS will prompt for a couple of items, and then will identify the dump with the title, failure reason, and other summary information. After that, use whatever commands and facilities IPCS offers to browse the dump. Remember, this dump being viewed is on magnetic media and can fairly easily be deleted, or lost. If analyzing an important problem, make a copy for backup. The COPYDUMP command is extremely easy to use, and creates a clean backup in case the primary dump is lost. If IBM requests a dump be shipped, COPYDUMP is the recommended facility to use to create that dump. IBM service people use MVS facilities to do their problem determination, so the dump is in a standard format.

Since IPCS was designed primarily for MVS use, many of the commands in the product format MVS control blocks. A CICS programmer really has no need to look at UCBs (unit control blocks) and other MVS control blocks. There are facilities, however, that can assist in the formatting of CICS control blocks. One of the advantages of IPCS in TSO is the ability to write command lists (CLISTs) that can execute any instructions. Many installations have written CLISTs that find the data areas relevant to CICS, and produce desired results. For example, a CLIST can find the pointer in the CSA to the active chains and equate symbols to all the TCAs (task control areas). Another CLIST could locate the pointer in the TCA to the storage areas chained off the control block, and identify all stor-

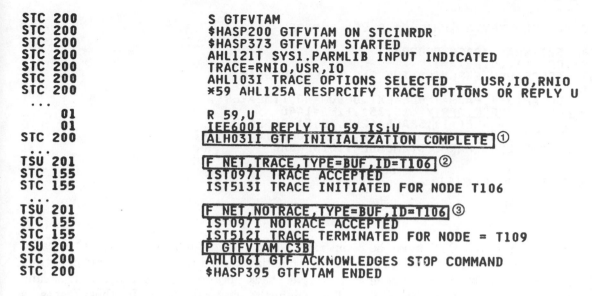

```
STC 200                     S GTFVTAM
STC 200                     $HASP200 GTFVTAM ON STCINRDR
STC 200                     $HASP373 GTFVTAM STARTED
STC 200                     AHL121T SYS1.PARMLIB INPUT INDICATED
STC 200                     TRACE=RNIO,USR,IO
STC 200                     AHL103I TRACE OPTIONS SELECTED ___ USR,IO,RNIO
STC 200                     *59 AHL125A RESPRCIFY TRACE OPTIONS OR REPLY U
...
    01                      R 59,U
    01                      IEE600I REPLY TO 59 IS;U
STC 200                     AHL031I GTF INITIALIZATION COMPLETE  ①
...
TSU 201                     F NET,TRACE,TYPE=BUF,ID=T106  ②
STC 155                     IST097I TRACE ACCEPTED
STC 155                     IST513I TRACE INITIATED FOR NODE T106
...
TSU 201                     F NET,NOTRACE,TYPE=BUF,ID=T106  ③
STC 155                     IST097I NOTRACE ACCEPTED
STC 155                     IST512I TRACE TERMINATED FOR NODE = T109
TSU 201                     P GTFVTAM.C3B
STC 200                     AHL006I GTF ACKNOWLEDGES STOP COMMAND
STC 200                     $HASP395 GTFVTAM ENDED
```

Figure 1-8    Commands to start GTF trace of terminals.

age "owned" by this transaction. In fact, CLISTs can do a great deal of the work for you in problem determination within IPCS. Many organizations have realized this, and either written many CLISTs of their own or located other installations that have already done so. Membership in national organizations can be very helpful in locating other CICS users and sharing information. In fact, the organizations of SHARE and GUIDE do exactly that. The CICS project within SHARE has compiled a large quantity of CLISTs from participating members, and offers them to other members who are interested. These resources can be very valuable and avoid redundant effort. CLISTs provide an incredible time-saving tool with IPCS to assist in problem determination.

**GTF.** The generalized trace facility is another resource in MVS that can assist with CICS problem determination. It is used fairly infrequently; however, it can be valuable when analyzing terminal and network problems. Terminal problems can be very difficult to debug, since much of what's going on is not in CICS, but in VTAM. Once CICS passes the data back to VTAM to present to the terminal screen, little is left in CICS to review. In the case of autoinstalled terminals, if the installation fails, some information can be located in the CICS log. Many times, however, important information is missing, information that only VTAM can provide. These problems can be assisted by the generalized trace facility. GTF can trace many events, especially network events, and can provide the missing pieces of network problems. GTF is fairly well documented in MVS Service Aids GC28-1159. One major function that GTF can provide is CICS termi-

nal buffer trace. Just as CICS trace facilities record and report all events in a CICS transaction, GTF terminal buffer traces can record and report all events in terminal input and output. The VTAM system programmers may need to be involved in this process, since they may be very familiar with GTF buffer traces. Basically, GTF provides the mechanism to record the data, and VTAM identifies the type of records to capture. In a typical problem, a terminal is experiencing failures, will not autoinstall, or will not display data properly on the screen. A VTAM buffer trace will identify every event in the process, and give the programmer more insight into the problem. In this problem, the first step would be to start GTF, the collector of the data. Figure 1-8 shows the MVS console commands necessary to start GTF. Once the trace parameters have been identified, GTF responds with

```
AHL103I GTF INITIALIZATION COMPLETE (1)
```

This indicates that the collector is ready to accept data. This procedure was initiated from the console via the OS START command, therefore is executing a procedure (PROC) from SYS1.PROCLIB. Figure 1-9 would be the member in SYS1.PROCLIB started by the commands in Figure 1-8. The dataset containing the trace records is shown (1), and would be the data definition (DD) in the batch job described later. After GTF signals that initialization is complete, VTAM must begin the buffer trace. Figure 1-8 contains the OS console commands to initiate a VTAM buffer trace (2) for a specific terminal (T106). After the desired interval, or the failure has been recreated, the trace is terminated with the NOTRACE request (3). This quies-

```
//GTFVTAM PROC MEMBER=GTFVTAM,UNIT=DASD,VOL=SYSPPS
//*
//*           VTAM EXTERNAL TRACE PROGRAM
//* REFER   SYS1.PROCLIB(GTFVTAM)
//* DOC     THIS PROCEDURE EXECUTES THE GTF TRACE PROGRAM.
//*
//IEFPROC EXEC PGM=AHLGTF,PARM='MODE=EXT,DEBUG=NO,TIME=YES',
//             REGION=2280K.DPRIY=(15,15),TIME=1440
//IEFRDER DD   DSN=GTF.TRACE(+1),SPACE=(CYL,(5,5),RLSE),①
//             DISP=(,CATLG),DCB=MODLDSCB,UNIT=&UNIT,VOL=SER=&VOL
//SYSLIB  DD   DSNAME=SYS1.PARMLIB(&MEMBER),DISP=SHR
```

Figure 1-9   SYS1.PROCLIB member for GTF trace.

ces the trace and recording stops. GTF must be quiesced, also, and can be done with the OS stop command, P GTF.stepname (4). The data has been recorded and can be reported with either the MVS service aid, AMDPRDMP, or the VTAM service aid, ACFTAP. ACFTAP is documented in the appropriate VTAM manuals. An example of using AMDPRDMP to format trace records is shown in Figure 1-10. Note the dataset name (1) from the previous recording procedure of GTFTRACE. Once reported, these trace entries can provide the exact sequence of data that was transferred between CICS and the terminal. It also displays the specific data streams that were transferred, and can provide insight into the cause of the failure. In MVS/ESA 3.1, GTF trace records are formatted with an IPCS command. See the IPCS manuals for proper syntax.

**OS DUMP Console Command.** Many times, unfortunately, CICS problems do not produce transaction dumps, or even system dumps. In these cases, CICS merely loops uncontrollably, or hangs in a suspended state. All efforts to release the wait or break out of the loop fail, and the CICS address space must be canceled. In situations of continuous operation and maximum availability, an installation is sometimes faced with the dilemma of getting the region back up and running properly first, and diagnosing the problem later. In these cases, a "snapshot" of the environment is required for later analysis. If the region is looping or in a wait, the CEMT SNAP function cannot produce a dump, since no new work is being dispatched. OS, however, has a function to dump any address space on command and write the dump to a SYS1.DUMPxx dataset. This could, at least, provide output to analyze the conditions at the time of the failure. To dump an address space (or CICS region) from the master console, enter the following command:

```
DUMP "title"
```

where "title" is any descriptive name to identify the dump. MVS will then prompt with:

```
xx IEE094D SPECIFY OPERANDS FOR DUMP COMMAND
```

Respond with the jobname of the CICS region to dump. A typical response would be

```
Rxx,CICSPROD,ALL
```

```
//VTAMPRNT JOB (),SYSTEMS,CLASS=N,MSGCLASS=X
//*
//* FOR PRINTING VTAM INTERNAL TRACE FROM GTF OUTPUT
//*
//AMDPRDMP EXEC PGM=IKJEFT01,PARM='AMDPRDMP'
//SYSPRINT DD SYSOUT=*
//PRINTER  DD SYSOUT=*
//INDEX    DD SYSOUT=*
//SYSUT1   DD SPACE=(4104,(4027,191)),UNIT=SYSDA
//SYSTSPRT DD DUMMY
//SYSTSIN  DD DUMMY
//SYSIN DD *
 EDIT J=PRDCICS,USR=(FE1),DDNAME=TAPE,START=(054,15.21.00),
 STOP=(054,15.22.00)
END
//TAPE     DD DISP=SHR,DSN=GTF.TRACE.G0112V00 ①
//
```

Figure 1-10   Sample job to format output from GTF trace.

```
//DB2LOGP JOB (),SYSTEMS,CLASS=N,MSGLEVEL=(1,1),
// MSGCLASS=A,REGION=2000K
//*
//******************************************************************
//* PRINT EVENT REPORT FOR DB2 PROBLEMS
//******************************************************************
//EVENTS   EXEC PGM=IFCEREP1,
//      PARM=('TYPE=S,PRINT=PS,ACC=N')
//SERLOG   DD  DSN=SYS1.LOGREC,DISP=OLD
//TOURIST  DD  SYSOUT=A,DCB=BLKSIZE=133
//EREPPT   DD  SYSOUT=A,DCB=BLKSIZE=133
//SYSUDUMP DD  SYSOUT=*
//SYSIN    DD  DUMMY
```

Figure 1-11   Sample job to print DB/2 software errors.

requesting that all portions of the address space are to be written to the dump dataset. When MVS has completed the process of writing the dump, a message will indicate that a dump has been written and identify which dump dataset suffix was used. The address space can then be canceled, and recovery procedures started. The snapshot of the region is contained in a system dump dataset and can then be processed with AMDPRDMP, or IPCS, or both. A complete description of this command can be found in MVS System Commands, GC28-1206.

**SYS1.LOGREC.** MVS has its own internal log, as does CICS, to record events that are operating-system related. Most of the entries in this log pertain to hardware failures, but software failures from certain subsystems are also recorded. DB2 is one product that records failures in SYS1.LOGREC. Since many installations use the CICS attach facility with DB2, this facility can be relevant to CICS problem determination. When problems or failures occur in CICS that are the result of a DB2 call, analysis becomes more complicated. The call is recorded in the CICS trace, but then the subsequent activity disappears to CICS. The events are recorded in the DB2 trace, but CICS does not get control again until the results are returned to the caller. This gap in the CICS trace sometimes leaves programmers at a loss when a failure occurs. A facility exists to locate the software failure records and report them. EREP (Environmental Recording Editing and Print program) is used to format SYS1.LOGREC data. Figure 1-11 shows the job that invokes the environmental report error program, EREP, and specifies the parameters necessary to select software events. The output from this program is covered fully in Chapter 7, Section 3 "DSNC Abends," which discusses a DB2 failure, an 0C7, a data exception. Refer to that material to discover the full steps necessary to diagnose DB2 failures in CICS.

### 1.2.3  CICS Supplied Transactions

There are a few transactions supplied by IBM to assist in problem determination. Some of these transactions assist application programmers, some assist system programmers. Of course, all IBM transactions start with the letter "C," and since CICS 1.7 are now documented in their own manual, CICS Supplied Transactions. Following are only a few of the more widely used ones; review the manual for a complete list of these transactions and how to use them. IBM will not only enhance these transactions in future releases, but add new transactions to provide more function and features.

**CEDF.** The execution diagnostic facility is a tried and true friend of the application programmer. This facility is used constantly during development and provides a number of commands for problem determination. IBM is aware of the significance of this facility and has consistently enhanced the transaction. An entire chapter has been dedicated to Interactive Tools, Chapter 9. Included in that chapter are two companion products, available from other vendors. Most programmers use a combination to develop and test in CICS. CEDF is discussed completely in that chapter, with examples of the screens most often utilized.

**CEDA,B,C.** The CEDx transactions replaced the singular CEDA transaction introduced in CICS 1.6 for the online definition of programs and transactions. Customers needed the ability to distinguish function within the resource facility, to have inquire capability without delete. In CICS 1.7, IBM provided the three transactions and the ability to protect execution of the most powerful level. The three transactions now separate function and capability of the resource definition facility.

These transactions are included in a discussion of problem determination because many problems are a result of incorrect or invalid definition of CICS resources. Although many installations still choose to assemble macro tables, such as the PPT, PCT, etc., serious consideration should be given to the migration to Resource Definition Online (RDO). IBM has made the direction very clear, as noted in the CICS/MVS 2.1 announcement. Although all table-supported resources have not been converted to RDO, there is no doubt that it is inevitable. IBM's announcement stated that resources supported via RDO will no longer be available in macro table format. Installations should convert while the bridge is in place to migrate existing tables into RDO. Further hesitation may cause more difficulty when all macro table support is removed. Utilization of RDO now, with resources currently available, will ease the trauma of new facilities when they arrive. The CEDx transactions are a good example of this. If an installation installs RDO support, it can give access to the appropriate personnel to maintain the resources. It can also give access to other personnel to browse, and therefore inquire into the status of CICS elements, such as programs and transactions. Some problems are the result of incorrect or invalid resource definitions. Examples of this would be incorrect TWA size, invalid program name within a transaction, or incorrect TIOAL (terminal input/output area length) of a terminal. If programmers are given access to view the contents of a resource, such as a program, transaction, or terminal definition, they may be able to detect this. Many installations require the application programmers to totally support their own test regions. This includes definition and support of all programs and transactions within these regions. Once the application is ready to be moved into production, the appropriate person merely copies the definitions from the test region to the production region. The process eliminates a great deal of redundant effort and reduces the possibility for error. For this reason, and many others, the CEDx transactions are valuable tools for application programmers, and can be used both in development and analysis. A complete explanation of both syntax and usage is contained in the manual, Resource Definition Online.

**CEMT.** The master terminal operator transaction is probably the most well-known CICS-supplied transaction. It has been available for many releases of CICS and was significantly enhanced in CICS 1.7. This transaction becomes important as a problem determination tool because it cannot only inquire, but modify existing CICS resources. CEMT has the ability to modify files specifications, load new copies of programs, alter system settings, invoke dump processing, and shut down the region, to name just a few. The complete range of function for the command can be found in CICS Supplied Transactions; however, a few important features related to problem determination will be highlighted. In releases of CICS prior to 1.7, file maintenance was accomplished with a combination of CEMT (to close the file) and ADYN (to deallocate the file). In CICS 1.7 and beyond, files are dynamically allocated to CICS when they are opened, or first reference. ADYN, therefore, is no longer necessary. CEMT was enhanced to include the elements necessary for the allocation to occur. CEMT now has elements of OBJECT (dataset name) and DISPOSITION (Share, Old or Mod). Since the default file status in the File Control Table (FCT) is now ENABLED,CLOSED, the files are not allocated to the CICS region until a request to open is detected. When CICS receives the request, it automatically invokes allocation, and the dataset name and disposition are utilized to create the appropriate control block. When the file is closed, this control block is actually deleted, and has to be recreated at next open.

This can be some additional overhead to CICS, but allows a great deal more flexibility in function. How many customers misspell a dataset name in the startup JCL when defining a new file to the test CICS? Prior to CICS 1.7, the region would be unable to locate the file, would return a JCL error, and the region would not initialize. How many installations were faced with a region that would not initialize in the morning because a production job the previous night abended and failed to recreate a CICS file? These problems, and others, are avoided by the new allocation process. If a file is not found, is unavailable, or otherwise unable to be opened, CICS returns an allocation failure to the CICS log and continues! An application programmer can create a new test file, with a new name, and immediately test with the new data. The steps would be

```
CEMT SET DA(ddname) CLO DIS    ... to close and
disable
CEMT SET OBJ(dataset name)     ... set to the
new name
CEMT SET DA(ddname) OPE ENA    ... to open and
enable
```

The new file is now accessible to the application for testing. There are many options available with these new dynamic facilities. File control is not the only facility enhanced.

Terminal control was also enhanced in CICS 1.7 and beyond. Using a combination of CEMT and CEDA, terminals can be dynamically defined or modified. Even if an installation is not using autoinstall, the definition of a printer can be created on the fly with CEDA, then SET INSERVICE with CEMT. This change surprised many people, however. Since the control blocks for the terminal and/or printer are not built until autoinstalled, or installed with CEDA, CICS has no knowledge of them. A request for CEMT INQ for a terminal or printer not installed yet will return a NOT FOUND. Dynamic creation of control blocks, such as files and terminals, will change the way resources are viewed. As IBM provides more of these functions, our perception of resources and problems viewed will have to change. The ability to respond and avoid problems, however, will grow with the enhancements.

### 1.2.4  CICS Monitors

Analyzing problems in a CICS region can be very frustrating. If there is no failure, we need to have a window into the region to see what's happening. CICS waits and loops are the most common problems that produce no external alert, no dump or abend code to research. The best way to diagnose these types of problems is with a monitor. These products provide us with various facilities to scan through the region, analyze existing conditions and resources, and possibly identify the cause of the problem. There are several vendors of monitors, including IBM. Most monitors have predefined screens to view the common conditions, such as active and suspend chains, subpool utilization, resource consumption, etc. They also come with the ability to create unique screens, to customize the product for specific applications. This can be especially helpful, since it gives the installation the ability to place critical or sensitive information in one place for quick reference.

Some of the monitors also come with a batch reporting facility to view trends from a previously defined interval. This is not as important in problem determination as it is in tuning. With an analysis of CICS over an extended period of time, trends can be seen in resource consumption and transaction activity, and can predict future requirements.

Your installation may not have any monitoring product. These products are quite expensive and are sometimes difficult to justify if budgets are limited. If you decide to purchase a monitor, analyze at least two for potential function. They all have different advantages; find the one that will offer the best tools to assist in solving problems.

**Non-IBM Products.** There are also a number of products on the market from various vendors that can be valuable tools in problem determination.

This chapter has discussed the service aids and tools that are delivered with either MVS or CICS, and are therefore already available. Other products are on the market that could supplement these resources, depending on the limits of the budget. Products are available to process and format dumps, maintain resources within the regions, and assist in program development and testing. As CICS evolves and future technologies are announced, additional products will be available to assist the installation. Develop skills in problem determination with the facilities that are always provided. In that way, you'll be prepared and able to use these skills in whatever installation you may be employed. Products that you become dependent upon may not have been purchased by your next employer. Also, using facilities that are part of the operating system or CICS will be supported from release to release. It is hoped that IBM will continue to provide the same function in future releases of the products.

## 1.3  METHODOLOGIES AND TECHNIQUES OF PROBLEM DETERMINATION

Methods of approaching problems are as varied as the problems themselves. Application failures and system failures utilize different techniques and tools, so have therefore been presented in two separate sections in this book. In each section, specific issues are covered that deal with the environment surrounding the problem. Since IBM produces different types of dumps, and provides various tools to analyze these dumps, a great deal of time is spent covering the dump types and contents.

In each section, specific failures are produced, failures that are typically common to most installations. In most failures, an illustration is provided entitled "Significant Items in a CICS . . . Failure." The figures contain items such as Abend Code, Probably Cause, Important Dump Items and other pieces that would be relevant in this particular type of failure. Use these illustrations to develop your methodologies for problem determination. You may discover additional information to assist in debugging and enhance the list already provided.

The preceding tools should be used whenever necessary to diagnose CICS problems. The first output from a failure is usually a dump, either transaction or system. The next chapter will discuss most portions of a dump and familiarize you with what is, and what is not, available.

# Formatted Transaction Dumps

When an application, or program, fails during execution within a CICS environment, documentation needs to be made available to assist in diagnosing the problem. CICS could take all storage created by the program and write it to a permanent location, possibly on disk, tape, or a printer. This storage, however, would be unformatted. It would merely contain the hexadecimal contents of the program and data that was being executed. Most programmers are not skilled, or do not care to spend the time it would take to convert this into meaningful information. For that reason, IBM has provided a formatting facility to convert the storage into somewhat readable results.

## 2.1 FORMATTED DUMP PROGRAM DFHFDP

The CICS formatted dump program produces output that isolates and separates most of the major control blocks in storage. These control blocks are portions of storage relevant to either the CICS system or the application program. The control blocks are identified by headings, and sometimes contain specific fields highlighted within the block of storage. Of course, these dumps do not contain the entire section of storage that makes up that CICS region, but rather, the portions that would be relevant to the application. Some types of dumps generated by DFHFDP map out portions of the entire CICS system. These are more relevant to total region failures or problems, and will be covered in a later chapter. The dumps discussed at this time are transaction dumps, or output from a single application failure. They contain, therefore, control blocks created by the application and CICS control blocks common to all applications. Transaction dumps are written to pre-allocated datasets, DFHDMPA or DFHDMPB. CICS begins writing to one of these datasets at initialization, depending on the type of startup of the region. When one dataset fills up, CICS can switch and begin writing to the alternate. At that time, or any other time required, a batch job can be run to print the contents of the dump dataset. A dump utility program, DFHDUP, is used to print the contents, and the dump dataset can then be emptied and reused. If not cleared, CICS merely begins writing over the existing contents when that dataset is opened for output next time. There is hope at this writing that IBM will enhance this utility to provide functions for selective printing of dumps, or suppression of unwanted abends. Future releases of CICS may provide additional facilities within DFHDUP, but CICS/MVS 2.1 requires that you process the entire dataset without options.

### 2.1.1 Invocation of DFHFDP

The formatted dump program is invoked by CICS for most transaction abends, and may optionally be invoked for ASRA and ASRB abends to produce a full formatted dump of the CICS region. The DUMP operand in the RDO entry for the transaction or the FDUMP parameter in the PCT macro will cause a formatted dump to be produced for ASRA or ASRB abends. In addition, the DFHFD macro or the EXEC CICS PERFORM SNAP command can be used by the programmer to request a dump if certain conditions are experienced. This is not a recommended procedure, however, for reasons explained below. Invocation of DFHFDP should be left to CICS. If programmers need to test for conditions and take precautions, HANDLE CONDITION facilities are available to attempt recovery from the condition.

When the formatted dump program is invoked, it must use operating system facilities to record all status of the CICS address space. Since it must use operating system facilities to perform the I/O of dumping storage to the dump dataset, it retains exclusive control of the CICS system until it completes. In other words, while the storage is dumping, DFHDMP does not relinquish control to CICS to process any other work. It issues special commands to insure that it is not abended and handles all interrupts during its execution. No additional transactions can execute. Programmers who code their own dump procedures, therefore, can lock out all other terminals and prevent any transactions from running while their dump is processing.

Once written to the dump dataset, DFHDMPA or DFHDMPB, the formatted dump utility can be used to produce printed output. The output is, as we previously explained, formatted into CICS control blocks. All portions of the dump will now be identified and explained in detail.

## 2.2    FORMAT AND CONTENT OF A TRANSACTION DUMP

All transaction failures produce a formatted dump containing most of the same control block areas. The content of these areas may be different, since different program code is being executed and different data is being manipulated. Once you become familiar with the format of the dump, any failure can be diagnosed more easily since you "know your way around." These dumps may be unfamiliar and intimidating at first, but like anything, once you become comfortable with the format and contents, you'll be able to find your way around like a pro. Depending on the type of failure, you may only need to reference a portion of the dump. Everyone develops different problem determination techniques, and may use some or all of the information contained in a dump to solve the problem. After you get used to looking at various components of a dump, you'll develop a sense of normal settings. In other words, some programmers who have worked with CICS for a number of years can look at certain portions of a dump and determine that something just doesn't look right. After all, the contents of most control blocks are merely hexadecimal representations of that block of storage. What is really supposed to be there? Is that block of user data storage what would be appropriate for this program? Does the trace table indicate normal logic for this program?

Only after a great deal of experience with dump debugging will you become able to answer these types of questions. When you look at many different dumps, you begin to see similarities. The best way to do this is to really get to know the components of a dump, where they can be found and what they should contain in normal conditions. The rest of this chapter is dedicated to identifying a transaction dump and many of the relevant components.

### 2.2.1    Control Blocks Produced and Where to Find Them

The first page of every dump contains a great deal of information relevant to the failure, and is always considered before proceeding any further. It may, in fact, give you enough information to solve the problem without going any further. That, unfortunately, happens very rarely. Since the first page is truly the starting point of most items you will use in problem determination, a good deal of time will be dedicated to describing each portion. Figure 2-1 contains the first page of a transaction abend.

The first line of a transaction abend identifies many critical pieces of information. From Figure 2-1, (1) PSICICT identifies the application identification, or APPLID, that this CICS region is known by VTAM. Many installations run multiple CICS regions, all of them managed by the IBM product that controls online access to address spaces, VTAM. Without getting into a deep technical discussion of VTAM, it should be sufficient to know that VTAM controls any address space that requires multiple user support, or multiple terminals having access to the same application concurrently. CICS is that address space, and since multiple copies of CICS may exist, VTAM manages each of them independently. This identifier (PSICICT) is the unique name that you can use as a reference to the specific CICS address space that handled this particular abend. This identifier was made available in transaction dumps starting with CICS 1.7, therefore will not appear in dumps prior to that release.

Moving to the right in line one is a descriptor **CODE=** with the contents of ASRA. This code will be the CICS abend code associated with this transaction abend. If generated by CICS, it will be a four-character code that can be referenced in the CICS manual, CICS Messages and Codes, for more description. If generated by a purchased product running in this CICS region, it must be researched in that particular vendor documentation. If it was generated by an application, it will only be documented if the programmer provided appropriate information about the abend code that was generated by the program. As previously discussed, this is not

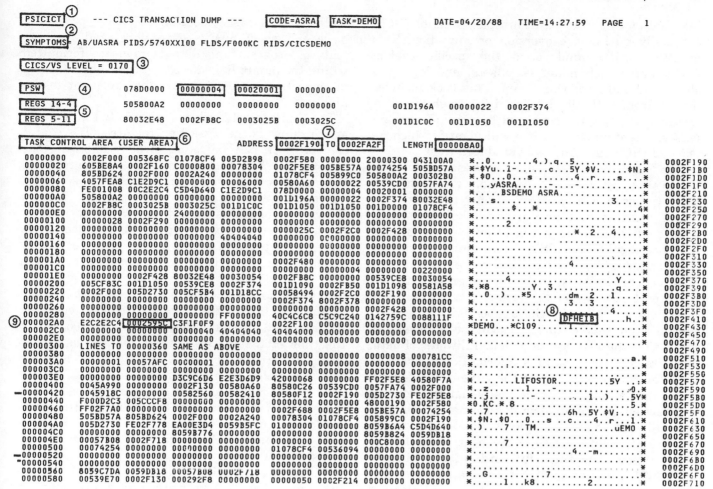

Figure 2-1    CICS transaction dump: page 1.

a recommended procedure for performance reasons. It also makes problem determination difficult, especially when you are attempting to diagnose a failure and the documentation on this abend code is unavailable, or not completely explained. It is hoped that this abend code is either in the IBM CICS Messages and Codes manual or in a vendor-supplied product codes manual.

The next descriptor code is **TASK=** and contains the value DEMO. This item is the transaction name that was attempting to execute at the time of the failure. This TRANSID would be found in the PCT, or the transaction entry in RDO. Transactions can execute many programs, and therefore may not be the definitive identity of the failing component. It does, however, give us additional insight into the system that was executing at the time of the failure.

Following this line to the right displays a time and date stamp entry for the failure. This date and time stamp indicate the exact entry in the system for the dump. Many times, application programmers do not see the dump output immediately upon the failure. This entry gives a specific reference to

both the date and the time of day that the failure occurred. This can be significant if you are attempting to diagnose a problem and wish to know exactly when the failure took place. On the far right of this line is the page number. Transaction dumps may be only a few or many pages, depending on options chosen, such as the number of trace table entries. This is merely a point of reference within this dump.

The second line of all dumps contains the Symptom String (2) for the failure. It contains some information which may be irrelevant, or merely interesting to most people. The only item in this line that is remotely important is the last entry. The content of this entry, CICSDEMO, is the program entry that was in control at the time of the abend. In other words, it was the executing module, which would be found in the PPT or program entry in RDO. This module, along with the TASK name from the previous line, gives us the specific program function that was attempting to execute at the time of the failure.

The third line (3) contains the CICS product level on behalf of which the abend was produced. Many installations need to run multiple levels of CICS, especially during a conversion or migration. This identifier will remind you of the specific level of CICS, and which manuals, offsets, and logic you should be using for this dump. This book includes dumps from both CICS 1.7 and 2.1 to show differences in the output generated by the different releases. The item on page one will identify which release of CICS the dump was produced from.

The fourth line (4) will only be present if the failure was a result of an exception condition. The PSW (program status word) is only relevant if an ASRA occurred and several additional items need to be contained in the dump. Other types of failures will not display the PSW, since program storage will not need to be analyzed for the cause of the failure. The PSW is explained in great detail in Chapter 4, ASRA abends, since it is critical to problem determination in those abends. For general purposes in this chapter, it will be sufficient to know that the PSW contains four fullwords of data. The first fullword contains information relevant to the status of processing at the time of the failure. This first fullword is normally ignored during transaction failure problem determination. The second fullword, in our example **00000004**, is normally the hexadecimal address of the next instruction to be executed. The third fullword, in our example **00020001**, contains the length of the instruction at the time of the abend and the program interrupt code for this abend. Since this relates entirely to program exception type of abends, any more detailed description will be deferred to Chapter 4. This data is very specific to the failure data and the relevance of the PSW will be covered in great detail.

The next two lines are the formatted contents of the registers. The register contents are formatted in another portion of the dump, which will be described later. In this location, however, we find the registers formatted in a peculiar sequence. You will notice that the registers are listed in the order of 14–4, and then 5–11 (5). The formatted dump program lists the registers in this order. You will notice that in this sequence, registers 12 and 13 are missing. They will never be listed in this representation of the registers, since they always contain the addresses of CICS control blocks that are formatted in the dump. Register 12 contains the address of the Common System Area (CSA), and Register 13 contains the address of the user area of the Task Control Area (TCA). Both of these control blocks are formatted within the dump, and they are not listed in the sequence of registers on page one. The other register contents may become relevant depending on the complexity of the problem. Many applications that are coded in Assembler require attention to the register settings. COBOL programs, however, use standard conventions, and the contents of program and data storage are formatted within the dump. Register contents will be analyzed in some transaction failures when relevant to the problem.

The first control block to be presented in a transaction dump is the Task Control Area (TCA). This control block can be found directly following the registers (6). The Task Control Area (TCA) contains two sections, the user area, and the system area. The system area actually precedes the user area in the control block, as we will see when we identify the addresses of these components. The user area, however, is presented first in the formatted transaction dump. This is probably done to make the user (or application) area available to the programmer in the formatted dump at the earliest possible time. It contains data that is specific to both the program and the data that was being executed at the time of the failure. As we will see later, the system area contains more CICS-related contents that are global to all applications. The TCA user area is also identified with some addresses. On the same line as the heading is the address of the starting location of the TCA user area (7). In our example, **0002F190** is the beginning address of this transaction's TCA user area. Also noted is **0002FA2F**, the ending address, and **000008A0** as the length. The TCA user area will always start at a location ending in 190 in CICS 1.7 and 2.1, since the length of the TCA system area is 190 bytes and begins at a doubleword boundary. In CICS 1.6, the TCA system area was 140 bytes, therefore all TCA user areas end with a location ending in 140. Although the TCA user area is mapped out, the contents may not be readily familiar. Certain portions of the TCA user area are important, depending on the type of failure that you are diagnosing. One portion that application programmers reference quite frequently is the EIB (Exec Interface Block). The EIB is identified within the TCA user area by the eyecatcher preceding the control block.

Notice 'DFHEIB' in the character representation of the control block (8). This marks the beginning of the EIB. This control block is discussed in great length in the next chapter. It can contain information to help diagnose the environment at the time of the failure. One highlighted area within the EIB begins at offset +12. This is the task number of the failing transaction. In the example, we see that task number 02595 (9) corresponds to the DEMO transaction. This will be important, especially if it becomes necessary to investigate the CICS trace table. Many tasks may be executing at the time of the failure. The trace entry contains the task number, so we can select only the entries relevant to

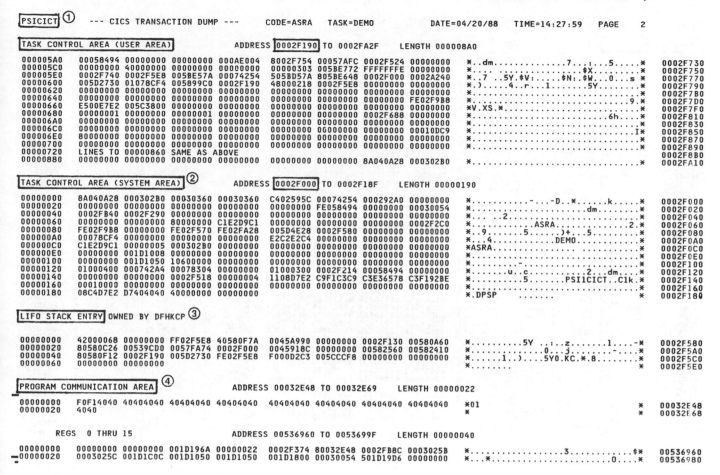

Figure 2-2   CICS transaction dump: page 2.

this task. Other contents of the TCA user area will be highlighted within following chapters to identify specific contents of the control block.

Figure 2-2 contains the second page of a transaction dump. Line one is repeated (1), which will show as the title line of every page within this dump. The remaining portion of the TCA user area is presented since it could not be fully represented on the first page. The second control block is then mapped, the TCA system area (2). Again, this is actually the first portion of the entire TCA, of which the user area has already been printed. The beginning address of this TCA system area in our example is **0002F000**. This agrees with the premise that the TCA user area is 190 bytes into the TCA. Remember in Figure 2-1, item (7), we identified the TCA user area starting at **0002F190**. The entire TCA, therefore, starts at location **0002F000**. The TCA system area contains information which is relevant to the CICS transaction, especially many pointers to other control blocks created on behalf of this task. One example is the COBOL dynamic storage area. At offset +40 is the address **0002FB40**. This block of storage will be used later

for specific application-related information. Several additional portions of the TCA system area will be identified when specific failures are diagnosed in following chapters.

The next portion of storage mapped in an application dump is LIFO storage (3). LIFO (Last In First Out) storage is specific to the application and is gotten by DFHKCP (the task control program of CICS) when calls are made to CICS management modules (programs that begin with DFH*). Since CICS may have to handle multiple calls, registers are saved upon invocation so that they can be restored upon return. This storage is managed by CICS, and therefore may not be important to the programmers since they do not create or control it. It does, however, provide a record of the depth of management module calls, and could be significant in diagnosing problems when the abend appears to occur in a CICS module.

The Program Communication Area (4) contains data that is built by the program to "pass" or communicate with another program. Many times a module transfers control, or links to another program, passing a communication area. This area

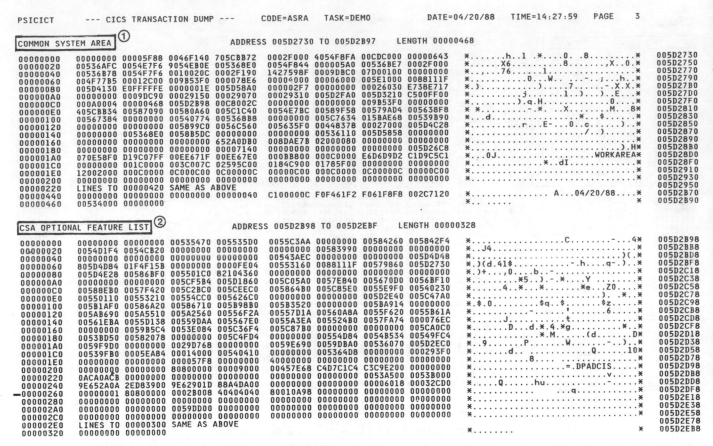

Figure 2-3  CICS transaction dump: CSA and CSAOPFL.

may contain data that will be needed by the other program for specific conditions or execution logic. The contents of this data area in the transaction dump are therefore mapped to assist the programmer in diagnosis of problems related to this Program Communication Area.

The next section of a dump is displayed in Figure 2-3. The Common System Area, or CSA (1), contains a great deal of information pertaining to the transaction. The CSA is actually the anchor control block, and contains pointers to most of the other control blocks in CICS. Although CICS builds one TCA for every transaction, there is only one CSA, one common area for all transactions. In addition to the pointers in the CSA, there are many status fields. The contents of the CSA are constantly being changed during execution, and many areas contain the status of various components of the region. For example, the CSA would detect if CICS was short of virtual storage or at maximum task limit. The CSA also keeps track of which task is currently being dispatched at any given time. CSA contents can be of great value in some areas of problem determination.

Following the CSA is extension called the CSA Optional Features List (2). This control block contains additional entries not available in the CSA.

Again, since it is still part of the common system area, this control block may be represented in every transaction dump, but exists as a single block of storage for all tasks to share.

Another important section of a transaction dump are the blocks of storage called "Transaction Storage." Figure 2-4 contains one entry that would be representative of those found within the listing. In this portion of a dump are contained all blocks of storage that were created by the program, or by CICS on behalf of the program. They are listed in the sequence that they were created during program execution, chained together by pointers from one block of storage to the next. The first block of storage is especially important, since it contains a control block that may be critical to diagnosing the problem. The first block of storage in our example is identified as Transaction Storage - User (1). This heading is merely the representation of the first byte in the control block that identifies the storage type. The first byte contains a hexadecimal 8C (2). Different types of storage are identified by different values in this first byte. Other storage types will appear in examples used in future chapters.

This first block of storage contains the control block Transaction Abend Control Block (TACB) (3). The TACB contains information pertaining to con-

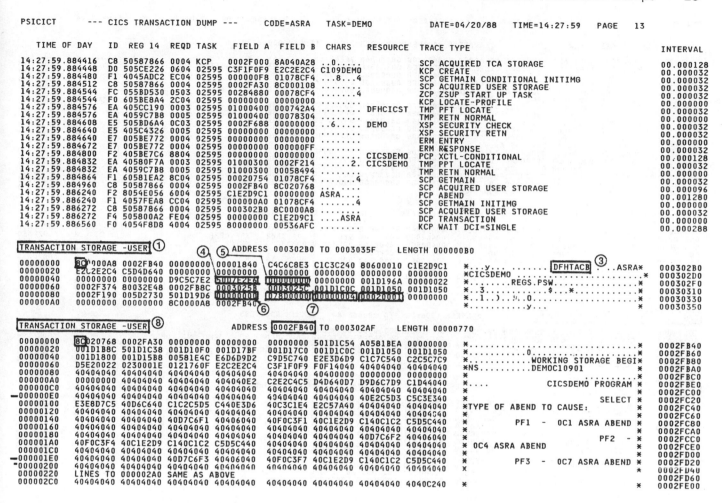

Figure 2-4   CICS transaction dump: user storage.

ditions at the time of the abend. Items contained in this control block are the abend type, or code, module name (also contained in the symptom string), and registers at the time of the abend. As mentioned previously, the registers are listed in the transaction dump in the first page. These formatted registers at the top of page one may be incorrect in certain failures. In some cases, during abend processing, these registers are reused and do not actually represent abend conditions. If the contents of specific registers are critical to the analysis of the problem, count on the contents in the TACB. Note, however, that the registers in the TACB are not formatted, or sequenced, as previously located on the first page of the dump. The best way to find the register contents is to locate the eyecatcher **REGS.PSW** within the contents of the control block. The hexdecimal representation of the eyecatcher is at offset **48** into the control block (4), ending with the hex **E6**, character W. The next fullword contains the contents of Register 0, and the other registers are followed in sequence, 2-15. Following in the example, then, Register 0 (5) con-

tains a fullword of zeros, as does Register 15 (6). Directly following the last register is the Program Status Word (7). Comparing this PSW with the formatted entry from page one [Figure 2-1, (4)], produces the same contents. Many times the PSW and the registers in the TACB are the same as those represented on the first page. Again, if this information is critical to the diagnosis of the problem, double check the contents, and trust the values in the TACB.

The next block of transaction storage is also identified as type "User," but actually is the first block of storage created by the application. As noted by the character representation of some of the storage contents (8), this contains the Working Storage section as built by the program. In the previous discussion of the TCA system area, a pointer to the program's dynamic storage area contained **0002FB40**. As the example shows, this transaction storage is indeed the COBOL dynamic storage area. The address in the title line, and the first entry in the far right column of addresses verifies the value. Other blocks of transaction storage may contain

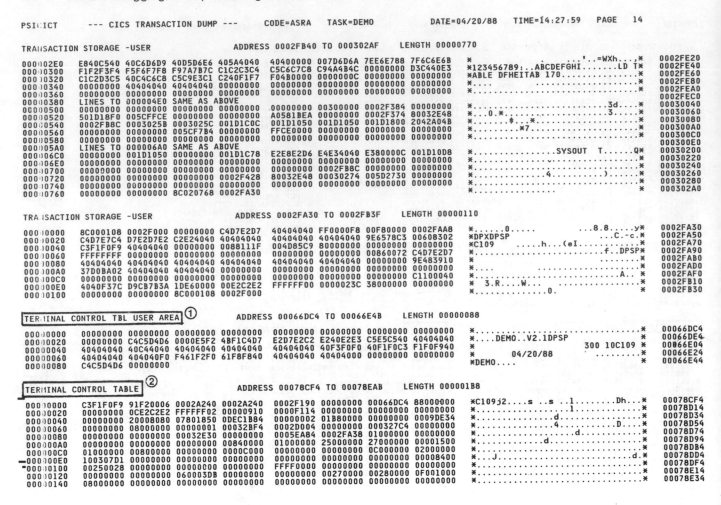

Figure 2-5   CICS transaction dump: TCTUA and TCT.

portions of data that were prepared by the application to be read. Most of the 8C type of storage is very application- related, and is used when diagnosing problems relating to data storage.

Another important section of data storage is presented on Figure 2-5, and relates to terminal storage. Two control blocks that may be relevant to problem determination are the Terminal Control Table (TCT) and an extension of it, the Terminal Control Table User Area (TCTUA). The TCT (1) is mapped for the terminal that was in control at the time of the failure. It contains information identifying the status of the terminal, which may be important if the problem is transmission- related. The TCTUA (2) may be even more important, since many installations use this control block to store CICS-related information that can be accessed by any transaction executed by that terminal. This control block is built at sign-on time, but may be written into, or read from, any time during the session.

One of the most critical blocks of storage within a dump is shown in Figure 2-6. The formatted dump

program identifies that module that was in control at the time of the failure, and attempts to map out that section of program storage. It is hoped that this block of program storage contains the instructions that were being executed to cause the failure. This block of storage is especially important in ASRA abends, since the failure is some type of program check. Several examples in the chapter covering ASRA abends reference this control block, and a great deal of time is spent analyzing its contents. Programmers reference this block of storage with output from the COBOL compile listing to diagnose many problems.

The last component of a transaction dump is represented in Figure 2-7 and could easily be one of the most important. Every program known to CICS, whether an IBM module or a user-written module, is listed in the module map at the end of every dump. This summary was made available only in CICS 1.7, so earlier releases will not contain this entry. This summary can be very valuable, since it contains items relevant to executed programs. The summary is in sequence by entry point

```
PSICICT      --- CICS TRANSACTION DUMP ---      CODE=ASRA   TASK=DEMO        DATE=04/20/88  TIME=14:27:59    PAGE  15

TERMINAL CONTROL TABLE                        ADDRESS 00078CF4 TO 00078EAB    LENGTH 000001B8
00000160  00000000 00000000 00000000 000000E0  28A14800 80002010 00000000 00000000   *........................*   00078E54
00000180  00000000 00000000 00078B34 0002BB85  00000000 000016CC D4000000 00000014   *................e.......M......*   00078E74
000001A0  00000000 00000000 00000000 00000000  00000000 00000000                     *........................*   00078E94

PSEUDO SIGN-ON TABLE ENTRY                    ADDRESS 0009DE34 TO 0009DE61    LENGTH 0000002E
00000000  002E4000 00000000 00000000 C0000000  00000000 00FFFFFF 00000002 000000E2   *........................*   0009DE34
00000020  C2E20008 40404040 40404040 0000                                            *........  ..*   0009DE54

TERMINAL STORAGE                              ADDRESS 0002A240 TO 0002A48F    LENGTH 00000250
00000000  85020248 00078CF8 02306040 40404040  40404040 404040E2 C2E2C4C5 D4D640D7   *e......8..-              CICSDEMO P*   0002A240
00000020  D9D6C7D9 C1D44040 40404040 40404040  40404040 40404040 40404040 40404040   *ROGRAM                  *   0002A260
00000040  40404040 40404040 40404040 40404040  40404040 40404040 40404040 40404040   *                        *   0002A280
00000060  40E2C5D3 C5C3E340 E3E8D7C5 40D6C640  C1C2C5D5 C440E3D6 40C3C1E4 E2C57A40   * SELECT TYPE OF ABEND TO CAUSE: *   0002A2A0
00000080  40404040 40404040 40404040 40404040  40404040 40404040 40404040 40404040   *                        *   0002A2C0
000000A0  40404040 40404040 40404040 40404040  40D7C6F1 40406040 40F0C3F1 40C1E2D9   *              PF1  -  0C1 ASR*   0002A2E0
000000C0  C140C1C2 C5D5C440 40404040 40404040  40404040 40404040 40404040 40404040   *A ABEND                 *   0002A300
000000E0  40404040 40404040 40404040 40404040  40404040 40404040 40404040 40404040   *                        *   0002A320
00000100  40D7C6F2 40406040 40F0C3F4 40C1E2D9  C140C1C2 C5D5C440 40404040 40404040   * PF2  -  0C4 ASRA ABEND *   0002A340
00000120  40404040 40404040 40404040 40404040  40404040 40404040 40404040 40404040   *                        *   0002A360
00000140  40404040 40404040 40404040 40404040  40D7C6F3 40406040 40F0C3F7 40C1E2D9   *              PF3  -  0C7 ASR*   0002A380
00000160  C140C1C2 C5D5C440 40404040 40404040  40404040 40404040 40404040 40404040   *A ABEND                 *   0002A3A0
00000180  40404040 40404040 40404040 40404040  40404040 40404040 40404040 40404040   *                        *   0002A3C0
000001A0  LINES TO 00000200 SAME AS ABOVE                                            *                        *   0002A3E0
00000220  40404040 40404040 40404040 40404040  40404040 40404040 40404040 00000000   *                     ....*   0002A460
00000240  00000000 00000000 85020248 00078CF8                                        *........e.....8*   0002A480
```

┌───────────────┐
│PROGRAM STORAGE│                             ADDRESS 001D1008 TO 001D2517    LENGTH 00001510
└───────────────┘

```
00000000  C4C6C8E8 C3F1F7F0 58F00010 58F0F000  58F0F0D0 58F0F004 58F0F014 58F0F00C   *DFHYC170.0...00..00..00..00..00.*   001D1008
00000020  58FF000C 07FF58F0 001058F0 F00058F0  F00458F0 F0D058F0 F01458F0 F00858FF   *.0...00..00..00..00...*   001D1028
00000040  00C858FF 018407FF 90ECD00C 185D05F0  4580F010 E2C2E2C4 C5D4D640 E5E2D9F1   *.H...d.....).0..0.CICSDEMO VSR1*   001D1048
00000060  0700989F F02407FF 96021034 07FE41F0  000107FE 001D1C0C 001D1050 001D1050   *..q.0..o......0...........*   001D1068
00000080  001D1800 00030054 001D18CC 001D1BCC  00000000 501D1C54 A0581BEA 00000000   *........................*   001D1088
000000A0  001D1B8C 501D1C38 001D10F0 001D17BF  001D17C0 001D1050 001D1050 001D1050   *........0..............*   001D10A8
000000C0  001D1800 001D15B8 00581E4C 001D17D0  F1F44BF0 F44BF0F9 C1D7D940 F2F06B40   *...........14.04.09APR 20, *   001D10C8
000000E0  F1F9F8F8 00000000 E6D6D9D2 C9D5C740  E2E3D6D9 C1C7C540 C2C5C7C9 D5E20022   *1988....WORKING STORAGE BEGINS..*   001D10E8
00000100  0230001E 0121760F 40404040 40404040  00000000 00000000 00000000 00000000   *........ ................*   001D1108
00000120  00000000 00000000 00000000 00000000  00000000 00000000 00000000 00000000   *........................*   001D1128
00000140  40404040 40404040 404040E2 C2E2C4C5  D4D640D7 D9D6C7D9 C1D44040 40404040   *          CICSDEMO PROGRAM   *   001D1148
00000160  40404040 40404040 40404040 40404040  40404040 40404040 40404040 40404040   *                        *   001D1168
00000180  40404040 40404040 40404040 40404040  40404040 40E2C5D3 C5C3E340 E3E8D7C5   * OF ABEND TO CAUSE:     SELECT TYPE*   001D1188
000001A0  40D6C640 C1C2C5D5 C440E3D6 40C3C1E4  E2C57A40 40404040 40404040 40404040   *                        *   001D11A8
000001E0  40404040 40404040 40D7C6F1 40406040  40F0C3F1 40C1E2D9 C140C1C2 C5D5C440   *        PF1  -  0C1 ASRA ABEND *   001D11C8
00000200  40404040 40404040 40404040 40404040  40404040 40404040 40404040 40404040   *                        *   001D11E8
00000220  40404040 40404040 40404040 40404040  40404040 40D7C6F2 40406040 40F0C3F4   *             PF2  -  0C4*   001D1208
00000240  40C1E2D9 C140C1C2 C5D5C440 40404040  40404040 40404040 40404040 40404040   * ASRA ABEND             *   001D1228
00000260  40404040 40404040 40404040 40404040  40404040 40404040 40404040 40404040   *                        *   001D1248
00000280  40404040 40D7C6F3 40406040 40F0C3F7  40C1E2D9 C140C1C2 C5D5C440 40404040   *    PF3  -  0C7 ASRA ABEND  *   001D1268
000002A0  40404040 40404040 40404040 40404040  40404040 40404040 40404040 40404040   *                        *   001D1288
```

Figure 2-6  CICS transaction dump: program storage.

of all modules known to CICS at the time of the abend. The fields in the summary represent the following:

Entry point (1) — the address of the first instruction to be executed at the time the program is entered, or run

Load point (2) — the address of the start of the module as it was loaded into CICS storage

Name (3) — the module name (from the PPT or RDO entry)

Vers'n (4) — the CICS version that the IBM module was shipped for

Time/Date (5) — the time and date stamp of the IBM module linkage

Note that in this example, as in many others, the address of the entry point is different from the address of the load point in some of the programs. This is important to take note of, since it will affect the location of failing instructions. In the sample program, CICSDEMO (6), while the load point of this program is **001D1008**, the entry point is **001D1050**. In order to accommodate high-level languages, CICS must incorporate a portion of program code in front of your program. In the output from a COBOL compile, there would be entries similar to Figure 2-8.

First, note that the linkage editor output contained an INCLUDE for DFHECI from the system library (SYSLIB) specification (1). This step places the execution control interface (ECI) code into the module, and therefore enables the execution interface program (EIP) of command level COBOL to execute instructions properly. If compiling a different high-level language, such as PL/1, or an ASSEMBLER program, this INCLUDEd component would be different, to handle the other language interface.

In the Cross Reference Table on that same page, the name of all code sections within the linked module are listed. DFHECI is identified, with a length of 48 bytes (2). The actual COBOL source that will be executed, therefore, begins 48 bytes into the load module. This can be verified by noting that the starting position of the program, CICSDEMO, is at location 48 (3). This offset into

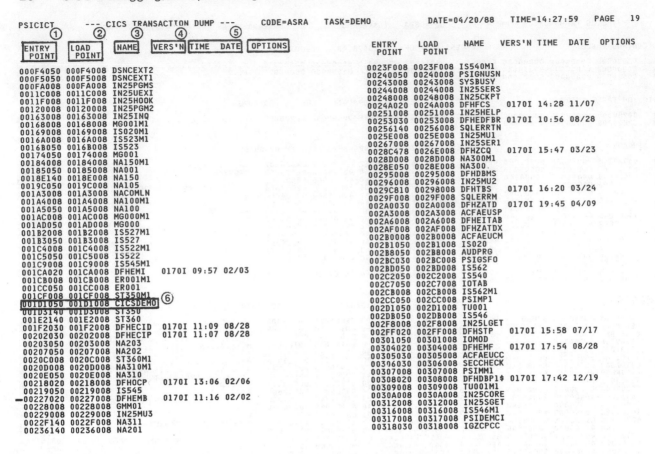

Figure 2-7   CICS transaction dump: module map.

the program may vary with COBOL release, CICS release and, of course, programming language used. Returning to Figure 2-7, program CICSDEMO (6), subtracting the entry point **001D1050**, from the load point **001D1008** verifies that the CICS prefix for this program is a hexadecimal value of 48. This explains the difference in value between the two addresses. But what about some of the other load modules? The entry directly preceding CICSDEMO is a program named ST350M1, with exactly the same addresses in both the entry point and load point. The program ST350M1 is actually a CICS map. Although maps are program load modules, they do not contain instructions that need to be interpreted by the command level interpreter, and therefore contain no prefix.

### 2.2.2  Formatted Trace Table Entries

Another portion of a dump contains all records of task execution during a particular interval. These trace records are stored in a trace table, which is built during CICS initialization. The size of this table is specified in the system initialization table

(SIT) or as a startup override. In a CICS region with high activity, the number of entries in a table should be large enough to contain the failure. Remember, not only the task experiencing the failure is writing entries into the trace. All activity in the region is being written to the table. A trace table of one thousand entries may appear large, but in fact, may only be enough to hold a very small interval of time. The trace table is filled in a "wrap" manner, which means when the table is filled, it begins overwriting entries at the start of the table. Trace must also be turned on via the SIT parameter TRACE, or can be started via the CEMT command once the region is initialized. In the previous chapter, auxiliary trace was explained. While auxiliary trace writes to an external dataset and is processed by the CICS utility DFHTUP, the internal trace facility must be specified in size prior to startup, and appears within formatted dumps from transaction or system failures. Both trace facilities produce standard trace records, however, and all trace entries are fully documented in the CICS Problem Determination Guide. Refer to this publication for complete syntax and format.

```
MVS/XA DFP VER 2 LINKAGE EDITOR          14:31:36  MON  JUL 18, 1988
JOB DPSPPIDA    STEP ASM        PROCEDURE LKED
INVOCATION PARAMETERS - LIST,LET,MAP,XREF
ACTUAL SIZE=(317440,86016)
 OUTPUT DATA SET PSIAD.LINKLIB IS ON VOLUME USER01
IEW0000      INCLUDE SYSLIB(DFHECI)  ①
IEW0000      NAME CICSDEMO(R)                                    50000000
IEW0132  DUMMY


                          CROSS REFERENCE TABLE


 CONTROL SECTION                  ENTRY

     NAME     ORIGIN   LENGTH ②      NAME     LOCATION    NAME     LOCATION    NAME     LOCATION    NAME     LOCATION
   DFHECI       00      48           DFHEI1       8     DLZEI01       8     DLZEI02       8     DLZEI03       8
                                     DLZEI04      8     DFHCBLI      26

   CICSDEMO     48 ③    C22
   ILBOCOM0*    C70     16D          ILBOCOM     C70

   ILBOSRV *    DE0     4A4          ILBOSRV0    DEA    ILBOSR5     DEA    ILBOSR3     DEA    ILBOSR      DEA
                                     ILBOSRV1    DEE    ILBOSTP1    DEE    ILBOST      DF2    ILBOSTP0    DF2
   ILBOBEG *   1288     188          ILBOBEG0   128A

   ILBOMSG *   1410     100          ILBOMSG0   1412


 LOCATION  REFERS TO SYMBOL  IN CONTROL SECTION            LOCATION  REFERS TO SYMBOL  IN CONTROL SECTION
    7F8           ILBOSRV0      ILBOSRV                        7FC          ILBOSR5       ILBOSRV
    800           DFHEI1        DFHECI                         804          DUMMY         $UNRESOLVED
    808           ILBOSRV1      ILBOSRV                        768          ILBOCOM0      ILBOCOM0
   116C           ILBOCOM       ILBOCOM0                      1180          ILBOSTT0      $UNRESOLVED(W)
   1170           ILBOCMM0      $UNRESOLVED(W)                1174          ILBOBEG0      ILBOBEG
   1178           ILBOMSG0      ILBOMSG                       117C          ILBOSND2      $UNRESOLVED(W)
   13C8           ILBOPRM0      $UNRESOLVED(W)
 ENTRY ADDRESS       48

 TOTAL LENGTH       1510
 ** CICSDEMO DID NOT PREVIOUSLY EXIST BUT WAS ADDED AND HAS AMODE 24
 ** LOAD MODULE HAS RMODE 24
 ** AUTHORIZATION CODE IS        0.


                          DIAGNOSTIC MESSAGE DIRECTORY
IEW0132 ERROR - SYMBOL PRINTED IS AN UNRESOLVED EXTERNAL REFERENCE.
```

Figure 2-8    COBOL linkage editor output.

Figure 2-9 contains a sample section of trace table from a transaction dump. It is usually found within the dump following the CSA and CSA Optional Feature List control blocks. The first page of the trace table would contain the section heading, Trace Table, and the addresses within storage containing the entries. The next entry would contain the Trace Header. The header record of the trace contains mostly addresses, such as the address of the first entry, the last entry, etc. Since this is a formatted trace table in the dump, these addresses are merely informational. If diagnosing a problem with an unformatted dump, it would be necessary to find this trace header, and then follow the addresses to the actual trace entries within storage. In most transaction failures, this will not be necessary. The headings on the next line identify the fields that will be shown within each formatted trace entry listed. These fields are

1. **Time-of-day stamp** — the time stamp of the trace entry in units of hour, minute, second, and microsecond. As you can see in the trace, CICS can execute many instructions per second.

2. **ID** — Trace identification entry. This identifies the type of trace entry, and is one hexadecimal byte.

3. **REG 14** — the contents of Register 14 at the time of this trace entry.

4. **REQD** — the type of request code if the entry relates to a CICS management or service program. This entries is unused for user entries.

5. **TASK** — the task identifier as found in the TCA system area, field TCADKTTA. This usually identifies either the CICS management module involved, or the task number of the user program executing.

6. **FIELD A/FIELD B** — these fields sometimes contain descriptive data pertaining to the trace entry. Reference each specific trace record type to see the specific content of these fields.

7. **CHARS** — the character representation of Field A and B, if the data can be represented in character format.

```
PSI1CICP      --- CICS TRANSACTION DUMP ---       CODE=AEIS   TASK=DEMO       DATE=10/10/88  TIME=08:09:20  PAGE  22
              ①    ②     ③    ④   ⑤            ⑥          ⑦     ⑧         ⑨                                      
          TIME OF DAY    ID   REG 14  REQD TASK    FIELD A    FIELD B   CHARS   RESOURCE  TRACE TYPE                          INTERVAL

08:09:20.763296  F0 505F617A C004 00028 80000000 005D3704 .....)..          KCP WAIT+CANCADDR DCI=SINGLE        00.000896
08:09:20.792544  D0 50666CDE 0904 KCP   00010001 3EA6CA0B                    KCP SYSTEM RESUME                  *00.029248
08:09:20.792768  D0 50666CDE 0504 00028 00000000 00000000 ........          KCP DISPATCH                        00.000224
08:09:20.792800  DE 405F5C60 0065 00028 01080000 000532B8 ........          SKP RETN NORMAL                     00.000000
08:09:20.792800  F0 6036DD0E 0204 00028 .0036DB90 00000000 ........          KCP DEQUEUE                         00.000032
08:09:20.792832  F5 4036DDBC 4265 00028 81020000 17080000 ........          FCP RETN DFHFCN ERROR               00.000032
08:09:20.792864  F1 5036D012 CC04 00028 00000043 01044004 ........          SCP GETMAIN INITIMG                 00.000032
08:09:20.792896  C8 5061D830 0004 00028 00048ED0 8C000058 ........          SCP ACQUIRED USER STORAGE           00.000032
08:09:20.792928  F1 6061CE5A 4004 00028 00053BD0 01044004 ........          SCP FREEMAIN                        00.000000
08:09:20.792928  C9 5061D86C 0004 00028 00053BD0 8C000408 ........          SCP RELEASED USER STORAGE           00.000032
08:09:20.792960  E0 6036D84A 0003 00028 009003B8 00048EF0 ........0         MGP DFH 00952 CSMT CONSOLE          00.000000
08:09:20.793024  F6 405F285E E103 00028 00000000 00000000 ........ CSMT     TDP APPL REQ CTYPE LOCATE           00.000064
08:09:20.793056  EA 40604854 0003 00028 01000600 000533DC ........ CSMT     TMP DCT LOCATE                      00.000032
08:09:20.793088  EA 40631A2C 0065 00028 01000600 00604458 .....-..          TMP RETN NORMAL                     00.000032
08:09:20.793088  F6 40604974 4003 00028 00000000 00000000 ........          TDP RETN APPL RESP NORMAL           00.000000
08:09:20.793120  F6 405F28A0 4003 00028 00000000 000531D8 .......Q CSMT     TDP APPL REQ PUT                    00.000032
08:09:20.793152  EA 40604974 4003 00028 01000600 000533DC ........ CSMT     TMP DCT LOCATE                      00.000000
08:09:20.793152  EA 40631A2C 0005 00028 01000600 00604458 .....-..          TMP RETN NORMAL                     00.000096
08:09:20.793248  F0 50606E44 C004 00028 20000000 0036DB90 ........          KCP WAIT+CANCADDR DCI=DISP          00.000032
08:09:20.793280  D0 50666CDE 0504 00028 00000000 00000000 ........          KCP DISPATCH                        00.000032
08:09:20.793312  F6 40604AC8 0005 00028 00000000 00000000 ........          TDP RETN APPL RESP NORMAL           00.000032
08:09:20.794560  E0 405F15E0 0005 00028 009003B8 80000000 ........          MGP DFH RETN 00952 CSMT CONSOLE     00.001248
08:09:20.794592  F1 5036D8B4 4004 00028 00048ED0 01044004 ........          SCP FREEMAIN                        00.000032
08:09:20.794624  C9 5061D86C 0004 00028 00048ED0 8C000058 ........          SCP RELEASED USER STORAGE           00.000032
08:09:20.794624  F0 7036CFAE 0204 00028 0404AE80 00000000 ........          KCP DEQUEUE                         00.000000
08:09:20.794656  F2 5036C2A0 1004 00028 00000000 00000000 ........ DFHFCS   PCP RETURN                          00.000032
08:09:20.794720  F1 60617A4E 4004 00028 00048E70 01044004 .....-..          SCP FREEMAIN                        00.000064
08:09:20.794720  C9 5061D86C 0004 00028 00048E70 89040058 ........          SCP RELEASED RSA STORAGE            00.000000
08:09:20.794752  F5 40610920 2065 00028 00000000 0000000C ........          FCP RETN ERROR                      00.000032
08:09:20.794784  E1 00000000 00F4 00028 0C000000 000060C .......           EIP STARTBR RESPONSE                00.000032
08:09:20.794784  F2 00669206 6004 00028 C1C5C9E2 00000000 AEIS....          PCP ABEND                           00.000000
08:09:20.794816  F1 40616818 CC04 00028 000000A0 01044004 ........          SCP GETMAIN INITIMG                 00.000032
08:09:20.794848  C8 5061D830 0004 00028 00048E70 8C0000A8 ........          SCP ACQUIRED USER STORAGE           00.000032
08:09:20.794848  F4 50616A52 FE04 00028 00000000 C1C5C9E2 ....AEIS          DCP TRANSACTION                     00.000000
08:09:20.794880  F0 505EF490 2004 00028 FE000000 00000000 ........          KCP CHAP                            00.000032
08:09:20.794912  D0 50666CDE 0504 00028 00000000 00000000 ........          KCP DISPATCH                        00.000352
08:09:20.795264  F0 405F0584 4004 00028 00000000 005D489C .....)..          KCP WAIT DCI=SINGLE                *00.015168
08:09:20.810432  D0 50666CDE 0904 KCP   00010001 3EA6CA12 ........          KCP SYSTEM RESUME                   00.000224
08:09:20.810656  D0 50666CDE 0504 00028 00000000 00000000 ........          KCP DISPATCH
```

```
TRANSACTION STORAGE -USER              ADDRESS 00048E70 TO 00048F1F     LENGTH 000000B0

─00000000  8C0000A8 00053000 00000000 00001840 C4C6C8E3 C1C3C240 80600010 C1C5C9E2 *...y.......... DFHTACB .-..AEIS*  00048E70
 00000020  C4C5D4D6 D7C7D440 00000000 00000000 00000000 00000000 00000000 00000000 *DEMOPGM ........................*  00048E90
 00000040  00000000 00000000 D9C5C7E2 50D7E2E6 2060EA14 0004A6B8 0004A474 0004A36C *........REGS.PSW.-....w...u...t.*  00048EB0
 00000060  0004A46C 0004A2BC 006696E1 00048BB0 00668380 00669050 00048C19 000482C0 *.u...s...c..........b.*          00048ED0
 00000080  00048190 0066A670 00669206 806691EE 0060EA14 00000000 00000000 04000000 *.a...w...k...j..-..............*  00048EF0
 000000A0  00000000 00000000 8C0000A8 00053000                                     *.........y....              *     00048F10
```

Figure 2-9   CICS formatted trace table entries.

8. **RESOURCE** — the name of the resource associated with the trace entry, if available. User trace entries can also set the value of this resource name.

9. **TRACE TYPE** — the interpreted description of the trace entry, as specified by the Trace ID.

The interval entry at the far right of the trace entry (10) merely notes the period-of-time interval since the last trace entry, usually in microseconds.

The first trace entries in the dump are actually the oldest. The time stamp entries will show the chronological sequence of activity from the oldest entry (that survived the wrap-around and hasn't been written over) to the last entry in the table. Logically, then, at the end of the trace would be the last transaction activity able to be recorded at the time of the failure. That is exactly the technique that most programmers use to locate trace entries that will be relevant to their analysis. Starting at the end and "backing up" would locate the trace entry that recorded the abend. Of course, that entry merely records the failure. If the scan continued back through the trace entries, it would display the activity that led up to the failure. These entries

could give clues and actually identify the instructions that produced the abend.

As a specific example, failures that occurred as a result of conditions that were not handled are excellent situations. They can very easily be resolved via the trace entries, which show the resource that was not available and the request that was not handled by the application. Figure 2-9 contains trace entries from a typical transaction dump. These situations are completely covered in following chapters. In particular, Chapter 5 deals with application file abends and conditions that were not handled properly. Trace entries such as those in Figure 2-9 will be analyzed in that chapter.

Trace entries can be very important in the analysis of a problem, and can give a step-by-step look at exactly what occurred directly preceding the failure. Future examples will analyze many more trace tables and use them to assist in problem determination.

In summary, the contents of a transaction dump can be very useful in problem solving. Although not all portions of a dump may be used in all problems, familiarization with the components can give access to data areas that may be useful.

# Application Programming

# 3

# Application Programming Issues

Although there are several programming languages available for use in CICS, most installations choose command-level COBOL as their programming standard. COBOL provides command interfaces, debugging tools such as CEDF, new functions in every release, and is clearly the supported product for future enhancements. For these reasons, most of the problem determination issues will deal with COBOL applications. This material applies equally to other languages that use EXEC interface facilities. This does not mean that PL/1 is not an effective and useful programming language. Some installations use PL/1 as the primary language for all CICS transactions. Other installations choose not to use high-level languages at all, and develop applications in Assembler language. For the most part, however, COBOL remains the industry standard and is the language discussed most thoroughly.

One of the most relevant issues in CICS application development, however, is the issue of macro-level coding. Macro coding was available long before command-level and was used extensively in the early releases of CICS. Many installations have hundreds of programs still written in macro-level code and are unable to spend the hours of programming time necessary to convert. Why should they convert programs that are, and have been, running perfectly well for so long? Should installations develop new applications in macro-level? Some macro-level vs. command-level issues will be discussed, especially from a problem determination perspective. Installations have to make their own choices and develop programming standards. Perhaps, however, if all the facts are known, the long-range plans can be made.

## 3.1 MACRO-LEVEL VS. COMMAND-LEVEL COBOL

Macro-level application programming, as previously stated, has been around for a long time. CICS macros gave programmers the ability to access control blocks and reference data areas within CICS internal storage. Not only were the programmers able to reference these areas, they were able to modify them. Some control blocks, or portions of control blocks, are designed to be read and/or updated by an application; others are not.

Applications that access restricted control blocks are creating dangerous support problems. For example, a macro could be used to access the Terminal Control Table (TCT) entry for a specific terminal. An alternative value could be moved into that data area. To CICS, therefore, the terminal entry now contained data that was placed into it by the application program. Another technique that was very popular in macro-level coding was to locate specific control blocks in CICS, such as table entries. Macro-level programs could scan the Program Control Table (PCT), and locate the transaction entry. As IBM changes these resources to be dynamic, through maintenance, new releases, or enhanced functions, these tables are no longer available. Resource Definition Online (RDO) creates definitions that are much different from the previous control table technique. In addition, CICS 1.7 introduced a new facility called "terminal autoinstall." Installations using this technique benefit by terminal control blocks are dynamically created during logon, and deleted when the terminal logs off. Any modifications to the terminal control blocks are erased during de-install, since the control blocks are constantly being recreated. Techniques used by macro-level programs may not be applicable in new CICS environments.

IBM introduced command-level facilities for many reasons. One obvious reason, as described above, is to avoid constant retrofitting of programs when new facilities are incorporated into CICS. The use of CICS commands isolates, or "externalizes," the program from the actual internals of the product. CICS developers can enhance the internals of the product and not affect the current applications. The commands, during pre-compile, are interpreted into proper expansions of the function being requested. Figure 3-1 contains a typical CICS command-level instruction and the result after being translated. The actual instruction as coded contains the typical syntax EXEC CICS command (1). In addition to the command, STARTBR, the statement contains appropriate parameters that, combined with the command, produce the entire request. The command requests a browse on file FILEA with a RIDFLD (request ID field). CICS commands can be identified in a compiled output listing by the asterisks (*) preceding the statement, thus making it into a comment. This indicates that the translator has located a command, commented out the source statement, and replaced it with the appropriate instructions to invoke the command through the EXEC interface. The command in the example has been replaced with a MOVE (2) and CALL containing the appropriate CICS data areas and values.

The EXEC block provides the layer between the programmer and CICS. This allows IBM to drastically change the internals of CICS without any need to recompile the application. Because this translation is performed by the translator at the time of compile, CICS takes care of inserting the correct values. These values can be, and sometimes are, different depending on the release of the product. The programmer may, at most, have to recompile the program to become compatible with the new release of CICS. In many cases, recompiling is not even necessary. This is one of the most important reasons that most installations are moving away from macros and converting to commands. To take advantage of new technologies, companies must install new releases of CICS that provide enhanced functions. Programs that contain macros may have to be converted, or even rewritten, to comply with the new release. Most installations are unwilling to apply programming staff to retrofit these applications. Migrations and conversions are time-consuming, time that could otherwise be spent on new application development. IBM's commitment to compatibility between releases with com-

mand level makes it very appealing to most installations.

### 3.1.1 Differences in Function and Future

Some of the differences in the two programming techniques have already been discussed. Probably the most important items are under the headings of "Depth of Programming Control" and "Compatibility Between Releases." From a problem determination viewpoint, these two topics become even more critical.

**Depth of Programming Control.** Programmers still code in macro-level to get function that is not available by command. They feel the need for programming control down to the control block level. True, many data areas within CICS are not accessible to a command-level programmer. If a programmer wishes to read the value of these items, there are no comparable commands to access the data. Another issue in CICS terminal control has always been the inability to select upper/lower case translation dynamically. Terminals are globally defined in the device definition for translation, and this value is set when the control block is built. Some installations have determined a need to modify this setting, depending on the application that is being executed. No commands are available to determine the existing value and modify the terminal to another setting. Programmers have, therefore, used macro-level facilities to access these control blocks and change the contents when necessary. Installations have some small number of utility subroutines that are called by normal applications. These routines "flip bits," or modify CICS resources in control blocks.

This depth of programming control has sustained the existence of macro-level coding. The control block dependent programs still exist, but the number is getting smaller and the functions are consolidated to a few programs outside the normal COBOL command code. IBM has a vehicle to remove these limitations. Installations can submit requirements to IBM, specifying the function required. Enhancements in new releases of CICS are direct responses to requirements that were submitted to IBM.

**Compatibility Between Releases.** IBM has committed to insure command-level programs are upward-compatible between releases. What does that mean? It means that programs that are written in command level will, when moved to the next upward release of CICS, execute without modifications. The installation will not need to commit time and resources

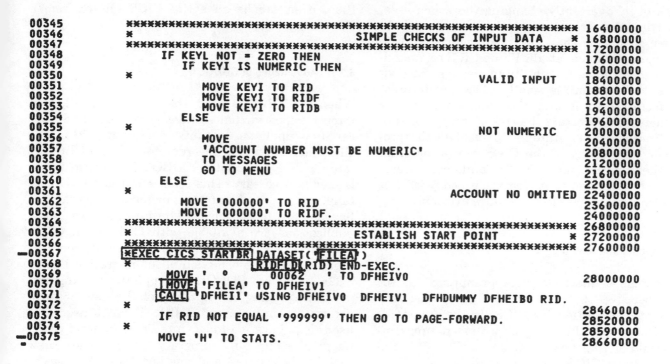

```
00345   ********************************************************** 16400000
00346   *                              SIMPLE CHECKS OF INPUT DATA  * 16800000
00347   ********************************************************** 17200000
00348         IF KEYL NOT = ZERO THEN                              17600000
00349            IF KEYI IS NUMERIC THEN                           18000000
00350   *                                          VALID INPUT     18400000
00351               MOVE KEYI TO RID                               18800000
00352               MOVE KEYI TO RIDF                              19200000
00353               MOVE KEYI TO RIDB                              19400000
00354            ELSE                                              19600000
00355   *                                          NOT NUMERIC     20000000
00356               MOVE                                           20400000
00357               'ACCOUNT NUMBER MUST BE NUMERIC'               20800000
00358               TO MESSAGES                                    21200000
00359               GO TO MENU                                     21600000
00360         ELSE                                                 22000000
00361   *                                    ACCOUNT NO OMITTED    22400000
00362            MOVE '000000' TO RID                              23600000
00363            MOVE '000000' TO RIDF.                            24000000
00364   ********************************************************** 26800000
00365   *                              ESTABLISH START POINT    *  27200000
00366   ********************************************************** 27600000
-00367  *EXEC CICS STARTBR DATASET( 'FILEA' )
00368   *                  RIDFLD(RID) END-EXEC.
00369         MOVE ' 0        00062   ' TO DFHEIVO                 28000000
00370         MOVE 'FILEA' TO DFHEIV1
00371         CALL 'DFHEII' USING DFHEIVO  DFHEIV1   DFHDUMMY DFHEIBO RID.
00372   *                                                          28460000
00373         IF RID NOT EQUAL '999999' THEN GO TO PAGE-FORWARD.   28520000
00374   *                                                          28590000
-00375        MOVE 'H' TO STATS.                                   28660000
```

Figure 3-1    Typical CICS command-level instructions.

to rewrite the program for compatibility. This can mean substantial savings in time and allow migration to new releases without conversions and outages. Macro-level programs may require much more effort to convert and test. Macros may change in the new release; data areas may change in size and content. Data areas that were used by the program may not even exist any longer. If the program depends on these data areas for function within the application, alternative programming techniques may need to be used. Function may have to be removed if the necessary data is now unavailable. The justification for macro-level and its depth of function within CICS internals may appear desirable. On the other hand, that function may be short-lived and unable to be continued. Installations face many decisions where function vies with support.

How do these topics relate to problem determination? While coding techniques may impact the ability to solve problems, the same techniques that provide function in macro-level may complicate failure analysis. The ability to not only reference but modify data areas within control blocks has been discussed. If a macro-level program can modify a data area or an address within storage, it can corrupt these areas with invalid values. CICS assumes that most of these control blocks are created and modified by CICS management modules. If, for example, a programmer was diagnosing a failure by referenc-

ing a portion of the CICS Common System Area, the CSA, it would be assumed that all contents of this control block were built by CICS services, and were therefore valid. If a macro-level program, for some reason, decided to modify the contents of a data area within the CSA (intentionally or unintentionally), would the programmer be aware of it? Since this control block is shared, or common, to all transactions, could any program be affected by the modification? Since the program did not make the modification, how would it know to accommodate the change? Modification of CICS data areas can be very dangerous and can affect many other applications. In fact, many program failures or even CICS failures are due primarily to inadvertent storage modifications. A full section on storage violations details this situation in a later chapter.

One of the most common results of storage corruption is a storage violation. Storage violations are very severe failures, and many times cause the entire CICS system to abend. They are very difficult to diagnose, since areas of storage have been corrupted, or overlayed, and the original contents destroyed. All CICS storage is connected through chains, or lists. When one of these chains is broken due to an overlay, pointers and addresses are lost. If the lost resource is critical to CICS execution, the region fails. Some storage violations are recoverable, depending on the contents and scope of the overlay. Programs that modify CICS data areas run the risk of inadvertently changing the wrong area, or inserting the wrong value. Great care needs to be taken to insure that any modification is made correctly, or not made at all. While CICS command-level programs have the ability to create storage violations, the exposure is smaller. IBM has incorporated facilities to isolate the program from the data, thereby minimizing the risk of storage corruption. Command-level statements insulate the programmer from many of the CICS control program areas, thereby reducing risk. The philosophy seems to be "if you can't get to it, you can't modify it." Not a bad technique, especially in failure avoidance.

### 3.1.2 Directions in Macro Level

The direction of macro-level programming was set on October 18, 1988, when IBM announced the Statement of Direction for CICS. In the announcement, IBM stated that support for macro programming would be removed in the *new CICS*. When the next version of CICS becomes available, it will no longer accommodate programs written with macros. IBM will provide a "bridge," or a vehicle to assist in the migration. CICS/MVS Version 2 will continue to run macro applications, and can be used by installations until all programs have been converted. The new CICS will have enhanced facilities, and these facilities cannot be provided if macro continues to be supported. If customers wish CICS to take advantage of new technologies and architectures, they must expect changes to be required for these enhancements.

Although there will be a period of time where macros will continue to co-exist with CICS commands, any future development with this facility should be reconsidered. Not only will macro-level restrict the application from new technologies — it could complicate problem determination and place the installation in a difficult support position.

## 3.2 COBOL II ISSUES

Installations are choosing to install and utilize COBOL II in CICS for several reasons. Even with MVS/XA, much of the CICS address space resides "below the line," or within the 16MB limitation. Programs are loaded into CICS storage within this limited area, and constantly contend for enough space to load and execute. If insufficient storage exists for these programs to remain, program compression results. The program is deleted from the dynamic area within CICS, and reloaded at next execution. Performance problems can result, and

there even can be an entire CICS failure from a short-on-storage condition.

### 3.2.1 Advantages of COBOL II

When COBOL II is used, the programs are loaded into extended virtual storage "above the line" and can free up large amounts of storage within the CICS address space. In order to utilize COBOL II into CICS 1.7 and later, COBOL II Release 2.0 or higher is necessary. This release of COBOL II contains many new features, including several enhancements for problem determination. Two new publications are available with COBOL II. C320-0562, IBM VS COBOL II Migration Guide contains a great deal of information about migration issues. SC26-4049, VS COBOL II Application Programming: Debugging covers many of the new problem determination features. COBOL II batch users can use this publication to learn the new interactive debugging facility. CICS programmers can also review FDUMP procedures, and reference any messages or codes produced during a failure. Some features have changed, or have been removed altogether. Following are highlights of COBOL II capabilities and features that may be productive for problem determination procedures.

**FDUMP Compiler Option.** Using this compiler option, the programmer can receive a formatted dump at abend time, either in a batch or CICS program. The formatted dump is not like the formatted transaction dump, or the formatted system dump produced by CICS, but rather a format of several application-related areas that may be significant to the problem. In addition to using the compile-time option, it is necessary to create a temporary storage queue for output. COBOL II will route the formatted dump output to this temporary storage queue, and CEBR, the CICS transaction, can be used to browse the queue. Abend information is also sent to the temporary storage queue and can be browsed for failure analysis. Remember, temporary storage allocated during testing is not freed automatically. The programmer must free temporary storage used, or this resource can become unavailable.

Figure 3-2 contains the abend information that is produced and sent to temporary storage, if requested. Entries within this abend information are

1. completion code, U101
2. PSW AT ABEND
3. Registers
4. Name of failing module NA001
5. Date and time stamp from compile time

```
COMPLETION CODE = U101   PSW AT ABEND = 00000000 00000000
                    GP REGISTERS AT ENTRY TO ABEND
REGS 0-3     000B122C  000B1780  000B4030  000B9030
REGS 4-7     000B4388  40000000  000B8BC0  00000000
REGS 8-11    000B1708  000B91B0  0025C10C  0025DA82
REGS 12-15   0025C0D0  000B5030  8025E0AE  00000000
  PROGRAM=NA001  COMPILED=07/14/88  16.39.08  TGT=000B5030
NO FILES USED IN THIS PROGRAM
CONTENTS OF BASE LOCATORS FOR WORKING-STORAGE:
    0-000B91B0     1-000BA1B0
CONTENTS OF BASE LOCATORS FOR LINKAGE SECTION:
    0-00000000   1-000BA1B0   2-000B1708   3-005D2870
    4-00258120   5-00259120   6-0025A120
NO VARIABLY LOCATED AREAS USED IN THIS PROGRAM
CONTENTS OF INDEXES:
    1-00000000   2-00000000   3-00000000   4-000000000
    5-00000000   6-00000000   7-00000000
END OF IBM VS COBOL II ABEND INFORMATION
```

Figure 3-2   IBM VS COBOL II Abend information.

6. Address of the TGT for the current program **000B5030**
7. Base locators of each active COBOL II program in the run unit

Much of this information is available in a transaction dump, or in the execution diagnostic facility, CEDF. All available facilities may be required, however, if the problem becomes difficult to diagnose. COBOL II provides some new functions that may be helpful.

## 3.3   DFHEIB — EXEC INTERFACE BLOCK (EIB)

The EXEC Interface Block (EIB) is a control block that is a conduit through which an application requests CICS services and CICS informs the application of the results. It provides the means of communication between the application and CICS. One of the advantages of using the EIB is the control-block independence that the facility provides. Data available through the EIB is provided to the program with no reference or knowledge of the internal structure of other CICS components. Remember, macro-level coding techniques have the ability to access the CICS control blocks, locate, and even change data areas. The EIB provides similar function, but through command facilities that are external to the actual control block structure. Of course, one of the limitations of the EIB is that not all data areas within the entire CICS system are accessible. (Hence the justification of macro-level in some in-

stallations.) Another limitation is the inability of the program to modify the data areas that are accessible. Of course, some people think of this as a blessing rather than a limitation. Data areas left intact are less prone to produce application or system failures.

### 3.3.1   Contents of the EIB

The EIB contents are documented in several CICS publications. As stated in the Application Programmer's Reference Manual (Command Level), the EIB contains valuable information for problem determination and dump debugging. Within the EIB available to the program are fields that identify date and time of execution, task number, terminal identification and cursor position, just to name a few. These fields can be used by the application even though they were not created by the task, and referenced by data name.

A complete listing of the EIB is provided in Table 3-1. This information is current to CICS/MVS 2.1. By design, the EIB will not change much over time except to add additional function, such as response codes. IBM enhances the EIB to contain additional data, making more information available to the programmer. Also, since all data in the EIB is referenced by data name, programs can remain intact from one release to another. Previous EIB contents remain available, and additional values can be utilized for enhanced function.

Other data items exist in the EIB that play an important role in problem determination. Three

| Field | Length | Description |
|---|---|---|
| EIBTIME | 4 | TIME IN 0hhmmss FORMAT |
| EIBDATE | 4 | DATE IN 00yyddd FORMAT |
| EIBTRNID | 4 | TRANSACTION IDENTIFIER |
| EIBTASKN | 4 | TASK NUMBER |
| EIBTRMID | 4 | TERMINAL IDENTIFIER |
| EIBRSVD1 | 2 | RESERVED FIELD |
| EIBCPOSN | 2 | CURSOR POSITION |
| EIBCALEN | 2 | COMMAREA LENGTH |
| EIBAID | 1 | ATTENTION IDENTIFIER |
| EIBFN | 2 | FUNCTION CODE |
| EIBRCODE | 6 | RESPONSE CODE |
| EIBDS | 8 | DATASET NAME |
| EIBREQID | 8 | REQUEST IDENTIFIER |
| EIBRSRCE | 8 | RESOURCE NAME |
| EIBSYNC | 1 | SYNCPOINT REQUESTED |
| EIBFREE | 1 | FREE REQUESTED |
| EIBRECV | 1 | RECEIVED REQUIRED |
| EIBSEND | 1 | RESERVED FIELD |
| EIBATT | 1 | ATTACH RECEIVED |
| EIBEOC | 1 | EOC RECEIVED |
| EIBFMH | 1 | FMHS RECEIVED |
| EIBCOMPL | 1 | DATA COMPLETE |
| EIBSIG | 1 | SIGNAL RECEIVED |
| EIBCONF | 1 | CONFIRM REQUESTED |
| EIBERR | 1 | ERROR RECEIVED |
| EIBERRCD | 1 | ERROR CODE RECEIVED |
| EIBSYNRB | 1 | SYNC ROLLBACK REQUESTED |
| EIBNODAT | 1 | NO APPL DATA RECEIVED |
| EIBRESP | 4 | INTERNAL CONDITION NUMBER |
| EIBRESP2 | 4 | MORE DETAIL ON RESPONSES |
| EIBRLDBK | 1 | ROLLED BACK |

Table 3-1   EXEC INTERFACE BLOCK contents.

fields, in particular, should be noted for many application problems. The EIB fields EIBFN (EIB Function Code), EIBRCODE (EIB Response Code), and EIBRESP (decimal number corresponding to the raised condition) contain very valuable information. These contain the CICS function the program has requested, and the return codes related to that request. After a request has been passed to CICS, CICS attempts to service the work. Regardless of the success or failure of the request, CICS passes control back to the application.

The EIBFN, or function code, contains information relating to the last function, or process, that was issued by the application. This function code is two bytes — the first byte identifying the management module responsible for the request, the second byte specifying the exact request within the function group. For example, all function codes can be grouped by the first byte. Following are just a few of the function code groupings:

| | |
|---|---|
| 04 | Terminal control |
| 06 | File control |
| 08 | Transient data |
| 0A | Temporary storage |
| 0C | Storage control |

A complete listing of all EIB function codes can be found in the Application Programmer's Reference Manual. Since the first byte identifies the request type and the second byte the specific request, this structure can be followed for all values. Following are a few EIB function codes and their values.

| | |
|---|---|
| 0402 | Terminal control — Receive |
| 0404 | Terminal control — Send |
| 0602 | File control — Read |
| 0604 | File control — Write |
| 060C | File control — Startbr |

0802   Transient data — Writeq Td
0C02   Storage control — Getmain

All EIBFN requests for terminal control start with 04; all requests for file control start with 06, etc. These do not need to be memorized, since they are well documented in several locations. After working with EIB function codes, however, programmers quickly recognize the more common requests and the typical response codes.

Now, the application issues a request for services; for example, a File control READ. The EIBRCODE, or response code, contains the response returned to the application after the command has been completed. A NORMAL response returns hexadecimal zeros, but a non-normal response returns a 6-byte value [COBOL PIC X(6)] with contents relating to the abnormal condition. Of course, non-normal responses can still be valid, depending on the request. If the request in our example issued a READ, and the file was available and all functions executed normally, the EIBRCODE would contain 6x'00', or six hexadecimal zeros. If the file was unable to be read, several different response codes could be returned in the EIBRCODE. Listed below are several responses that can be returned from a File Control request.

06 01   DSIDERR
06 02   ILLOGIC
06 08   INVREQ
06 0C   NOTOPEN
06 0D   DISABLED

A complete listing of these EIBRCODEs can be found in several different publications. If the EIBRCODE contained the values 0601, defined as DSIDERR, the programmer would research a dataset identification error. Most times, this error is caused by a program request to read a dataset when the dataset has not yet been defined to CICS. The dataset has to be defined in the File Control Table (FCT) before it can be referenced by the program. If the EIBRCODE contained 060D, defined as DISABLED, research a dataset that could not be opened because it was disabled. CICS 1.7 placed some additional function into file control, and a disabled file could mean many different problems. The file, however, is unavailable to the application until some action is taken.

When the programmer receives an EIBRCODE other than zeros, meaning an abnormal response, alternative measures can be taken. Almost all of the information in the EIBRCODE can be used by the application to take alternative action within the program. The use of HANDLE CONDITION is the normal method of passing control to another section

of the program in these situations. The use of HANDLE CONDITION gives the programmer the opportunity to analyze the EIBRCODE and take whatever measures are necessary. A complete discussion of HANDLE CONDITION follows later in this chapter. The combination of EIBRCODE and the ability to handle the condition gives the programmer dynamic access to results of requests and analysis of some problems.

### 3.3.2   Enhancements in CICS/VS 1.7

Several enhancements were made available in CICS/VS 1.7. These functions gave the programmer the ability to use new command facilities in the release and check for new status flags. In CICS 1.7, programmers were given the ability to inquire on resources and determine the status of those resources. For example, the program could inquire on the status of a file and determine if the file was open, closed, enabled, disabled, etc. Conditions returned from this command could be used by the program to execute different logic during execution. An enhancement in this release also provided access to the JES SPOOL via command facilities. A programmer could code COBOL commands to inquire into the output SPOOL and manipulate the output from CICS. The return from these commands are new function codes and response codes from conditions relating to the inquire and set facilities in CICS 1.7.

As IBM offers new functions in coming releases and versions of CICS, the interface facility will be enhanced to give programmers access to the function and the conditions that can be raised from the new environment.

## 3.4   USE OF HANDLE CONDITIONS

One of the most common occurrences in programming is the exceptional condition, or the fact that a certain condition has occurred within the execution of the program that may not be desirable. When commands execute and attempt to process the data or operation that was requested, many situations can occur that will keep the instruction from executing normally. Of course, the application can stay out of the way and allow the natural course of the process to continue. In most cases, this leads to an abnormal termination of the program, an ABEND. The programmer may not wish the program to terminate at this time, and instead, may wish to follow some alternative course of action. If the programmer wishes to take alternative action, there are several options available. One option, the HAN-

DLE condition technique, can be used to test for the conditions in effect at the time of the test and vary the execution of the program accordingly. Other alternatives are to use the IGNORE CONDITION or NOHANDLE option, and take no action for specific conditions. Still another is to not code a HANDLE or IGNORE at all, and intentionally allow any situation to proceed.

In addition, CICS 1.7 improved the programmer's ability to handle conditions. CICS commands now may contain two additional options: RESP and RESP2. Use of these options within the command allows the programmer to test for conditions and accommodate responses. Use of RESP and RESP2 allows a test for a primary and secondary return code, thereby accommodating specific conditions without using HANDLE CONDITION.

### 3.4.1   Prevention of Unacceptable Conditions

Many times, during execution of a program, a situation arises that is not normal to the successful completion of the program. Dozens of these situations are possible and probable in the daily processing of CICS activity. A programmer cannot only test for these conditions, but can take a number of different actions, depending on the condition that has arisen. This chapter is not going to discuss all possible combinations, nor the specific syntactical alternatives that can be taken. In the realm of problem determination, it will be adequate to cover some options that may be available, and how these options can assist in avoiding failures and unacceptable conditions.

A critical control block called the Exec Interface Block (EIB) can be useful in these conditions. Within the EIB are several fields, including the EIBFN (function code), EIBRCODE (return code), and the EIBRESP (response). All COBOL programs have commands available to test the contents of these fields. After a command is executed, the EIB is updated to reflect the request that was made (EIBFN) and the results of that request (EIBRCODE and EIBRESP). The programmer may, at this time, inquire into the contents of these fields and take any action necessary based on the contents. This can be a powerful tool to control the flow of processing. Not only can the program detect the conditions that exist, but can take any number of alternative actions for various conditions. Assume, for example, a program that requires one specific condition that would be critical to the successful completion of the transaction. Any other conditions would be noted, but could follow alternative processing. This situation could be accommodated by the following example:

```
EXEC CICS HANDLE CONDITION
ERROR(ERROUTN)
DISABLED(DISROUTN) END-EXEC.
```

In this example, the application has determined that a file control request that returns a DISABLED condition must be passed to a special routine (DISROUTN) for processing. Any other condition that arises will be handled by the generic routine ERROUTN. This is merely one simple example of the many combinations that can be used to handle exceptional conditions that arise during execution. Several examples in following chapters will describe various failures, and how this tech-nique can be used to contain the outcome. Chapter 5 covers several AEIx abends, and how specific handling of those conditions can avoid the abend and continue processing when necessary.

### 3.4.2   HANDLE ABEND and EXEC CICS DUMP

During the handling of an abnormal condition, the application may choose to intercept the failure, or even invoke dump processing itself. Handling of failures and application dump processing should be approached with great care. Once the application takes control at time of failure, the results may complicate problem determination, and in fact make problem resolution even more difficult.

Use of the HANDLE ABEND command passes control to a user-written exit routine. The installation must create this routine, and accommodate all standard requirements of application failure. The routine must prevent recursive abends, since failure to accommodate this critical condition can cause a failure in the entire region. If intersystem communication is being used, a failure in the remote system may be handled, but following requests to remote resources may not be processed. In addition, if the failure results from a BMS command, cleanup of CICS control blocks will occur, and unpredictable (and undesirable) results will result. Extreme care should be taken with this facility, and should only be used if necessary.

Applications can also generate their own transaction dumps. Use of the CICS command ABEND will terminate a task and produce a dump with the four-character code specified by the application. CICS creates a dump of the main storage associated with the task, with the four-character identifier as the abend code in the dump. Of course, the danger in this procedure is the lack of documentation concerning the failure and what caused it. Most abend codes are documented in the appropriate CICS Messages and Codes manual. This code, of course, will not be found, and any explanation of the abend is left to the conscience of the programmer producing the dump. Many installations do not allow this type of procedure, since dumps produced may be difficult to diagnose, especially if the programmer is no longer available. Most installations leave dump creation to CICS and attempt to handle most conditions as well as possible.

An even more dangerous process, if not utilized with extreme caution, is the DUMP command. The request to dump main storage, via the DUMP command, allows specific areas of global CICS storage to be dumped. These requests can create significant performance problems, since many CICS functions must be suspended while the DUMP request is processed. In addition, several EIB fields, such as EIBFN and EIBRCODE will be overwritten in the Task Control Area (TCA) as a result of this command. This could complicate problem determination, since critical information was overlayed and destroyed. This command should be used with extreme caution and avoided if possible. Again, use of HANDLE CONDITION should attempt to avoid the failure and continue processing, if at all possible.

## 3.5  IGNORE AND NOHANDLE CONDITIONS

On some occasions, a programmer may want to intentionally bypass handling of conditions and allow processing to continue. The use of IGNORE and NOHANDLE will allow this type of processing. The command IGNORE (condition) will specify that no action is to be taken, and returns control to the instruction directly following the failing command. In this way, conditions can be bypassed, and processing can continue. The parameter NOHANDLE can also be used with CICS commands to specify that no action should be taken. This parameter can be used in addition to the IGNORE command to control the scope of specific conditions. In other words, a command can be executed, with the NOHANDLE condition. If the condition for NOHANDLE is not met, control is passed along, and a HANDLE command can then take effect. The combination of these two facilities can be useful in "filtering" certain conditions to create maximum results.

Another condition that may require special handling, or lack of it, is the case of commands that produce exceptional conditions that need to be allowed. Commands such as ALLOCATE, JOURNAL, READQ TD and WRITEQ TS create conditions that may or may not need to be handled. These commands request services that would suspend the task until the resource becomes available. An installation may wish to allow this suspension and wait for the resources. The program may also use an option of these commands that request NOSUSPEND and therefore automatically handle the suspend request. If no exceptional condition handling is specified, the task will be suspended and wait on the availability of the resource that is required to continue processing.

Installations may intentionally, or unintentionally, fail to handle exceptional conditions during processing. A few of these situations will be covered in subsequent chapters to determine if handling the conditions is indeed the best course of action or if the transaction should be allowed to ABEND.

# 4

# ASRA Abends

ASRA ABENDS are normally caused by a program interrupt, which means the normal program execution was interrupted by an abnormal condition. If FDUMP=ASRA was specified in the DFHPCT macro or the RDO entry for the transaction, the formatted dump program is invoked. A dump is written to the DFHDMPx (A or B) dataset currently opened by the CICS region. CICS services creates a transaction abend control block (TACB) to contain relevant information about the failure. This control block would contain information such as abend code, program status word (PSW), name of the program that was active at the time of the failure, and other pieces that will be incorporated into the formatted dump.

Programmers who have experience in the batch environment have possibly diagnosed similar failures in batch programs. If a batch program experiences a program check or data exception, the job abends with a S0C4 or a S0C7. Programmers then take the dump produced at job termination and diagnose the problem. CICS, however, cannot abend the job, or address space, of the CICS region, so it must produce comparable diagnostic information and proceed with its processing. The formatted dump of ASRAs, therefore, will contain information similar to the batch program dumps, but is constructed somewhat differently. These 0Cx abends can be diagnosed somewhat similarly, therefore, utilizing the program check type (the x in 0Cx) to key in on the specific situation. Listed below are just some of the program check types and their descriptions:

## 4.1 EXCEPTION CONDITIONS HANDLED BY ASRA

0001 — Operation exception
0002 — Privileged operation exception
0003 — Execute exception
0004 — Protection exception
0005 — Addressing exception
0006 — Specification exception
0007 — Data exception
0008 — Fixed-pt overflow exception
0009 — Fixed-pt divide exception
000A — Decimal-divide exception

When diagnosing various abends, particular items within the dump may be more important than others. In the analysis of various problems, each problem type will be summarized by abend code, the probable cause of the failure, and the important dump items. Figure 4-1 identifies these items for an ASRA.

### 4.1.1 Important Items for Analysis

Now that we have discussed the process that CICS has gone through at the time of the failure, and has produced the transaction dump, we will analyze the important items in the dump for this particular type of failure. These pieces contain the information that will identify the cause, and how to correct the problem.

```
ABEND CODE: ASRA
PROBABLE CAUSE: Program check or data exception


IMPORTANT DUMP ITEMS: PSW
                      SYMPTOM STRING
                      TRACE TABLE
                      PROGRAM STORAGE
                      SOURCE PROGRAM CLIST
```

Figure 4-1  Significant items in an ASRA dump.

**PSW — Program Status Word.** The PSW can be found in the formatted dump in Figure 4-2 (1). Following the identifier (PSW) are four fullwords of data. A fullword is four bytes, or characters, so the PSW is actually 16 bytes long. Only two of the four fullwords are actually relevant to an application abend — the second and third ones. The second fullword contains the address (in hexadecimal) of the next instruction to be executed (2). This is particularly important, since it would be the next program instruction to execute if the failure had not occurred. Logically, therefore, the instruction directly preceding this address is the one that caused the failure. Finding this address and identifying the program instruction at the time of the abend will be critical in determining the cause of the failure. The third fullword actually contains two pieces of data. It is broken down into two halfwords, as follows:

```
aaaa/bbbb
```

aaaa = the length of the instruction at the time of the abend
bbbb = the program interrupt code for this abend

The length of the instruction becomes more important if the program was written in ASSEMBLER or if the source is unavailable, since the instruction actually has to be constructed from the hexadecimal representation in the dump. Most COBOL programmers have access to their compiled source, however, so this may not be necessary. The next two bytes contain the interrupt code, was described earlier. This code will show the actual type of failure, such as a 0001 for an operation exception or a 0007 for a data exception. Once the type of exception is identified, the programmer can direct his attention to causes specific to this type. The value of these two pieces of information (the next instruction to be executed and the program check type) can be different for various ASRAs. As shown in the following examples of ASRAs, the next instruction to be executed may be extremely valuable in a protection exception (type 0004). It may, however, contain a value that is not even a legitimate address, as in an operation exception (type 0001).

**Symptom String.** The symptom string can be found on the second line of the dump (3) and contains several items that are either merely interesting or not relevant. Most programmers ignore most of the entries and go directly to the end of the line, the item after the last slash (/). This item contains the program name (4), or actually the module name, from the PPT or RDO entry in control at the time of the failure. Figure 4-2 shows that the program CICSDEMO was the failing module. This program name and the address from the PSW are two very important pieces for use in the search for the cause of the failure.

**Trace Table.** The trace table is formatted in every transaction dump and contains an entry for all activity within the CICS region during a specified interval. The trace table within the dump, therefore, contains not only the entries from the program being anlayzed, but every other transaction that was executing at the time. CICS regions with very high transaction loads, 10–20 transactions per second, for example, can create trace tables with many entries of other transactions. In addition, as previously covered, trace tables wrap. CICS regions with high transaction activity require trace tables that are large enough to keep trace entries for an adequate interval without being written over. A trace table of 1000 entries in such a region may record entries only for one second without wrapping.

Programmers should insure that the trace table for their region is large enough to contain the entries required for problem determination. The trace table is usually found in the fifth or sixth page of a transaction dump. An example of a trace table can be seen in Figure 4-3. In the case of an ASRA, an entry can be found in the trace for a trace identification of F2, field A containing the hexadecimal C1E2D9C1, character ASRA (1). This entry identifies the ABEND invoked by CICS and can be used as a pointer to see exactly what was happening before the failure. Many programmers use the trace table to back up after the ABEND, see what programs were executed, what files were accessed prior to the ASRA. Of course, make sure the entries tracked belong to the correct transaction. The task number in the F2 ASRA trace entry identifies the transaction (2) and should be used to select only the entries relevant to the failing transaction.

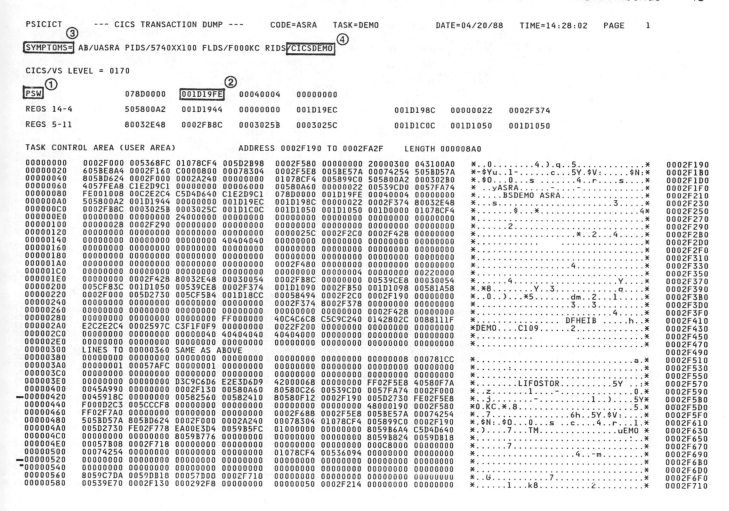

Figure 4-2  ASRA abend: page 1.

**Program Storage.** CICS formatted dump program attempts to place into the dump as much relevant information as possible to assist in problem identification. The last blocks of storage, usually near the end of the dump, are program storage areas that were moved into the dump from CICS dynamic storage area at the time of the failure. Figure 4-4 contains a portion of program storage from a transaction dump. The first line, containing the PROGRAM STORAGE identifier, also contains two addresses and a length (1). The first address, a fullword, is the load point of the active module or program at the time of the abend (2). This can be verified by locating the program in the module summary at the end of the dump. The module summary, at the end of every transaction dump, lists each module known to CICS at the time of the failure, and both the entry and load points. Figure 4-5 identifies an example of a module summary. These

entries are in sequence by hexadecimal load-point address. Note that in some entries the load point and entry point are the same address (1). This is not always the case, however. When calculating offsets into a module, always reference the module map and verify the correct entry point of the module.

The second address in the Program Storage identification line, another fullword, is the address of the module end (3). The length is therefore calculated and shown at the end of this first line (4). The following pages in the dump are the blocks of storage from the program. On the left side of the page are listed the program offset references to assist the programmer in locating any specific offsets into the program (5). On the right side are the actual addresses through program storage through the ending address, already identified in the first line (6). From this block of program storage, in combina-

PSICICT   --- CICS TRANSACTION DUMP ---    CODE=ASRA  TASK=DEMO        DATE=04/20/88   TIME=14:28:02   PAGE    9

| TIME OF DAY | ID | REG 14 | REQD | TASK ② | FIELD A ① | FIELD B | CHARS | RESOURCE | TRACE TYPE | INTERVAL |
|---|---|---|---|---|---|---|---|---|---|---|
| 14:27:59.884640 | E5 | 405C4326 | 0005 | 02595 | 00000000 | 00000000 | ........ | | XSP SECURITY RETN | 00.000032 |
| 14:27:59.884640 | E7 | 005BE772 | 0004 | 02595 | 00000000 | 00000000 | ........ | | ERM ENTRY | 00.000000 |
| 14:27:59.884672 | E7 | 005BE772 | 0004 | 02595 | 00000000 | 000000FF | ........ | | ERM RESPONSE | 00.000032 |
| 14:27:59.884800 | F2 | 405BE7C6 | 8804 | 02595 | 00000000 | 00000000 | ....... | CICSDEMO | PCP XCTL-CONDITIONAL | 00.000128 |
| 14:27:59.884832 | EA | 40580F7A | 0003 | 02595 | 01000300 | 0002F214 | ......2. | CICSDEMO | TMP PPT LOCATE | 00.000032 |
| 14:27:59.884832 | EA | 4059C7B8 | 0005 | 02595 | 01000300 | 00058494 | ........ | | TMP RETN NORMAL | 00.000032 |
| 14:27:59.884864 | F1 | 60581EA2 | 8C04 | 02595 | 00020754 | 01078CF4 | .......4 | | SCP GETMAIN | 00.000096 |
| 14:27:59.884960 | C8 | 50587866 | 0004 | 02595 | 0002FB40 | 8C020768 | ........ | | SCP ACQUIRED USER STORAGE | 00.001280 |
| 14:27:59.886240 | [F2] | 8054E056 | 6004 | [02595] | C1E2D9C1 | 00000000 | ASRA.... | | PCP ABEND | 00.000000 |
| 14:27:59.886240 | F1 | 4057FEA8 | CC04 | 02595 | 000000A0 | 01078CF4 | .......4 | | SCP GETMAIN INITIMG | 00.000000 |
| 14:27:59.886272 | C8 | 50587866 | 0004 | 02595 | 000302B0 | 8C0000A8 | ........ | | SCP ACQUIRED USER STORAGE | 00.000000 |
| 14:27:59.886272 | F4 | 505800A2 | FE04 | 02595 | 00000000 | C1E2D9C1 | ....ASRA | | DCP TRANSACTION | 00.000000 |
| 14:27:59.886560 | F0 | 4054F8D8 | 4004 | 02595 | 80000000 | 00536AFC | ........ | | KCP WAIT DCI=SINGLE | 00.000288 |
| 14:27:59.894208 | FD | 0000010C | 0104 | 02595 | 004F77B5 | 004F77D7 | .......P | | ... REPEAT 00010 TIMES | 00.007648 |
| 14:28:00.305024 | F1 | 60581388 | 4004 | 02595 | 0002FB40 | 01078CF4 | .......4 | | SCP FREEMAIN | *00.410816 |
| 14:28:00.305056 | C9 | 505878A2 | 0004 | 02595 | 0002FB40 | 8C020768 | ........ | | SCP RELEASED USER STORAGE | 00.000032 |
| 14:28:00.305088 | F2 | 405801A8 | 0204 | 02595 | 00000000 | 00000000 | ....... | DFHDBP1$ | PCP XCTL | 00.000032 |
| 14:28:00.305120 | EA | 40580F7A | 0003 | 02595 | 01000300 | 0002F214 | ......2. | DFHDBP1$ | TMP PPT LOCATE | 00.000032 |
| 14:28:00.309888 | EA | 4059C7B8 | 0045 | 02595 | 01000300 | 00040 2E4 | .......U | | TMP RETN NORMAL | 00.004768 |
| 14:28:00.309920 | CB | 70308056 | 0044 | 02595 | 00000000 | 00000000 | ........ | | DBP DYN BACKOUT | 00.000032 |
| 14:28:00.309952 | FC | 403080D6 | 0203 | 02595 | 21005B00 | 01078CF4 | ..$....4 | | ZCP ZLOC RECOVER REQ | 00.000032 |
| 14:28:00.309952 | FC | 605AC93E | 4203 | 02595 | 21005B00 | 01078CF4 | ..$....4 | | ZCP ZSYN SYNCPOINT RECOVER | 00.000000 |
| 14:28:00.309984 | FC | 405AC9DC | 0235 | 02595 | 21005B00 | 00078CF4 | ..$....4 | | ZCP RETN ZLOC NORMAL | 00.000032 |
| 14:28:00.309984 | F2 | 503081F6 | 0204 | 02595 | 00000000 | 00000000 | ....... | DFHACP | PCP XCTL | 00.000000 |
| 14:28:00.310016 | EA | 40580F7A | 0003 | 02595 | 01000300 | 0002F214 | ......2. | DFHACP | TMP PPT LOCATE | 00.000032 |
| 14:28:00.310048 | EA | 4059C7B8 | 0005 | 02595 | 01000300 | 0003FFB4 | ........ | | TMP RETN NORMAL | 00.000000 |
| 14:28:00.310048 | DC | 7040EE74 | 0044 | 02595 | C1C3D7D0 | C1E2D9C1 | ACP.ASRA | | ACP | 00.000032 |
| 14:28:00.310080 | F1 | 6040F148 | 4004 | 02595 | 00032E30 | 01078CF4 | .......4 | | SCP FREEMAIN | 00.000032 |
| 14:28:00.310112 | C9 | 505878A2 | 0004 | 02595 | 00032E30 | 93000040 | ........ | | SCP RELEASED SHARED STORAGE | 00.000032 |
| 14:28:00.310144 | FC | 5040F53C | 0103 | 02595 | 00042000 | 00078CF4 | .......4 | | ZCP ZARQ APPL REQ WAIT COND | 00.000000 |
| 14:28:00.310144 | F0 | 405BB32C | 4004 | 02595 | 20000000 | 00536AFC | ........ | | KCP WAIT DCI=DISP | 00.000032 |
| 14:28:00.310176 | FC | 405BB264 | 0105 | 02595 | 00000000 | 0002A240 | ........ | | ZCP RETN ZARQ APPL REQ | 00.000000 |
| 14:28:00.310208 | F2 | 5040FBA0 | 8104 | 02595 | 00000000 | 00000000 | ....... | DFHPEP | PCP LINK-CONDITIONAL | 00.000032 |
| 14:28:00.310208 | EA | 40580F7A | 0003 | 02595 | 01000300 | 0002F214 | ......2. | DFHPEP | TMP PPT LOCATE | 00.000000 |
| 14:28:00.310240 | EA | 4059C7B8 | 0005 | 02595 | 01000300 | 00041924 | ........ | | TMP RETN NORMAL | 00.000032 |
| 14:28:00.310240 | F1 | 40580B76 | 8904 | 02595 | 00030050 | 01078CF4 | ..&....4 | | SCP GETMAIN | 00.000000 |
| 14:28:00.310272 | C8 | 50587866 | 0004 | 02595 | 0002FB40 | 89030058 | ........ | | SCP ACQUIRED RSA STORAGE | 00.000032 |
| 14:28:00.310272 | F2 | 5042519C | 1004 | 02595 | 00000000 | 00000000 | ....... | DFHPEP | PCP RETURN | 00.000000 |
| 14:28:00.310304 | F1 | 40580FE2 | 4004 | 02595 | 0002FB40 | 01078CF4 | .......4 | | SCP FREEMAIN | 00.000032 |
| 14:28:00.310304 | C9 | 505878A2 | 0004 | 02595 | 0002FB40 | 89030058 | ........ | | SCP RELEASED RSA STORAGE | 00.000032 |
| 14:28:00.310336 | E0 | 5040FD48 | 0003 | 02595 | 018008BC | 81078CF4 | .......4 | | MGP DFH 02236 CSMT | 00.000064 |
| 14:28:00.310400 | F1 | 40586D38 | CC04 | 02595 | 00000400 | 01078CF4 | .......4 | | SCP GETMAIN INITIMG | 00.000000 |
| 14:28:00.310432 | C8 | 50587866 | 0004 | 02595 | 0002FB40 | 8C000408 | ........ | | SCP ACQUIRED USER STORAGE | 00.000000 |
| ─14:28:00.310432 | F6 | 6055186E | E103 | 02595 | 00000000 | 00000000 | ....... | CSMT | TDP APPL REQ CTYPE LOCATE | 00.000032 |
| ─14:28:00.310464 | F1 | 40586D38 | CC04 | 02595 | 00000400 | 01078CF4 | .......4 | | SCP GETMAIN INITIMG | 00.000000 |
| 14:28:00.310464 | C8 | 50587866 | 0004 | 02595 | 00030360 | 8C000408 | ...-.... | | SCP ACQUIRED USER STORAGE | 00.000032 |
| 14:28:00.310496 | EA | 40563A84 | 0003 | 02595 | 01000600 | 0002FCCC | ........ | CSMT | TMP DCT LOCATE | 00.000000 |
| 14:28:00.310496 | EA | 4059C7B8 | 0005 | 02595 | 01000600 | 00563750 | .......& | | TMP RETN NORMAL | 00.000000 |
| 14:28:00.310496 | F6 | 40563CF8 | 0005 | 02595 | 00000000 | 00000000 | ........ | | TDP RETN APPL RESP NORMAL | 00.000032 |
| 14:28:00.310528 | F1 | 60586F22 | 4004 | 02595 | 00030360 | 01078CF4 | .......4 | | SCP FREEMAIN | 00.000000 |
| 14:28:00.310528 | C9 | 505878A2 | 0004 | 02595 | 00030360 | 8C000408 | ...-.... | | SCP RELEASED USER STORAGE | 00.000032 |
| ─14:28:00.310560 | F6 | 405518B4 | 4003 | 02595 | 00000000 | 0002F948 | .......9. | | TDP APPL REQ PUT | 00.000000 |
| ─14:28:00.310560 | F1 | 40586D38 | CC04 | 02595 | 00000400 | 01078CF4 | .......4 | | SCP GETMAIN INITIMG | 00.000032 |
| 14:28:00.310592 | C8 | 50587866 | 0004 | 02595 | 00030360 | 8C000408 | ...-.... | | SCP ACQUIRED USER STORAGE | 00.000000 |
| 14:28:00.310592 | EA | 40563BA4 | 0003 | 02595 | 01000600 | 0002FCCC | ........ | CSMT | TMP DCT LOCATE | 00.000000 |

Figure 4-3    ASRA abend: trace table entries.

tion with the address identified in the PSW, the programmer can calculate the exact instruction that was in control at the time of the abend.

**Calculating the Abending Instruction.**   To identify the failing instruction, one simple calculation is done from the previously identified addresses. The address in the PSW was the address about to be executed. The entry-point address in the module summary is address 0 relative to program execution. Therefore, the following calculation produces the desired result:

```
  PSW ADDRESS
- PROGRAM ENTRY POINT ADDRESS
  ─────────────────────────────
  OFFSET INTO PGM OF FAILING INSTRUCTION
```

Remember, this calculation is performed with hexadecimal addresses, therefore must be done in hexadecimal. The resulting value can be used with the hexadecimal offsets on the left side of the program storage entries to locate the exact instruction.

Using the examples already highlighted, then, subtract the program entry-point address [Figure 4-5 (2)], from the PSW address [Figure 4-2 (2)]. These calculations will be performed later in the chapter, when analyzing specific ASRAs. Once located, the block of program storage is still in hexadecimal and is difficult to relate to actual COBOL source statements. There may be some significant information within that section of the module, however, that can give additional keys to what is actually going on. Many programmers find the offset value in program storage, and then look through the translated character representation on the right portion of the page. Sometimes useful information can be located and used later to assist in identifying the specific environment that was active at the time of the failure. To find the instruction in readable COBOL source statements, however, the best source is the

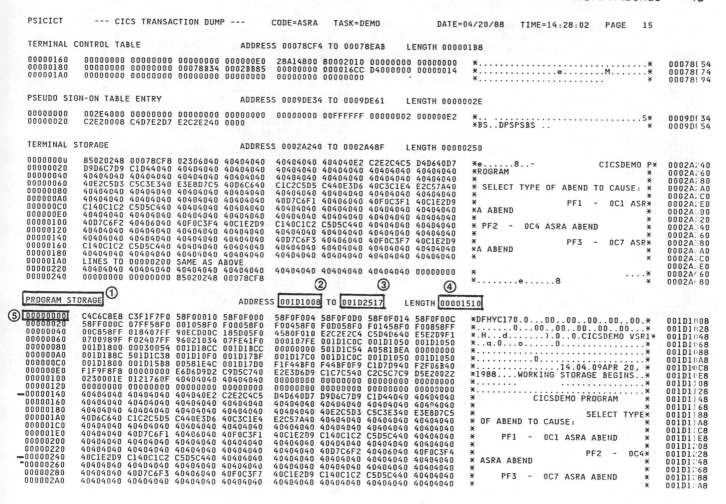

Figure 4-4   ASRA abend: program storage.

condensed listing (CLIST) from the program compile.

**CLIST — Condensed Listing.** The CLIST, or condensed listing, contains a cross reference of the procedure portion of the program. This listing cross-references the verbs within the program, the location of the first instruction of each verb sequentially within the listing of the source statements, and the hexadecimal offset into the program of this location. From this listing, a programmer can take a hexadecimal offset from a dump and directly locate the instruction in the source.

To obtain a CLIST at compile time, specify CLIST in the compile options. NOCLIST is the compiler default, so it must be overridden to obtain the desired output. Check the installation-selected compile options. Some companies choose to provide procedure libraries (PROCLIBS), and the PROC

that executed for COBOL compiles may contain the CLIST selection. A request for a CLIST will contain a condensed listing with entries that relate to the COBOL source. Figure 4-6 is an example of output from a CLIST. Following are the items in that CLIST and a description of each:

1. The compiler-generated source statement number. This number refers to the COBOL statement as sequenced by the compiler. These statement numbers can be found in the program listing on the left of every source statement.
2. The verb contained in the procedure division. This verb is used in the statement number identified in column 1.
3. The relative hexadecimal location of the instruction within the module.

```
PSICICT    --- CICS TRANSACTION DUMP ---      CODE=ASRA   TASK=DEMO         DATE=04/20/88  TIME=14:28:02   PAGE  19

ENTRY    LOAD      NAME   VERS'N TIME  DATE OPTIONS          ENTRY    LOAD      NAME   VERS'N TIME  DATE OPTIONS
POINT    POINT                                               POINT    POINT

000F4050 000F4008 DSNCEXT2                                   0023F008 0023F008 IS540M1
000F5050 000F5008 DSNCEXT1                                   00240050 00240008 PSIGNUSN
000FA008 000FA008 IN25PGMS                                   00243008 00243008 SYSBUSY
0011C008 0011C008 IN25UEXI                                   00244008 00244008 IN25SERS
0011F008 0011F008 IN25HOOK                                   00248008 00248008 IN25CKPT
00120008 00120008 IN25PGM2                                   0024A020 0024A008 DFHFCS    0170I 14:28 11/07
00163008 00163008 IN25INQ                                    00251008 00251008 IN25HELP
00168008 00168008 MG001M1                                    00253030 00253008 DFHEDFBR  0170I 10:56 08/28
00169008 00169008 IS020M1                                    00256140 00256008 SQLERRTN
0016A008 0016A008 IS523M1                                    0025E008 0025E008 IN25MU1
0016B050 0016B008 IS523                                      00267008 00267008 IN25SER1
00174050 00174008 MG001                                      0028C478 0026E008 DFHZCQ    0170I 15:47 03/23
00184008 00184008 NA150M1                                    0028D008 0028D008 NA300M1
00185050 00185008 NA001                                      0028E050 0028E008 NA300
0018E140 0018E008 NA150                                      00295008 00295008 DFHDBMS
0019C050 0019C008 NA105                                      00296008 00296008 IN25MU2
001A3008 001A3008 NACOMLN                                    0029C810 00298008 DFHTBS    0170I 16:20 03/24
001A4008 001A4008 NA100M1                                    0029F008 0029F008 SQLERRM
001A5050 001A5008 NA100                                      002A0030 002A0008 DFHZATD   0170I 19:45 04/09
001AC008 001AC008 MG000M1                                    002A3008 002A3008 ACFAEUSP
001AD050 001AD008 MG000                                      002A6008 002A6008 DFHEITAB
001B2008 001B2008 IS527M1                                    002AF008 002AF008 DFHZATDX
001B3050 001B3008 IS527                                      002B0008 002B0008 ACFAEUCM
001C4008 001C4008 IS522M1                                    002B1050 002B1008 IS020
001C5050 001C5008 IS522                                      002B8050 002B8008 AUDPRG
001C9008 001C9008 IS545M1                                    002BC030 002BC008 PSIGSFO
001CA020 001CA008 DFHEMI    0170I 09:57 02/03               002BD050 002BD008 IS562
001CB008 001CB008 ER001M1                                    002C2050 002C2008 IS540
001CC050 001CC008 ER001                                      002C7050 002C7008 IOTAB
001CF008 001CF008 IS350M1 ①                                002CB008 002CB008 IS562M1
② 001D1050 001D1008 CICSDEMO                                002CC050 002CC008 PSIMP1
001D3140 001D3008 ST350                                      002D1050 002D1008 TU001
001E2140 001E2008 ST360                                      002DB050 002DB008 IS546
001F2030 001F2008 DFHECID   0170I 11:09 08/28               002F8008 002F8008 IN25LGET
00202030 00202008 DFHECIP   0170I 11:07 08/28               002FF020 002FF008 DFHSTP    0170I 15:58 07/17
00203050 00203008 NA203                                      00301050 00301008 IOMOD
00207050 00207008 NA202                                      00304020 00304008 DFHEMF    0170I 17:54 08/28
0020C008 0020C008 ST360M1                                    00305030 00305008 ACFAEUCC
0020D008 0020D008 NA310M1                                    00306030 00306008 SECCHECK
0020E050 0020E008 NA310                                      00307008 00307008 PSIMM1
00218020 00218008 DFHOCP    0170I 13:06 02/06               00308020 00308008 DFHDBP1$  0170I 17:42 12/19
00219050 00219008 IS545                                      00309008 00309008 TU001M1
00227020 00227008 DFHEMB    0170I 11:16 02/02               0030A008 0030A008 IN25CORE
00228008 00228008 GMM01                                      00312008 00312008 IN25SGET
00229008 00229008 IN25MU3                                    00316008 00316008 IS546M1
0022F140 0022F008 NA311                                      00317008 00317008 PSIDEMCI
00236140 00236008 NA201                                      00318030 00318008 IGZCPCC
```

Figure 4-5   ASRA abend: module map.

Many of these items will become much easier to understand by relating them to the actual program. They will also provide the final pieces of information necessary when diagnosing a failure. The best teacher is experience, so let's take the information covered and apply it to some actual ASRA failures.

## 4.2   ASRA ABEND - 0004 PROTECTION EXCEPTION

A protection exception is recognized by the operating system when an attempt is made to access a location in storage that is protected from the type

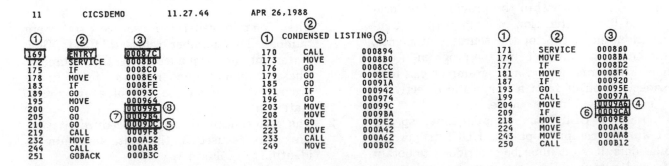

Figure 4-6   COBOL compile condensed list output.

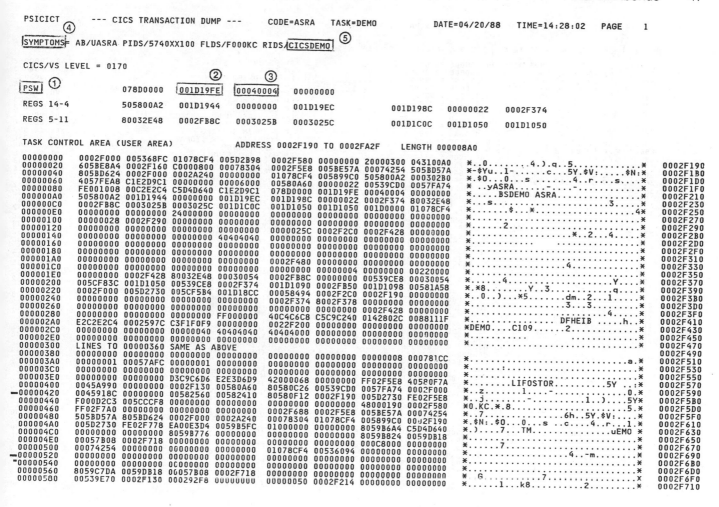

Figure 4-7    ASRA 0C4 abend: page 1.

of access requested. Storage is managed by the operating system by "protect keys," and the requestor must be in the same protect key as the storage that is being requested. Some areas of storage, called "low storage," typically in the range of 0–511, are protected by the operating system because they are reserved for privileged operations. Other areas of storage are protected from either read or write access to protect the operating system, or other address spaces, from being corrupted. Attempts to fetch or execute from protected areas will produce a protection exception, and will cause an abend in the requesting program with a interrupt code of 0004. Source statement verbs such as MOVE (in COBOL) or LOAD (in ASSEMBLER) will very often produce protection exceptions, since they are fetching or referencing portions of storage that are invalid or protected.

This section will look at a dump of this type of failure, locate the important dump items, and identify the cause of the failure.

### 4.2.1    Important Items for Analysis

Figure 4-7 contains selected pages from an ASRA 0004 dump. Refer to this example throughout this discussion of protection exception failures. The first item in the dump to locate is the PSW (1). Page one contains the PSW and four fullwords of information. The second fullword (2) contains the address of the next instruction to be executed. It contains a **001D19FE**, therefore this address should be noted as one to locate in program storage later. The third fullword (3) contains the length of the failing instruction, and the interrupt code. Note that its con-

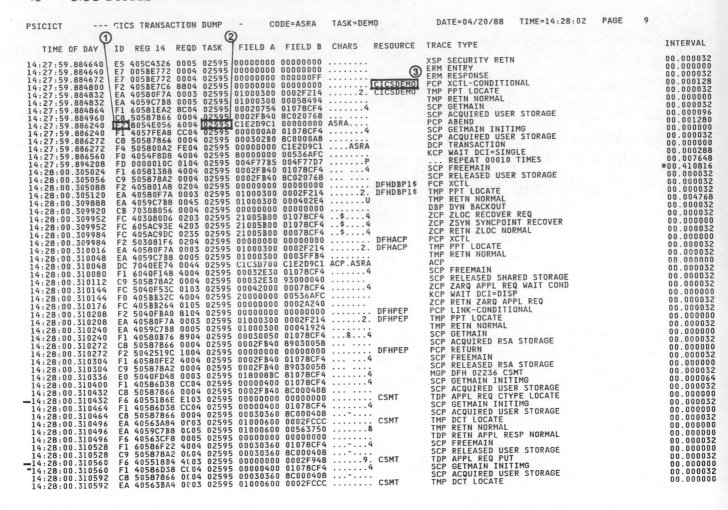

Figure 4-8   ASRA 0C4 abend: trace table entries.

tents are 00040004, a protection exception abend, with an instruction length of 0004. This validates the exception type and may be important when attempting to find the exact instruction that caused the failure.

The next item to locate in the dump is the symptom string (4). It can be found on the same page. The last entry in the string is CICSDEMO (5). This is the program, or module, that was in control at the time of the failure. This program name will be important to look for in the trace table, and it will be necessary to produce a CLIST of this program when it was compiled to identify the failing instruction.

Further into the dump is the trace table. The trace can be thousands of entries; however, it is necessary to find the section of the trace that contains the abend. Figure 4-8 contains the trace entry identifying the ASRA, an F2 trace ID (1), time stamp 14:27:59.886240 by Task number 02595 (2).

This task number, therefore, is the one to identify in any preceding trace entries for reference to other activity before the failure. Moving backward in the trace are the entries identifying a transfer control (XCTL) to program CICSDEMO (3), a normal return from locating the program in the PPT or RDO resource, storage control requesting storage (GETMAIN), and then the ASRA. These entries further validate the suspicion that program CICSDEMO is causing the failure, but do not provide much more information to assist in detecting the cause.

The next item to locate in the dump is the section of program storage. Figure 4-9 contains the first reference to program storage, with a load point address of **001D1008** (1). Looking to the right in this area is the CICS prefix area of the program and then the eyecatcher CICSDEMO (2), matching the program name found in the symptom string. This is, indeed, the section of program storage required.

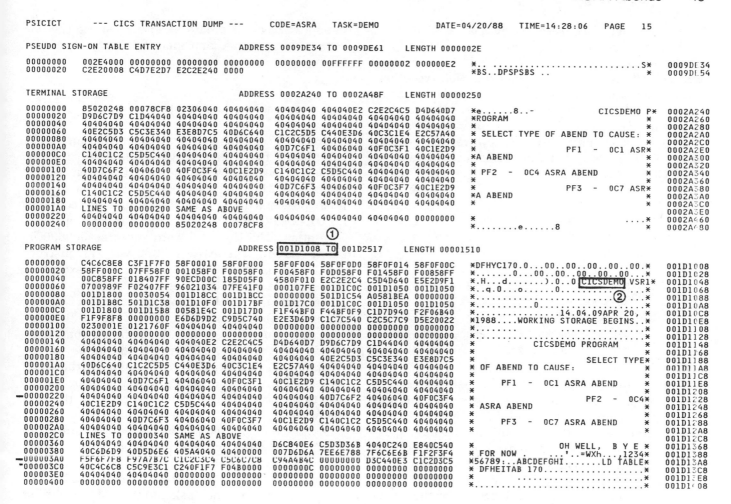

Figure 4-9   ASRA 0C4 abend: program storage.

At this point, it will be necessary to calculate the offset into the program of the failing instruction utilizing the formula previously defined. Subtracting the program entry-point address [located in the module summary at the end of the dump, Figure 4-5, Entry Point for CICSDEMO (2)] from the address in the PSW, produces

$$
\begin{array}{r}
001DF1FE \\
-\quad 001D1050 \\
\hline
9AE
\end{array}
$$

The next instruction to be executed was at hexadecimal location 9AE in the program. Locating that offset in program storage is possible, within the dump, but the instruction is impossible to identify. The next step is to locate the CLIST of this program when it was last compiled, and find this offset in the program map listing.

### 4.2.2   Review of the Failure and COBOL Source

The CLIST provided was produced at compile time of the program CICSDEMO. Since the offset calculated was 9AE, this listing contains the instruction required. The cross reference (Figure 4-6) shows hexadecimal locations 0009A6 (4), then 0009B4 (5), as highlighted in the listing. Since 0009B4 is higher than the offset calculated, take the address preceding the one identified and then go back into the actual source statements. The hexadecimal address 0009A6 references instruction 204, a verb of MOVE. This type of verb is one of the ones identified earlier as a possible culprit in a protection exception, since it would be performing a compare function. Locating statement 204 from the COBOL compiled listing output produces

```
203        MOVE 0 TO RECORD-POINTER.
204        MOVE LOW-VALUES TO RECORD-TEXT.
```

### 4.2.3  Location of the Problem and Solution

The attempt to move LOW-VALUES to the variable RECORD-TEXT is causing the protection exception, and contains an address that is unavailable to the program. In the preceding instruction, the program is setting RECORD-POINTER to a value of zeros. This is not necessarily invalid; however, the section of the COBOL program that defines the data area of RECORD-TEXT contains

```
01    DFHCOMMAREA.
      03  COMM-CONTROL      PIC 99.
      03  COMM-TEXT         PIC X(32).
01    BLL-CELLS.
      03  FILLER            PIC S9(8) COMP.
      03  RECORD-POINTER    PIC S9(8) COMP.
01    RECORD-AREA.
      03  RECORD-TEXT       PIC X(50).
      03  RECORD-CHAR REDEFINES RECORD-TEXT
          PIC X OCCURS 50.
```

The pointer in the BLL cells establishes addressability to all storage requested by the program. This pointer must contain an address to an area of storage that the program can use during execution. This program moved zeros to the pointer and, by doing so, pointed the program to low core for GETMAINED storage. When the program then attempted to move LOW-VALUES, or for that matter, anything, to that data area, RECORD-TEXT, an 0C4 resulted. No program is able to store in that area of storage, since it is fetch-protected by the operating system. This is a common failure when programmers attempt to use BLL cells to keep track of areas of storage referenced that are external to their program (in this case, the CICS address space). These addresses must be managed carefully or 0C4s result.

## 4.3  ASRA ABEND - 0007 DATA EXCEPTION

A data exception is recognized by the operating system when the sign or digit codes of operands in decimal instructions are invalid. It can also be caused by operand fields in operations that overlap incorrectly. Most of these types of failures are caused during arithmetic operations in the programs. Since these operations utilize packed fields, COBOL verbs performing arithmetic are located during analysis of the problem. Sometimes comparison of data from one type of field to another, perhaps from decimal to binary, can cause exceptions in the data type. Data exceptions are very common failures in programming and can be diagnosed fairly easily. This section will look at a data exception, locate the important dump items, and identify the cause of the failure.

### 4.3.1  Important Items for Analysis

Figure 4-10 contains selected pages from an ASRA 0007 dump. Refer only to this example during the discussion of data exceptions. The first item in the dump should be the PSW (1), located on line four as in our previous dump. The second fullword contains **001D1A26** (2) and will be noted for later address calculation. The third fullword contains 00060007, a data exception ABEND (0007), with an instruction length of 0006. This validates the exception type, and the instruction length if required.

The next item in the dump, the symptom string, contains a module name of CICSDEMO (3). It identifies the program, or module name in control at the time of the failure. This program name will be a valuable item to know when analyzing the trace table, and a CLIST of this program will be necessary to perform the search as described in the earlier ASRA.

The trace table section as shown contains the ASRA abend entry. Figure 4-11 identifies the trace entry identifying the ASRA, an F2 trace ID, at time stamp 14:28:06.277440 by task number 02599 (1). This is, therefore, the task number of the failing transaction, and other entries should be disregarded. Moving backward in the trace are entries very similar to the entries located in the previous ASRA. They identify the module name, but do not provide much additional information to diagnose the cause of the failure.

The next step is to locate the section of program storage containing the module identified in the symptom string. Figure 4-12 contains the first reference to program storage, and the load point address of this module, **001D1008** (1). Looking to the right, in the character representation of program storage is the CICS prefix area, and then the eye-catcher module name CICSDEMO. This verifies that the program storage contains the necessary module. Now, calculate the offset into the program of the failing instruction. Subtracting the program entry-point address (from the module summary, Figure 4-5) from the address in the PSW:

```
  001D1A26
- 001D1050
  ─────────
       9D6
```

The next instruction to be executed was at hexadecimal location A1E in module CICSDEMO. Lo-

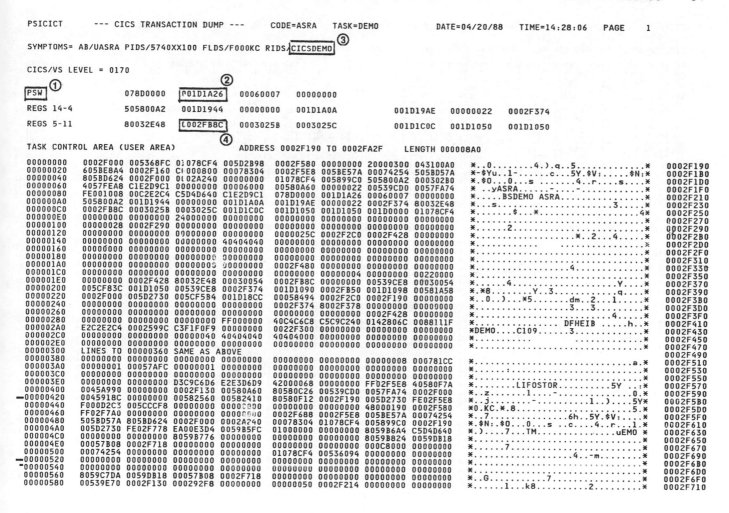

Figure 4-10   ASRA 0C7 abend: page 1.

### 4.3.2   Review of the Failure and COBOL Source

cate that offset in program storage, mark the position for later verification, and locate the CLIST listing of this program.

The CLIST provided (Figure 4-6) was produced at compile time of the program CICSDEMO. Looking down the cross reference are hexadecimal locations 9CA (6) and then 9DC (7). Since 9DC is higher than the offset calculated, take the preceding one. The hexadecimal address of 9CA references instruction 209, a verb of IF. This type of verb was identified as a potential culprit of data exceptions, and may be comparing data of different types. Looking at the entire statement:

```
IF WORK-MONTH = 10 THEN ......
```

Locating the variable WORK-MONTH in the compile summary after the source statements would produce a reference similar to

| INTRNL NAME | LVL | SOURCE NAME | BASE | DISPL |
|---|---|---|---|---|
| DNM=1-426 | 02 | WORK-MONTH | BL=1 | 050 |

This is a reference to the contents of the general "registers," or registers that contain pointers to data names utilized by the program. The reference to WORK-MONTH in the above glossary from compiler output shows that it has been assigned to base locator 1 (BL=1), with a displacement of 050 bytes. In other words, the sum of the value in base locator 1 and the hexadecimal offset 50 is the address of variable WORK-MONTH. Further into the compiled output, the compiler shows register assignments utilized at compile time.

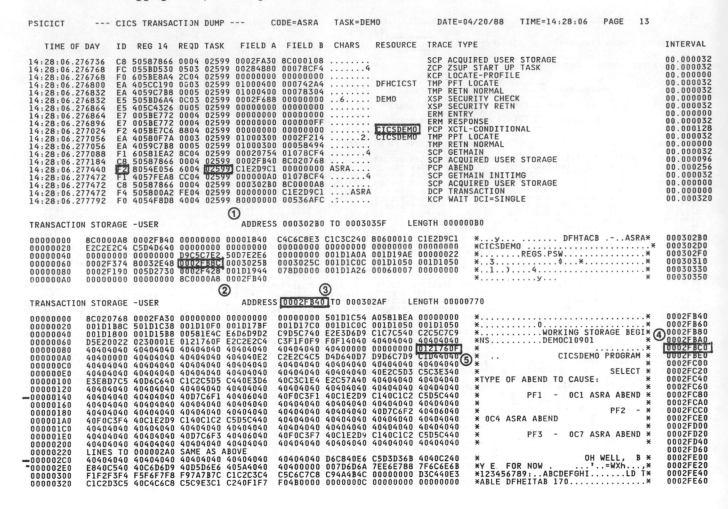

Figure 4-11    ASRA 0C7 abend: trace table and user storage.

The Register Assignment Table lists the registers assigned at compile time to each base locator (BL). It contains

```
REG 6    BL = 1
```

This means that the address contained in register 6 points to the beginning of all storage owned by BL 1. Looking back at the beginning of the dump, where register assignments are identified (Figure 4-10) Register 6 contains **0002FCB8C** (4). Chapter Three discussed that these registers are not always correct for the failure. Register contents should always be validated within the TACB (Transaction Abend Control Block). At the end of the trace table is the first block of transaction storage, the TACB. Figure 4-11 shows the portion of the dump containing the TACB. Counting six registers past the PSW, the contents of Register 6 at the time of the abend

contains the same contents, **0002FB8C** (2). This is the correct address and can be used to find the offset for the variable in storage needed. The previous reference to this variable identified the displacement, 050, as the pointer to WORK-MONTH. It is, therefore, possible to locate the actual data currently stored by making the appropriate calculation:

```
   0002FB8C
 +       50
   0002FBDC
```

Looking again at Figure 4-11, directly after the TACB is another section of transaction storage, with a starting address of **0002FB40** (3). It is possible to perform the calculation to find the piece of storage needed, or simply refer to the addresses down the right side of the page to find the exact

```
PSICICT    --- CICS TRANSACTION DUMP ---    CODE=ASRA   TASK=DEMO         DATE=04/20/88   TIME=14:28:02   PAGE   15

TERMINAL CONTROL TABLE                    ADDRESS 00078CF4 TO 00078EAB    LENGTH 000001B8

00000160    00000000 00000000 00000000 000000E0    28A14800 80002010 00000000 00000000   *................................*   00078E54
00000180    00000000 00000000 00078B34 0002BB85    00000000 000016CC D4000000 00000014   *................e........M.......*   00078E74
000001A0    00000000 00000000 00300000 00000000    00000000 00000000                     *..........................      *   00078E94

PSEUDO SIGN-ON TABLE ENTRY                ADDRESS 0009DE34 TO 0009DE61    LENGTH 0000002E

00000000    002E4000 00000000 00000000 00000000    00000000 00FFFFFF 00000002 000000E2   *.. .............................S*   0009DE34
00000020    C2E20008 C4D7E2D7 E2C2E240 0000                                               *BS..DPSPSBS ..                  *   0009DE54

TERMINAL STORAGE                          ADDRESS 0002A240 TO 0002A48F    LENGTH 00000250

00000000    85020248 00078CF8 02306040 40404040    40404040 404040E2 C2E2C4C5 D4D640D7   *e......8..-           CICSDEMO P*   0002A240
00000020    D9D6C7D9 C1D44040 40404040 40404040    40404040 40404040 40404040 40404040   *ROGRAM                          *   0002A260
00000040    40404040 40404040 40404040 40404040    40404040 40404040 40404040 40404040   *                                *   0002A280
00000060    40E2C5D3 C5C3E340 E3E8D7C5 40D6C640    C1C2C5D5 C440E3D6 40C3C1E4 E2C57A40   * SELECT TYPE OF ABEND TO CAUSE: *   0002A2A0
00000080    40404040 40404040 40404040 40404040    40404040 40404040 40404040 40404040   *                                *   0002A2C0
000000A0    40404040 40404040 40404040 40404040    40D7C6F1 40406040 40F0C3F1 40C1E2D9   *            PF1  -  0C1 ASR*   0002A2E0
000000C0    C140C1C2 C5D5C440 40404040 40404040    40404040 40404040 40404040 40404040   *A ABEND                         *   0002A300
000000E0    40404040 40404040 40404040 40404040    40404040 40404040 40404040 40404040   *                                *   0002A320
00000100    40D7C6F2 40406040 40F0C3F4 40C1E2D9    C140C1C2 C5D5C440 40404040 40404040   * PF2  -  0C4 ASRA ABEND         *   0002A340
00000120    40404040 40404040 40404040 40404040    40D7C6F3 40406040 40F0C3F7 40C1E2D9   *            PF3  -  0C7 ASR*   0002A360
00000160    C140C1C2 C5D5C440 40404040 40404040    40404040 40404040 40404040 40404040   *A ABEND                         *   0002A3A0
00000180    40404040 40404040 40404040 40404040    40404040 40404040 40404040 40404040   *                                *   0002A3C0
000001A0    LINES TO 00000200 SAME AS ABOVE                                                                                    0002A3E0
00000220    40404040 40404040 40404040 40404040    40404040 40404040 40404040 00000000   *                          ....*   0002A460
00000240    00000000 00000000 85020248 00078CF8                                          *........e......8        *   0002A480
```

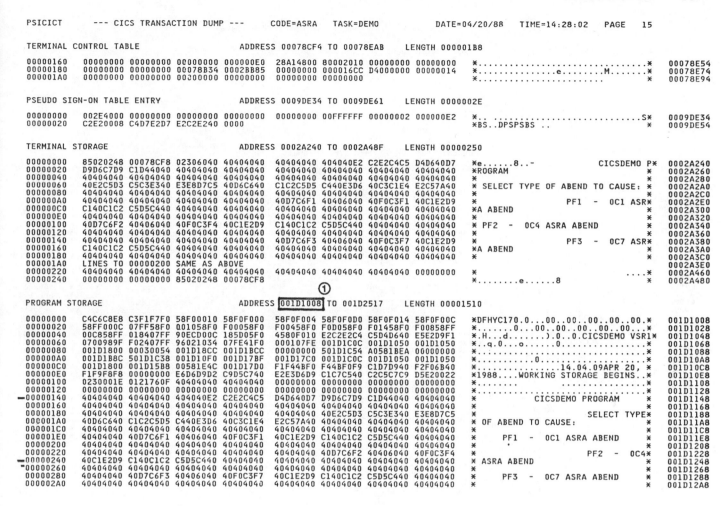

```
                                                    ①

PROGRAM STORAGE                           ADDRESS [001D1008] TO 001D2517    LENGTH 00001510

00000000    C4C6C8E8 C3F1F7F0 58F00010 58F0F000    58F0F004 58F0F0D0 58F0F014 58F0F00C   *DFHYC170.0...00..00..00..00..00.*   001D1008
00000020    58FF000C 07FF58F0 001058F0 F00058F0    F00458F0 F00D58F0 F01458F0 F00858FF   *........0...00..00..00..00...00..*   001D1028
00000040    00C858FF 018407FF 90ECD00C 185D05F0    4580F010 E2C2E2C4 C5D4D640 E5E2D9F1   *.H...d.......).0..0.CICSDEMO VSR1*   001D1048
00000060    0700989F F02407FF 96021034 07FE41F0    000107FE 001D1C0C 001D1050 001D1050   *..q.0...o.......0................*   001D1068
00000080    001D1800 00030054 001D18CC 001D1BCC    001D1C54 A0581BEA 00000000           *................................*   001D1088
000000A0    001D1B8C 501D1C38 001D10F0 001D17BF    001D17C0 001D1C0C 001D1050 001D1050   *...........0....................*   001D10A8
000000C0    001D1800 001D15B8 00581E4C 001D17D0    F1F44BF0 F44BF0F9 C1D7D940 F2F06B40   *...........<....14.04.09APR 20, *   001D10C8
000000E0    F1F9F8F8 00000000 E6D6D9D2 C9D5C740    E2E3D6D9 C1C7C540 C2C5C7C9 D5E20022   *1988....WORKING STORAGE BEGINS..*   001D10E8
00000100    0230001E 0121760F 40404040 40404040    00000000 00000000 00000000 00000000   *.............. .................*   001D1108
00000120    00000000 00000000 00000000 00000000    00000000 00000000 00000000 00000000   *................................*   001D1128
00000140    40404040 40404040 404040E2 C2E2C4C5    D4D640D7 D9D6C7D9 C1D44040 40404040   *           CICSDEMO PROGRAM     *   001D1148
00000160    40404040 40404040 40404040 40404040    40404040 40404040 40404040 40404040   *                                *   001D1168
00000180    40404040 40404040 40404040 40404040    40404040 40E2C5D3 C5C3E340 E3E8D7C5   *                    SELECT TYPE*   001D1188
000001A0    40D6C640 C1C2C5D5 C440E3D6 40C3C1E4    E2C57A40 40404040 40404040 40404040   * OF ABEND TO CAUSE:             *   001D11A8
000001C0    40404040 40404040 40404040 40404040    40404040 40404040 40404040 40404040   *                                *   001D11C8
000001E0    40404040 40D7C6F1 40406040 40F0C3F1    40C1E2D9 C140C1C2 C5D5C440 40404040   *    PF1  -  0C1 ASRA ABEND      *   001D11E8
00000200    40404040 40404040 40404040 40404040    40404040 40D7C6F2 40406040 40F0C3F4   *                    PF2  -  0C4*   001D1208
00000240    40C1E2D9 C140C1C2 C5D5C440 40404040    40404040 40404040 40404040 40404040   * ASRA ABEND                     *   001D1248
00000260    40404040 40404040 40404040 40404040    40404040 40404040 40404040 40404040   *                                *   001D1268
00000280    40404040 40D7C6F3 40406040 40F0C3F7    40C1E2D9 C140C1C2 C5D5C440 40404040   *    PF3  -  0C7 ASRA ABEND      *   001D1288
000002A0    40404040 40404040 40404040 40404040    40404040 40404040 40404040 40404040   *                                *   001D12A8
```

Figure 4-12   ASRA 0C7 abend: program storage.

address. The closest address is **0002FBC0** (4), so take that line and, since that address is actually the second fullword on the left side of the page, locate the exact address, **0002FBDC**. As noted in Figure 4-11, the contents of this address is 0121760F (5).

### 4.3.3   Location of the Problem and Solution

Of course, this can immediately be identified as packed data. The IF statement, therefore, is attempting to compare packed data with decimal data, which caused the data exception. This situation was caused by, previously in the program, moving a 77-level item, defined as COMP-3 (packed) to a group item, an 01-level. This move does not unpack the data, so it remained in packed format within the variable storage. Locating the

data within transaction storage immediately identified it as improper format and solved the mystery of the data exception.

## 4.4   ASRA ABEND - 0001   OPERATION EXCEPTION

An operation exception is recognized by the operating system when an attempt is made to execute an instruction with an invalid operation code. This could mean that the operation code does not exist, or may not be executable on the existing CPU. Some special-purpose Assembler instructions are designed for new technologies in CPUs, such as expanded storage. These instructions, therefore, cannot execute on computers that do not have the hardware so support them. In most CICS programs,

```
PSICICT      --- CICS TRANSACTION DUMP ---      CODE=ASRA   TASK=DEMO        DATE=04/20/88   TIME=16:27:59   PAGE   1

SYMPTOMS= AB/UASRA PIDS/5740XX100 FLDS/F000KC RIDS/CICSDEMO

CICS/VS LEVEL = 0170
```

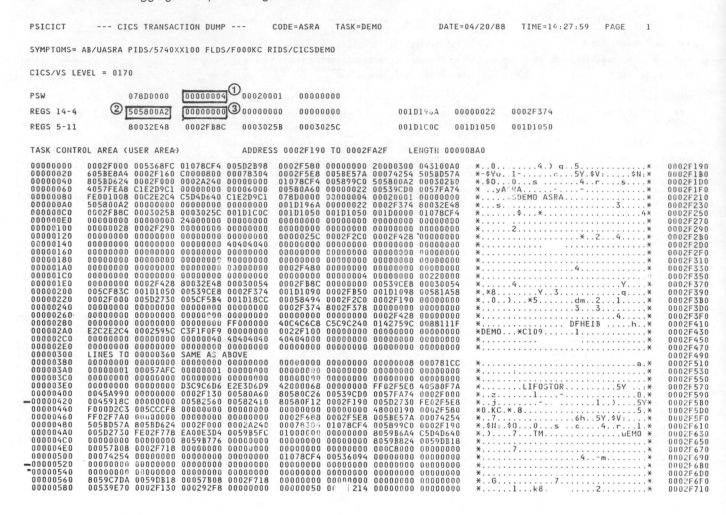

Figure 4-13   ASRA 0C1 abend: page 1.

however, COBOL programs do not utilize these instructions, and operation exceptions are usually the result of an attempt to execute an operation code that does not exist. In most cases, this is caused by an invalid address being loaded into the PSW at execute time. Further research usually locates the problem as errors at compile time that were unnoticed or ignored. The linked module then has invalid or missing linkage and, when loaded to attempt to execute, produces an operation exception.

### 4.4.1   Important Items for Analysis

Figure 4-13 contains selected pages from an ASRA 0001 dump. Refer to this example during the discussion of operation exceptions. Locating the PSW immediately displays unusual results compared to the other ASRAs diagnosed. The second fullword contains **00000004** (1). This cannot be the address of a legitimate instruction, so how can the problem be diagnosed? These are, obviously, different from previous ASRAs and must be treated somewhat differently.

Since the second fullword of the PSW cannot be used to find the cause of the problem, what other source could be used? In most dumps, registers point to locations that are significant to the execution of the program. As previously discussed, registers such as 12 and 13 point to critical control blocks in CICS processing, the CSA, and the TCA chains. Two other registers are sometimes significant, registers 14 and 15. In many cases, these registers point to the address that the transaction was called from, and the address that the caller wishes to branch to. In cases such as an operation exception, these registers can be helpful in diagnosing the problem. In this example, in the two registers

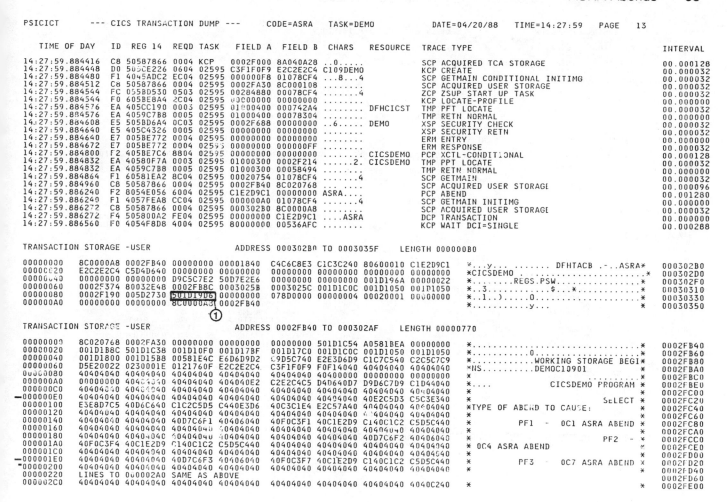

Figure 4-14   ASRA 0C7 abend: user storage.

in the summary at the beginning of the dump, R14 contains **505800A2** (2), and R15 contains **00000000** (3). Remember, however, these registers may not be correct, and must be validated from the TACB further into the dump.

Using Figure 4-14, at the time of the failure, R14 contains **501D19D6** (1) and R15 is a fullword of zeros. The caller at the time of the failure was at location **1D19D6**. The high-order bit of the address in a situation such as this is omitted, since it probably contains irrelevant information in the construction of the address. This address is within the range of storage identified in the dump as belonging to CICSDEMO, as previously identified from the first line of program storage address ranges. It may therefore be assumed that the module CICSDEMO was attempting to execute at the time of the failure. What action was being attempted? It is sometimes necessary to return to the compile listing. Before doing that, investigate the contents of R14.

Register 14, in most cases, points to the address of the instruction to which control will be returned after execution. This address, **001D19D6**, happens to also point to a portion of the module in question. What instruction would be executed from this register? With the technique used with previous calculations:

```
  001D19D6
- 001D1050
     996
```

### 4.4.2   Review of the Failure and COBOL Source

Within the CLIST from Figure 4-6, that address directly references statement 200 (8). Returning to

```
MVS/XA DFP VER 2 LINKAGE EDITOR              09:55:22  THU  APR 13, 1989
JOB DPSPPIDB   STEP CBL        PROCEDURE LKED
INVOCATION PARAMETERS - LIST,LET,MAP,XREF
ACTUAL SIZE=(317440,86016)
OUTPUT DATA SET PSISP.SYSTEMS.LOADLIB IS ON VOLUME CICS21
IEW0000    INCLUDE SYSLIB(DFHECI)                         50000000
IEW0000    NAME CICSDEMO(R)
IEW0132   DUMMY
```

```
                            CROSS REFERENCE TABLE


   CONTROL SECTION                 ENTRY

     NAME     ORIGIN  LENGTH         NAME    LOCATION    NAME    LOCATION    NAME    LOCATION    NAME    LOCATION
   DFHECI      00      48
                                   DFHEI1       8      DLZEI01      8      DLZEI02      8      DLZEI03      8
                                   DLZEI04      8      DFHCBLI     26
   CICSDEMO    48      BFA
   ILBOCOMO*   C48     173
                                   ILBOCOM     C48

   ILBOSRV *   DC0     4D4
                                   ILBOSRV0    DCA     ILBOSR5     DCA     ILBOSR3     DCA     ILBOSR      DCA
                                   ILBOSRV1    DCE     ILBOSTP1    DCE     ILBOST      DD2     ILBOSTP0    DD2
   ILBOBEG *   1298    1DC
                                   ILBOBEG0    129A
   ILBOMSG *   1478    100
                                   ILBOMSG0    147A


   LOCATION  REFERS TO SYMBOL  IN CONTROL SECTION          LOCATION  REFERS TO SYMBOL  IN CONTROL SECTION
      7D0        ILBOSRV0         ILBOSRV                     7D4        ILBOSR5          ILBOSRV
      7D8        DFHEI1           DFHECI                      7DC        DUMMY            $UNRESOLVED
      7E0        ILBOSRV1         ILBOSRV                     738        ILBOCOMO         ILBOCOMO
      1154       ILBOCOM          ILBOCOMO                    1168       ILBOSTT0         $UNRESOLVED(W)
      1158       ILBOCMM0         $UNRESOLVED(W)              115C       ILBOBEG0         ILBOBEG
      1160       ILBOMSG0         ILBOMSG                     1164       ILBOSND2         $UNRESOLVED(W)
      13D8       ILBOPRM0         $UNRESOLVED(W)
   ENTRY ADDRESS     48
   TOTAL LENGTH      1578
   ** CICSDEMO REPLACED AND HAS AMODE 24
   ** LOAD MODULE HAS RMODE 24
   ** AUTHORIZATION CODE IS        0.



                            DIAGNOSTIC MESSAGE DIRECTORY
   IEW0132 ERROR - SYMBOL PRINTED IS AN UNRESOLVED EXTERNAL REFERENCE.
```

Figure 4-15   COBOL linkage editor output.

the COBOL source statements from compile time would display the statements:

```
198    0110-0C1.
199    CALL 'DUMMY'.
200    GO TO 0130-SEND-SCREEN.
```

The statement directly preceding 200 is a call to an external reference DUMMY. This must be the instruction that is causing our failure. This can be further validated by returning to the compile listing of the program, CICSDEMO, and locating the last step in the listing, the linkedit step. In Figure 4-15 is the output from the invocation of the linkage editor, and on the last line is the linkage editor warning message (1):

```
IEW0132 ERROR - SYMBOL PRINTED IS AN UNRESOLVED
EXTERNAL REFERENCE
```

### 4.4.3  Location of the Problem and Solution

On the eighth line of that same page is the IEW0132 message from the linkedit step (2) and the module name, DUMMY, that the linkage editor was unable to resolve. Notice that this message ends in a numeric of 2, so will consequently create a condition code of 0008 in the jobstep. A programmer, however, can decide to execute the step (linkedit) regardless of content of condition code. This has happened, as validated by the output from the linkage editor (3):

```
TOTAL LENGTH        1510
** CICSDEMO REPLACED AND HAS AMODE 24
```

In this example, even though the linkage editor produced a message identifying an unresolved external reference, the module was linked and replaced the previous version. At execution time, if this unresolved module was called, the linkage section of the program had no idea where to load the program from and failed, since there was no valid instruction to execute. Many operation exception failures are caused by errors that occurred at the time the module was linked. These errors went unnoticed, or uncorrected, and caused failures later on when the module attempted to execute. Always retain the compile listing and the linkedit step of the module when last maintained. This information can be invaluable when diagnosing failures.

This chapter has analyzed three different types of ASRA abends, and it has become apparent that although they contain uniquely different types of failures ASRA abends have many similarities. As programmers spend more time diagnosing problems, they find that the techniques utilized in one problem can assist in diagnosing others. The phrase "they all start to look alike" may not be totally accurate, but as diagnostic skills improve, soon things "pop out" as questionable situations. Following are chapters that cover other types of failures and additional techniques that can be used to diagnose and resolve problems.

# 5

# Typical Application File Abends

Many failures in CICS applications are results of file status, or actually, inappropriate file status. In most cases, the programmer may not have the ability to change the status of the file and will merely react to the lack of availability of the resource. In some cases, the resource, or file, may not be available for a very good reason, and the programmer needs to accommodate these conditions. Take, for example, an installation that processes most of its business via CICS. This installation may have an extensive network, with offices throughout the country, or even throughout the world. These types of networks are becoming not only technically feasible, but affordable. In many cases, having a terminal in a specific geographic region may give that company the competitive edge to be successful. If the company is centralized, or processes most of the work in one large data center, the computer may be in New York, while the terminal may be in California, or even Hawaii. The situation requires CICS to be executing in one time zone, and accommodating customers in any other. "Continuous operations" is a very important concern to many installations.

When a company requires continuous operations, it poses some problems for many operational issues. If CICS needs to be up for extended periods of time, even 24 hours, how do normal down time functions happen? Most installations bring CICS down at some point during the night for normal backup of files and batch processing. If CICS doesn't come down, how can these backups and offline processes occur? The answer is to remove the resources from the online system, perform required processing, and then return the resources. Unfortunately, if these resources are files, any transactions that may execute during the time the file was removed from CICS may have a problem. What does an application do if the file is not available? Of course, this

becomes an installation decision, even a programming standard. Most companies choose to place appropriate condition-handling routines into the application. For example, the application could detect the file state and notify the CICS operator that the file was not available at that time. A previous chapter discussed HANDLE CONDITION processing techniques. These conditions may not be handled, however, and may in fact choose to be ignored. An entire category of CICS abend codes deals with the failures that occur as a result of these conditions. This chapter will cover only a few, and only those that relate to file conditions. These tend to be the most common, and therefore the ones that may be experienced. Before covering these failures, however, an understanding of CICS abend codes and messages is required. An awareness of these messages and codes, and how IBM uses them, will facilitate diagnosis.

## 5.1 CICS ABEND CODES AND MESSAGES

When CICS detects a condition that is not handled, or one that cannot be recovered, it produces a CICS message attempting to describe the problem, or a CICS transaction dump with an abend code, or both. These messages are standard IBM message format and always start with the letters DFH. There are many stories and rumors concerning the selection of DFH as the CICS prefix, including the use of the initials of the original developer of the CICS product during its infancy. Wherever DFH came from, it remains the prefix for all CICS/MVS messages. The remainder of the message number contains the four numerics unique to the message. The first digit of these numbers, however, indicates which CICS management module is producing the message. In the CICS Messages and Codes manual, the messages are in numeric sequence, and also grouped into categories. The first group begins with DFH03xx, DFHKCP. These messages would deal with issues of CICS task control. In addition, DFH09xx messages pertain to DFHFCP, file control; and DFH10xx messages pertain to DFHTCP, terminal control. In this way, the message category can produce insight into content and purpose of the message. Beyond the messages in this manual are the CICS transaction abend codes. These are listed alphabetically and begin with the letter A. The short explanation that follows the code attempts to provide some insight into potential causes of this failure and possible action to take. The description is by no means complete, but gives a starting point into analysis.

A dump may be produced that contains an abend code not documented in this manual. How can this happen? All CICS-produced failures, that is, produced by the product CICS, are documented. As discussed in previous chapters, an application can choose to produce a dump and create its own abend code. These, of course, will never be found in an IBM manual. Hopefully, the programmer was considerate enough to document this abend code for the installation. An installation may also have vendor products running in CICS, or in purchased packages. These applications, which are usually purchased, are installed into CICS regions and supported by the vendor. Most products come with a technical support or operations manual that contains messages that the product produces, and abend codes that could occur during utilization. These abend codes must be researched within the specific vendor documentation.

## 5.2  AEIx ABENDS

When CICS returns a condition (other than NORMAL), it is usually the symptom of a problem that needs to be accommodated by the application. It may also not be a problem at all, merely that the resource is not available at the current time. Numerous conditions may be experienced by an application. As previously discussed in Chapter 3, the programmer may decide to handle all conditions globally with a generic error routine. The programmer may also choose to select specific conditions for a specialized routine, or may not handle the condition at all. If a condition arises for which there is no routine to take over, CICS produces an abend, with a corresponding abend code. The abend codes of the format AEIx are used to identify the condi-

tion not handled by the failing task. In Figure 5-1 a program was used and conditions raised.

The program is a very simple one; in fact, it is provided by IBM in the sample library that comes with the product. These samples give installations some starter programs to use and test with the product during installation, if needed. The program attempts some simple file processing and utilizes a single map. Notice in Figure 5-1 that the program establishes certain conditions that will be handled during execution of this application. The programmer has decided to specifically handle the conditions of MAPFAIL and NOTFND, and process all other conditions with the generic ERROR routine. This is fairly common in many programs. The program will be modified, however, to intentionally not handle certain conditions and review the failures that result. The first change made to this program is to remove the generic ERROR condition that is currently being handled. Figure 5-2 shows the same portion of the program, with the new contents. Notice that both MAPFAIL and NOTFND are still being handled. Any other conditions, however, are not accommodated, and will therefore cause an abend.

After making the above change and recompiling the program, the application will, for the most part, execute as it always had. If, however, conditions arise during execution of the program, there are no provisions to avoid a transaction failure. In the category of potential file problems, there are a number of conditions that could be raised during execution. Some of the most common are

- The file will not open, usually as a result of a previous open failure that left the file in the DISABLED state.
- The file was explicitly closed via an application request, or by the CEMT SET command to close the file, which left the file in the UNENABLED state.
- The file has somehow been deleted and is no longer in the MVS catalog: open fails and the file is left DISABLED.
- One of the associations or alternate indexes has been deleted: if the index is upgradeable, and is unavailable, the request to open the base cluster will fail.

In any of these cases, the end result is that the file is unavailable for processing. These are just a few of the conditions that can cause a file to be unavailable to the application. The application can choose to handle the condition and take alternative action. In the failure below, no handle was used, and an abend resulted.

```
EDIT ---- DPSPPID.CICS.PGM(PGM) - 01.11 --------------------- COLUMNS 001 072
COMMAND ===> _                                              SCROLL ===> CSR
084000       *                              FILEA RECORD DESCRIPT'N
088000       01  FILEA.   COPY DFH$CFIL.
092000       *                              GENERAL MENU MAP
096000                     COPY DFH$CGA.
100000       *                              BROWSE FILEA MAP
104000                     COPY MAPA.
108000       *
112000       *
116000        PROCEDURE DIVISION.
120000            EXEC CICS HANDLE CONDITION
128000                          MAPFAIL (SETUP)
132000                          NOTFND(NOTFOUND) END-EXEC.
136000       *
140000            EXEC CICS RECEIVE MAP('MENU') MAPSET('DFH$CGA') END-EXEC.
144000       *
148000            EXEC CICS HANDLE AID
152000                          CLEAR(SMSG)
156000                          PF1 (PAGE-FORWARD)
160000                          PF2 (PAGE-BACKWARD) END-EXEC.
164000       ***************************************************************
168000       *                    SIMPLE CHECKS OF INPUT DATA       *
172000       ***************************************************************
```

Figure 5-1   Typical CICS COBOL handle condition instructions.

The situations raised in these examples are all from CICS 1.7 and later. Prior to CICS 1.7, file processing was handled much differently. The enhancements to file control program in CICS 1.7 allowed a much greater flexibility in file states. Files can be dynamically allocated and, in fact, are in a CLOSED state after CICS initialization. This is normal, and the preferred method in most cases. At first reference, CICS builds the appropriate control blocks and OPENs the file to the requestor. During this process, when the file is first opened, the application is unaware that the file was CLOSED and, in fact, does not receive any notification by CICS. The open is processed, and the application proceeds with its request. If, during this process, the file cannot be opened, a condition is passed back to the application. Programmers need to be aware of the changes to file processing that were introduced in CICS 1.7. The changes are completely documented in the CICS Release Guide and the Application Programmer's Reference Manual.

## 5.3   AEIS ABEND

The DISABLED condition became much more relevant in CICS 1.7. Since the meaning of file status changed, the condition of the file as OPENED vs. DISABLED had to be handled differently by the application. Also, as continuous operations issues began to surface, some files needed to be removed from the online system for various reasons for short

```
EDIT ---- DPSPPID.CICS.PGM(PGM) - 01.11 -------------------- COLUMNS 001 072
COMMAND ===> _                                              SCROLL ===> CSR
084000      *                                     FILEA RECORD DESCRIPT'N
088000        01  FILEA.    COPY DFH$CFIL.
092000      *                                     GENERAL MENU MAP
096000                      COPY DFH$CGA.
100000      *                                     BROWSE FILEA MAP
104000                      COPY MAPA.
108000      *
112000      *
116000        PROCEDURE DIVISION.
120000            EXEC CICS HANDLE CONDITION
128000                         MAPFAIL (SETUP)
128100                         ERROR(ERRORS)
132000                         NOTFND(NOTFOUND) END-EXEC.
136000      *
140000            EXEC CICS RECEIVE MAP('MENU') MAPSET('DFH$CGA') END-EXEC.
144000      *
148000            EXEC CICS HANDLE AID
152000                         CLEAR(SMSG)
156000                         PF1 (PAGE-FORWARD)
160000                         PF2 (PAGE-BACKWARD) END-EXEC.
164000      ***************************************************************
168000      *                                  SIMPLE CHECKS OF INPUT DATA    *
```

Figure 5-2   Modified handle condition instructions.

periods of time. Starting in CICS 1.7, files that were CLOSED explicitly, either by an application or via the CEMT command, changed in more than one category. Once an operator issued the command:

```
CEMT SET DA(FILEA) CLOSED
```

CICS acknowledged that the closed was an explicit one, therefore one that was specifically requested. This differentiated a file that was still unreferenced since CICS initialization (therefore CLOSED) from a file that had been requested to be closed. Files that were closed explicitly were not only placed into a file state of CLOSED, but also DISABLED or UNENABLED. In CICS 1.7 this new state of UN-ENABLED returned the same condition as DISABLED from a program request, but indicated that the CLOSE had been a result of direct action. In other words, CICS acknowledged that the file was CLOSED for some specific reason, and therefore would not allow the OPEN to process without additional action, returning a NOTOPEN condition.

This process is a totally new facility in CICS 1.7, and requires an installation to rethink the handling of files. Take, for example, a file that uses the new facilities for dynamic allocation and open processing. The file state after CICS initalization is CLOSED, ENABLED. This is the norm, and is the default state of the file if CICS 1.7 File Control Table defaults are used. At first reference, the file is allocated and opens. The file then becomes

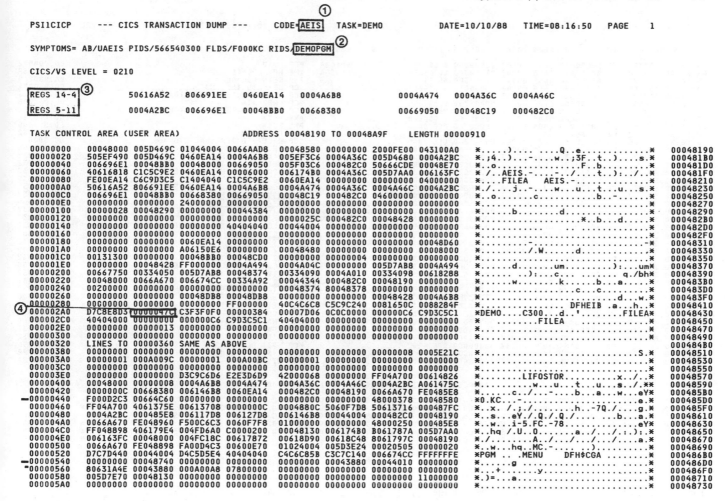

Figure 5-3   CICS AEIS abend: page 1.

OPEN, ENABLED. If, however, the installation chooses to CLOSE the file, or make the file unavailable for a period of time, it issues the command:

```
CEMT SET DA(FILEA) CLOSED
```

The file is then not only CLOSED, but placed into the state of UNENABLED. A file that is either DISABLED or UNENABLED cannot be opened, either by an application request or even via the CEMT command. The file must first be set to the ENABLED status before an implicit or explicit open can be processed. CICS assumes that since an external source set the file to an UNENABLED or DISABLED status, it will reject the OPEN. This is not necessarily a problem, but a condition that needs to be understood by all installations moving to CICS 1.7 and beyond.

The description of the AEIS abend code in the CICS manual describes an exception condition, similar to the AEIx abends, for which no handle condi-

tion was present. In reality, an AEIS abend will result from a file request against a file that is currently either DISABLED or UNENABLED. In the sample program, the HANDLE for the ERROR condition was removed. During testing, the file FILEA was explicitly CLOSED via the CEMT command. The status of the file was then CLOSED, UNENABLED. When the program attempted to execute, the file could not be OPENED, and the AEIS resulted. How can these type of abends be analyzed? Figure 5-3 contains the first page of the transaction dump that was produced from the AEIS. Using the techniques discussed on previous failures, the abend code AEIS (1) from program DEMOPGM (2) is identified.

Since this is not an 0Cx type of abend, no PSW appears in the dump. The registers (3) are probably not significant, since program storage is not the issue. The EIB will identify the task number to reference in the trace table. As identified in Chapter 2, the task number is at offset +12 into the EIB. In

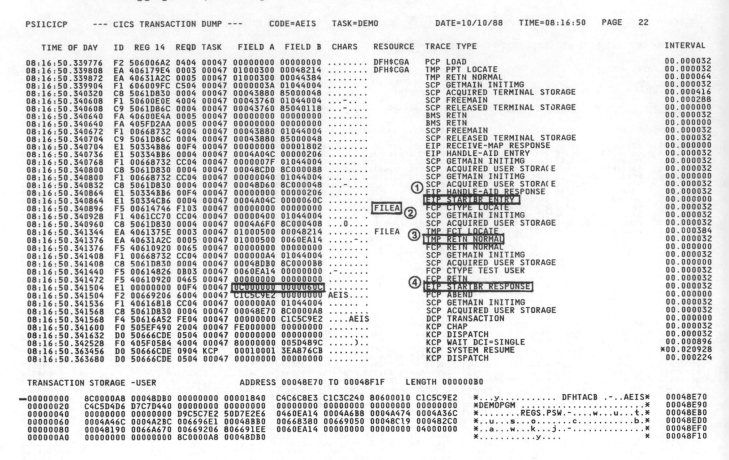

Figure 5-4   CICS AEIS abend: trace table entries.

this dump, the task number is 47 (4). Most AEIx type of abends are diagnosed from the trace table within the dump. Figure 5-4, contains the last page of the trace table. The trace entries can be validated as relevant by the task number previously found in the EIB. The EIB task number was 00047, which matches these trace entries. The last request for a file in the dump is indicated by the STARTBR trace entry (1). It can be assumed that this is the request unable to complete successfully. In the next trace entry (2) the browse request specifies file FILEA, since file control program issued a locate for that dataset from within the File Control Table (FCT). The response from the FCT LOCATE appears normal (3), therefore the definition within the table existed and was correct. The next entry, however, (4) is the response from the STARTBR request. This response is NOT normal and is immediately followed by the AEIS abend in the trace table. Notice in the trace entry:

```
EIP STARTBR RESPONSE
```

the values of FIELD A and FIELD B:

| FIELD A | FIELD B |
|---------|---------|
| 0C000000 | 0000060C |

As documented in the CICS Problem Determination Guide, an E1 type trace entry contains the following information in these fields:

```
FIELD A - Response code, zeroes indicate no ex-
ceptional condition

FIELD B - Command code
```

Of course, the response code is NOT zeros. The command code **060C** is, indeed, the command code for a file control STARTBR. The interpreted field in the trace identified the command. The response code, however, when researched, identifies a **0C** response from a file control request as NOTOPEN. Since CICS had no HANDLE CONDITION set for this response in the program, it could not return control to the application and processed the AEIS dump.

If the HANDLE instruction was returned to the program, as it was originally found, the NOTOPEN

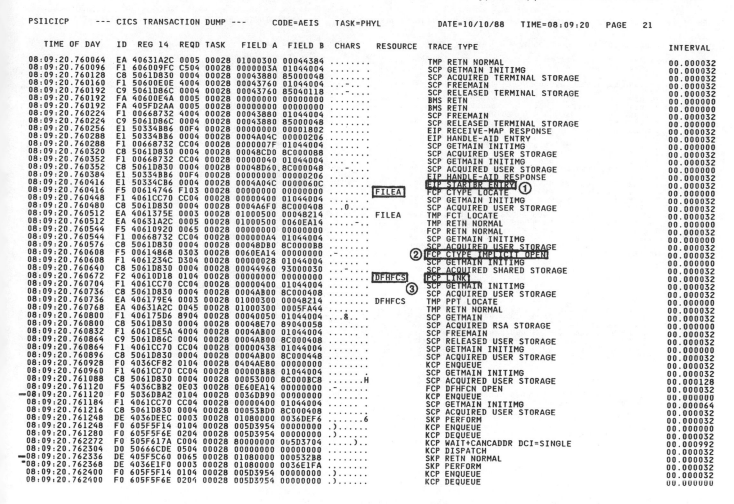

```
PSI1CICP    --- CICS TRANSACTION DUMP ---    CODE=AEIS   TASK=PHYL        DATE=10/10/88  TIME=08:09:20   PAGE  21

  TIME OF DAY    ID  REG 14  REQD TASK  FIELD A  FIELD B  CHARS    RESOURCE  TRACE TYPE                                INTERVAL
08:09:20.760064  EA 40631A2C 0005 00028 01000300 00044384 ........          TMP RETN NORMAL                          00.000032
08:09:20.760096  F1 606009FC C504 00028 0000003A 01044004 ........          SCP GETMAIN INITIMG                      00.000032
08:09:20.760128  C8 5061D830 0004 00028 00043880 85000048 ........          SCP ACQUIRED TERMINAL STORAGE            00.000032
08:09:20.760160  F1 50600E0E 4004 00028 00043760 01044004 ...-...           SCP FREEMAIN                             00.000032
08:09:20.760192  C9 5061D86C 0004 00028 00043760 85000118 ...-....          SCP RELEASED TERMINAL STORAGE            00.000032
08:09:20.760192  FA 40600E4A 0005 00028 00000000 00000000 ........          BMS RETN                                 00.000000
08:09:20.760192  FA 405FD2AA 0005 00028 00000000 00000000 ........          BMS RETN                                 00.000000
08:09:20.760224  F1 00668732 4004 00028 00043880 01044004 ........          SCP FREEMAIN                             00.000032
08:09:20.760224  C9 5061D86C 0004 00028 00043880 85000048 ........          SCP RELEASED TERMINAL STORAGE            00.000000
08:09:20.760256  E1 50334B86 00F4 00028 00000000 00001802 ........          EIP RECEIVE-MAP RESPONSE                 00.000032
08:09:20.760288  E1 50334BB6 0004 00028 0004A04C 00000206 ........          EIP HANDLE-AID ENTRY                     00.000032
08:09:20.760288  F1 00668732 CC04 00028 0000007F 01044004 ........          SCP GETMAIN INITIMG                      00.000032
08:09:20.760320  C8 5061D830 0004 00028 00048CD0 8C000088 ........          SCP ACQUIRED USER STORAGE                00.000032
08:09:20.760352  F1 00668732 CC04 00028 00000040 01044004 ........          SCP GETMAIN INITIMG                      00.000000
08:09:20.760352  C8 5061D830 0004 00028 00048D60 8C000048 ...-....          SCP ACQUIRED USER STORAGE                00.000032
08:09:20.760384  E1 50334B86 0004 00028 00000000 00000206 ........          EIP HANDLE-AID RESPONSE                  00.000032
08:09:20.760416  E1 50334CB6 0004 00028 0004A04C 0000060C ........          EIP STARTBR ENTRY ①                      00.000032
08:09:20.760416  F5 00614746 F103 00028 00000000 00000000 ........  FILEA   FCP CTYPE LOCATE                         00.000000
08:09:20.760448  F1 4061CC70 CC04 00028 00000400 01044004 ........          SCP GETMAIN INITIMG                      00.000032
08:09:20.760480  C8 5061D830 0004 00028 0004A6F0 8C000408 ...0....          SCP ACQUIRED USER STORAGE                00.000032
08:09:20.760512  EA 4061375E 0003 00028 01000500 00048214 ........  FILEA   TMP FCT LOCATE                           00.000000
08:09:20.760512  EA 40631A2C 0005 00028 01000500 0060EA14 .....-..          TMP RETN NORMAL                          00.000000
08:09:20.760544  F5 40610920 0065 00028 00000000 00000000 ........          FCP RETN NORMAL                          00.000000
08:09:20.760544  F1 00668732 CC04 00028 000000A4 01044004 ........          SCP GETMAIN INITIMG                      00.000032
08:09:20.760576  C8 5061D830 0004 00028 00048DB0 8C000088 ........          SCP ACQUIRED USER STORAGE                00.000032
08:09:20.760608  F5 00614868 0303 00028 0060EA14 00000000 .-......          FCP CTYPE IMPLICIT OPEN ②                00.000032
08:09:20.760608  F1 4061234C D304 00028 00000028 01044004 ........          SCP GETMAIN INITIMG                      00.000000
08:09:20.760640  C8 5061D830 0004 00028 00044960 93000030 ...-....          SCP ACQUIRED SHARED STORAGE              00.000032
08:09:20.760672  F2 40610D18 0104 00028 00000000 00000000 ........  DFHFCS  PCP LINK ③                               00.000032
08:09:20.760704  F1 4061CC70 CC04 00028 00000400 01044004 ........          SCP GETMAIN INITIMG                      00.000032
08:09:20.760736  C8 5061D830 0004 00028 0004AB00 8C000408 ........          SCP ACQUIRED USER STORAGE                00.000032
08:09:20.760736  EA 406179E4 0003 00028 01000300 00048214 ........  DFHFCS  TMP PPT LOCATE                           00.000000
08:09:20.760768  EA 40631A2C 0045 00028 01000300 0005FA44 ........          TMP RETN NORMAL                          00.000032
08:09:20.760800  F1 406175D6 8904 00028 00040050 01044004 ...&....          SCP GETMAIN                               00.000032
08:09:20.760800  C8 5061D830 0004 00028 00048E70 89040058 ........          SCP ACQUIRED RSA STORAGE                 00.000000
08:09:20.760832  F1 6061CE5A 4004 00028 0004AB00 01044004 ........          SCP FREEMAIN                             00.000032
08:09:20.760864  C9 5061D86C 0004 00028 0004AB00 8C000408 ........          SCP RELEASED USER STORAGE                00.000032
08:09:20.760864  F1 4061CC70 CC04 00028 00000438 01044004 ........          SCP GETMAIN INITIMG                      00.000000
08:09:20.760896  C8 5061D830 0004 00028 0004AB00 8C000448 ........          SCP ACQUIRED USER STORAGE                00.000032
08:09:20.760928  F0 4036CF82 0104 00028 0404AE80 00000000 ........          KCP ENQUEUE                              00.000032
08:09:20.760960  F1 4061CC70 CC04 00028 00000BB8 01044004 ........          SCP GETMAIN INITIMG                      00.000032
08:09:20.761088  C8 5061D830 0004 00028 00053000 8C000BC8 .......H          SCP ACQUIRED USER STORAGE                00.000128
08:09:20.761120  F5 4036CBB2 0E03 00028 0E60EA14 00000000 .-......          FCP DFHFCN OPEN                          00.000032
—08:09:20.761120  F0 5036DBA2 0104 00028 0036DB90 00000000 ........          KCP ENQUEUE                              00.000000
08:09:20.761184  F1 4061CC70 CC04 00028 00000400 01044004 ........          SCP GETMAIN INITIMG                      00.000064
08:09:20.761216  C8 5061D830 0004 00028 00053BD0 8C000408 ........          SCP ACQUIRED USER STORAGE                00.000032
08:09:20.761248  DE 4036DEEC 0003 00028 01080000 0036DEF6 .......6          SKP PERFORM                              00.000032
08:09:20.761248  F0 605F5F14 0104 00028 005D3954 00000000 .)......          KCP ENQUEUE                              00.000000
08:09:20.761280  F0 605F5F6E 0204 00028 005D3954 00000000 .)......          KCP DEQUEUE                              00.000032
08:09:20.762272  F0 605F617A C004 00028 80000000 0u5D3704 .....).. KCP WAIT+CANCADDR DCI=SINGLE                       00.000992
08:09:20.762304  D0 50666CDE 0504 00028 00000000 00000000 ........          KCP DISPATCH                             00.000032
—08:09:20.762336  DE 405F5C60 0065 00028 01080000 000532B8 ........          SKP RETN NORMAL                          00.000032
—08:09:20.762368  DE 4036E1F0 0003 00028 01080000 0036E1FA ........          SKP PERFORM                              00.000032
08:09:20.762400  F0 605F5F14 0104 00028 005D3954 00000000 .)......          KCP ENQUEUE                              00.000032
08:09:20.762400  F0 605F5F6E 0204 00028 005D3954 00000000 .)......          KCP DEQUEUE                              00.000000
```

Figure 5-5   CICS AEIS abend: trace entries containing open.

condition would have been handled by the generic ERROR routine. The programmers could also have entered a specific handle for this condition if they did not wish to pass control to the ERROR routine. In this case, any NOTOPEN condition is not properly handled and will produce an abend.

## 5.4    AEIS FAILURES FROM DELETED FILES

Figure 5-5 and 5-6 contain the last two pages of the trace table in a related dump. The circumstances creating this failure are similar, yet need to be separated from the previous failure. Page 21 in the dump is the first reference to the open request for the file. The request for STARTBR is made (1), and FILEA is identified as the entry in the FCT. After the file is located in the table, file control program makes note that the file requires open processing, since it is now CLOSED. This is indicated in the

trace entry (2) requesting the IMPLICIT OPEN. File control then attempts to process the open (3).

On the next page of the trace, page 22 (Figure 5-6), is displayed the return from the open request. The REQD field (1) contains **4265**. In the Problem Determination Guide, trace type F5 indicates that if byte one and two of this REQD field contains **42**, the trace entry has logged a DFHFCN error from file control. Field A will contain the DFHFCN return code, and FIELD B will contain additional error information. The documentation also notes that corresponding information is sent to the CICS console. These entries can be seen in the trace (2). Message DFH0952 will be routed to the CSMT destination. Also displayed are the return from file control (3), as an ERROR, and then the response to the STARTBR immediately following. Again, FIELD A in the STARTBR response should contain the condition as in the previous failure. We can see that FIELD A contains **0C000000**. The previous

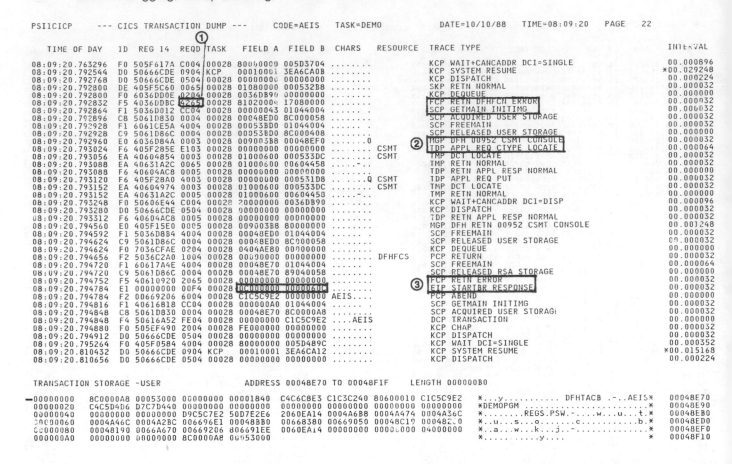

Figure 5-6    CICS AEIS abend: trace entries containing open failure.

failure contained **0C**. This condition **0C** represents a NOTOPEN state, or actually, an inability to open. Remember, a CLOSED file will be opened by CICS, if possible. In this case, CICS attempted an OPEN and was unable to complete successfully.

In the CSMT log, or wherever the CSMT messages are routed, the following entry would be found:

```
DFH0952I  DYNAMIC ALLOCATION OF FILE   FILEA
FAILED. RETURN CODE -
0004,1708  12:52:17
```

The creation of this message was noted in the trace entry, and the contents of FIELD A and FIELD B were moved into this message as return codes. These two return codes are the most common within this message, since allocation failures are mainly caused by the inability to locate the file. These return codes, 1708, are caused by the inability of MVS to locate the file in the catalog.

Two important new features of CICS can now be handled by the application:

1. DISABLED files can be handled as a specific condition, and may need to be accommodated with a special routine. These files can later be ENABLED and made available to the application.
2. CLOSED files are automatically opened by CICS; this does not raise any abnormal conditions to the application. Failure to open will return a NOTOPEN condition and usually means a more serious file inavailability.

## 5.5   MANIPULATION OF FILES BY APPLICATIONS

A new facility in CICS 1.7 provides a great deal of function and power to an application. In this release, CICS enhanced the ability of an application to inquire and modify CICS resources. With command-level facilities, an application can inquire into the status of any resource. Much like the CEMT transaction, this facility will allow INQUIRE into a resource, and pass back existing conditions of the resource to the application. Now, rather than attempting to execute a command, such as STARTBR, and waiting for the condition to return from the request, the application can interrogate the resource to determine the condition. The application may decide, based on the status of the resource, to execute different logic within the program.

This new facility also allows, much like the CEMT transaction, that the resource be changed, or SET to another status. Resources such as files and terminals can be set to alternative values by the application. This can be a very dangerous technique for a normal application, since it is actually modifying CICS resources. It is not documented in the CICS Application Programmer's Reference Manual for this reason. In the manual that contains documentation for this facility, IBM warns of the use of these new functions and advises their use only for systems types of applications. Many installations are securing these facilities and restricting their use. If an installation has a need for the function, however, this is a very powerful tool. These types of enhancements to the COBOL command facility give installations more choices, and ability to respond to new CICS requirements.

# 6

# Typical Application Terminal Abends

CICS is constantly sending and receiving requests from terminals. A great deal of the work performed by CICS concerns data transmissions, both inbound and outbound. Data must be received, processed, and mapped back out to the appropriate terminal. During this process, a number of events can occur that induce errors and pose problems for the application. Some are not caused by the application, but must be handled by the application program. The method of handling these problems is sometimes as different as handling file problems. Just as terminals come in a variety of models and types, the problems generated can be as complicated as the networks that some installations are building. The nature of hardware problems and the asynchronous nature of timing while terminal requests are being processed cause problems. Terminal problems happen asynchronously from the application, sometimes after the application has completed.

Terminals can be grouped into two categories, VTAM controlled, and non-VTAM. Of course, with IBM's Statement of Direction, BTAM terminals will no longer be supported after CICS/MVS 2.1. For that reason, VTAM is the recommended network protocol, and the primary focus of this chapter. CICS has different routines to handle these different types of terminals, since the capabilities are very different. The systems initialization table, SIT, contains entries to identify the types of terminals that need to be supported in CICS.

An installation can remove the modules that are not necessary for terminals unused in their network. The routine DFHTACP is invoked when errors are detected in non-VTAM terminals. DFHZNAC is the routine for error handling of VTAM terminals. These routines, however, only provide minimal error processing. For the most part, if not enhanced, they simply produce a generic abend if any type of error is detected. Installations generally provide user-written routines to supplement these IBM-provided procedures.

## 6.1 TEP AND NEP FOR TERMINAL PROBLEMS

The IBM-supplied program DFHTEP can be enhanced for error handling of non-VTAM terminals and DFHZNEP, for VTAM terminals. These programs can be used in much the same way that HANDLE CONDITION is used in application program processing. Let us use DFHZNEP as an example. If an error is detected, perhaps a terminal is unavailable at this time, a specific error code is returned to DFHZNEP. The installation can code appropriate instructions into this program to detect this error and take corrective action. The error condition is passed to the program in a one-byte field, and the NEP (node error program) can choose alternative action. A sample NEP is shipped with CICS, but it simply returns control back to the caller. Installations must customize this routine to provide any true functionality. It is important to realize that most terminal abends occur on out-bound transmissions, after the application has successfully completed and returned control to CICS. Since there is no application to notify and take action, these error programs must be used to process any error condition, if necessary.

The NEP can also take advantage of VTAM sense codes that are returned to CICS. The CICS-VTAM interface provides a small "indicative dump" that contains information relevant to the problem. Since the VTAM sense codes are provided, this information can be used to diagnose the problem and determine the cause of the terminal failure. Some installations choose to intercept these situations via the NEP. The NEP can analyze the sense codes and take action, perhaps notification to a network console that would be monitoring terminal outages.

Another common procedure would be to specify an interval, usually a few seconds, and retry the failing request. If successful, the transmission can proceed. If unsuccessful after several repetitions, the terminal can be taken out of service to avoid redundant failures, and appropriate notification can be sent.

If the environment is non-VTAM, the program NACP (network abnormal condition program) would be used. Full documentation on NEP and NACP can be found in the CICS Customization Guide.

## 6.2    3270 DATA STREAMS

Typical 3270 data streams can be either inbound (data keyed in from the terminal) or outbound (data being sent to the terminal), and are usually diagnosed very differently. A 3270 data stream is generated by the CICS facility BMS (basic mapping services). This consists of a merge of the data in the physical map and a symbolic mapping of application data from the program. Although inbound and outbound data streams contain slightly different information and structure, outbound data streams tend to cause the most problems, and the most failures. This will become more obvious as the contents are analyzed.

### 6.2.1    Outbound Data Streams

These data streams consist of commands, or orders (usually a set buffer address, SBA), structured fields (SF), write control characters (WCC), and character data. A typical outbound data stream would look similar to the following:

```
-----I----I----I----------I----I----I---------
WCC   SBA  SF   DATA       SBA  SF   DATA
```

The contents of these fields would vary, of course, depending on the type of data being transmitted. Some typical buffer control orders, or commands, used in 3270 data transmission are

```
SBA    Set Buffer Address
SF     Start Field
PT     Program Tab
RA     Repeat to Address
EUA    Erase Unprotected Fields
SFE    Start Field Extended
```

```
MF     Modify Field
SA     Set Attribute
```

Take, for example, an SBA command. How is that recognized within a data stream? The format of an SBA order is

```
X'11rrcc'
```

where rr corresponds to the row number and cc the column number within the 3270 screen. The numbers are not the physical positions on the screen, but a logical placement. The hexadecimal 11 represents the actual command code, the rest of the SBA positions the address. If an SBA of

```
X'114040'
```

was detected, it would represent a Set Buffer Address at Row 1, Column 1. Note, however, that row and column numbers vary by terminal model. The 3270 Reference Manual contains all possible combinations for different devices.

A Start Field order (SF) instructs the controller (hardware) that the next byte is an attribute byte. The command code for SF is hexadecimal 1D, so a typical SF would appear as:

```
X'1Daa'
```

where "aa" represents the field attributes. Since the field attributes must fit in a one-byte field, it is "mapped" into bit patterns that are interpreted. The mapping of field attributes are

```
BIT    Field Description
0,1    Determined by the contents of 2-7
 2     0=Unprotected
       1=Protected
 3     0=Alphanumeric
       1=Numeric, causes numeric lock in KB
4,5    00=Display/not light pen detectable
       01=Display/light pen detectable
       10=Intensified/pen detectable
       11=Non-display (dark)
 6     Reserved, must be zero
 7     MDT - Modified Data Tag
       0=Field has not been modified
       1=Field has been modified
```

Therefore, if an SF of X'1D50' was encountered, 50 would map out to 01010000. Bits 1 and 3 are turned on, or contain a binary 1. The field attributes describe an unprotected numeric field.

New 3270 devices sometimes have the ability to produce extended features, such as color, reverse video, or highlighting. In these devices, field attributes are extended and require a two-byte attribute. The second byte of a standard attribute byte is used, and can contain hexadecimal values such as 41 (extended highlighting), 42 (extended colors), or 43 (programmed symbols).

The combination of these data stream commands, or orders, produces a typical, and we hope, correct 3270 data stream. A segment of an outbound data stream is presented below and broken into its components. The WCC (write control character) is not shown, but would precede the example.

```
X'1140401DF9C1C2C3C4C540F1F2F311C1401DC813'


X'114040'    SBA Row 1, Column 1
X'1DF9'      SF Attributes of Bright, Protected
             MDT (Modified Data Tag) On
X'C1C2C3C4C540F1D2F3'
             Data 'ABCDE 123'
X'11C140'    SBA Row 2, Column 1
X'1DC8'      SF Attributes of Bright, Unprotected
X'13'        Insert Cursor
```

### 6.2.2  Inbound Data Streams

These data streams are similar, since they contain SBA and SF orders with attribute bytes. They, however, contain an AID byte rather than a WCC byte at the beginning of the segment. The AID byte would contain codes to represent the interrupt key pressed by the terminal operator, such as CLEAR, ENTER, etc. The AID is available to the program in two places, the TCTTEAID field of the TCTTE or the EIBAID in the EIB. This could be used by the program to determine which key was used, and to execute different logic in the program. Many times, the MDT attribute is investigated, since the program may only wish to acknowledge data fields that have been modified. Most inbound data streams are not the cause of program checks and abends, since the data can be analyzed and screened by the program.

In summary, outbound 3270 data streams are the major cause of terminal problems, and for several reasons. Some installations purchase compression packages to optimize transmissions. These packages can interfere with the data streams. Data streams are very dependent on device model and type, and maps that display on one device may cause failures on a different device. The program must know the characteristics of the device. Programmers must be careful to match the BMS map to the physical map. If the map is changed and recompiled, but the program is not, a mismatch will

usually cause unpredictable and undesirable results.

With so many potential pitfalls, how does a programmer avoid terminal failures? Installation standards and constant attention are the best defense against invalid data streams. Of course, failures occur and must be diagnosed. Two typical examples of invalid data streams are discussed later in this chapter. Hopefully, these examples will provide insight into the cause of ATNI failures and how to debug them.

## 6.3  ATNI ABENDS

When the Node Error Program, NEP, fails to handle the error condition, an abend results. The abend code is normally ATNI. As documented in CICS Messages and Codes, this abend indicates that NEP or NACP has decided to terminate the task. The error can be caused from a variety of situations. Some are hardware failures, but they can also be caused by incorrect device definition in the TCT or TYPETERM entry in RDO. Many ATNI abends are caused by invalid data streams. The data attempting to be transmitted to the terminal may contain invalid entries, or unsupported functions. These ATNIs can be resolved by correcting the definition of the device, or insuring that the applications fields do not contain data which could be interpreted as 3270 instructions.

If the error is a hardware failure, there is little the application can do to resolve it. ATNI transaction dumps, therefore, are of minimal value since they show only that an error has occurred, and are seldom analyzed unless caused by invalid data streams. In addition to the ATNI abend, additional information is written to the CSMT destination that may document the failure. VTAM error codes and sense codes are usually the most valuable pieces of information in terminal failures. If experiencing ATNI abends, work with others, such as operations or network staff, to determine the cause of the problem.

## 6.4  VTAM SENSE CODES

When network failures are detected, VTAM passes information to CICS. This information can be handled by the error routines or are sent to the CSMT destination for output. The messages produced will be in the format DFH34xx or DFH24xx, since they are generated by DFHZNAC. Although hundreds of messages can be produced in this category, most contain sense data within the message. This sense data can be analyzed and contribute to the debugging effort, since at times the sense data is the only information that is relevant to the failure. The sense data displayed will be in the format:

```
'SENSE RECEIVED xxyy zzzz'


xx - VTAM system sense information byte
     08 - request reject
     10 - request error
     20 - state error
     40 - request header usage error
     80 - path error


yy - VTAM system sense modifier byte


zzzz - user sense information
```

The value for the VTAM sense modifier byte (yy) will vary depending on the sense information byte (xx). Some of the most common sense codes are

```
1003 - Function not supported
```

This sense code could mean that a function requested by a control character, or a request unit is not supported by the existing device types. Hardware limitations in devices and controllers restrict the level of function an application may execute.

```
0831 - LU component disconnected
```

This sense code is displayed if the device attached to the communications controller cannot be contacted. Normal reasons for this situation would be that the terminal has been powered off, or that the cable connections have been broken.

Many other sense codes can be returned. Printers sometimes present significant problems. The differences between LU1-type printers and LU3-type printers and page sizes can generate many different sense codes. A complete listing of all sense codes can be found in the VTAM Messages and Codes manual. This manual may be necessary to diagnose terminal problems.

## 6.5   TERMINAL PROGRAM CHECKS

Many terminal problems are created by data streams passed from the application. This data is received from the host, but produces an error since it violates standard VTAM protocols. The program check returns a PROG XXX to the device, where XXX can be type 401-499. Some of these program checks are documented in Appendix B at the end of this book. A complete list of program check types and descriptions can be found in the 3274 Control

Unit Description and Programmer's Guide, GA23-0061. While the program check type usually appears at the bottom of the terminal, additional information is written to the CSMT destination, and an ATNI abend can be produced. While that ATNI dump may contain relevant information, the program check type and the VTAM sense codes written to CSMT may also be significant. It may also be necessary to utilize a VTAM buffer trace to analyze the data stream and locate the failing portion. Two of these program checks are included in this chapter to identify relevant debugging items and how to resolve these problems.

## 6.6   CICS AUTOINSTALL PROBLEMS

Starting with CICS 1.7, a new facility was introduced to allow the automatic installation of terminals into a CICS region without having an explicit definition of that device in the TCT. Installations were freed from the tedious and time-consuming definition of each terminal in a macro, and reassembling that table every time a new terminal was installed. In fact, the terminal control table could be entirely removed and all terminals defined via RDO or autoinstall. This was truly welcomed by most customers, but forced them to rethink the status of devices. Prior to autoinstall, the TCT was a static table and contained all terminal definitions, whether the user was signed on or not. In fact, some applications actually looked at terminal control blocks to check status conditions, or modify the terminal control table user area (TCTUA).

With autoinstall, the TCT is not built until the user signs on. This can save large amounts of virtual storage, since the control blocks are not built until needed. It poses a new situation for an application, however, since it does not guarantee that data will be available at all times. Applications that went looking for a terminal may now receive new response codes from devices that have not yet signed on. In addition, applications that built or modified the user area (TCTUA) must be aware of the timing of creation of the control blocks and their deletion. While an application can reference and modify the TCTUA during execution, the control block is deleted at log-off time. When the user reestablishes the session, the control blocks are rebuilt, including the TCTUA. The prior modification no longer exists. In addition, each TCTUA may be created with a different length, as specified by the autoinstall model or installation exit.

The use of the TCTUA can still be accommodated, but may have to be changed. IBM provides a program that is invoked at autoinstall time, DFHZATDX. This is a routine that can be enhanced, or replaced by an installation. Chapter 11, System Programming Issues, contains some information about this module and how an installation may customize the routine. An installation that requires data in the TCTUA could use this module to build the user area during autoinstall. A program could be executed during sign on to build the user area. The application must remember, however, that any data stored in the user area is lost when the control blocks are deleted, and must be rebuilt.

## 6.7    TERMINAL FAILURES — TWO EXAMPLES

While many terminal failures are hardware-created, some are caused by the application and the data stream being transmitted to the device. These failures usually produce transaction dumps. Figure 6-1 displays all items that may be relevant in debugging these type of failures.

Of course, the first point of failure is at the device. The failure displays the program check at the bottom of the terminal. In the first example, the user experienced a PROG 402 at the device. The documentation on a program check type 402 describes:

> "An invalid (out of range) address was received following an SBA, RA, or EUA order: or an MF order addressed a nonfield attribute location."

The recommendation for recovery of this failure is to merely RESET the program check indicator on the device, and retry the operation. Since this is probably a data stream error, a recurrence is likely. Further investigation will be required. Since many messages are sent to the CSMT destination in these failures, the next step would be to locate the output for potential importance. Figure 6-2 contains the section of the CICS CSMT log with the output.

The first CICS message in the output is DFH3406I, indicating a parameter error (1). The explanation given in the CICS Messages and Codes manual describes an error caused by an invalid function in the data received. The contents of the description identifies the application program as the cause of the problem.

The message also contains a sense code of 1005 (2). This sense code is also described in the VTAM Messages and Codes manual as a parameter error. It goes further to document this sense code as caused by invalid data following an SBA (set buffer address) or other control function. Obviously, this failure is caused by invalid contents in the data stream attempting to be transmitted. Very possibly,

```
ABEND CODE:  ATNI

PROBABLE CAUSE:  Invalid data stream or hard-
ware failure

IMPORTANT DUMP ITEMS:    Trace Table
                         TCTTE
                         TIOA

OTHER RELEVANT ITEMS:    CSMT messages
                         VTAM sense contents
                         Program Check Type
```

Figure 6-1    Significant items in an ATNI abend.

an invalid block of data is being interpreted as an SBA, and contains a binary 11.

The DFH3406I message also contains a few CICS control blocks that may be relevant to the failure. Following the message are the RPL (request parameter list), TCTTE (terminal control table terminal entry) and the TCTTEXTN (TCTTE extension). Most significant, however, is the TIOA (3). The TIOA (terminal input/output area) contains data relevant to terminal I/O operations. It is created by storage control much the same way as user storage is created on behalf of the task. This storage is chained to the TCTTE, while user storage is chained to the TCA. The portion of the TIOA displayed is not the entire contents, but merely four fullwords, or 16 bytes of data. The full block of terminal storage can be found within the dump. In some cases, the TIOA shown in the CICS message will be adequate to diagnose the problem. In this case, however, it contains valid data and the dump must be used. The last line of the CSMT output displays the message that an ATNI abend has been detected, and that a transaction dump has been produced.

Previous analysis of transaction dumps used many task-related control blocks, such as the TCA, and the storage chained off the task. Since ATNI abends are primarily terminal-related, the control blocks related to the task are not as important. The trace table contains entries that track the flow of the transaction, therefore may contain information relevant to the analysis. Figure 6-3 contains a section of the trace table prior to the ATNI abend. Notice that MAPA, a BMS map, has been loaded (1), the map was sent (2), and that data appears to have been transmitted (3). Immediately after the trace entry type 'EE' (4), from DFHZCP (VTAM) containing the send, is the corresponding trace entry to receive the data (5), with a negative response code. Obviously, while transmitting the data

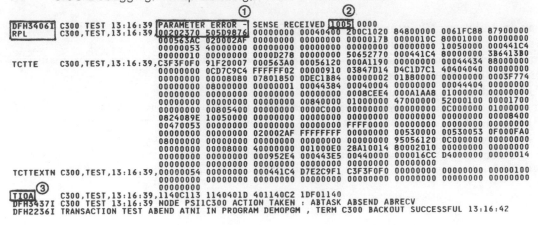

```
                                          ①                    ②
DFH3406I  C300 TEST 13:16:39 PARAMETER ERROR - SENSE RECEIVED 1005 0000
RPL       C300,TEST,13:16:39 00202370 505D9876 00000000 00040400 200C1020 84800000 0061FC88 87900000
                             000563AC 020002AF 00000000 00000000 0000017B 0000010C 80001000 00000000
                             00000053 40000000 00000000 00000000 00000000 00000000 10050000 000441C4
                             00000010 00000000 0000D278 00000000 50652770 000441C4 80000000 3B6413B0
TCTTE     C300,TEST,13:16:39,C3F3F0F0 91F20007 000563A0 00056120 000A1190 00000000 00044434 88000000
                             00000000 0CD7C9C4 FFFFFF02 00000910 03847D14 D4C1D7C1 40404040 00000000
                             00000000 00008080 07801850 0DEC1B84 00000002 01BB0000 00000000 0003F774
                             00000000 08000000 00000001 00044384 00040004 00000000 00044404 00000000
                             00000000 08000000 00000000 0008CEE4 000A1AA8 01000000 00000000
                             00000000 00000000 00000000 00840000 01000000 47000000 52000100 00001700
                             00000000 00805400 00000000 0000C000 00000000 00000000 0C000000 01000000
                             0824089E 10050000 00000000 00000000 00000000 00000000 00000000 00008400
                             00470053 00000000 00000000 00000000 00000000 FFFF0000 00000000 00000000
                             00000000 00000000 020002AF FFFFFFFF 00000000 00530000 00530053 0F000FA0
                             08000000 00000000 00000000 00000000 00000000 95056120 0C000000 00000000
                             00000000 00008000 40000000 001000E0 28A10014 80002010 00000000 00000000
                             00000000 00000000 000952E4 000443E5 00440000 000016CC D4000000 00000014
TCTTEXTN  C300,TEST,13:16:39,00000054 00000000 000441C4 D7E2C9F1 C3F3F0F0 00000000 00000000 00000100
                             00000000
TIOA ③    C300,TEST,13:16:39,1140C113 1140401D 401140C2 1DF01140
DFH3437I  C300 TEST 13:16:39 NODE PSI1C300 ACTION TAKEN : ABTASK ABSEND ABRECV
DFH2236I  TRANSACTION TEST ABEND ATNI IN PROGRAM DEMOPGM , TERM C300 BACKOUT SUCCESSFUL 13:16:42
```

Figure 6-2   CICS DFH3406I message and contents.

```
PSI1CICP    --- CICS TRANSACTION DUMP ---    CODE=ATNI   TASK=TEST        DATE=11/07/88   TIME=13:16:39   PAGE   16


   TIME OF DAY   ID  REG 14  REQD TASK  FIELD A  FIELD B  CHARS   RESOURCE  TRACE TYPE                               INTERVAL

13:16:38.333248  EA 406179E4 0003 00086 01000300 000A1214 ........ MAPA ①  TMP PPT LOCATE                           00.000032
13:16:38.333280  EA 40631A2C 0005 00086 01000300 00044AD4 .......M          TMP RETN NORMAL                          00.000032
13:16:38.333312  F2 406006DA 0804 00086 00000000 00000000 ........          PCP DELETE                               00.000032
13:16:38.333312  EA 406179E4 0003 00086 01000300 000A1214 ........ DFH$CGA  TMP PPT LOCATE                           00.000000
13:16:38.333344  EA 40631A2C 0005 00086 01000300 00044A74 ........ DFH$CGA  TMP RETN NORMAL                          00.000032
13:16:38.333376  F1 40600FAA 8504 00086 000A025E 010441C4 .......D          SCP GETMAIN                              00.000032
13:16:38.333408  C8 5061D830 0004 00086 00056120 850A0278 ../.....          SCP ACQUIRED TERMINAL STORAGE            00.000032
13:16:38.333568  FC 5060167E 0103 00066 00810000 000441C4 .......D          ZCP ZARQ APPL REQ ERASE WRITE            00.000160
13:16:38.333600  FC 4065300C 0105 00086 00810400 00056120 ......./          ZCP RETN ZARQ APPL REQ ERASE WRITE DEFER 00.000032
13:16:38.333632  FA 40600E4A 0005 00086 00000000 00000000 ........          BMS RETN                                 00.000032
13:16:38.333632  FA 405FD2AA 0005 00086 00000000 00000000 ........          BMS RETN                                 00.000000
13:16:38.333664  E1 50367EE0 00F4 00086 00000000 00001804 ........     ②   EIP SEND-MAP RESPONSE                    00.000032
13:16:38.333664  E1 50368238 0004 00086 000A1BFC 00001802 ........          EIP RECEIVE-MAP ENTRY                    00.000000
13:16:38.333696  F1 6061CE5A 4004 00086 000A2B40 010441C4 .......D          SCP FREEMAIN                             00.000032
13:16:38.333728  C9 5061D86C 0004 00086 000A2B40 8C000408 ........          SCP RELEASED USER STORAGE                00.000032
13:16:38.333728  FA 005FF912 0003 00086 00020509 00000020 ........     ③   BMS MAP MAPSET WAIT IN                   00.000000
13:16:38.333760  FA 405FD28C 0003 00086 00020509 00000020 ........          BMS MAP MAPSET WAIT IN                   00.000032
13:16:38.333792  FC 506009B8 0103 00086 00140000 000441C4 .......D          ZCP ZARQ APPL REQ READ WAIT              00.000032
13:16:38.333824  FC 7064F7F8 1804 00086 00534880 000441C4 .......D          ZCP ZSDS SEND                            00.000032
13:16:38.333856  FC 5064F8B8 1D04 00086 00474880 000441C4 .......D          ZCP ZSDR SEND RESPONSE                   00.000032
13:16:38.333888  F0 6065134E 0D04 00086 0003F890 00000000 ..8.....          KCP ATTACH HTA                           00.000032
13:16:38.334112  F0 7065312C 4004 00086 13000000 000441C4 .......D          KCP WAIT DCI=TERMINAL                     00.000224
13:16:38.334144  D0 50665608 0A04 00086 00000000 00000000 ........          KCP SUSPEND                               00.000032
13:16:38.334912  D0 50666CDE 0904 KCP   00010000 622CFB63 ........          KCP SYSTEM RESUME                         00.000768
13:16:38.335360  D0 50666CDE 0504 TCP   00000000 00000000 ........     ④   KCP DISPATCH                             00.000448
13:16:38.336128  EE 70651588 2214 TCP   00532126 010441C4 .......D 020002AF VIO SEND CD OIC DATA RQE1               00.000768
13:16:38.336160  EE 70651588 0024 TCP   017BF5C3 1140C113 .5C. A.  020002AF VIO DATA                                00.000032
13:16:38.336192  FC 7065184C 1604 TCP   00480080 190441C4 .......D          ZCP ZRVS RECEIVE SPECIFIC                00.000032
13:16:38.336192  F1 6064E3A0 E304 TCP   00000100 000441C4 .......D          SCP GETMAIN CONDITIONAL INITIMG          00.000000
13:16:38.336224  C8 5061D830 0004 TCP   000563A0 85000118 ........          SCP ACQUIRED TERMINAL STORAGE            00.000032
13:16:38.336256  F0 6065134E 0D04 TCP   0003F890 00000000 ..8.....          KCP ATTACH HTA                           00.000032
13:16:38.337216  F0 40652830 4004 TCP   40000000 005D1D50 ....).&           KCP WAIT DCI=LIST                         00.000960
13:16:38.407424  D0 50666CDE 0904 KCP   00010000 622CFB64 ........     ⑤   KCP SYSTEM RESUME                        *00.070208
13:16:38.407648  D0 50666CDE 0504 TCP   00000000 00000000 ........          KCP DISPATCH                              00.000224
13:16:38.407968  EE 70651588 2314 TCP   005300EE 010441C4 ......D  020002AF VIO RECEIVE RESP DATA - RQE1            00.000320
13:16:38.408000  EE 70651588 2334 TCP   00D5C5C7 10050000 .NEG..   020002AF VIO NEGATIVE RESP CODE                  00.000032
13:16:38.408064  F1 40651AA4 5704 TCP   00000000 C3E2D5C5 ....CSNE          KCP                                      00.000064
13:16:38.408096  F1 406646C2 EA04 TCP   00000950 010441C4 ....&...D          SCP GETMAIN CONDITIONAL INITIMG          00.000032
13:16:38.408192  C8 5061D830 0004 TCP   00A4000 8A040958 ........          SCP ACQUIRED TCA STORAGE                 00.000096
13:16:38.408288  D0 50665608 0604 00087 00000000 C3E2D5C5 ....CSNE          KCP CREATE                                00.000096
13:16:38.408352  EA 40664B58 0003 TCP   0C000100 005D3D20 .....).  CSNE     TMP PCT TRANSFER                          00.000064
13:16:38.408512  EA 40631A2C 0035 TCP   0C000100 00000000 ........          TMP RETN NORMAL                           00.000160
13:16:38.408576  F0 40652830 4004 TCP   40000000 005D1D50 ....).&           KCP WAIT DCI=LIST                         00.000064
13:16:38.408640  D0 50666CDE 0504 00087 40000000 005D1D50 ........          KCP DISPATCH                              00.000064
13:16:38.408672  F2 50651AC4 8104 00087 00000000 00000000 ........ DFHZNAC  PCP LINK-CONDITIONAL                      00.000416
13:16:38.409088  EA 406179E4 0004 00087 01000300 000A4214 ........ DFHZNAC  TMP PPT LOCATE                            00.000032
13:16:38.409120  EA 40631A2C 0045 00087 01000300 0005E034 ........          TMP RETN NORMAL                           00.000160
13:16:38.409280  F1 406175D6 8904 00087 00000050 00000000 ....&...          SCP GETMAIN                                00.000032
13:16:38.409312  C8 5061D830 0004 00087 000A4960 89000058 ...-....          SCP ACQUIRED RSA STORAGE                  00.000096
13:16:38.409408  F1 4061CC70 CC04 00087 00000418 00000000 ........          SCP GETMAIN INITIMG                        00.000032
13:16:38.409440  C8 5061D830 0004 00087 000A49C0 8C000428 ........          SCP ACQUIRED USER STORAGE                 00.000064
13:16:38.409472  F2 504BD392 2024 00087 004BDC0A 00000000 ........          PCP SETXIT,ROUTINE                         00.000000
13:16:38.409472  F1 604BD3AC CC04 00087 0000029C 00000000 ........          SCP GETMAIN INITIMG                        00.000000
13:16:38.409536  C8 5061D830 0004 00087 000A4DF0 8C0002A8 ..(0....          SCP ACQUIRED USER STORAGE                 00.000064
13:16:38.409568  F1 504BD3CC CD04 00087 00000498 00000000 ........          SCP GETMAIN INITIMG                        00.000032
```

Figure 6-3   CICS ATNI abend: trace table entries.

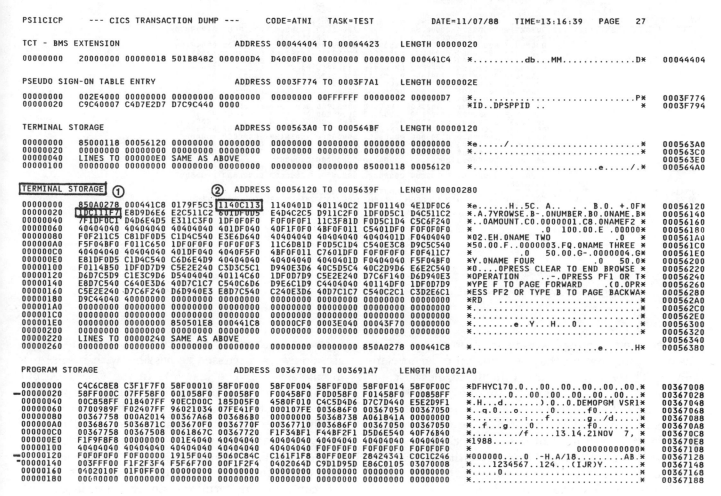

Figure 6-4  CICS ATNI abend: terminal storage.

an error was detected. CICS then dispatches CSNE, the CICS transaction for CICS-VTAM error handling. If the installation had written a NEP (node error program) to handle the situation, it would have been given control. In this case, no customized NEP was available, so CICS produces messages and the ATNI abend.

The TCTTE was already reproduced in the DFH3406I message, but could be located in the dump for further investigation. More important, however, would be to locate the TIOA and investigate the entire contents. The TIOA is located in a formatted transaction dump after the TCTTE, and is titled Terminal Storage. Figure 6-4 contains the two blocks of terminal storage created for this terminal. The second entry (1) relates to the failure, since the contents of the TIOA in the CSMT message can be matched to the contents. The first four bytes in any transaction storage contain the storage type and length. The next four bytes always contain the address to the next block of storage in the

chain. In a TIOA, the third fullword contains information relating to terminal control. Finally, the fourth fullword begins the actual data.

Note that the fourth fullword in the contents of terminal storage (2) matches the first entry in the TIOA from the message [Figure 6-2 (3)]. The storage in the dump, however, contains the entire TIOA. The contents can be analyzed for the entry causing the failure. Note that at offset +20 into this storage is a one byte field **1D** (1). This field contains a command SF (start field) within the data being transmitted; however the SF is not preceded by an SBA, which is the normal protocol for a 3270 datastream. In fact, the entire fullword at this location is '1DC111F7'. An SBA is imbedded within the data, preceded by the SF. This is obviously not valid in an outbound data stream, as documented by the program check and the VTAM sense codes. This invalid data could have been erroneously inserted by the program by moving packed or binary data into a character field. Only character data is

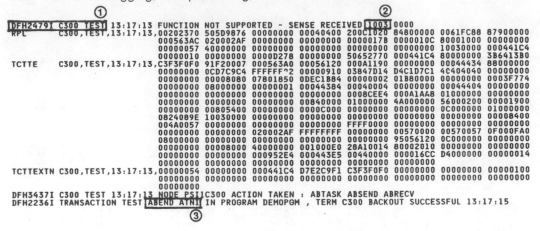

Figure 6-5   CICS DFH2479I message and contents.

allowed, and nondisplay data may produce a hexadecimal combination that becomes an order or command. These failures are difficult to diagnose for this exact reason. The program may execute correctly, and then suddenly fail. Perhaps a single record contained just the right data to translate into hexadecimal representations of a SBA or some other command. These terminal failures must be diagnosed with the dump to analyze the contents of the TIOA and find the invalid data.

In the second example, the type of program check experienced was a 471. The documentation on this type of program check describes:

> "An extended data stream function cannot be executed...."

and continues to list several unsupported and invalid field types and formats that may cause this problem. The results are basically the same as the type 402, and the cause is, again, an invalid data stream. The symptoms are slightly different, especially in the messages produced.

Figure 6-5 contains the output written to the CSMT log. In this failure, the message DFH2479I is produced (1). This message identifies the error as an application request for a function that is not supported. The VTAM sense data (2) contains 1003, also documented as an error "Function Not Supported." While the previous problem produced symptoms relating to invalid parameters, this data stream appears to contain control characters that request an unsupported function. Remember, in a

previous section of this chapter, extended data streams were discussed as possible with special terminal features. The last line in the CSMT output identifies the ATNI abend (3), and the dump can be analyzed for this invalid data stream.

Within the dump, the trace table would identify many of the same entries as the previous ATNI abend. Terminal storage must be investigated to locate the data within the TIOA for content. Figure 6-6 contains the terminal storage associated with this device. In the second entry, which is the TIOA, the data stream appears very similar to the contents of the previous failure. At offset +20, however, is the one-byte field containing a **29**. This value relates to a command SFE (Start Field Extended). The problem, however, is that the device does not contain the facilities for extended attributes. The request is returned to CICS, since the request cannot be accommodated. Again, programs must be aware of the characteristics of the device being utilized. Extended features may be available and valid on some devices, but not on others. The request for SFE could have been incorrectly coded into the application, or may have merely been invalid binary data in the field that accidently mapped into a command. In either case, this request cannot be processed, and produced the ATNI failure.

In summary, although many ATNI abends are unrelated to the application, this is not always the case. The resolution to data stream-related ATNI abends usually involves identifying the invalid contents of the TIOA (the 3270 data stream) and removing the cause.

```
PSI1CICP    --- CICS TRANSACTION DUMP ---    CODE=ATNI   TASK=TEST         DATE=11/07/88   TIME=13:17:13   PAGE   27

TCT - BMS EXTENSION                      ADDRESS 00044404 TO 00044423    LENGTH 00000020

00000000   20000000 00000018 501B8482 000000D4  D4000F00 00000000 00000000 000441C4  *..........db...MM.............D*  00044404

PSEUDO SIGN-ON TABLE ENTRY               ADDRESS 0003F774 TO 0003F7A1    LENGTH 0000002E

00000000   002E4000 00000000 00000000 00000000  00000000 00FFFFFF 00000002 000000D7  *. .........................P*    0003F774
00000020   C9C40007 C4D7E2D7 D7C9C440 0000                                            *ID..DPSPPID ..           *         0003F794

TERMINAL STORAGE                         ADDRESS 000563A0 TO 000564BF    LENGTH 00000120

00000000   85000118 00056120 00000000 00000000  00000000 00000000 00000000 00000000  *e...../.....................*     000563A0
00000020   00000000 00000000 00000000 00000000  00000000 00000000 00000000 00000000  *............................*     000563C0
00000040   LINES TO 000000E0 SAME AS ABOVE                                                                                 000563E0
00000100   00000000 00000000 00000000 00000000  00000000 00000000 85000118 00056120  *........................e...../.* 000564A0

TERMINAL STORAGE                         ADDRESS 00056120 TO 0005639F    LENGTH 00000280

00000000   850A0278 000441C8 0179F5C3 1140C113  1140401D 401140C2 1DF01140 4E1DF0C6  *e......H..5C. A.. . . B.0. +.0F*  00056120
00000020   2901111F7 E8D9D6E6 E2C511C2 601DF0D5  E4D4C2C5 D911C2F0 1DF0D5C1 D4C511C2  *.A.7YROWSE.B-.0NUMBER.B0.0NAME.B*  00056140
00000040   7F1DF0C1 D4D6E4D5 E311C3F0 1DF0F0F0  F0F0F0F1 11C3F81D F0D5C1D4 C5C6F240  *..0AMOUNT.C0.0000001.C8.0NAMEF2 *  00056160
00000060   40404040 40404040 40404040 401DF040  40F1F0F0 4BF0F011 C5401DF0 F0F0F0F0  *               .0   100.00.E .00000* 00056180
00000080   F0F211C5 C81DF0D5 C1D4C540 E3E6D640  40404040 40404040 4040401D F0404040  *02.EH.0NAME TWO         .0  *       000561A0
000000A0   F5F04BF0 F011C650 1DF0F0F0 F0F0F0F3  11C6D81D F0D5C1D4 C540E3C8 D9C5C540  *50.00.F..0000003.FQ.0NAME THREE *   000561C0
000000C0   40404040 40404040 401DF040 4040F5F0  4BF0F011 C7601DF0 F0F0F0F0 F0F411C7  *         .0    50.00.G-.0000004.G*   000561E0
000000E0   E81DF0D5 C1D4C540 C6D6E4D9 40404040  40404040 4040401D F0404040 F5F04BF0  *Y.0NAME FOUR         .0   50.0*     00056200
00000100   F0114B50 1DF0D7D9 C5E2E240 C3D3C5C1  D940E3D6 40C5D5C4 40C2D9D6 E6E2C540  *0....0PRESS CLEAR TO END BROWSE *   00056220
00000120   D6D7C5D9 C1E3C9D6 D5404040 40114C60  1DF0D7D9 C5E2E240 D7C6F140 D6D940E3  *OPERATION    ..-.0PRESS PF1 OR T*   00056240
00000140   E8D7C540 C640E3D6 40D7C1C7 C540C6D6  D9E6C1D9 C4404040 40114DF0 1DF0D7D9  *YPE F TO PAGE FORWARD    .(0.0PR*   00056260
00000160   C5E2E240 D7C6F240 D6D940E3 E8D7C540  C240E3D6 40D7C1C7 C540C2C1 C3D2E6C1  *ESS PF2 OR TYPE B TO PAGE BACKWA*   00056280
00000180   D9C44040 40000000 00000000 00000000  00000000 00000000 00000000 00000000  *RD .........................*      000562A0
000001A0   00000000 00000000 00000000 00000000  00000000 00000000 00000000 00000000  *............................*      000562C0
000001C0   00000000 00000000 00000000 00000000  00000000 00000000 00000000 00000000  *............................*      000562E0
000001E0   00000000 00000000 850501E8 000441C8  00000CF0 0003E040 00043F70 00000000  *.......e..Y..H...0...........*      00056300
00000200   00000000 00000000 00000000 00000000  00000000 00000000 00000000 00000000  *............................*      00056320
00000220   LINES TO 00000240 SAME AS ABOVE                                                                                 00056340
00000260   00000000 00000000 00000000 00000000  00000000 00000000 850A0278 000441C8  *........................e...H*     00056380

PROGRAM STORAGE                          ADDRESS 00367008 TO 003691A7    LENGTH 000021A0

 00000000   C4C6C8E8 C3F1F7F0 58F00010 58F0F000  58F0F004 58F0F0D0 58F0F014 58F0F00C  *DFHYC170.0...00..00..00..00..*     00367008
-00000020   58FF000C 07FF58F0 001058F0 F00058F0  F00458F0 F0D058F0 F01458F0 F00858FF  *.......0...00..00..00..00...*      00367028
 00000040   00C858FF 018407FF 90ECD00C 185D05F0  4580F010 C4C5D4D6 D7C7D440 E5E2D9F1  *.H...d.......).0..0.DEMOPGM VSR1*   00367048
 00000060   0700989F F02407FF 96021034 07FE41F0  000107FE 003686F0 00367050 00367050  *..q.0..o.......0.......f0.......*   00367068
 00000080   00367758 000A2014 00367A68 003686B0  00000000 50368738 A061841A 00000000  *........:..f.......g../d.....*      00367088
 000000A0   00368670 5036871C 003670F0 0036770F  00367710 003686F0 00367050 00367050  *..f..g...0.......f0.........*       003670A8
 000000C0   00367758 00367508 0061867C 00367720  F1F34BF1 F44BF2F1 D5D6E540 40F76B40  *......./f....13.14.21NOV 7, *       003670C8
 000000E0   F1F9F8F8 00000000 001E4040 40404040  40404040 40404040 40404040 40404040  *1988......     000000000000*        003670E8
 00000100   40404040 40404040 40404040 40404040  40404040 F0F0F0F0 F0F0F0F0 F0F0F0F0  *              000000000000*         00367108
-00000120   F0F0F0F0 F0F00000 1915F040 5060C84C  C161F1F8 80FF0E0F 28424341 C0C1C246  *000000....0 .-H.A/18.......AB.*     00367128
-00000140   003FFF00 F1F2F3F4 F5F6F700 00F1F2F4  0402064D C9D1D95D E86C0105 03070008  *....1234567..124...(IJR)Y.......*   00367148
 00000160   0402010F 01F0FF00 00000000 00000000  00000000 00000000 00000000 00000000  *.....0.....................*       00367168
 00000180   00000000 00000000 00000000 00000000  00000000 00000000 00000000 00000000  *.....0.....................*       00367188
```

Figure 6-6   CICS ATNI abend: terminal storage.

# Typical Miscellaneous Application Abends

As already discussed, many problems can occur during execution of an application. Previous chapters have covered program check abends and those related to both file and terminal issues. Many simply do not fall into those categories, yet need to be understood. This chapter will cover some of these other failures, and identify the most relevant items for successful problem determination.

## 7.1  AICA ABENDS

An application may not abend, but may be in such a state that CICS takes corrective action. The product has a facility to detect looping conditions within a task; in other words, the task has been executing for longer than the maximum value (defined in the SIT) without invoking task control. Applications need to issue task control requests, thereby returning control to the CICS dispatcher. If not, CICS determines that the task is in a looping condition, and removes the task from the active chain. The SIT parameter will be investigated later; for now, it will be assumed that an application is experiencing an AICA abend. Figure 7-1 contains the summary of typical dump items relevant to a CICS AICA abend.

### 7.1.1  Debugging AICA Abends

**Trace Table.** If the trace table contains adequate entries, it will contain the entries for the task during the loop. If the trace table is too small, or trace has not been turned on, the problem may need to be recreated with auxiliary trace turned on. With a sufficiently large auxiliary trace, the application and the looping conditions should be trapped.

```
ABEND CODE:  AICA

PROBABLE CAUSE:  RUNAWAY TASK, LOOPING APPLICA-
TION

IMPORTANT DUMP ITEMS:  TRACE TABLE
                       TASK CONTROL AREA (TCA)
                       COMMON SYSTEM AREA (CSA)
```

Figure 7-1  Relevant dump items for AICA.

Before interrogating the trace, identify the task number of the executing transaction. If the trace contains entries from many transactions, reference only the entries for the runaway task. In the transaction dump, the TCA system area offset +12 displays the transaction number. Use this value to find relevant trace entries. Once the task number is known, look at the trace entries for this task. Try to determine the flow of control within the application from the last call to CICS task control until the AICA. The trace provides a listing of all requests made by the transaction, therefore identifies the last CICS request. Look for a very large time inverval within the trace entries, or a process with excessive entries, indicating the loop.

The application should be designed to invoke the dispatcher regularly. Some CICS requests, such as GETMAIN and FREEMAIN, do not go through the CICS dispatcher. Also, file control requests do not cause the CICS timer to be reset until AFTER the request is complete. If the file response time is excessive, access time to the data may exceed the maximum value. Data should be organized and accessible to the application, or AICA abends can result. If the application cannot provide sufficiently low file access time, the value in the SIT may have to be increased.

**Task Control Area.** The TCA contains relevant information, such as the task number. It may also need to be referenced if the trace is unable to provide results concerning the loop. Two fields, TCAPCPSW and TCAATAC, may contain data relevant to the loop. TCAPCPSW, at +90 into the TCA user area, contains the PSW at the time the runaway task condition was detected. This is only true if CICS detected the failure in an application module. In this case, the PSW points to the application code executing when the interval expired.

TCAATAC, at +F4 into the TCA user area is the TCA abnormal termination abend code. It becomes significant if the task was executing within a CICS service module at the time of the failure. It then contains the address of the last CICS service call from the application.

If either of these fields point to DFHEIP, the return address within the application can be found at offset +C within a save area pointed to by the TCA system area, TCAPCHS, the high-level language save area.

**CICS System Area.** The CSA contains a value that may need to be referenced in AICA failures. CSAICRUN, at +1B4 contains the number of runaway tasks that have been flushed, or abended. This can provide a cumulative number of runaway tasks that have been detected by CICS since initialization.

### 7.1.2   ICVR Value in SIT

The timer previously mentioned is specified in the SIT via the ICVR parameter. This value becomes the maximum time, in milliseconds, that a CICS task is allowed to execute without invoking the CICS dispatcher. Installations may need to tune this value, since some applications may need additional time for file access; tasks should not be allowed to remain on the active chain for unlimited periods of time. If an installation has excessive AICA abends and the tasks were not looping, this number may need to be increased. The CICS default is adequate for most environments, but may need to be increased or decreased depending on specific needs.

## 7.2   APCT ABENDS

These abends typically occur most often during testing, or when an application has just been moved into production. They are both easy to analyze, and to resolve. An APCT failure is the result of an ability to execute a specific module. The inability to execute can have several causes:

DEFINITION — program (or map) has not yet been defined to CICS
DISABLED — program (or map) is disabled for some reason
EMPTY — program (or map) has a zero length

If the module has a zero length, CICS obviously cannot execute such as program. Determine the reason for this length, specifically checking both the map of the module from the LINKLIB and possibly the output from the last compile of this program. The step to LINK this program should indicate the status and size of the module when created.

### 7.2.1   Lack of Definition

If CICS attempts to load a program and is unable to locate the resource from a previous definition, an APCT abend results. If the installation is still assembling PPT tables, add this definition to the table, assemble, and then recycle the region to make the resource known to CICS. This can frequently happen during testing, or when a new application has been moved into production. On occasion, a program or map failed to be defined to the new region. Unfortunately, if the installation is still using macro tables and not RDO definitions, CICS is unable to utilize this definition until the next startup. Tables are only loaded during initialization; therefore, new entries are not available until the next time CICS initializes.

If, however, RDO (resource definition online) is used for program and transaction definition and this problem is experienced, the entry can be made immediately available. Once the program or map that is not defined has been identified, use the CEDA or CEDB transaction to DEFINE this new entry. Remember, it must be defined to an existing group, or a new group. Since groups can only be INSTALLed, or loaded into CICS, if all entries in the group are inactive, it may be necessary to temporarily define this program to a new group for easy installation. The program can later be added to its appropriate group for documentation and continued support. After defining the program or map with RDO, execute

```
CEDA INSTALL GROUP(groupname)
```

The defined resource is immediately available to the online system, and can then be utilized by the application. While RDO makes defining resources extremely easy, it also allows a programmer to respond to missing resources immediately. Many installations cannot, or do not wish to, wait until CICS recycles before a new program or map is available to the system. RDO will become the standard facility for resource definition in future releases.

### 7.2.2  Disabled Programs

APCT abends can also result from a program that is defined, but for some reason, disabled to CICS. The program can become disabled for several reasons:

* The program status in the definition contained DISABLED.
* The program abended and was placed into a DISABLED condition.
* The program was disabled as a result of a failed NEWCOPY.

If, for some reason, the installation wishes to define the program or map, but does not wish it to be executed at this time, it can define the resource in the PPT or via RDO and indicate a status of DISABLED. Until this program or map is changed, via resource modification or CEMT SET, it is unexecutable. Any attempt to execute will result in an APCT abend.

The program may abend, with an APCC or APCI for example. These failures will cause the module to be placed in a DISABLED condition since the required support for the program was not in the system. All subsequent attempts to execute the program will result in an APCT abend, since the program has been DISABLED.

A program may also become DISABLED as a result of loading a new copy of the module into the system. If changes are made to the program and it is relinked into an RPL library, the changes can immediately be made available to CICS. The process is accomplished via the CEMT SET command against the program, requesting that the new copy of the module now be used, such as:

```
CEMT SET PROG(PROG1) NEWCOPY
```

CICS will attempt to rebuild the pointer to the new copy of the module for all future requests. If, however, the program is active, or is currently being used by an application, CICS is unable to resolve the copy of an active module, and DISABLEs the program. All subsequent requests for the program will produce an APCT failure. Of course, you must use the CEMT command to ENABLE the program after these types of situations, since the module is truly executable. Installations that have dynamic program changes should be aware of this, and insure that the NEWCOPY request did not place the program into a DISABLEd state.

## 7.3  DSNC ABENDS

Many installations are installing DB/2, IBM's relational data base. This product can be used in cooperation with CICS, via the CICS Attach Facility in DB/2. The application uses a new CICS table, the RCT (Resource Control Table) to identify the connections between the CICS system and the DB/2 system. When the application executes in the CICS system as a normal task, it can request data from a DB/2 database. DB/2 uses the Task Related User Exit (TRUE) facility in CICS to pass control to the resource manager, respond to the database request, and return control to the task. The application has replaced the EXEC CICS READ, or other file control request for VSAM services with an EXEC CICS SQL type request to a DB/2 database. The application then can HANDLE the response from DB/2, which, in some cases, may be an SQL return code.

This CICS Attach Facility allows installations to continue most CICS development, rewriting the application when necessary to migrate the function into database support. It provides an efficient use of DB/2 from CICS, since applications can be preprocessed, and 'BOUND' prior to execution. The BIND process in DB/2 allows the application to have all database functions defined and all linkage between the program and the DB/2 facilities in place. When executed, the static definitions are followed, and provide optimum efficiency and response time.

For many application and system programmers, however, procedures for debugging change dramatically. Take, for example, the CICS trace entries. When the DB/2 request is detected, CICS passes control to the resource manager, dispatches other work, and then, when notified by DB/2 that the request is complete, regains control from the resource manager to complete this task. The task, while waiting for control to return, remains on the CICS active chain in a WAIT FOR DB/2 state. This poses two new problems in debugging.

First, these tasks remain on the active chain until the DB/2 request is returned. Inefficient, or excessive requests to DB/2 can leave tasks on the active chain for extended periods of time, severely impacting AMXT (active maximum tasks). Other tasks may be unable to dispatch, since AMXT has been reached. Installations using DB/2 should watch the shutdown statistics for the number of times AMXT has been reached, and insure that these applications are not remaining active unnecessarily.

Second, previous chapters discussed the use of the trace table for a large percentage of failures. It has very valuable information for debugging many different types of abends. Unfortunately, any problems with applications that occurred during the time the DB/2 request was being accommodated do not appear in the trace. What results, in effect, is a "hole" in the trace during that time. CICS is unaware of the processing, and unable to produce any diagnostics. There are two facilities that must be used when debugging DB/2 problems in a CICS application. One is the system LOGREC, which contains the software program checks in DB/2 failures. The other is DB2/PM, the performance monitor, which can be utilized to trace all DB/2 activity. Since DB2/PM is mainly a performance monitor, this chapter will not discuss the facility. Installations may need to use the trace to determine excessive resource consumption or performance issues in the DB/2 call. Reference the DB2/PM publications for more information about the product.

### 7.3.1   SYS1.LOGREC Use in DB/2 Failures

When CICS detects a failure in the portion of the program using DB/2, it produces a transaction dump with the abend code DSNC. This abend code can be found in the CICS Messages and Codes manual, but merely notes the DB/2 origin and refers the reader to the DB/2 Messages and Codes manual. In fact, the transaction dump provides minimal information, since the abend occurred in another address space. In most DB/2 failures, the information necessary to resolve the problem is recorded in another facility. Chapter 1 mentioned briefly the job needed to format DB/2 abends. Figure 1-11 (from Chapter 1) contains a sample of the job that would need to be executed to format the entries. Since DB/2 failures are recorded into SYS1.LOGREC, this job is necessary to locate the failing entries. The two examples of the DB/2 failure are represented by Figures 7-2 and 7-3 to provide a closer look at them. Figure 7-2 contains the formatted LOGREC entry for a DB/2 program check. Note at the top of the page (1) the version and release of the product are identified. On the second line, the ASID (address space identification) can be used to insure which DB/2 system produced

the abend. In this example, 0034 (2) is the ASID. Many installations run both a production and a test DB/2 system, and both may produce failures into LOGREC. The System Abend Code is displayed (3), much as the PSW in an ASRA contains the program check type. The Jobname (4) would identify which CICS region made the failing request, and the Module (5) displays the DB/2 system module involved during the failure. The remaining information may be difficult to utilize since it contains registers and addresses within the DB/2 address space which are very difficult to map for relevance. The next page of the output, Figure 7-3, repeats some of the same information and gives an abend code of 04E (1). All DB/2 failures, in CICS or not, will produce an abend code of 04E or 04F. This is another way of locating DB/2 abends within LOGREC, since all system program checks will be formatted in this report.

In addition to the abend code, this page now has an Abend Reason Code (2) of **00E7000D**. This code can be found in the DB/2 Messages and Codes manual, and contains the description:

```
An application-supplied decimal datum has an in-
valid format
```

The Problem Determination portion of the abend description identifies Registers 2–4, 8 and 9 as pointers to parameter lists. The parameter lists contain fields identifying the call, the caller, and various other relevant fields. It is then possible to return to the 04E abend information and locate these registers from the section REGS AT TIME OF ERROR (3). Locate these parameter lists and find the specific statement number at time of failure. Just as the statement number in an ASRA was identified and traced back to the source listing, it is possible to locate this statement number in the DB/2 Pre-compiler listing. The other registers give pointers to the variables with bad data.

Although the process is very different, DB/2 provides information to assist in problem determination. Each DB/2 Abend Reason Code may contain different procedures and areas to locate. Debugging DB/2 failures takes on various directions depending upon the type of failure, so note the specific instructions for each abend in the manuals.

## 7.4   TYPICAL IMS ABENDS

Many installations run both CICS and IMS for their transaction processing. IMS is IBM's DB/DC product, database datacommunication facilities, and has been used extensively for high-volume non-relational database processing. CICS has the ability to

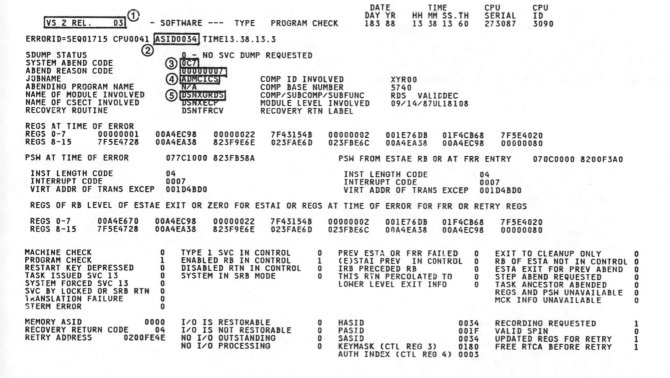

```
                                            DATE      TIME      CPU     CPU
                                            DAY YR    HH MM SS.TH  SERIAL  ID
   VS 2 REL.   03   - SOFTWARE --- TYPE  SOFTWARE(SVC 13)  183 88  13 38 13 60  273087  3090

ERRORID=SEQ01716 CPU0042 ASID0034 TIME13.38.13.4

SDUMP STATUS              ① 0 - NO SVC DUMP REQUESTED
SYSTEM ABEND CODE           04E
ABEND REASON CODE           00E7000D ②
JOBNAME                     ADMCICS        COMP ID INVOLVED       XYR00
ABENDING PROGRAM NAME       N/A            COMP BASE NUMBER       5740
NAME OF MODULE INVOLVED     DSNXGRDS       COMP/SUBCOMP/SUBFUNC   RDS  VALIDDEC
NAME OF CSECT INVOLVED      DSNXECP        MODULE LEVEL INVOLVED  09/14/87UL18108
RECOVERY ROUTINE            DSNTFRCV       RECOVERY RTN LABEL

REGS AT TIME OF ERROR ③
REGS 0-7    80000000   8004E000   801EA51C   001EA590   00000007   05020003   01F4CB68   7F5E4020
REGS 8-15   001E76DB   00A4EA38   823F9E6E   023FAE6D   023FBE6C   00A4EA38   7F4314D4   00E7000D

PSW AT TIME OF ERROR       077C1000 823FA876        PSW FROM ESTAE RB OR AT FRR ENTRY    070C0000 8200F3A0

   INST LENGTH CODE        02                          INST LENGTH CODE        02
   INTERRUPT CODE          000D                        INTERRUPT CODE          000D
   VIRT ADDR OF TRANS EXCEP  FF6F408A                  VIRT ADDR OF TRANS EXCEP  FF6F408A

   REGS OF RB LEVEL OF ESTAE EXIT OR ZERO FOR ESTAI OR REGS AT TIME OF ERROR FOR FRR OR RETRY REGS

   REGS 0-7    80000000   8004E000   801EA51C   001EA590   00000007   05020003   01F4CB68   7F5E4020
   REGS 8-15   001E76DB   00A4EA38   823F9E6E   023FAE6D   023FBE6C   00A4EA38   7F4314D4   00E7000D

MACHINE CHECK          0   TYPE 1 SVC IN CONTROL    0   PREV ESTA OR FRR FAILED   0   EXIT TO CLEANUP ONLY        0
PROGRAM CHECK          0   ENABLED RB IN CONTROL    1   (E)STAI PREV  IN CONTROL  0   RB OF ESTA NOT IN CONTROL  0
RESTART KEY DEPRESSED  0   DISABLED RTN IN CONTROL  0   IRB PRECEDED RB           0   ESTA EXIT FOR PREV ABEND    0
TASK ISSUED SVC 13     0   SYSTEM IN SRB MODE       0   THIS RTN PERCOLATED TO    0   STEP ABEND REQUESTED        0
SYSTEM FORCED SVC 13   0                                LOWER LEVEL EXIT INFO     0   TASK ANCESTOR ABENDED       0
SVC BY LOCKED OR SRB RTN 1                                                             REGS AND PSW UNAVAILABLE    0
TRANSLATION FAILURE    0                                                               MCK INFO UNAVAILABLE        0
STERM ERROR            0

MEMORY ASID         0000   I/O IS RESTORABLE        0   HASID              0034   RECORDING REQUESTED         1
RECOVERY RETURN CODE  00   I/O IS NOT RESTORABLE    0   PASID              001F   VALID SPIN                  0
                           NO I/O OUTSTANDING       0   SASID              001F   UPDATED REGS FOR RETRY      0
                           NO I/O PROCESSING        0   KEYMASK (CTL REG 3) 0180  FREE RTCA BEFORE RETRY      0
                                                        AUTH INDEX (CTL REG 4) 0003
```

Figure 7-2   Formatted DB/2 LOGREC entry: page 1.

```
                                            DATE      TIME      CPU     CPU
                                            DAY YR    HH MM SS.TH  SERIAL  ID
   VS 2 REL.   03 ① - SOFTWARE --- TYPE  PROGRAM CHECK  183 88  13 38 13 60  273087  3090

ERRORID=SEQ01715 CPU0041 ASID0034 TIME13.38.13.3
                              ②
SDUMP STATUS              0 - NO SVC DUMP REQUESTED
SYSTEM ABEND CODE        ③ 0C7
ABEND REASON CODE          00000007
JOBNAME                  ④ ADMCICS        COMP ID INVOLVED       XYR00
ABENDING PROGRAM NAME       N/A            COMP BASE NUMBER       5740
NAME OF MODULE INVOLVED  ⑤ DSNXGRDS       COMP/SUBCOMP/SUBFUNC   RDS  VALIDDEC
NAME OF CSECT INVOLVED      DSNXECP        MODULE LEVEL INVOLVED  09/14/87UL18108
RECOVERY ROUTINE            DSNTFRCV       RECOVERY RTN LABEL

REGS AT TIME OF ERROR
REGS 0-7    00000001   00A4EC98   00000022   7F43154B   00000002   001E76DB   01F4CB68   7F5E4020
REGS 8-15   7F5E4728   00A4EA38   823F9E6E   023FAE6D   023FBE6C   00A4EA38   00A4EC98   00000080

PSW AT TIME OF ERROR       077C1000 823FB58A        PSW FROM ESTAE RB OR AT FRR ENTRY    070C0000 8200F3A0

   INST LENGTH CODE        04                          INST LENGTH CODE        04
   INTERRUPT CODE          0007                        INTERRUPT CODE          0007
   VIRT ADDR OF TRANS EXCEP  001D4BD0                  VIRT ADDR OF TRANS EXCEP  001D4BD0

   REGS OF RB LEVEL OF ESTAE EXIT OR ZERO FOR ESTAI OR REGS AT TIME OF ERROR FOR FRR OR RETRY REGS

   REGS 0-7    00A4E670   00A4EC98   00000022   7F43154B   00000002   001E76DB   01F4CB68   7F5E4020
   REGS 8-15   7F5E4728   00A4EA38   823F9E6E   023FAE6D   023FBE6C   00A4EA38   00A4EC98   00000080

MACHINE CHECK          0   TYPE 1 SVC IN CONTROL    0   PREV ESTA OR FRR FAILED   0   EXIT TO CLEANUP ONLY        0
PROGRAM CHECK          1   ENABLED RB IN CONTROL    1   (E)STAI PREV  IN CONTROL  0   RB OF ESTA NOT IN CONTROL  0
RESTART KEY DEPRESSED  0   DISABLED RTN IN CONTROL  0   IRB PRECEDED RB           0   ESTA EXIT FOR PREV ABEND    0
TASK ISSUED SVC 13     0   SYSTEM IN SRB MODE       0   THIS RTN PERCOLATED TO    0   STEP ABEND REQUESTED        0
SYSTEM FORCED SVC 13   0                                LOWER LEVEL EXIT INFO     0   TASK ANCESTOR ABENDED       0
SVC BY LOCKED OR SRB RTN 0                                                             REGS AND PSW UNAVAILABLE    0
TRANSLATION FAILURE    0                                                               MCK INFO UNAVAILABLE        0
STERM ERROR            0

MEMORY ASID         0000   I/O IS RESTORABLE        0   HASID              0034   RECORDING REQUESTED         1
RECOVERY RETURN CODE  04   I/O IS NOT RESTORABLE    0   PASID              001F   VALID SPIN                  0
RETRY ADDRESS     0200FE4E   NO I/O OUTSTANDING     0   SASID              0034   UPDATED REGS FOR RETRY      1
                           NO I/O PROCESSING        0   KEYMASK (CTL REG 3) 0180  FREE RTCA BEFORE RETRY      1
                                                        AUTH INDEX (CTL REG 4) 0003
```

Figure 7-3   Formatted DB/2 LOGREC entry: page 2.

communicate to IMS and utilize the DL/1 databases within CICS applications. These applications can have complicated debugging procedures, much like DB/2, since CICS is accessing data that it may not truly own. Installations must use both CICS and IMS facilities to analyze these problems.

All failures in IMS or DL/1 processing within CICS produce dumps that are AD** format. Each abend may require different techniques, depending on the failure. Some of the most common abends are ADLA and ADLD.

### 7.4.1   ADLA Abends

When a CICS application fails during transaction processing as a result of a DL/1 abend, an ADLA abend occurs. The transaction is terminated, and a message DFH3901 is sent to the destination defined for CSMT. The message will display as:

```
DFH3901   TRANSACTION transid DL/I ABEND
abendcode
```

The transid in the message will identify the transaction that experienced the failure. Abendcode is the DL/I pseudoabend code and must be located in IMS/VS Messages and Codes manual for a complete description. The description of the abend in the IMS manual should give more detail concerning the cause.

A CICS dump results, but since the failure is actually with IMS facilities, it may contain minimal information for analysis. In these failures, information from the IMS address space is recorded into the CICS journal. The IMS utility program should be used to format the transaction data recorded.

This output may contain addition information to debug the failure.

### 7.4.2   ADLD Abends

These failures are a result of deadlock conditions. In VSAM, we could have deadlock conditions within the data; however, CICS is unable to resolve the deadlock. VSAM deadlocks produce transactions that must be manually purged, and are ususally detected only from the resources that have been locked, backing up other requests.

In IMS, the lock manager (IRLM) can be given maximum time values to allow resources to be locked. When a request exceeds that value, it can be selected for termination. In this manner, locks can be given maximum time for resource retention, and released if necessary. An ADLD abend indicates that a program isolation deadlock has been detected by the system. This transaction has been selected for abnormal termination, and results in the abend and subsequent transaction dump. The trace may be helpful to identify the resources requested prior to the deadlock. Messages may also be produced in IMS to indicate the deadlock condition and the subsequent abnormal termination of the lock.

In summary, since CICS can accommodate both a variety of applications and products, the problem determination techniques for these various situations will take various procedures. This chapter has identified only a few that may be experienced. Use the Messages and Codes manuals from CICS and all appropriate products to locate all documentation concerning the failure.

# Interactive Debugging Facilities

There are several debugging facilities that can be used within CICS. Interactive debugging provides many advantages, especially during application development. Several facilities have already been discussed, including service aids that can be used in problem determination. Most of the debugging features discussed so far have been used after the fact, or after the failure has occurred. Transaction dumps have been analyzed in great depths to diagnose failures. Auxiliary trace can be implemented to discover where the problem lies. These facilities provide documentation about the existing environment at the time of the failure. Both IBM and several vendors provide facilities to utilize during the development process, or during a failure, to examine the problem as it occurs. These interactive debugging facilities can supplement other techniques to provide the most information available to solve the problem. The facility that IBM provides, as part of the CICS product, is called the Execution Diagnostic Facility, or EDF. Also discussed will be two of the other popular non-IBM products used in many installations.

## 8.1 CEDF

EDF allows testing of a command-level application online, within CICS, as it executes. Applications that are in development, or need to be tested with EDF, must be compiled with the translator option EDF. This option is usually the default; however, check the compiler options to insure the default status. EDF is supplied, without charge, as part of the CICS product. It is invoked via a CICS-supplied transaction, CEDF. Of course, this system function must have been installed with all the appropriate

program and transaction resources defined. Since CEDF is a CICS-supplied transaction, it is documented in the CICS-Supplied Transactions manual. The single page in the manual is far from adequate if assistance is required with the facility. It is documented more thoroughly in the Application Programmer's Reference Manual, Command Level. A few of the functions that EDF supplies will be covered here, with a discussion of how they can supplement the techniques already learned.

### 8.1.1 Invoking EDF

EDF can be started by entering the transaction CEDF, or using an appropriate PF key if one has been assigned to the transaction. EDF can be executed on the same terminal as the transaction that is being tested, or can be tested with transactions executing on a different terminal. If a terminal number is not specified, it will default to the existing terminal. If the command

```
CEDF C300
```

is used, EDF will monitor the transaction at terminal C300, a four-character terminal (termid) known to CICS.

When invoking EDF, the facility will return a message:

```
THIS TERMINAL: EDF MODE ON
```

If an alternate terminal has been requested, as in the previous CEDF command, the facility will return:

```
TERMINAL C300: EDF MODE ON
```

```
TRANSACTION: MMM1①   PROGRAM: PSIMP1②    TASK NUMBER: 0000126③ DISPLAY: 00④
STATUS:    PROGRAM INITIATION⑤

     EIBTIME      = 73952
     EIBDATE      = 88264
     EIBTRNID     = 'MMM1'
  ⑥  EIBTASKN     = 126
     EIBTRMID     = 'C301'

     EIBCPOSN     = 4
     EIBCALEN     = 0
     EIBAID       = X'7D'                          AT X'00044452'
     EIBFN        = X'0000'                         AT X'00044453'
     EIBRCODE     = X'000000000000'                 AT X'00044455'
  ⑨ EIBDS        = '.........'
 +   EIBREQID     = '.........'



 ENTER:   CONTINUE⑧
 PF1 : UNDEFINED        PF2 : SWITCH HEX/CHAR⑦   PF3 : END EDF SESSION
 PF4 : SUPPRESS DISPLAYS PF5 : WORKING STORAGE     PF6 : USER DISPLAY
 PF7 : SCROLL BACK      PF8 : SCROLL FORWARD⑩     PF9 : STOP CONDITIONS
 PF10: PREVIOUS DISPLAY PF11: UNDEFINED           PF12: UNDEFINED
```

Figure 8-1   CEDF output: program initiation.

### 8.1.2   EDF Commands and Screens

After requesting the CEDF transaction, clear the screen (to remove the response), and key in the transaction to diagnose. The facility will gain control and display a screen similar to Figure 8-1. This screen contains information provided by EDF at program initiation. EDF gains control at transaction initialization after the EIB has been built. Some of the relevant items on the display are

1. Transaction: the transid, or PF key that initiated the task
2. Program: the program invoked by the above transaction
3. Task number: assigned by CICS for the length of the task
4. Display: the relative location within the EDF session
5. Status: the status of the program in this display
6. EIB fields: contents of EIB fields at this time
7. Key assignments: functions associated with PF keys

In this example, the task is at program initiation. To continue the EDF session, press the ENTER key (8). Notice also that a "+" sign appears at the bottom of the EIB field listings (9). This sign will indicate that additional information can be available within this display. In other words, there are more EIB fields that can be displayed than are shown on this single screen. As specified in the lower PF key assignments, PF8 can be used to scroll forward (10). If PF8 is requested from this screen, the next screen of EIB fields that were available would be displayed. Using the combination of PF7/PF8 keys, it is possible to scroll back and forth within this display.

If ENTER is pressed, EDF will continue to the next screen, Figure 8-2, which is actually the first EXEC CICS command encountered within the program. The first line of the display remains the same as the previous one. The STATUS, however, is now ABOUT TO EXECUTE COMMAND (1). EDF intercepts the execution of the application at the start of every EXEC CICS command, before the requested action has been performed. Notice that EDF displays the command being executed (2) and the contents of all relevant parameters being used by the command. Also displayed is the hexadecimal offset into the program of this instruction (3), the relative line number within the program (4), and the EIB function code associated with this request (5). Provided, therefore, are the potential instruction to be executed and the data that will be executed with the instruction.

If ENTER is pressed from this screen, it will execute the command that is displayed. The next display (Figure 8-3) verifies that the command has been executed (1). It returns the values of all relevant fields, especially two at the bottom of the screen. The RESPONSE (2) is returned with the associated EIB response code (3). The wording in the RESPONSE field is merely a translated representation of the value in the EIBRESP. It provides an

```
TRANSACTION: MMM1    PROGRAM: PSIMP1       TASK NUMBER: 0000139   DISPLAY:  00
STATUS: ABOUT TO EXECUTE COMMAND
EXEC CICS JOURNAL ②
  JFILEID (4)
  JTYPEID ('CP')
  FROM ('.....h.<MMM1....C30110   DPSPPID 6007    2990')
  LENGTH (44)




OFFSET: X'000AEC' ③    LINE:01158 ④          EIBFN=X'1402' ⑤


ENTER:   CONTINUE
PF1 : UNDEFINED              PF2 : SWITCH HEX/CHAR      PF3 : UNDEFINED
PF4 : SUPPRESS DISPLAYS      PF5 : WORKING STORAGE      PF6 : USER DISPLAY
PF7 : SCROLL BACK            PF8 : SCROLL FORWARD       PF9 : STOP CONDITIONS
PF10: PREVIOUS DISPLAY       PF11: UNDEFINED            PF12: ABEND USER TASK
```

Figure 8-2   CEDF output: prior to command execution.

instant look at the results of the command execution and the ability to see it "as it happens."

Other features available at this point are various contents and representations of data. In the previous display, the contents of all entries was displayed in the character representation. Note in that example, the FROM field (4). CICS attempts to display character representations of the data stored within the field. Of course, many times there is no character that can be translated. To display the actual hexadecimal contents, as would be represented

in a dump, use PF2 (5), and switch the display to the alternative representation. Figure 8-4 contains the same data as the previous figure, but switched with PF2. Notice that contents of fields are now in hex, a length of X'002C' (1), rather than 44. It may be necessary to use this facility during testing to debug contents of fields that are not character-format.

Other features available in EDF at this point could be viewing the previous display (2), viewing working storage of the program (3), or ending the

```
TRANSACTION: MMM1    PROGRAM: PSIMP1       TASK NUMBER: 0000149   DISPLAY:  00
STATUS: COMMAND EXECUTION COMPLETE ①
EXEC CICS JOURNAL
  JFILEID (4)
  JTYPEID ('CP')
④ FROM ('.....h.<MMM1....C30110   DPSPPID 6007    2990')
  LENGTH (44)




OFFSET:X'000AEC'    LINE:01158             EIBFN=X'1402'
RESPONSE: NORMAL ②                        EIBRESP=0 ③

ENTER:   CONTINUE
PF1 : UNDEFINED              PF2 : SWITCH HEX/CHAR ⑤    PF3 : END EDF SESSION
PF4 : SUPPRESS DISPLAYS      PF5 : WORKING STORAGE      PF6 : USER DISPLAY
```

Figure 8-3   CEDF output: after command execution.

```
PF7 : SCROLL BACK          PF8 : SCROLL FORWARD      PF9 : STOP CONDITIONS
PF10: PREVIOUS DISPLAY      PF11: UNDEFINED           PF12: ABEND USER TASK

 TRANSACTION: MMM1    PROGRAM: PSIMP1      TASK NUMBER: 0000149    DISPLAY:  00
 STATUS:   COMMAND EXECUTION COMPLETE
 EXEC CICS JOURNAL
   JFILEID (X'0004')                                     AT X'0007A648
   JTYPEID (X'C3D7')                                     AT X'0007A64C
   FROM (X'0074331C0088264CD4D4D4F10000149CC3F3F0F1F1F04040'...)  AT X'000A9EA8
   LENGTH (X'002C')  ①                                   AT X'0007A650




 OFFSET:X'000AEC'     LINE:01158        EIBFN=X'1402'
 RESPONSE: NORMAL                       EIBRESP=X'00000000'

 ENTER:  CONTINUE
 PF1 : UNDEFINED            PF2 : SWITCH HEX/CHAR ③   PF3 : END EDF SESSION ④
 PF4 : SUPPRESS DISPLAYS    PF5 : WORKING STORAGE ③   PF6 : USER DISPLAY
 PF7 : SCROLL BACK      ②   PF8 : SCROLL FORWARD      PF9 : STOP CONDITIONS
 PF10: PREVIOUS DISPLAY     PF11: UNDEFINED           PF12: ABEND USER TASK
```

Figure 8-4   CEDF output: hexadecimal representation.

EDF session (4). Notice that some keys are undefined within this EDF session, PF1 and PF11. EDF suppresses the execution of various functions within the session by removing availability to that function key. For example, PF3 is always the function key to end the EDF session. If EDF is in a status that does not allow session termination, PF3 will indicate "Undefined." The session must be continued until the PF3 key indicates "End EDF Session." At that time, use the PF3 key to terminate the session.

Another function available during development or testing is to move through the session without displaying every command within the application. PF4 can be used to suppress displays during the EDF session. If, from Figure 8-1, it was necessary to move directly into another part of the program, PF4 would be used. When this key was used, a screen similar to Figure 8-5 would appear. This display indicates that task termination has been reached (1) and that CICS is ready to complete all execution of this task. A prompt at the bottom of the screen indicates whether to continue the EDF session. If the default is taken, (NO), then EDF will terminate the transaction and the EDF session. If the reply is overtyped with YES, then EDF will continue to monitor the session and take control at the initiation of the next task.

This facility gives the programmer opportunities to review the status of the program during execution. If, during the EDF session, abnormal conditions occur, the programmer has the ability to freeze the program and inspect portions of program or data storage. If a program is failing, it would be possible to recreate the problem within an EDF session and attempt to resolve the problem on the fly. This can be much more productive than processing a dump, possibly waiting for it to print, and then scanning the trace to determine the location of the failing instruction.

### 8.1.3   Correlation with Dump Content

Chapter Four analyzed three program failures by locating portions of both program and data within the dump. The programmer could choose not to print the dump and to view the failure via CEDF. In many cases, the cause of the failure can be diagnosed interactively, thus saving time and paper. Of course, the failure must be consistent and reproducible in a CICS region with CEDF active. Many failures are inconsistent and cannot be reproduced in a test region under the control of an EDF session. It will be assumed that one of the failures in Chapter Four is consistent and can be diagnosed CEDF facilities. Figure 8-6 is an example of an EDF screen produced by the 0Cx abend.

Notice that in this EDF screen, the transaction identifier (1) and program name (2) are identified, and the unique task number is identified (3) if further investigation requires that a dump be produced. Several EIB fields are displayed (4) and may

```
TRANSACTION: MMM1                           TASK NUMBER: 0000159   DISPLAY:  00
STATUS:  TASK TERMINATION ①
```

```
TO CONTINUE EDF SESSION REPLY YES                           REPLY: NO
ENTER:   CONTINUE
PF1 : UNDEFINED            PF2 : SWITCH HEX/CHAR     PF3 : END EDF SESSION
PF4 : SUPPRESS DISPLAYS    PF5 : WORKING STORAGE     PF6 : USER DISPLAY
PF7 : SCROLL BACK          PF8 : SCROLL FORWARD      PF9 : STOP CONDITIONS
PF10: PREVIOUS DISPLAY     PF11: UNDEFINED           PF12: UNDEFINED
```

Figure 8-5   CEDF output: task termination.

be investigated further if necessary. The PSW is produced (5), which would correspond to the PSW contained within the ASRA dump. This could be used in the same way as previously described to calculate the failing instruction. From this screen, PF12 could be utilized to investigate contents of the registers at the time of the abend (6). PF5 could be used to locate the Working Storage contents of the program for potential relevance to the failure (7). All items that were previously investigated via the formatted dump can now be viewed online, and analysis can be accomplished at the actual time of the failure. If the abend can be reproduced, this can be a substantial time-saving facility to reference data areas in real time, rather than printing and locating these areas in a dump.

```
TRANSACTION: TEST ① PROGRAM: CICSDEMO ② TASK NUMBER: 0000188 ③ DISPLAY:  00
STATUS:   AN ABEND HAS OCCURRED
     COMMAREA       = '01
     EIBTIME        = 114155
     EIBDATE        = 88333
     EIBTRNID       = 'TEST'
     EIBTASKN       = 188
     EIBTRMID       = 'C301'

  ④ EIBCPOSN       = 0
  ④ EIBCALEN       = 34
     EIBAID         = X'F2'                              AT X'0004D442'
     EIBFN          = X'0000'                            AT X'0004D443'
     EIBRCODE       = X'000000000000'                    AT X'0004D445'
     EIBDS          = '........'
 +   EIBREQID       = '........'
  OFFSET:X'1C89CA'                       INTERRUPT: PROTECTION
  ABEND :   ASRA                          PSW: X'078D0000 001C89CE 00040004' ⑤

ENTER:   CONTINUE
PF1 : UNDEFINED            PF2 : SWITCH HEX/CHAR     PF3 : END EDF SESSION
PF4 : SUPPRESS DISPLAYS    PF5 : WORKING STORAGE ⑦   PF6 : USER DISPLAY
PF7 : SCROLL BACK          PF8 : SCROLL FORWARD      PF9 : STOP CONDITIONS
PF10: PREVIOUS DISPLAY     PF11: UNDEFINED           PF12: REGISTERS AT ABEND ⑥
```

Figure 8-6   CEDF output: abend output.

Although extensive documentation is not available for the CEDF facility, the process is very function-key oriented, and contains an online HELP facility. The best teacher is experience, and programmers who use this facility often become productive in short periods of time.

Of course, some installations choose to purchase additional packages that supplement or replace CEDF. Many are available, but two of the most widely used products are described in the following sections. Installations that seek additional products to supplement CEDF should investigate several, and select the one that provides the best facilities for their needs.

## 8.2   INTERTEST® *

The product InterTest is a licensed facility of On-Line Software International. Many installations license InterTest to supplement or replace CEDF for interactive problem determination. InterTest has many more functions than EDF, and can be used in many additional situations. In fact, InterTest has facilities to view not only program execution and the related areas of program and data storage, but can view (and alter) CICS system areas. Since this product is very popular and used by so many CICS installations, some of the functions of InterTest will be discussed, and how the produce can be utilized as an alternative to processing dumps.

### 8.2.1   Usage and Invocation

InterTest contains several facilities in addition to simple dump avoidance. The three main transactions used by most programmers are CNTL, CORE, and FILE. CNTL is the facility for monitoring the execution of a program, thereby diagnosing problems during execution. CORE is the facility for viewing portions of storage within the CICS address space. Of course, storage can also be changed with this transaction. As previously discussed in the section on macro-level coding, modifying portions of storage, especially CICS system areas, is dangerous and not advised. In some instances, however, when well controlled and in a test region during development, this function can be desirable. FILE is the facility to manipulate data known to CICS. In the most current release of InterTest, this data can even be a DB2 database. InterTest can be

a very valuable tool when diagnosing problems relating to data or file problems.

The purpose of this chapter is not to cover all functions and facilities of the product. If licensed, the documentation from the vendor would contain detailed instructions for use. Some of the highlights, however, will be covered and utilized with the 0Cx abend.

### 8.2.2   Commands and Screens

CNTL.  The control facility must be activated after the CICS region is initialized. If CNTL has not been activated, a message will indicate that it must be started. This facility is very menu-oriented, and friendly, since the menus identify the functions available and do not require knowledge of command syntax. The main menu is presented as a result of the CNTL command and is shown in Figure 8-7. The facility provides many options, and gives the programmer the ability to control almost any situation during program execution. Again, since the intent is to recreate the failure previously diagnosed via an application dump, option 10 would be chosen to monitor a particular program. Specify the program or transaction name in the appropriate location. For this example, CICSDEMO will be monitored, since it was the failing program identified in the previous dump. Once selected, InterTest executes the request and returns the command that was constructed from the menu selections. The result:

```
CNTL=ON,PROG=CICSDEMO
```

would be displayed from the request. This allows the programmer to get familiar with the syntax and key the command in directly, bypassing the menu. After this request and InterTest has responded that the request has been processed, execute the program to produce the failure. Figure 8-8 displays the abend screen produced by the 0C4 failure. Many of the areas of storage that were located within the dump are contained within the screen. Note that the failing instruction address **01C89CA** (1) corresponds to the PSW address found from a dump. Note that execution of the program was suspended at location **+0097A**. This corresponds to the location previously calculated via the manual method. InterTest not only detects the error, but performs the calculation to identify the instruction that has produced the failure. Many other items are also available from this point. The BLL cells at the time the

---

*      InterTest is a registered trademark of On-Line Software International, Inc.

```
      OSI InterTest MONITORING COMMAND BUILDER - FUNCTION SELECTION
Select function by number: __
For functions 10-23, enter S to set or R to remove: _

 10  Monitoring                20  Replace Options        30  Status Display
 11  Unconditional Breakpoints 21  Protect Options        31  Utility Functions
 12  Conditional Breakpoints   22  Special Options        32  System-Wide Functions
 13  Request Breakpoints       23  Composite Support      33  Resume Task Execution


For functions 10-30, enter Program Names or Transaction Codes or Terminal Names

     Program Names     _____ _____ _____ _____ _____ _____ _____
     Transaction Codes _____ _____ _____ _____ _____ _____ _____
     Terminal Names    _____ _____ _____ _____ _____ _____ _____


Press ENTER key with data to process command or select PF key:
1 Help      2 CNTL     3 End        4 Source     5 CORE=Task     6 CORE=Bkpt
7 FILE      8 Prev     9            10           11 CORE=Syst    12 Status
```

Figure 8-7    InterTest output: monitoring. Reprinted with permission. Copyright © On-Line Software International, Inc., 1988. All rights reserved.

failure was detected (2), the task number (3), a log of the instructions that were executed previous to the current (4), are noted. In addition, the execution is frozen, and the programmer has the ability to diagnose other areas of CICS that may be relevant to the problem.

Many programmers find this facility superior to CEDF, since it provides many additional functions and features. Of course, the ability to diagnose problems in a timely manner is enhanced by additional tools. Another facility of InterTest could be of significant value.

CORE. The CORE facility allows the programmer to view, and alter if desired, areas of storage within the CICS address space. This could be of significant value if it is necessary to analyze the contents of control blocks related to the task. Figure 8-9 displays the menu presented via the CORE command. Again, the programmer is removed from the actual syntax of the command, and can merely select areas of CICS or programs that need to be analyzed. Key in the control block name, or specific address if desired. Many times, when diagnosing a problem, the contents of the CSA are relevant for many reasons. This facility provides the ability to view specific fields within the control block for relevant values. A specific terminal can be anaylzed and the related areas of storage can be viewed if terminal-related failures are being diagnosed.

Realize, however, that CICS is a very dynamic environment, and the contents of many of these

```
 CNTL=GO,TASK=00071,A        at +009AA        pgm=CICSDEMO, addr=2B29FA ①
06 ABP: target beyond permitted storage. System damage prevented.
  Mon.as CICSDEMO        Pgm CICSDEMO Trx FIL  Fac C301 Trm     in.....out
Task 00071 at +009AA             CWK=04C04C    TIOA 043760      +0087C  +0089E
② BLLs: / 0 00044428  1 80050828  2 0004C734  3 00000000        +008A0  +008CA
    ③ 4 00000000  5 00000000  6 00000000  7 00000000            +008D2  +008E2
      8 00000000  9 00000000 10 00000000 11 00000000            +008F4  +00918
     12 00000000 13 00000000 14 00000000 15 8C040768 C.C.0      +00920  +0092E
Nxt 92 00 E000      at +009AA  Prev 58 E0 D224 ④    at +009A6   +0093C  +00940
    Press ENTER to execute the default command on line 1,       +0099C  curr.
    OVERTYPE it, or use any of the following PF KEYS:
 1 Help 2 CNTL 3 Report   4         5 CORE=Task 6 CORE=Bkpt
 7 FILE 8 Bktr 9 1 instr 10        11 Override 12 Resume
```

Figure 8-8    InterTest output: abend output. Reprinted with permission. Copyright © On-Line Software International, Inc., 1988. All rights reserved.

```
        OSI InterTest CORE COMMAND BUILDER - SYSTEM-RELATED AREAS   (CORE=Syst)

Specify AREA, ADDRESS, TABLE or PROGRAM to be displayed or changed:

   CICS AREA:   ____      CSA, PCT, PPT, FCT, TCT, DCT, SIT     ADDRESS: _____
                          PAM, TRT, OPFL, ATRT, ADCH, SDCH

   CICS TABLE entry:   PPT _____  FCT _____  PCT ____  TCT ____  DCT ____

      To display PROGRAM:   _____     ENTER L to load, D to delete or M for map: _

Optional offset: _____

Scan value: _____        Data  Formats
Scan range: _____        B to scan backwards: _       ----------------
                                                        . P' ' = Packed .
To VERIFY and/or CHANGE data:                           . X' ' = Hex    .
Existing data: _____        . C' ' = Char   .
    New data: _____        ----------------

Press PF12 (structure display) or ENTER (dump display), or select PF key:
1 Help       2 CNTL       3 End       4 Source     5 CORE=Task    6 CORE=Bkpt
7 FILE       8            9 BMSG      10           11 CORE=Syst   12 Structure
```

Figure 8-9   InterTest output: CORE. Reprinted with permission. Copyright © On-Line Software International, Inc., 1988. All rights reserved.

control blocks change quickly in a very active system. Unless the system can be frozen, the values viewed may change quickly as a result of other transactions executing. This ability to view CICS data areas, however, can be a powerful tool when analyzing a problem.

FILE.   The facility to view data is provided via the FILE transaction. Many installations prefer FILE over CECI, the CICS-supplied transaction, since it has enhanced functions. Many problems are data-related, and many failures are the direct result of invalid or missing data. This facility provides the ability to view existing contents of files, change values, and even add or delete records. Many times, the ability to browse a suspect file will reveal the contents that are producing the failure. Figure 8-10 displays the results of the FILE request. The pro-

```
DATATYPE= FC FILEID=           MODE=       LOG=OFF TODEST=        PASSWORD=
FUNC=         SUBFUNC=         RETMETH=    ARGTYP=  SRCHTYP=
MESSAGE=
 RETNRCID=                                                        CHGELEN=
   RCID=
   DATA=                                                          SIZE= 0000
FORMAT= D 00112233 44556677 8899AABB CCDDEEFF   *0123456789ABCDEF*
LOC 0000  ........ ........ ........ ........    ................



               InterTest Release 3.0.000

                    COPYRIGHT 1985
           On-Line Software International, Inc.
                ALL RIGHTS RESERVED
           (800) 526-9045      (201) 592-0009


--------------------------------------------------------------------------------
 1 Help       2 Format C   3 End      4 BEGB      5 PREV     6 DataType DL
[7 Page bwd] [8 Page fwd]  9 Caps Off 10 Top      11 Bottom  12
```

Figure 8-10   InterTest output: FILE. Reprinted with permission. Copyright © On-Line Software International, Inc., 1988. All rights reserved.

grammer would then identify the file name, function, and key (if known) to view the requested record. Once located, move backward or forward within the file with the appropriate PF key. If a record needs to be added, or deleted, the correct function must be specified. Reference the product documentation for complete steps necessary. Remember, the file must be defined to CICS with the appropriate file control authority. A file that is specified in the File Control Table (FCT) as "read and browse only" cannot be updated. InterTest is an application that executes within CICS, and is only allowed add, delete, and update capability if the file contains those specifications in the FCT.

This section has covered only a fraction of the function that is available within InterTest. It can be a very valuable tool in problem determination, and may be used to supplement or replace your utilization of CEDF. This chapter is not meant to promote any particular products, but to make programmers aware of the numerous tools that are available to assist them in their jobs.

## 8.3   CICS ABEND-AID

The product CICS Abend-AID is a licensed facility of COMPUWARE Corporation and allows a programmer to view complete diagnostic reports of transaction failures online rather than printing and analyzing dumps. CICS Abend-AID also analyzes the problem, and produces diagnostic information in easily-read narratives. This can be a significant advantage, since not only is the output from the failure available immediately, but removes the manual and time-consuming process of dump analysis. Instead of printing large volumes of output from a dump, most of which is unnecessary and irrelevant, the programmer can browse various screens to review all diagnostic information that is important to the specific transaction failure.

One extremely useful function of CICS Abend-AID is the Report Directory. The directory displays all existing abends, and allows the programmer to selectively access a particular abend report. After selecting a report online, the product provides screens with diagnostic information about the failure. The abend location is calculated, and supporting facts are supplied, such as probable cause and action that should be taken. The programmer can then access relevant data such as trace table entries, program storage, file content, and more. These detailed diagnostics coupled with direct accesses into a report can save great amounts of time in debugging.

### 8.3.1   Commands and Screens

After invoking CICS Abend-AID and entering a specific transaction, the programmer is provided with a Report Directory, as displayed in Figure 8-11. This directory contains all transaction failures detected by CICS during execution. Within the directory are fields to identify the failure, such as transaction identification (1), terminal (2), unique abend number (3), abend code (4), date and time stamp (5), program name (6) and net name of the terminal (7). These items allow exact identification and specific selection of the requested abend report. Instead of processing the entire dump dataset, the programmer can elect to view or print a single abend report. This directory can also provide problem tracking and a view of timely history of problems within CICS regions. One quick look at the report directory can show a trend of any specific transaction or abend during the day.

After selecting a specific entry, a diagnostic section pertaining to the failure is presented. Figure 8-12 contains a representative entry for an ASRA type of abend. Note that this screen interprets the type of ASRA (1) as a data exception, and provides a narrative description of the problem as might be found in a messages and codes manual. It pinpoints the failing instruction (2), including its offset within the program. Chapter Four spent a great deal of time explaining the process that a programmer would need to use to accomplish this task. CICS Abend-AID performs the process automatically.

Other sections of the report are available to further diagnose the problem. Figure 8-13 contains the COBOL information provided to futher diagnose the cause of the error. The product identifies the fields in error and the contents of these fields (1). Again, the manual process requires that the programmer cross-reference the dump, the program source, and attempt to tie all sources together.

Other facilities, including EDF, allow the programmer to locate the EIB at the time of the error. EDF, if requested, displays the EIB, but produces an unformatted display of the control block and requires that the programmer know the layout, or map, of the storage. If the contents of a specific field are required, the calculation must be made with the offset into the EIB, and the hexadecimal contents retrieved. Figure 8-14 contains the CICS Abend-Aid representation of the EIB. Notice that the control block is formatted, and contents translated. The programmer is not required to know at which offset into the EIB to find the function code (EIBFN), or what function is represented by **060E**. This data is provided and translated (1), so that the requestor is immediately aware that the failing instruction was READNEXT.

| ① TRAN | ② TERM | ③ REPORT | ④ ABEND | ⑤ DATE | TIME | ⑥ PROGRAM | ⑦ NETNAME |
|--------|--------|----------|---------|--------|------|-----------|-----------|
| 8 CCAD | MS04 | 3499 | ASRA | 07/16/88 | 14:40:14 | CCAASRA | TERM004 |
| CCAD | MS04 | 3498 | AEIM | 07/15/88 | 17:02:26 | CCAAEIM | TERM004 |
| CCAD | MS04 | 3497 | AEIP | 07/15/88 | 15:09:45 | CCAAEIP | TERM004 |
| CCAD | MS04 | 3495 | ASRA | 07/15/88 | 14:36:22 | CCAASMB | TERM004 |
| CCAD | MS17 | 3494 | ASRA | 07/15/88 | 12:25:04 | CCAAPL1 | TERM017 |
| CCAD | MS04 | 3493 | ASRA | 07/15/88 | 11:36:17 | CCAADLI | TERM004 |
| DB2D | MS31 | 3492 | DSNC | 07/15/88 | 11:14:04 | SQLDEMO | TERM031 |
| DB2D | MS04 | 3491 | 0818 | 07/14/88 | 17:41:21 | SQLDEMO | TERM004 |
| DB2D | MS31 | 3486 | 0811 | 07/14/88 | 16:21:10 | SQLDEMO | TERM031 |
| DB2D | MS31 | 3485 | 0303 | 07/14/88 | 16:19:36 | SQLDEMO | TERM031 |

```
PF 1=HELP 2=PRT 3=END 4=REP        5=DIR        7=UP 8=DOWN 9=PAGE 0
CMD-->
```

Figure 8-11   Abend/Aid output: report directory.

```
CODE=ASRA   TASK=CCAD   PROGRAM=CCAASRA        07/15/88   14:04:14   TERM=MS04

                    C I C S / A B E N D - A I D
      (C) COPYRIGHT 1984 COMPUWARE CORPORATION ALL RIGHTS RESERVED
                        RELEASE 880315-R 3.2.4


        *****************************①:*********************
        *      DIAGNOSTIC SECTION - [ASRA] DATA EXCEPTION      *
        ****************************************************
```

THE DATA EXCEPTION IS CAUSED WHEN A PACKED FIELD HAS AN INVALID
DIGIT (NOT 0-9), OR ITS LAST BYTE CONTAINS AN INVALID SIGN
(NOT F, C, OR D).

THE SUBTRACT INSTRUCTION IN ERROR IS LOCATED AT OFFSET [0007C0] ② IN
PROGRAM CCAASRA.

```
   PF 1=HELP 2=PRT 3=END 4=REP   003499 5=DIR 6=MENU   7=UP 8=DOWN 9=PAGE
   CMD-->
```

Figure 8-12   Abend/Aid output: diagnostic section.

```
CODE=ASRA   TASK=CCAD   PROGRAM=CCAASRA      07/15/88  14:04:14   TERM=MS04
                       COBOL INFORMATION

              *  NOTE BOTH FIELDS ARE IN ERROR
```

THE EXTERNAL DECIMAL DATA FIELD CAUSING THE ERROR IS LOCATED IN WORKING
STORAGE ADDRESSED BY PROGRAM CCAASRA. THE FIELD IN ERROR CAN BE FOUND
IN THE PROGRAM'S "DMAP" AT DISPLACEMENT 0000003A FROM THE START OF BL
CELL 1. THIS FIELD CONTAINS X'F1F2F04F4F7C7C'.


THE EXTERNAL DECIMAL DATA FIELD CAUSING THE ERROR IS LOCATED IN WORKING
STORAGE ADDRESSED BY PROGRAM CCAASRA. THE FIELD IN ERROR CAN BE FOUND
IN THE PROGRAM'S "DMAP" AT DISPLACEMENT 00000041 FROM THE START OF BL
CELL 1. THIS FIELD CONTAINS X'7C7C7C7CF9F2'.
                                      ①

```
PF 1=HELP 2=PRT 3=END 4=REP  003499 5=DIR 6=MENU  7=UP 8=DOWN 9=PAGE
CMD-->
```

Figure 8-13   Abend/Aid output: COBOL information.


Many failures require that the trace table be investigated for potential relevance. Figure 8-15 contains the table as represented by the product. Notice that not only are the most recent entries displayed first (instead of having to go to the end of the table and back up), but the entries are translated into an English narrative of the contents. Many programmers find this preferable to the trace table entries within a dump, which must be translated for contents. Of course, these interpreted

```
CODE=ASRA   TASK=CCAD   PROGRAM=CCAASRA      07/15/88  14:04:14   TERM=MS04


        *************************************************
        *     NEXT SEQUENTIAL INSTRUCTION SECTION     *
        *************************************************

   THE NEXT SEQUENTIAL INSTRUCTION TO BE EXECUTED IN PROGRAM CCAASRA
   WAS AT DISPLACEMENT 0007C6.

   THE PROGRAM WAS COMPILED ON 06/20/88 AT 17:30:44 AND IS 00092A
   BYTES LONG. IT IS PART OF LOAD MODULE CCAASRA WHICH WAS LOADED
   FROM CWX0102.BKS.LOADLIB.

   IT WAS LINK EDITED ON 06/20/88 AND IT IS 001470 BYTES LONG.

   THE LAST CALL OR 'EXEC CICS' COMMAND WAS ISSUED FROM PROGRAM
   CCAASRA AT DISPLACEMENT 000838.



PF 1=HELP 2=PRT 3=END 4=REP  003499 5=DIR 6=MENU  7=UP 8=DOWN 9=PAGE
CMD-->
```

Figure 8-14   Abend/Aid output: EIB.

```
CODE=ASRA   TASK=CCAD   PROGRAM=CCAASRA       07/15/88  14:04:14  TERM=MS04

              ************************************************
              *  ┌───────────┐                              *
              *  │TRACE TABLE│ WITH MOST CURRENT ENTRIES FIRST  *
              *  └───────────┘                              *
              ************************************************

COMMAND LEVEL REQUEST FOR FILE CONTROL READ NEXT TO FILE CCATEST
THE RETURN WAS TO PROGRAM CCAASRA - DISPLACEMENT 00083A.

COMMAND LEVEL REQUEST FOR STORAGE CONTROL GETMAIN - USER STORAGE FOR
0078 BYTES WAS ACQUIRED AT ADDRESS 00043730
THE RETURN WAS TO PROGRAM CCAASRA - DISPLACEMENT 000A60.

COMMAND LEVEL REQUEST FOR TERMINAL CONTROL RECEIVE FROM TERMINAL
THE RETURN WAS TO PROGRAM CCAARSA - DISPLACEMENT 000980.

COMMAND LEVEL REQUEST FOR EXEC INTERFACE HANDLE CONDITION
THE RETURN WAS TO PROGRAM CCAASRA - DISPLACEMENT 000AA4.

COMMAND LEVEL REQUEST FOR FILE CONTROL READ NEXT TO FILE CCATEST
THE RETURN WAS TO PROGRAM CCAASRA - DISPLACEMENT 00083A.

  PF 1=HELP 2=PRT 3=END 4=REP  003499 5=DIR 6=MENU  7=UP 8=DOWN 9=PAGE
  CMD-->
```

Figure 8-15   Abend/Aid output: trace table.

trace entries can produce three or four lines for each native trace table entry. A large trace table for a very active CICS system can produce an extremely large number of lines. CICS Abend-AID's trace table provides only those entries relevant to the abending task, filtering out the unnecessary entries.

Many programmers need to reference program storage, including the Working Storage section of their program. This information is formatted by BL cell and displacement for reference of any field. Figure 8-16 displays information concerning the next instruction to be executed, including the program load library attributes (1). The compile and link

```
CODE=ASRA   TASK=CCAD   PROGRAM=CCAASRA       07/15/88  14:04:14  TERM=MS04

              *********************************************
              *          EXECUTE INTERFACE BLOCK  (EIB)   *
              *********************************************

EIBTIME    17.46.03                 EIBDATE    88/172
EIBTRNID   CCAD                      EIBTASKN     0138
EIBTRMID   MS04                      EIBCPOSN     0065
EIBCALEN   00000                     EIBAID     7D - ENTER
EIBFN      060E          - ┌────────┐①
                           │READNEXT│
EIBRCODE   000000000000 - └────────┘
EIBDS      CCATEST                   EIBREQID   ........
EIBRSRCE   CCATEST                   EIBSYNC    00
EIBFREE    00                        EIBRECV    00
EIBATT     00                        EIBEOC     00
EIBFMH     00                        EIBCOMPL   00
EIBSIG     00                        EIBCONF    00
EIBERR     00                        EIBERRCD   00000000
EIBSYNRB   00                        EIBNODAT   00

  PF 1=HELP 2=PRT 3=END 4=REP  003499 5=DIR 6=MENU  7=UP 8=DOWN 9=PAGE
  CMD-->
```

Figure 8-16   Abend/Aid output: next sequential instruction.

```
CODE=ASRA   TASK=CCAD   PROGRAM=CCAASRA      07/15/88  14:04:14   TERM=MS04


            ************************************
            *         PROGRAM SECTION          *
            ************************************


                ****************************
                *   LINK TRACE SUMMARY     *
                ****************************


   PROGRAM     CSECT                        PROGRAM     CSECT     RETURN

   CCAASRA     CCAASRA   **LINKED TO BY**   CCAMENU     CCAMENU   000CCA
   CCAMENU     CCAMENU   **LINKED TO BY**   SYSTEM




   PF 1=HELP 2=PRT 3=END 4=REP   003499 5=DIR 6=MENU  7=UP 8=DOWN 9=PAGE
   CMD-->
```

Figure 8-17   Abend/Aid output: program section.

edit information is provided to assist in determining that the correct source listing is being referenced and the proper version of the program was executed. If this program was executed as a result of a LINK, a trace of these connections is summarized in the Link Trace Summary, Figure 8-17. The Working Storage of the program is available, as displayed in Figure 8-18, and may be investigated for contents relevant to the failure.

Many other sections of the report can be used to futher diagnose the abend. If the failure is terminal-related, terminal control blocks can be viewed, including the TCTUA. If the problem appears to be file-related, file control blocks can be investigated,

```
CODE=ASRA   TASK=CCAD   PROGRAM=CCAASRA      07/15/88  14:04:14   TERM=MS04

*********************************************************************
*            WORKING STORAGE PRINT FOR PROGRAM CCAASRA             *
*          THE PROGRAM WAS COMPILED ON 06/20/88 AT 17:30:44        *
*                 THIS IS THE ABENDING PROGRAM                     *
*********************************************************************


            ***************************************************
            *    WORKING STORAGE REFERENCED BY BL CELL 1      *
            *            FOR PROGRAM CCAASRA                   *
            ***************************************************

ADDRESS  DISPL   -------------HEX DATA--------------   --DISPLAY DATA--
000ED69C 00000   0050F0F6 F0F2F2F9 F8F4F5D5 E8D50000   *. 060229845NYN..
000ED6AC 00010   F4F0F1F4 F0F0F3F9 F1F2D1D6 C8D5E2E3   *4014003912JOHNST
000ED6BC 00020   D6D5C56B 40D9C5C7 C9D5C1D3 C440C24B   *ONE, REGINALD B.
000ED6CC 00030   40404040 40404040 4040F1F2 F04F4F7C   *          120]]@
000ED6DC 00040   7C7C7C7C 7CF9F2F2 F3F4F4F2 F3F4F440   *@@@@@9223442344
000ED6EC 00050   40404040 40404040 40404040 40404040   *
000ED6FC 00060   00000000 00000000 007D6D6A 7EE6E788   *.........'_.=WXH

   PF 1=HELP 2=PRT 3=END 4=REP   003499 5=DIR 6=MENU  7=UP 8=DOWN 9=PAGE
   CMD-->
```

Figure 8-18   Abend/Aid output: working storage section.

including all file storage chained off the TCA storage chain. Of course, actual contents of the information are provided as interpreted data, not merely the unformatted contents of control blocks. If the failure occurred in a CICS transaction performing DB/2 calls, a great deal of DB/2 data is also available from the report, some of which is not available in a dump. In a normal CICS environment utilizing the DB/2 attach facility, all DB/2 diagnostic information must be investigated in external sources such as SYS1.LOGREC, or in the DB/2 address space. This facility provides a single point of access to all information relevant to a DB/2 abend. The time savings could be significant.

This section has covered only a fraction of the functions available within CICS Abend-AID. The vendor can supply additional information if an installation wishes to evaluate the product for purchase. Again, this chapter is not meant to promote any particular product, but to make programmers aware of alternative tools available for problem determination and dump debugging.

# Common Programming Errors Not Causing Abends

In the course of development and testing, many conditions arise that were not planned, and are not desirable. We would like to develop a new application and have it work right the first time. This is not only idealistic, but probably impossible. During development, however, conditions are sometimes experienced that were not intended. Many times testing produces situations that are not abends, therefore do not fail and produce a dump. These can be extremely difficult to debug, since there is no abend code, no messages to assist during problem determination. Some of the most common situations in this category are program loops, file deadlocks, string waits, and other data-related problems when resources are not released. This chapter will cover a few of these and identify tools and/or techniques that can be used when a dump is not available.

## 9.1 CONVERSATIONAL VS. PSEUDO-CONVERSATIONAL PROGRAMMING

During design of an application, the flow of programs and the processing environment need to be considered. In CICS, an application communicates with a terminal. When a request is transmitted from a keyboard, the application processes the request, and transmits the response back to the display. This is truly a simplification of the process, but in fact, CICS is constantly in send–receive mode. After the application processes either the send or receive, however, it makes a choice. Should this program retain control and wait for the next interrupt, or should it release control and start back up when new work appears? This choice in-

volves two different coding techniques, called "conversational" and "pseudo-conversational"

Conversational transactions use a technique to converse, or sustain a send–receive arrangement until all communication is complete. This could be compared to a telephone conversation. From the time the phone is picked up until hung up, the communication continues and the line is busy to anyone else. In CICS, the control blocks, such as the TCA and all related storage, are built and remain until the transaction terminates. While this may save some overhead of task initiation and termination, it holds all storage related to the task during the entire time. It also holds a place on the CICS chains during this time, possibly keeping another task from being dispatched. Conversational transactions can produce problems in a system from resource retention and elongated response times.

While attempting to debug conversational transactions, since no dump has been produced, the auxiliary trace facility can be utilized. Since these tasks may remain active for long periods of time, the CICS internal trace may not contain adequate entries for the length of the transaction. An auxiliary trace can be created large enough to contain all entries. If transaction storage is being analyzed, it may be necessary to force an abend via CEDF or an intentional program check. During the EDF session, an option is available to abend the current transaction with a user-defined abend code. In the transaction dump, it will be possible to follow all storage created on behalf of the task. Perhaps excessive storage was created and never released during execution of the transaction. Again, conversational programs may affect other applications and their ability to reuse CICS resources.

Pseudo-conversational transactions use a technique that produces the same appearance at the terminal, but releases resources during the time between communications. If the analyzer is a typical CICS terminal user, a request is keyed, the result appears on the screen, and a period of time is spent analyzing the results. This "think" time can be seconds or minutes, depending on the user. In a high transaction-rate CICS region, the transaction rate can be 20–30 transactions per second. Releasing these resources between tasks can make them available to other transactions.

Resources can be released to CICS by returning control at the end of the task. The CICS command to do this is

```
    RETURN
TRANSID(name)
COMMAREA(data-area)
LENGTH(data-value)
```

The application returns control to the next higher logical level or to CICS. The TRANSID option can be used to specify the next transaction to be associated with that terminal. In addition, a COMMAREA can be used to pass data to the new task that will be started. Other techniques can be used to RETURN control to CICS, creating a temporary storage record to use for re-initiation of the new transaction.

Whichever method of program control is used, pseudo-conversational programming can prevent excessive resource consumption by an application. Consult the Application Programmer's Reference manual for further information concerning program control techniques.

## 9.2    TRANSACTION LOOPING

When debugging, note that an application that contains a loop produces a situation that will not produce a dump unless specifically requested. If the transaction remains active for long periods of time, it can be purged with the CEMT command. This does not provide the information necessary to resolve the problem, however. One solution would be to monitor the execution of the application with CEDF and attempt to locate the instruction chain that continues to execute. This could provide insight into the series of program statements containing the loop. An auxiliary trace of the application may also be produced, and would contain the statements within the loop. Again, the task can be abended from within CEDF to produce a dump. In a low-volume CICS region, the trace within the dump may contain the instruction chain that shows the loop.

## 9.3    DEADLOCKS AND STRING WAITS

Some of the most common problems in browse-type applications occur when resources are not released at the proper time. Deadlocks and string waits can occur when an application fails to release a resource, or requests a resource that is not available. The number of concurrent accesses available to a VSAM file is specified by the FCT parameter, STRNO. Depending upon the request, an access may retain one or more strings of a VSAM file for an extended period of time. If an application executes a request, for example GET for update, against a VSAM file, the string is held until the PUT is complete.

Requests for VSAM files that would exceed the string count previously specified cause the task to wait until a string is released by another transaction. An ECB (event control block) is created for the WAIT and is posted after a string is released, resulting in the task re-dispatch. If experiencing a great deal of string waits, increase the STRNO value for that file. The STRNO value may be correct, however. Strings may be held by applications because of incorrect programming techniques. One of the most common mistakes involves the browse operation. If an application uses the following sequence:

```
STARTBROWSE ...
GETNEXT ...
GETNEXT ...
ENDBROWSE
GET/UPDATE
```

the string is released from the STARTBROWSE by the ENDBROWSE before the next string is acquired with the GET. If the application fails to issue the ENDBROWSE before requesting the GET for update, two strings are held for the request. When the PUT is issued, both strings are released.

### 9.3.1    Debugging String Waits

If experiencing excessive string waits, especially in one particular VSAM file, determine which tasks are holding those strings and why. Strings can be identified by the existence of a VSWA block of storage. Each VSWA represents one string held by the task. In order to identify all VSWAs in existence for any particular VSAM file, take a snapshot of the CICS address space at the time of the problem and look for these blocks of storage. A transaction dump will only identify task-related storage for that specific task. All storage for all tasks and a total system dump will be necessary. The following steps can be followed:

1. Use CEMT to produce a SNAP dump of the region, or the OS DUMP command to write a SDUMP to a SYS1.DUMPxx dataset. An unformatted dump will be preferable, since the PRDMP exit or IPCS can be used to look into the problem.
2. Once the dump has been produced, use PRDMP with the KCP option to map out all task-related storage. Review the task summary to identify all active and suspended transactions, since the VSWAs created by these tasks will be relevant.
3. Follow the portion of the report titled "Task and User Related Storage" to locate VSWAs. The first control block will always be the TCA and will contain an 8A in the first byte. All storage following will be task-related. VSWAs can be identified by 8F in the first byte. These 8F blocks of storage were created from VSAM file control requests. At offset +20 into the VSWA is the ACB address. Every VSWA located may not have been created for the file being diagnosed with string waits. Identify the ACB address of the file being analyzed, and use only the VSWAs with that ACB. IPCS may be required to look up these ACB addresses, finding the ACB for the VSAM file with string waits.
4. Once all the VSWAs for the correct file have been identified, analyze the tasks that have created these VSWAs. Does one application contain a large number, and is therefore holding several strings? Is that task suspended for some reason, and therefore not releasing the strings?

Only after analysis of all tasks, and the strings held by each, will the offending task be identified. We hope this investigation will uncover the culprit.

In summary, many problems may need to be analyzed that are not actually failures. Proper coding techniques and reasonable utilization of resources during application execution will avoid many of the problems covered in this chapter.

# System Programming

# Formatted vs. Unformatted Dumps

Dumps can be produced from CICS as a result of a failure or by an explicit request. There are several options, especially in release 1.7 and later, that allow a user to select the type of dump that is produced and the location that the dump is written to. The dumps discussed in this chapter are not transaction dumps, as was covered in Chapter 2. These dumps are full system dumps, containing more than just the transaction dumps pertaining to a particular task. The system dump contains control blocks and storage areas of all tasks in the region at the time of the dump. Of course, depending on the options that are chosen, the dump may contain every piece of storage known to CICS, or a portion of that data. CICS produces two types of system dumps:

Formatted dumps
Partition dumps

Both types will be discussed in great detail, but first, we will determine how to select each one and what results are produced with those selections.

Beginning in CICS 1.7, the system initialization table (SIT) provided the ability to select the default dump parameters, including the new SDUMP option. The options in the SIT are

NO — Produce an operating system abend dump, but only if the region abnormally terminates or is canceled. A data definition (DD) must be placed in the CICS JCL for a SYSUDUMP, SYSMDUMP or SYSABEND.

PARTN — Produce a dump of the CICS partition, or region.

SNAP — If coded with PARTN, produce a SNAP dump to DFHSNAP.

SDUMP — If coded with PARTN or FULL, issue an MVS SDUMP macro to write a dump to the MVS system dump dataset.

FORMAT — Produce a formatted dump to the CICS dump dataset.

Utilizing a combination of these parameters in the SIT, or overriding them with the CEMT command when requesting a dump, will produce the specific type of dump output necessary for various problems. What type of storage is contained within these different dump types? Of course, it is important to produce a dump that contains all entries necessary to analyze the problem. Each of the two types of system dumps identified earlier, formatted and partition dumps, has advantages and disadvantages.

**Formatted Dumps.** A formatted dump contains most of the storage areas and control blocks known to CICS at the time of the failure. In addition, the output is segmented, or formatted, into the separate areas. Many people prefer these types of dumps because the areas within the dump are isolated, have titles, and are easier to read. Major control blocks are identified and easy to locate. Formatted dumps are followed by indexes of control blocks and both CICS and user modules to assist in locating these items within the dump.

**Partition Dumps.** Partition dumps can be region, SNAP, or SDUMP type dumps. Each contain a little different information; however, all are unformatted.

CICS Region Dump. These dumps are produced by CICS, therefore contain all storage known to CICS. They are unformatted, except for the interpreted version of the trace table, and are written to the CICS dump dataset.

SNAP Dump. The MVS SNAP dump is produced by the MVS SNAP macro, therefore contains all data from the CICS region plus some MVS storage including storage subpools, job pack area and link pack area. This dump is unformatted and is written to the DFHSNAP dataset as specified in the startup JCL.

SDUMP Dump. The SDUMP dump is produced by the MVS SDUMP macro, therefore also contains MVS storage areas. These dumps contain the entire CICS address space, CICS private storage areas, and the MVS nucleus and common areas. This dump is also unformatted and is written to an MVS system dump dataset in the format of SYS1.DUMP-xx.

Most installations choose to use either the unformatted SDUMP or the formatted dump, depending on their type of failure or support needs. Both of these dump types will be analyzed to determine which can provide the optimum information to assist in problem determination.

## 10.1    FORMATTED DUMP PROGRAM DFHFDP

When the CICS dump control program, DFHDCP, gets control during a failure, it can pass control to formatted dump program DFHFDP to produce formatted output. If the installation wishes to produce a formatted dump of the region at failure, or with the CEMT SNAP command, FORMAT should be specified in the SIT parameter. This will cause the formatted dump program to analyze all storage in the region at the time of the failure, and format any and all control blocks, including all chained storage. This mapped version of the address space will be written to one of the dump datasets, DFHDMPA or DFHDMPB, whichever is active at the time of the failure. Many people prefer formatted dumps, since they are actually organized, with all storage areas formatted and identified with appropriate titles. Realize, however, that formatted dumps only contain the portions of storage that are chained, or connected to the primary control blocks. Formatted dump program can only identify storage that is referenced, or pointed to via addresses from one control block to another. Formatted dumps DO NOT contain all portions of storage known to CICS. If the failing component, or address, is within the formatted dump, you will be able to locate the fail-

ure and detect the probable cause. If, while diagnosing the failure, any reference is made to a portion of unformatted storage, or an address that does not exist within the formatted areas in the dump, there is no access to that storage. A customer may be unable to resolve the problem or diagnose the cause without all the pieces of the puzzle.

Another reason that formatted dumps may not be desirable for system problems was previously mentioned in Chapter 2, diagnosing formatted transaction dumps. Since formatted dumps are written to DFHDMPA or DFHDMPB, the only way to process them is to use the IBM utility, DFHDUP. This utility is without a great deal of function and flexibility, and does not provide the ability to selectively process the dumps within the datasets. To produce the output of a formatted dump, ALL dumps in the dataset must be processed. The entire output must be printed, or viewed within the JES SPOOL. This is difficult and unnecessary. Possibly IBM will enhance this facility to make formatted dump processing more functional.

Once a formatted dump has been requested, or received automatically via the options chosen when a failure occurs, the dump can be printed or viewed from a terminal. Unfortunately, there is no facility for direct reference of any items within the dump except for an editor "find" facility. In other words, if the trace table needs to be located, the customer would have to issue a FIND command from within the output viewing facility for a keyword of TRACE. Many people either print the formatted dump or use unformatted dumps with IPCS (Interactive Problem Control System). IPCS will be covered later in this chapter, including the functions in the product that make problem determination simpler. As previously stated, formatted dumps contain all storage that is chained off the major control blocks, storage that CICS can format as the major components of the product. The output from a formatted CICS region dump is shown in Figure 10-1. This is a sample from a requested CEMT SNAP command that specified FULL, FORMAT in the options. The first page of a formatted dump indicates CICS SYSTEM DUMP (1) and gives a time and date that the dump was produced (2). The Symptom String, as in other dumps, contains the name of a program module in control at the time of the failure (3). This program, DFHEMTD, however, is the CICS module used to invoke the CEMT SNAP command, so is not significant in the analysis of the problem in this example. The first control blocks formatted in the dump are the Common System Area (CSA) (4) and the CSA Optional Features List (5). These areas are further detailed by some significant data areas within the control block. IBM formats some data areas by indicating the field name,

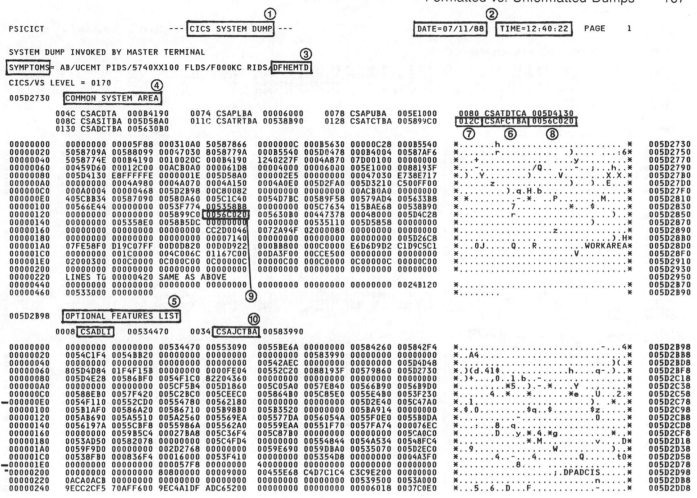

Figure 10-1   CICS formatted dumps: page 1 of 2.

offset into the control block, and contents. Take, for example, the pointer to the File Control Table. The data name is indicated, CSAFCTBA (6), the offset into the control block is 012C (7), and its contents are **0056C020** (8). This can be verified by finding the offset within the control block. On the far right of the page is the reference to offset **00000120**. The exact address (12C) would be the fourth fullword over to the right of that offset. At this location (9) is a fullword with the value of **0056C020**. This could have been located manually; however, the purpose of a formatted dump is to attempt the mapping out of important areas in the dump automatically. Customers are not forced to identify all relevant components of control blocks for themselves. Many people find this extremely helpful, and therefore use formatted dumps most often.

In the control block, Optional Features List, there are other data areas that could be relevant to problem solving. Two items are formatted, CSADLI and CSAJCTBA (10). These pointers could be im-

portant in analyzing problems relating to DL/1 databases, or if the pointer to the Journal Control Table is needed.

Another page in a formatted dump is represented by Figure 10-2. As shown in the dump, control blocks for Class Maximum Task Counters (1), Program Check / Abend Trace Table (2), and the System Initialization Table (3) are mapped. There are no individual data areas mapped within these control blocks. It would be necessary, then, to refer to the CICS Data Areas Manual to identify any contents within these control blocks. The Program Check / Abend Trace Table may be very relevant in some failures. Several system failures will be used in following chapters, and the contents of this table will be relevant. Many other control blocks are also formatted in these dumps, including all resources controlled by table macros or Resource Definition Online facilities (RDO). Program Control Table entries could be utilized to identify specific contents of a program. The status of a particular file within the

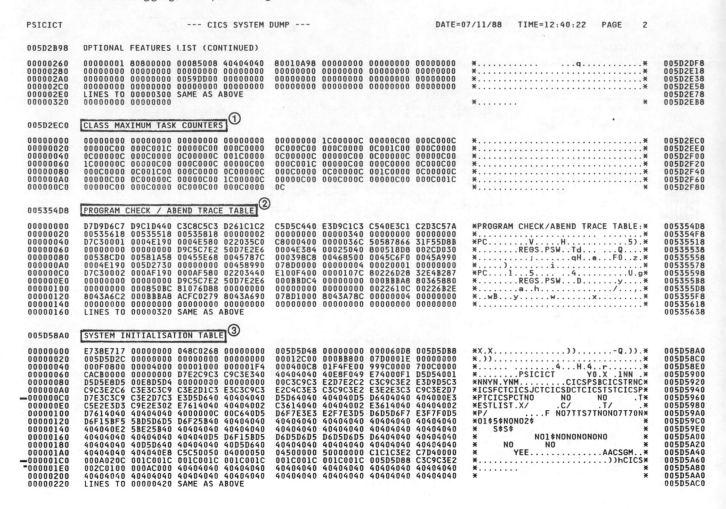

Figure 10-2   CICS formatted dumps: page 2 of 2.

region could be analyzed by locating its entry in the File Control Table control blocks mapped within the dump. All resources defined to the region at the time of the dump are mapped out, and can be located within the specified entries of the control blocks.

Areas more critical to the problem, however, may be the control blocks relating to the task in control at the time of the failure. These control blocks are called Task Control Areas (TCAs) and can be found further into the formatted dump. Figure 10-3 contains the portion of a formatted dump representing a task within the CICS region at the time of the failure. A TCA is built for every task when it is first dispatched by CICS, and remains whether that task is active or has been suspended. A task, therefore, may be analyzed as the suspected cause of a failure. While a formatted transaction dump describes a specific transaction, or task, a formatted dump of the entire region would contain ALL tasks that were attached at the time of the failure. If at-

tempting to diagnose the contents of this particular task, data areas associated with that task are conveniently mapped out. One relevant item may be the TCATCPC (1), or the transaction identification. In this example, the contents are SDF (2), or the IBM Screen Definition Facility product. This product creates CICS screens and generates the Basic Mapping Services, BMS, maps automatically without coding the native macros.

This information is found within the TCA System Area. The TCA contains two areas, the User Area and the System Area. The System Area also identifies the TCAPCTA, or program pointed to by the transaction (3). The first portion of the TCA (4) also known as the TCA User Area, contains additional information that may be relevant to the status of the task. The TCASVMID (5) defines the services that the task is requesting, and the TCATCTR (6) identifies that status of the task. Several of the other areas mapped may be significant, and, of course, can be analyzed for relevant information. At

```
PSICICT                  --- CICS SYSTEM DUMP ---                    DATE=07/11/88  TIME=12:40:22  PAGE  363

 000A1320    LIFO STACK ENTRY

             ---  OWNED BY DFHKCP
 00000000    42000068 00000000 FF0A1388 5042F046   00000000 00000000 00000000 504303BE   *..........h..0..............*   000A1320
 00000020    00000000 5042F022 00000000 00000000   000C0000 005D2B98 00000000 00000000   *........0...........).q.....*   000A1340
 00000040    00000000 000A1190 005D2730 FE0A1388   F000D2C3 005CCCF8 00000000 00000000   *.........)......h0.KC.*.8...*   000A1360
 00000060    00000000 00000000                                                           *........                   *   000A1380

 000A2280    JOURNAL CONTROL AREA

 00000000    9B000098 000A1000 00000000 00000000   00000000 00000000 00000000 00000000   *...q.......................*   000A2280
 00000020    00000000 00000000 00000000 00000000   00000000 00000000 00000000 00000000   *..........................*    000A22A0
 00000040    LINES TO 00000060 SAME AS ABOVE                                                                              000A22C0
 00000080    00000000 00000000 00000000 00000000   00000000 00000000 9B000098 000A1000   *.........................q..*   000A2300

 000A1290    LOAD LIST AREA

 00000000    00000028 000A1290 00000000 00000000   00000000 00000000 00000000 00000000   *..........................*    000A1290
 00000020    00000000 00000000 00000000 00000000                                         *...............             *   000A12B0

 000A2320    USER STORAGE

 00000000    8C001778 000A2280 00000000 00000000   00000000 00000000 00000000 00000000   *..........................*    000A2320
 00000020    00000000 00000000 00000000 00000000   00000000 00000000 00000000 00000000   *..........................*    000A2340
 00000040    LINES TO 00001740 SAME AS ABOVE                                                                              000A2360
 00001760    00000000 00000000 00000000 00000000   00000000 00000000 8C001778 000A2280   *..........................*    000A3A80

 000A12C0    TABLE ELEMENT LOCAL LOCK BLOCK

 00000000    00000000 00000008 00000000 00000000   00000000 00000000 00000000 00000000   *..........................*    000A12C0
 00000020    00000000 00000000 00000000 00000000   00000000 00000000 00000000 00000000   *..........................*    000A12E0
 00000040    00000000 00000000                                                           *........                   *   000A1300

 0004A910    DISPATCH CONTROL AREA

       0008 DCATCQC  00000000      0014 DCATCAA  00050190      0018 DCATCDC  13

 00000000    81000070 00000000 00000000 0004A230   0004A070 00050190 13400113 04053AB4   *a..............s...........*    0004A910
 00000020    00000000 00000000 00000000 00000000   00000000 01008000 00000000 00000000   *..........................*    0004A930
 00000040    00000000 00000000 00000000 00000000   00000000 00000000 00050450 00000001   *..........................*    0004A950
 00000060    00099040 00000001                                                           *...  ....                  *   0004A970

 00050190    │TASK CONTROL AREA│④

       0000 TCASYAA  00050000      0008 TCAFCAAA 01053AB4      0014 TCATCQA  00053AB4      005C TCASCSA  400B2CA0
       0080 TCAFCAA  00000014      0080 TCATDAA  00000014      0080 TCATSDA  00000014      00F0 TCAJCAAD 00000000
       0018 TCATCEI  13
       │001D TCASVMID 8108│⑤                                 │0019 TCATCTR  TASK WAIT│⑥

 00000000    00050000 00000000 01053AB4 005D2B98   00050518 00053AB4 13400100 04810800   *............).q..........a..*   00050190
 00000020    705BB384 405BA3D8 405BB648 00000058   00589C98 00000000 00050000 505BAE9A   *.$.d $tQ $........q........$.*  000501B0
```

Figure 10-3   CICS formatted dumps: TCA system area. (Page 1 of 2.)

the end of the formatted dump is the entire summary of all control blocks that were formatted, Figure 10-4. This summary is in sequence by address within the dump, and identifies the starting address of the control block (1), the page within the formatted dump where this control block can be located (2), and the control block type (3).

Realize that the identity of the control block is not available. There are many TCAs, for example, within a dump. The control block type merely gives a visual reference of all control blocks of a particular type if you wish to search for a particular one. The next summary at the end of a formatted dump is similar to the summary that you find in transaction dumps starting in CICS 1.7. The module summary, Figure 10-5, identifies the entry point (1), load point (2), and module name (3) of all load modules known to the CICS region at the time of the failure. It can be very helpful in locating a failing module when a particular control block points to an address, and the module needs to be identified.

Many other control blocks are mapped into a formatted dump; only a few have been covered within the examples shown in this chapter. If formatted dumps are used for problem determination, become familiar with the output generated by the facility, and "know your way around." The best way is to use CEMT to produce a dump, and get familiar when the situation is not critical. The worst ways to learn dump formats and contents is during a critical failure, when the installation is experiencing an outage. Spend time during a stress-free learning experience. In fact, make the time. The time will be much more productive.

## 10.2   UNFORMATTED DUMPS

Since formatted dumps have several limitations, including missing sections of storage that may be important in diagnosing a problem, many system programmers are beginning to use unformatted dumps. An enhancement in CICS 1.7 gave more

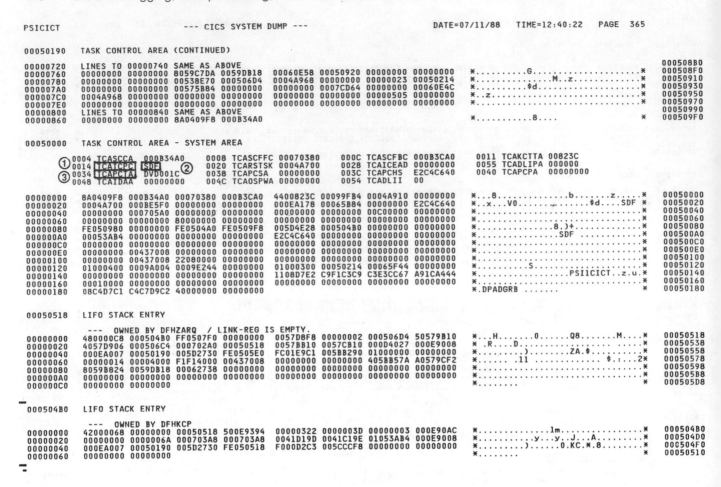

Figure 10-3   CICS formatted dumps: TCA system area. (Page 2 of 2.)

flexibility in dump selection with the new SIT parameter SDUMP. Prior to CICS 1.7, unformatted dumps could be requested in some situations and written to a SYSMDUMP dataset for processing. The content of these dumps is established at system IPL time from entries in system parameters. The existing status of these parameters can be determined by using the command:

```
DISPLAY DUMP,OPTIONS
```

from any console. Figure 10-6 contains the results of this command. The complete description of this message can be found in the MVS Messages and Codes manual, IEE857I. As shown, however, the display indicates the current system dump options. These can be changed with the CHNGDUMP command, or by overriding the options as a result of the DUMP command. Note that the SYSMDUMP options are different from the SDUMP options.

Make sure that your dump contains all data areas necessary to properly resolve the problem.

SYSMDUMP datasets are pre-allocated and identified to the CICS region via DD statements in the startup JCL. Whether SDUMP or SYSMDUMP datasets are used for unformatted output, similar techniques are available for processing the dump. Since these dumps are unformatted, all appropriate control blocks and storage areas must be located. IBM has some facilities to accomplish this. IPCS is probably one of the most popular products for unformatted dump analysis, and was discussed in great detail in Chapter 1.

IPCS is IBM's strategic product in problem determination. As previously stated, MVS/ESA will use IPCS exclusively to process any system dumps. As IPCS is enhanced, new functions will further assist systems programmers in their analysis of problems. IPCS will process any unformatted dump, therefore both SYSMDUMPs and SDUMPs can be analyzed

```
PSICICT                        --- CICS SYSTEM DUMP ---                        DATE=07/11/88   TIME=12:40:22   PAGE  418
        ①      ②      ③
   ┌ADDRESS┐ ┌PAGE┐ ┌C.B.┐ ERROR      ADDRESS   PAGE  C.B.  ERROR      ADDRESS   PAGE  C.B.  ERROR      ADDRESS   PAGE  C.B.  ERROR
   └───────┘ └NO ┘ └TYPE┘ COUNT                 NO    TYPE  COUNT                NO    TYPE  COUNT                NO    TYPE  COUNT
```

| ADDRESS | PAGE NO | C.B. TYPE | ERROR COUNT | ADDRESS | PAGE NO | C.B. TYPE | ERROR COUNT | ADDRESS | PAGE NO | C.B. TYPE | ERROR COUNT | ADDRESS | PAGE NO | C.B. TYPE | ERROR COUNT |
|---|---|---|---|---|---|---|---|---|---|---|---|---|---|---|---|
| 00005368 | 28 | MRSD | | 00049754 | 178 | SNIB | | 0004FE04 | 188 | TCTTE1 | | 0005BA44 | 82 | DSG | |
| 00005594 | 28 | MRSD | | 00049FE4 | 172 | CCE | | 0004FFC5 | 188 | BIND | | 0005C6F4 | 93 | SKT | |
| 000057F8 | 26 | TDST | | 0004A000 | 403 | DCA | | 0004FFE5 | 190 | BIND | | 0005C764 | 93 | DSG | |
| 00005848 | 26 | MWCA | | 0004A070 | 361 | DCA | | 00050000 | 365 | TCA | | 0005C934 | 93 | DSG | |
| 00005920 | 26 | MBCA | | 0004A0E0 | 401 | DCA | | 00050190 | 363 | TCA | | 0005D1C4 | 81 | DSG | |
| 00005998 | 27 | MBCB | | 0004A150 | 358 | DCA | | 00050420 | 367 | PCL | | 0005E644 | 79 | DSG | |
| 000059CC | 27 | MBCB | | 0004A1C0 | 412 | DCA | | 00050450 | 390 | TMLL | | 000601B4 | 92 | DSG | |
| 00005A00 | 26 | MBCB | | 0004A230 | 391 | DCA | | 000504B0 | 365 | LFS | | 000605C4 | 91 | DSG | |
| 00005A38 | 27 | MQCB | | 0004A310 | 415 | DCA | | 00050518 | 365 | LFS | | 000609D4 | 91 | DSG | |
| 00005A44 | 27 | MQCB | | 0004A380 | 409 | DCA | | 00050A00 | 370 | USER | | 00060DE4 | 88 | DSG | |
| 00005A50 | 27 | MQCB | | 0004A3F0 | 26 | VCT | | 00050B10 | 370 | USER | | 000611F4 | 77 | DSG | |
| 00005A60 | 27 | MRCA | | 0004A410 | 26 | IDX | | 00050B80 | 369 | USER | | 00061FE4 | 73 | DSG | |
| 00005B08 | 27 | ACB | | 0004A684 | 173 | SNTTE | | 00050B88 | 390 | TMLL | | 00062FF5 | 197 | BIND | |
| 00005B50 | 28 | MRCB | | 0004A6C4 | 178 | SNTTE | | 00050BE0 | 368 | USER | | 00063584 | 76 | DSG | |
| 00005B74 | 28 | MRCB | | 0004A7C4 | 187 | SNTTE | | 00050E70 | 389 | USER | | 00064924 | 75 | DSG | |
| 00005B90 | 27 | MRCB | | 0004A800 | 14 | ICE | | 00051000 | 411 | TCA | | 00066004 | 72 | DSG | |
| 00005BB0 | 28 | TDVSWA | | 0004A870 | 14 | ICE | | 00051190 | 409 | TCA | | 00067504 | 71 | DSG | |
| 00005CA4 | 28 | TDVSWA | | 0004A8D4 | 184 | SNTTE | | 00051488 | 412 | PCL | | 00068984 | 70 | DSG | |
| 00005D98 | 27 | TDVSWA | | 0004A910 | 363 | DCA | | 000514B8 | 411 | EIS | | 00069CF4 | 68 | DSG | |
| 000060D8 | 3 | SIPCOM | | 0004A9F4 | 182 | SNTTE | | 0005171C | 412 | TMLL | | 0006B274 | 67 | DSG | |
| 00016000 | 96 | UET | | 0004AA34 | 186 | SNTTE | | 00051780 | 411 | LFS | | 0006C824 | 66 | DSG | |
| 00047030 | 13 | PAM | | 0004AA84 | 181 | SNTTE | | 00052004 | 90 | DSG | | 0006DD84 | 65 | DSG | |
| 00047250 | 13 | MAP1 | | 0004AAC4 | 180 | SNTTE | | 00052414 | 89 | DSG | | 0006F2C4 | 64 | DSG | |
| 0004764B | 14 | MAP2 | | 0004AB04 | 184 | SNTTE | | 00052824 | 89 | DSG | | 0006FFF5 | 199 | BIND | |
| 00048000 | 17 | TSUT | | 0004AB44 | 192 | SNTTE | | 000538F4 | 177 | TCTTE1 | | 00070000 | 386 | USER | |
| 00048F20 | 17 | TSUTE | | 0004ABC4 | 191 | SNTTE | | 00053AB4 | 186 | TCTTE1 | | 000703A0 | 367 | USER | |
| 00048F30 | 17 | TSUTE | | 0004AC04 | 190 | SNTTE | | 00053C75 | 187 | BIND | | 00070540 | 389 | PCL | |
| 00048F40 | 18 | TSUTE | | 0004AC44 | 189 | SNTTE | | 00053C94 | 186 | TCTTEX | | 000705A0 | 366 | PCL | |
| 00048F50 | 18 | TSUTE | | 0004B240 | 359 | TIOA | | 00053D70 | 96 | EPB | | 000705D0 | 390 | USER | |
| 00048F60 | 18 | TSUTE | | 0004B720 | 358 | TIOA | | 00053DB0 | 96 | EPB | | 000705D8 | 390 | TMLL | |
| 00048F70 | 18 | TSUTE | | 0004B940 | 359 | TIOA | | 00054004 | 61 | DSG | | 00070680 | 389 | USER | |
| 00048F80 | 18 | TSUTE | | 0004BC20 | 360 | TIOA | | 00054FE5 | 176 | BIND | | 000706A0 | 390 | USER | |
| 00048F90 | 18 | TSUTE | | 0004C004 | 359 | RPL | | 00055000 | 360 | TCA | | 000706C0 | 386 | USER | |
| 00048FA0 | 18 | TSUTE | | 0004C094 | 358 | RPL | | 00055190 | 360 | TCA | | 00070740 | 386 | USER | |
| 00048FB0 | 18 | TSUTE | | 0004C1B4 | 358 | RPL | | 00055290 | 361 | PCL | | 00070780 | 386 | USER | |
| 000491C4 | 190 | SNIB | | 0004D004 | 47 | DSG | | 000552C0 | 361 | TMLL | | 00070830 | 386 | USER | |
| 00049225 | 189 | BIND | | 0004DCC4 | 171 | TCTTE1 | | 00055320 | 361 | LFS | | 00070870 | 386 | USER | |
| 00049244 | 189 | TCTTEX | | 0004DE84 | 171 | TCTTEX | | 00056280 | 361 | JCA | | 00070910 | 389 | USER | |
| 00049370 | 145 | FCSBK | | 0004DF44 | 172 | TCTTEX | | 00057004 | 86 | DSG | | 00070930 | 389 | USER | |
| 00049474 | 182 | SNIB | | 0004DFE5 | 175 | BIND | | 00057DC4 | 84 | DSG | | 00070950 | 389 | USER | |
| 000494D5 | 182 | BIND | | 0004E000 | 412 | USER | | 00058BF4 | 37 | SKT | | 00070970 | 389 | USER | |
| 000494F5 | 178 | BIND | | 0004F004 | 46 | DSG | | 00058BF4 | 316 | PCT | | 00070990 | 389 | USER | |
| 00049544 | 182 | TCTTEX | | 0004FB00 | 144 | FCSBK | | 00058D24 | 48 | SKT | | 000709B0 | 389 | USER | |
| 000495A5 | 172 | BIND | | 0004FC04 | 183 | SNIB | | 00058D94 | 87 | SKT | | 000709D0 | 389 | USER | |
| 000495C5 | 195 | BIND | | 0004FC65 | 183 | BIND | | 00058FE4 | 78 | DSG | | 000709F0 | 388 | USER | |
| 000495D4 | 178 | TCTTEX | | 0004FC84 | 183 | TCTTEX | | 00059FF5 | 196 | BIND | | 00070A10 | 388 | USER | |
| 00049604 | 172 | SNIB | | 0004FDA4 | 187 | SNIB | | 0005A584 | 83 | DSG | | 00070A30 | 390 | USER | |

Figure 10-4   CICS formatted dumps: control block summary.

with the facility. IPCS functions, however, currently map only MVS control blocks. The installation will, therefore, have to create the process of mapping CICS control blocks. As mentioned in the previous chapter, command lists (CLISTs) are available through the IBM User Group SHARE. The CICS project provides a software exchange tape that contains software that members have contributed. There are CLISTs on the tape for most current releases of CICS to process these unformatted dumps within IPCS, and create the symbols and pointers needed.

In addition to online processing of unformatted dumps, there are facilities to produce printed formatting of both SYSMDUMPs and SDUMPs. Starting in CICS 1.7, IBM provides a facility to process these dumps and produce a report with many critical areas formatted. In addition to the usual control blocks mapped out by the formatted dump program, this facility reports the status and contents of the active and suspended DCA and TCA chains. This program, DFHPDX, is far superior to a formatted dump program since it not only gives a visual check of the active tasks at the time of the failure, but takes each task and formats all storage chained off that transaction. This TCA summary is an excep-

tional view of conditions at the time of the failure, and can save hours in the diagnostic process. The facility is so important that an entire chapter is dedicated to making everyone aware of the program and how to utilize the function. The combination of IPCS and DFHPDX give a system programmer very powerful tools to use in problem determination.

### 10.2.1 SYSMDUMP

Prior to CICS 1.7, when IBM provided the facilities to direct output to a system dump dataset, alternative methods needed to be used to request an unformatted dump. Of course, many system programmers never wanted an unformatted dump, since it was merely a large section of address space storage, and meaningless without any tools for formatting. Some people, however, found facilities like IPCS, and wrote command lists (CLISTs) to process these SYSMDUMPs. In some failures, the formatted dumps did not contain adequate information, and critical sections of storage were omitted. SYSMDUMPs allow all portions of a CICS address space to be dumped, therefore available, when diag-

```
PSICICT                        --- CICS SYSTEM DUMP ---                    DATE=07/11/88  TIME=12:40:22  PAGE  424
    ①        ②       ③
 ┌───────┐ ┌───────┐ ┌──────┐
 │ ENTRY │ │ LOAD  │ │ NAME │ VERS'N TIME  DATE  OPTIONS        ENTRY   LOAD    NAME   VERS'N TIME  DATE  OPTIONS
 │ POINT │ │ POINT │ └──────┘                                   POINT   POINT
 └───────┘ └───────┘
 00027BA8  00027AC0  DFHTRP                    40              002A2050 002A2008 PSIPUTIL
 000D3008  000D3008  DVD020                                    002A6020 002A6008 DFHEMF   0170I 17:54 08/28
 000E0008  000E0008  DVDDCT                                    002A7030 002A7008 SECCHECK
 000E1008  000E1008  DVDCMDT                                   002A8008 002A8008 GMM01
 000E5008  000E5008  DVDSGEN                                   002A9050 002A9008 PSIGNUS
 000E6008  000E6008  DVD990C                                   002AC008 002AC008 PSISIGN
 000E7008  000E7008  DVD904C                                   002AD008 002AD008 IS779M1
 000E8008  000E8008  DVD901                                    002AE008 002AE008 SYSBUSY
 000E9008  000E9008  DVD900C                                   002AF140 002AF008 IS779
 000EB008  000EB008  DVD001C                                   002B7030 002B7008 PSIGSFO
 00143008  00143008  M2XTBL01                                  002B8050 002B8008 NA105
 00164008  00164008  M2XTBL00                                  002BF008 002BF008 PSIDEMCI
 00166008  00166008  M2XTBLFX                                  002C0008 002C0008 NACOMLN
 001C2050  001C2008  IS1000L                                   002C1008 002C1008 NA100M1
 001E0050  001E0008  IS546                                     002C2050 002C2008 NA100
 001FE008  001FE008  IN25UEXI                                  002C9050 002C9008 CASEALTR
 00209008  00209008  IN25HOOK                                  002CB008 002CB008 ACFAEUCM
 0020B008  0020B008  IN25PGM2                                  002CC008 002CC008 DFHZATDX
 00219008  00219008  IS546M1                                   002D1810 002CD008 DFHTBS   0170I 16:20 03/24
 0021A050  0021A008  NA202                                     002F2478 002D4008 DFHZCQ   0170I 15:47 03/23
 0021F050  0021F008  IS548                                     002F3030 002F3008 DFHZATD  0170I 19:45 04/09
 00226008  00226008  IN25DB2                                   002F6030 002F6008 ACFAEUCC
 0022F008  0022F008  IS548M1                                   002F7008 002F7008 PSIACFUC
 00230008  00230008  IOMOD                                     002F8050 002F8008 PSICSSN
 00233008  00233008  IN25FLE                                   002FB008 002FB008 DVD142
 00237050  00237008  IS540A                                    002FC008 002FC008 DVD140
 0023C050  0023C008  IS402100                                  00301008 00301008 DVD130
 0024B050  0024B008  IOTAB                                     00304008 00304008 DVD120
 0024F008  0024F008  IS540M2                                   0030D008 0030D008 IGZCPAC
 00250008  00250008  IS540M2                                   003286D0 003286D0 CFTNALPO
 00251008  00251008  IN25UCOM                                  003D78D8 003D7890 CFTNS030
 00252008  00252008  IN25CORE                                  003FB148 003FB130 DFHACP   0170I 13:09 10/10
 0025B008  0025B008  IN25LGET                                  00401710 00401710 DFHEITMT
 00266008  00266008  IN25SGET                                  004033F8 004033D0 DFHEMTD  0170I 11:23 08/28
 00278020  00278008  DFHOCP   0170I 13:06 02/06                00410108 004100E0 DFHEMTP  0170I 11:22 08/28
 00279020  00279008  DFHEMB   0170I 11:16 02/02                00410DA0 00410DA0 DFHNET
 0027A008  0027A008  IN25SER1                                  004114D8 004114C0 DFHPEP   0170I 16:51 08/28
 00284008  00284008  IS549M1                                   00414978 00414960 DFHZNAC  0170I 17:55 06/30
 00285050  00285008  IS549                                     00419080 00419060 DFHZNEP  0170U 16:25 01/11
 00289050  00289008  DSNCEXT2                                  004196B0 004196B0 DVD902
 0028A050  0028A008  DSNCEXT1                                  0041A180 0041A180 DVD910
 0028C008  0028C008  IN25PGMS                                  00425DF8 00425DD0 PSIGSFSR
─00294008  00294008  IS540M1                                   00430020 00430008 DFHSTP   0170I 15:58 07/17
 00295050  00295008  IS540                                     00432008 00432008 DVD920
 0029C008  0029C008  PSIMM1                                    00435008 00435008 DVD932
 0029D050  0029D008  PSIMP1                                    00437008 00437008 DVD911
 002A0008  002A0008  PSIUTIL                                   0043A030 0043A008 IGZCPCC
```

Figure 10-5   CICS formatted dumps: module map.

```
 SDSF SYSLOG 3641.107 PSI1 DATE 11/21/88 LINE  16,428    COLUMNS  51 130
 COMMAND INPUT ===>                                      SCROLL ===> PAGE
 0010 ┌──────────────┐
 0010 │D DUMP,OPTIONS│
      └──────────────┘
 0010 IEE857I 12.09.14 DUMP OPTIONS 140
 0010    SYSABEND- ADD PARMLIB OPTIONS SDATA=(LSQA,TRT,CB,ENQ,DM,IO,ERR,SUM),
 0010                       PDATA=(SA,REGS,LPA,JPA,PSW,SPLS)
 0010    SYSUDUMP- ADD PARMLIB OPTIONS SDATA=(TRT,CB,ENQ,DM,ERR), PDATA=(SA,
 0010                       REGS,LPA,JPA,PSW,SPLS,SUBTASKS)
 0010    SYSMDUMP- ADD PARMLIB OPTIONS (NUC,SQA,LSQA,SWA,TRT,RGN,LPA,CSA,SUM,
 0010                       GRSQ)
 0010    SDUMP- ADD OPTIONS (ALLPSA,NUC,SQA,LSQA,RGN,LPA,TRT,CSA,SWA,SUMDUMP,
 0010                       Q=YES)
 0010 $HASP395 MICRO05   ENDED
 0010 $HASP250 MICRO05   IS PURGED
 0010 $OJ4771
 0010 $HASP000 OK
 0010 $HASP317 TKLSRBK   0004 DATA SETS RELEASED
 0010 $HASP250 TKLSRBK   IS PURGED
 0010 IEA989I SLIP TRAP ID=X33E MATCHED
 0010 M N20E07 BDCSC52 LOGGED OFF FROM TP14B207
 0010 $OJ4853
 0010 +GSF0100 - GSF SUCCESSFULLY INITIALIZED AT 000AB008
 0010 $HASP000 OK
 0010 $HASP317 TRCLCASE 0006 DATA SETS RELEASED
```

Figure 10-6   MVS command to display dump options.

```
 .   .   .   .   .   .   .   .   .   .   .   .   .   .   .   .   .   .   .   .   .
------------------------- DATA SET INFORMATION  -------------------------
COMMAND ===> _


DATA SET NAME: [DFH.SYSMDUMP]


GENERAL DATA:                              CURRENT ALLOCATION:

     Volume serial:        PAK208              Allocated Cylinders     75

     Device type:          3380                Allocated extents:      1

     Organization:         PS

     Record format:        F

     Record length:        4104

     Block size:           4104             CURRENT UTILIZATION:

     1st extent Cylinders: 75                  Used Cylinders:         0

     Secondary Cylinders:  0                   Used extents:           0



     Creation date:        1988/05/11

     Expiration date:      ***NONE***
```

Figure 10-7    Dataset format for SYSMDUMP.

nosing a very difficult problem. SYSMDUMP processing was discussed in Chapter 1, but will be repeated to combine all unformatted dump issues.

Datasets that will ultimately contain SYSMDUMPs must be pre-allocated and defined to the CICS region before output can be requested. SYSMDUMPs should be defined with characteristics similar to SYS1.DUMP datasets. Use the same DCBs for the SYSMDUMP, but calculate the requirement for space. Many CICS address spaces are very large, and the amount of space allocated for the SYS1.DUMP dataset may not be adequate for a region dump. If the amount of space is insufficient to write the CICS address space at the time of a failure, a B37 abend will result. This indicates that the dataset was not large enough to contain the address space, and the dump will not contain all storage from the region failure. A large CICS address space, for example with a region size of nine megabytes, may require a dump dataset as large as 75 cylinders (3380 disk type). Overestimate on my calculations, since an underallocated dump dataset may produce unfortunate results. No one wants to recreate a failure because the dump dataset was too small and failed to contain critical areas of storage. Figure 10-7 illustrates a typical

file allocation for a SYSMDUMP dataset. The space allocation may vary, depending on the size of the CICS region you wish to accommodate.

Once the file has been allocated, it must be identified to CICS via a DD statement in the JCL. The statement will appear as

```
//SYSMDUMP  DD  DSN=CICS.SYSMDUMP,DISP=SHR
```

whatever dataset naming convention is used at the installation. CICS will then be able to allocate this dataset at region initialization, and open it for output when necessary in case of a failure. Realize, however, that a single dataset has been allocated for a single region. If multiple regions wish to use SYSMDUMP processing, a different dataset must be allocated to avoid sharing the files. The files could be technically shared, but one failure would overwrite the contents from the previous failure. Another situation to consider is the possibility of multiple failures within the same region. Consider the scenario of a region failure and the subsequent creation of an unformatted dump into the CICS dump dataset, SYSMDUMP. Normal course of action would be to immediately attempt recovery and

```
                         D D,T
                         IEF196I IEF285I SYS1.DUMP01
                         IEF196I IEF285I VOL SER NOS = PAK208
                         IEE853I 13.26.25 SYS1.DUMP TITLES
                         SYS1.DUMP DATASET AVAILABLE=004 AND FULL=001
                              DUMP01 TITLE=COMPON=IOS,COMPID=SC1C3,ISSUER=IECVPST
                                DUMP TAKEN TIME=20.33.49 DATE=07/21/88
                         NO DUMP DATA AVAILABLE FOR THE FOLLOWING EMPTY SYS1.DUMP DATASETS
                         00,02-04
```

Figure 10-8   OS dump display command and output.

bring the region back up again. If, after recovery, the region initializes and then sustains another failure, the SYSMDUMP dataset would be reused, and the dump from the initial failure would be lost. How can you avoid that? Create a SYSMDUMP dataset as a generation data group (GDG) index, with some appropriate number of entries. Then specify the statement in the startup CICS JCL as

```
//SYSMDUMP  DD  DSN=CICS.SYSMDUMP(+1),
//              DISP=(NEW,CATLG)
```

Every time CICS writes a dump to this dataset, it creates an entirely new generation, retaining the previous copy. Of course, this is going to require more disk space to accommodate the number of SYSMDUMP generations specified. The installation would also have to manually manage the generations, insuring the processing of the correct generation for the correct failure. It does, however, provide an adequate facility to avoid loss of previously created dumps. Installations become very creative when faced with technical challenges.

### 10.2.2   SDUMP

SDUMP processing allows CICS to write to the SYS1.DUMP datasets, using operating system dump facilties to produce the dump. These system dump datasets can be managed very easily, and IBM has several facilities to back up, process, and analyze the output. If the request is SDUMP processing, via the SIT parameter, most CICS system failures are written to one of these datasets. For example, if a CICS region detects a storage violation and the SIT option specifies that recovery should be attempted, the storage violation will be dumped to one of the SYS1.DUMP datasets, and processing continues. If the storage violation is severe and CICS is unable to continue processing, a 501 type abend occurs, and that failure is written to a system dump dataset. Unformatted dumps, es-

pecially in storage violation conditions, provide more information and more storage than formatted dumps. These dumps can be viewed via IPCS for problem determination. As installations move toward MVS/ESA, SDUMPs will need to be analyzed with IPCS as the standard in CICS system problem determination.

SDUMPs can be analyzed with the IBM-supplied program DFHPDX, using the same procedure as previously described. This involves running a batch job to format requested control blocks, and is invoked via AMDPRDMP. Remember, this will change with MVS/ESA since AMDPRDMP is no longer supported. The facility is fully described in a later chapter dedicated to the process.

SDUMPs are pre-allocated datasets to the CICS region, but are not identified to CICS via a statement within the startup JCL. Since operating system components are invoked to write storage to these dump datasets, they need only be identified to OS. These files must be allocated and defined to the operating system via system parameters in SYS1.PARMLIB.

Note that the record length in a SYS1.DUMPxx dataset would be typical of an MVS/XA 2.2 environment. In MVS/ESA, dump processing has been enhanced and requires a larger block size. Consult with the operating system release documentation, or other MVS system programming staff, to determine the specifications for your specific environment.

Typically, since the operating system uses these dump datasets for component failures, several have probably been allocated and made available to OS. What and how many currently exist? The OS DISPLAY command will identify the existing data datasets with the following syntax:

```
DISPLAY DUMP,TITLE
```

or

```
D D,T
```

```
D D,T
IEF196I IEF285I SYS1.DUMP00
IEF196I IEF285I VOL SER NOS = PAK208
IEF196I IEF285I SYS1.DUMP01
IEF196I IEF285I VOL SER NOS = PAK208
IEE853I 13.30.21 SYS1.DUMP TITLES
SYS1.DUMP DATA SETS AVAILABLE=003 AND FULL=002
      DUMP00 TITLE=CICS DUMP - ID = CICSPROD - REASON = CEMT
         DUMP TAKEN TIME=13.26.41 DATE=07/25/88
      DUMP01 TITLE=COMPON=IOS,COMPID=SC1C3,ISSUER=IECVPST
         DUMP TAKEN TIME=20.33.49 DATE=07/21/88
NO DUMP DATA AVAILABLE FOR THE FOLLOWING EMPTY SYS1.DUMP DATASETS
02-04
```

Figure 10-9   Dump display command after CICS dump creation.

Figure 10-8 shows the operating system command entered and the results as they would appear on the console. Note that the display returns the number of dump datasets used and full, with a title of the dump contents. If the display returns results that indicate that all dump datasets are full and none are available, then a failure will produce no dump output. A message would be displayed indicating all dump datasets are full, and no dump will be produced. If using SDUMPs, put some procedure in place to insure at least one dump dataset is always empty in case its needed. Existing dumps can be copied, for example to tape, and then that dump dataset can be cleared for reuse. Investigate any operational procedures that may exist in your installation to insure available dump datasets.

Assume, then, that at least one dump dataset is available for CICS in case of a failure. If an SDUMP is produced, which dataset was used? Figure 10-9 represents another DISPLAY command after a CICS failure has occurred. In this example, the dump was produced as a result of a CEMT SNAP request. Notice that the operating system used the next available dump dataset, SYS1.DUMP00. This dump was available in Figure 10-8; now it contains the output from the CEMT request. Note also, that the operating system attempts to document the failure. The display identifies the CICS region (1) that produced the dump, and a short title or description of the cause. If there are multiple CICS address spaces, this will be important information to identify the region that produced the dump.

Since it is now known that SYS1.DUMP00 contains the storage at the time of the failure, use the appropriate tool to diagnose the problem. If DFHPDX is used to locate task chains or control blocks, this dataset will be the DD (data definition) name in the job to process. If IPCS is used, the SETDEF command will identify this dataset as the dump to analyze. As stated earlier, these SDUMP datasets can be cleared by operations personnel at any time. If this dump contains critical information, and the problem may be worked on for an extended period of time, copy this dump to a safe place. The COPYDUMP command of IPCS works perfectly to assist in saving your dump into an alternate location, either tape or disk. Reference IPCS command documentation to locate the exact syntax and options of this feature.

In summary, each installation will choose which dump format is the most productive. Perhaps attempting to use all three, formatted dumps, SYSMDUMP, and SDUMP — would be a good idea to start with. After getting familiar with the process, and content of each one, the most appropriate type can be selected.

# 11

# System Programming Issues

System programmers have numerous responsibilities in an installation. Technical personnel are usually responsible for CICS product support, maintenance, availability, reliability, and performance of the major operating system components. Of course, they also support the applications that provide all online business for their installation. The system programmer is the end of the line for problem determination. Any failures that cannot be resolved by applications support or operations end up in technical support. For this reason, the system programmer must have all the tools, knowledge, and technique at their fingertips to react to any situation. Companies can, and do, lose hundreds or thousands of dollars an hour when the online systems are not available.

Technical support staff must insure the availability and reliability of operating system components in every way possible. IBM ships the base product code, other vendors provide packaged software, and application programmers create new systems. The system programmer must be able to identify and resolve problems that come from many sources. In many cases, the final solution is out of their control. How can you support a dynamically changing CICS environment? In many installations, a change control or project management system can localize the impact of changes within the installation. There are many other items that can assist with the control of a changing environment and minimize outages.

Some external sources can be managed, such as the changes to the CICS product itself. Maintenance of CICS is an entire topic that will be discussed later. Of course, if IBM is making changes to the product, it will be difficult to control those changes. A sound maintenance philosophy is always

the best defense. Other external sources should be controlled, such as programming standards and problem determination tools and techniques. Some of these issues will be covered under the category of "Self-Inflicted Problems." Chapter 3 covered, in great detail, the issues of macro vs. command-level programming. Conversion of macro programs to command will contribute substantially to problem avoidance.

Many installations continue to customize CICS functions. Fortunately, or unfortunately, CICS has historically been shipped with most of its functions still available in source code format. Installations, and in particular, system programmers, have taken advantage of this. Since the source exists for a management module, the system programmer can add code, or modify the provided source, and assemble the revision into executable modules. IBM has already announced that CICS will gradually become OCO, object code only. By removing the source from customers, IBM can improve the integrity of the product. This will also remove the customer's ability to modify any CICS functions.

Other issues that may become significant to technical support are multiregion operation (MRO) and intersystem communication (ISC). Many system programmers feel that having one or two CICS regions poses enough support problems. If an installation needs to, or decides to implement multiple CICS systems that communicate with each other, totally unique issues arise. Those issues will be covered in the the Intersystem Communication section.

Of course, no system programming issues are complete without the subject of data areas. Many system programmers hold CICS internals close to their hearts. Many hard-core system programmers feel that if they are not chasing control blocks in a dump, or in the live system, they are not in touch with the product. Well, IBM may change all of that with OCO. When the source is no longer available, and IBM ceases to publish CICS Data Areas, chains will be difficult to chase. The following section will discuss several issues relating to data areas, and will identify some new items in CICS 1.7 that can assist in analyzing certain problems.

## 11.1   SELF-INFLICTED PROBLEMS

Most never like to admit that perhaps some of the problems and failures experienced may, indeed, have been self-inflicted. The CICS environment is so complex that some failures are difficult to diagnose, and changes to one component may surface in another area. There is no easy way to avoid this, other than never making changes to CICS, which, as we know, is impossible. Some proper methodologies and planning may be the best defense against self-inflicted problems. As previously mentioned, your installation should put a change control or project management system into place. This would provide awareness of new programs and systems that were implemented. Other techniques can also be used for CICS facilities that tend to affect availability of the system.

### 11.1.1   Program List Table (PLT) Processing

The PLT provides a facility to execute programs at CICS initialization and shutdown. The initialization programs are executed while CICS is initializing, before the terminal control program receives control. In other words, they are executed before the message:

```
DFH1500:   CONTROL IS BEING GIVEN TO CICS
```

In CICS 2.1, PLT programs run under the initialization task and may not have access to the TWA (transaction work area) during execution. Many installations use PLT programs to reestablish an environment for online applications requiring application-dependent data.

A danger in PLT programs exists, however, since CICS assumes that these programs are important to the initialization of the system. Failures that occur during execution of PLT programs cause CICS to abort initialization. This may be the desired result, but severely impacts availability. Does the installation really want to keep the CICS region from initializing because one application program

abends? Another danger in PLT processing is the management of these programs. Typically, installations place user-written programs in the PLT. A system programmer may not be aware of a new version of these programs into CICS. If suddenly one morning, CICS failed during initialization, would the system programmer know that a new copy of a PLT program went in the night before?

While PLT processing provides a valuable opportunity to set up procedures during initialization, it must be managed carefully. A CICS system failure described in Chapter 12 was caused by a PLT program that abended. This may provide some techniques to use to diagnose these failures and resolve the problem.

### 11.1.2   Recursive Abends

Another application-related situation that can cause an entire system failure is a recursive abend. When CICS detects a problem, it attempts to pass control to an abend routine and then produce a transaction dump with all appropriate control blocks for that task. Previous chapters have covered several transaction abends and the components within those dumps. Some applications prefer to take control of the situation and handle the failure with alternative processing. Chapter Three discussed the HANDLE CONDITION processing that is available. The application can also HANDLE ABEND and attempt to handle the abend within the program. This may or may not be desirable, since the application assumes responsibility to handle the abend correctly.

The dangerous condition arises when an application attempts to handle the abend, and then experiences a failure itself during execution of the abend-handling routine. If any processing is attempted during the routine that is handling the abend, an exposure exists. During that processing, for example, the program may experience a program or data check, an ASRA. CICS then detects that an abend occurred during processing of an abend. A message is displayed:

```
DFH0405  ABEND XXXX HAS BEEN ISSUED WHILE PRO-
CESSING ABEND XXXX  FOR THE SAME TASK, TRANSAC-
TION XXXX
```

CICS then is unable to recover from the abnormal condition, and the entire CICS system comes crashing down. A normal transaction failure which would have produced a transaction dump has now caused the entire CICS region to fail. Instead of one user experiencing an application abend, all processing within the CICS region is terminated and all users experience the outage.

Although applications may need to handle abend conditions, use the facility wisely and cautiously. Such error processing routines must be carefully designed and thoroughly tested with the most extensive range of error conditions.

### 11.1.3 Storage Corruption

Probably the most frustrating failure to diagnose is when storage has been corrupted and a storage violation occurs. Of course, this is self-inflicted, but by whom? The installation may have requested storage recovery via the SIT, and avoided an entire outage. If not, or if the corruption was severe enough to be unrecoverable, a system dump is produced. One example of a storage violation is covered in Chapter 13, but every one is different. The failure shows the blocks of storage that were overwritten, but that is merely the victim, not the criminal. Sometimes the program will corrupt its own storage. The challenge is finding the program that caused the overlay.

Corruptions of storage are probably the most difficult problems to diagnose, so most of that chapter will be spent on a storage violation failure. Of course, prevention is always the best protection. Proper coding techniques, testing, and standards will always be the best defense against storage corruption.

## 11.2 OBJECT CODE ONLY (OCO)

There has been a great deal of discussion recently concerning IBM's direction toward object code only (OCO) support. In a few years the discussion will be a moot point, since most of CICS will be distributed and supported this way. In the meantime, however, what can installations do to position themselves, and how will OCO affect support of the product?

### 11.2.1 OCO Issues

Most issues dealing with OCO fall within two categories:

1. Customization — use of source to provide enhanced function
2. Problem determination — access to data areas to diagnose problems

**Customization.** The first issues deal with installations that have used the source code of the product

to customize particular modules and provide enhanced function. For a multitude of reasons, installations promise, or are pressured into providing, facilities within their online systems that the base product does not contain. Perhaps there are genuine business needs to provide these facilities. In any case, system programmers take the source as shipped from IBM and insert new code, or modify existing instructions, to customize the functions. These enhanced functions may be very justifiable. However, when the source is no longer available, this process may become impossible. Installations are faced with the grim reality of loss of this customized function. The only alternative is to submit requirements to IBM that would provide the same function in the base product. Since the statement of direction is clear, if the business indeed requires facilities that are now being provided with source code changes, installations should submit their requirements to IBM.

**Problem Determination.** Other issues that will arise with OCO deal with problem determination techniques and tools. Many system programmers now use the CICS Data Areas to inspect dumps and attempt to diagnose failures. The specification of data areas within the product are the only tools, other than the source, that allow the inspection of control blocks and validation of fields within the control blocks. If both source and mapped control blocks are removed from support, unformatted dumps will be impossible to use for problem determination. Formatted dumps only display the control block; understanding the data contained within the control block requires the map.

### 11.2.2 IBM Tools, PRDMP and IPCS

IBM has begun to respond by providing the PRDMP facility to format the SDUMPS, as discussed in Chapter 14. But, as noted, this is primarily a batch processing facility, and formats out only the provided data areas. If additional contents of the system dump are required, you must use IPCS to access these portions of storage. Most customers have written their own CLISTs to format these areas of storage, and chase the chains. If IBM does not provide an online formatting facility for IPCS and removes the documentation of these data areas, problem determination will become much more difficult.

IPCS has been declared IBM's direction in all system dump processing, and will no doubt be enhanced to assist in system-level debugging.

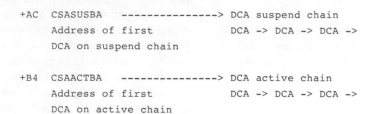

```
        CSA

  +AC   CSASUSBA    ---------------> DCA suspend chain
        Address of first            DCA -> DCA -> DCA ->
        DCA on suspend chain


  +B4   CSAACTBA    ---------------> DCA active chain
        Address of first            DCA -> DCA -> DCA ->
        DCA on active chain
```

Figure 11-1    CSA pointers to DCA chains.

## 11.3    CRITICAL CICS CONTROL BLOCKS

When faced with a failure, systems programmers have no alternative but to pore through the dump and try to locate the failing component. If it is a straightforward failure, such as a program check, this may not be extremely difficult. In most cases, however, especially in wait and loop conditions, the dump is merely a huge block of storage with no overt abend. The system programmer must search through various portions of the dump and attempt to locate something that looks suspicious. It would be wonderful to take these failures, run some program against them, and have a report produced with a pointer "**THE PROBLEM IS HERE.**" Unfortunately, every problem is different and must be analyzed uniquely. Many system programmers develop a technique, however. They use a methodology to follow common steps for similar failures, locating certain control blocks and checking values. Many times these critical data areas contain values that don't seem right, or point to addresses that are obviously invalid. Everyone approaches debugging differently, but perhaps some of the following techniques may provide additional information.

### 11.3.1    Finding Your Way Through Data Areas

The publication CICS Data Areas contains documentation on all CICS system areas for that specific release. Be sure to use the manual that corresponds to the correct release. This manual is a licensed publication, therefore is only available if the installation has a license for that release. This manual may eventually cease to be available. As the product goes OCO, data areas most likely will not be published.

The control blocks are in alphabetic sequence within the manual, and the beginning of every area contains an alphabetic listing of fields with corresponding offsets within the control block. If the name of the field is known, this reference will provide an index to locate it directly. Which control blocks are the most important for debugging? Of course, the one to locate first is the Common System Area, the CSA, since it points to practically everything else. It will not be possible to cover CICS internals in great depth, but the majority will be highlighted to analyze a CICS failure.

### 11.3.2    CSA — The Pointer to Everything Else

How do you find the CSA? If the output is a formatted dump, it will already be identified in the heading. If the request was an unformatted dump, there are several techniques to locate the CSA. Of course, the simplest would be to use the PRDMP facility against the unformatted dump. The first control block formatted by that facility is the CSA. Also, in the existing CICS region that produced the dump, the CSA is always built in the same place during initialization. Until changes are made to the region that affects the creation of system areas, the address remains the same. In the CICS Problem Determination Guide, Chapter 2.4 Control Block Linkages, there are additional techniques that can be used.

Once the CSA is found, pointers are available that contain addresses to the next major control blocks, the active and suspend chains. At offset +0B4 in the CSA is the pointer to the active Dispatch Control Area (DCA). Figure 11-1 illustrates the relationship of the CSA to both the active and suspend DCA chains. The DCA is built when the task is first attached by CICS, and contains a record of the dispatching priority and current status of the task. When the task is ready to be dispatched for the first time, another control block, the Task Control Area (TCA) is built. The TCA becomes the anchor for all work performed on behalf of this task. Figure 11-2 illustrates the relationship of the DCA and the TCA that is chained from it. Most transaction dumps map out the TCA and all related storage, since the dump was created on behalf of one task. CICS system dumps contain all TCAs in existence at the time of the failure. An active CICS

```
DCA   Dispatch Control Area


                                        +0  TCA system area

+14   DCATCAA       --------------- +190 TCA user area
      Address of TCA user area


NOTE: The pointer to the TCA is the address of the user
area portion of the control block. The TCA actually begins
190 bytes (hexidecimal) prior to this address, with the TCA
system area (CICS 1.7 and 2.1).
```

Figure 11-2   DCA pointer to TCA user area.

region can contain dozens of TCAs. For this reason, locating all TCAs in an unformatted dump is not a small task. DFHPDX is explained in great detail in Chapter 14, and is an excellent tool to locate some of these data areas.

After locating the TCA chain within the dump, debugging may take different directions depending on the failure. Chapter 12 will cover several different failures. It may be necessary to identify specific values of fields within the CSA and to analyze specific TCAs, based on their status. Initial steps, however, should usually consist of

1. Location of the CSA, and several key fields within
2. Location of the active and suspend DCA chains
3. Location of the active and suspend TCA chains

From here on, the specific failure, wait, or loop condition determines the next direction of problem solving. The CICS system failures that are covered in subsequent chapters describe several different techniques to consider.

## 11.4   AUTOINSTALL ISSUES

In CICS 1.7, IBM provided a new facility to dynamically allow terminals into a CICS region without any explicit definition in a TCT. This process is called autoinstall, and revolutionized the support of

VTAM terminals in CICS. Chapter 6 briefly covered autoinstall, highlighting some application considerations that autoinstall produced. This facility has even more implications to system programmers, especially since it finally freed them from TCT assemblies every time a new device needed to be defined to a region.

Autoinstall was very confusing at first to many users, especially since the process seemed so magical, and was difficult to trace. Some system programmers spent hours diagnosing autoinstall failures, some made new friends in Raleigh because they were on the phone for long conversations with Level 2. The facility has now been demystified, and much more thoroughly documented. An excellent publication, GG66-0288 CICS Autoinstall is available, and is highly recommended to anyone attempting to use the facility. Several pieces of the autoinstall puzzle are essential, not only for successful implementation, but for diagnosing problems.

### 11.4.1   DFHZATDX

IBM provides a "user replaceable module," DFHZATDX, with the product that autoinstalls all devices. This routine can be used as supplied by IBM, and many installations are able to do just that. If the installation wishes to enhance or customize the autoinstall process, it can modify this program to add functions. This program uses the autoinstall models to build the appropriate terminal

```
09/24/88 01611239 INSTALL TERMINAL(C300);

DFH5935I INSTALL FOR TEMINAL: C300, NETNAME: TRM1C300, MODEL_NAME:
DFHLU2  , SUCCESSFUL
```

Figure 11-3   Autoinstall messages.

```
DFH5987I BEST FAILURE FOR NETNAME: LOC72A  . WAS MODEL NAME: MAI2  ①
② CINIT BIND:  01020271 40200000 00000000 00000000  00000000 00000000 000008C1 C4D4F1C3
MODEL BIND:  ③ C9C3E2
                010303B1 B0308000 00000000 00028000  00000018 5018507F
④ MISMATCH BITS: 000101C0 F0108000 00000000 0002
DFH2411I ↑↑↑↑ CSNE  9:15:46 LOC72A ATTEMPTED INVALID LOGON
DFH2410I CD21 CSNE  9:15:52 NODE UNRECOVERABLE. VTAM LOSTERM ERROR CODE 14
TCTTE   CD21,   , 9:15:52,C3C4F2F1 91F20007 00137568 00000000 00000000 00000000 0010E4B4 88000000
                00000000 0CD1D7E6 FFFFFF00 00000910 00047D14 C7D4D4F0 F1404040 00000000
                00000000 00008080 07801850 07801850 00000000 01B30000 00000000 00180DF4
                00000000 08000000 00000001 001046E4 00000000 00000000 000E70A4 00000000
```

Figure 11-4    Autoinstall messages after failure to install.

control blocks. There are different models for each distinct type of terminal, and this program attempts to find a best-fit model. For many reasons, this routine may not be successful in the creation of the terminal. Figure 11-3 shows messages that appear in the log if the autoinstall process was successful. The first line of the message indicates the date and time stamp of the request, and the terminal identifier used (1). The second line contains the VTAM net name that was provided by the network for the autoinstall request (2) and the autoinstall model name that was used to complete the process (3).

### 11.4.2  Autoinstall Messages

If the process was not successful, a different message will appear. The message was not available when autoinstall first shipped, which made debugging failures extremely frustrating. Fortunately, IBM recognized that assistance was needed to analyze autoinstall failures, and created the following message. Figure 11-4 shows the content of an autoinstall failure message. The module DFHZATDX attempts to find an appropriate model, the best fit, and identifies the one that was selected (1). In this example, MAI2 was used. As explained in the CICS Messages and Codes manual, the failure was caused by the mismatch between the terminal definition sent by VTAM and the terminal definition in CICS. The entry from VTAM is indicated by the CINIT BIND (2), and contains the hexadecimal representation of the bind image. The entry from CICS is indicated by the MODEL BIND (3), and contains the hexadecimal representation of the autoinstall model. The message then provides an entry of MISMATCH BITS (4), a line of data produced during the analysis of these two bind images. An entry of anything other than "0" in this line indicates a mismatch in that position between the VTAM entry and the CICS entry. In other words, the message has analyzed the failure, and points to the entries in the two bind images that are incompatible.

Prior to this message, analysis was much more difficult. VTAM traces had to be executed to capture the bind image sent from VTAM. The Restart Dataset (RSD) had to be dumped to locate the entry for the autoinstall model and the bind image that was created. Of course, this can still be done, but IBM has provided a very helpful facility to show all the relevant information within this message.

What should be done when the entries are incompatible? One bind image or the other can be changed to produce a match. If the model is incorrect, it can be changed by modifying the TYPETERM entry corresponding to the autoinstall terminal definition. However, this TYPETERM may be valid for other terminals, and is merely being selected incorrectly. In that case, modifications can be made to the selection program, DFHZATDX, to choose a different model for these devices. VTAM definitions can be investigated. These bind images are created from the logmode table in VTAM. Assistance from the VTAM system programmer may be required to identify the logmode entry, and decide whether this definition needs to be modified.

The above message is fully documented in SC33-0514, CICS Messages and Codes for CICS/MVS 2.1. Since this message was not produced when CICS 1.7 first shipped, it does not appear in the 1.7 manuals. It was provided via the service process, PTF PL19502, and documented in the cover letter. Since CICS did not update their manuals with TNLs (technical newletters) until recently, the 1.7 publications do not document this message. Fortunately, CICS/MVS 2.1 manuals are now updated when necessary, and the TNLs can be inserted into the manuals to keep them current. A long overdue requirement has finally been accommodated.

## 11.5  INTERSYSTEM COMMUNICATION ISSUES

Many installations are now finding the need to support many CICS systems. If these systems need to share resources, or communicate with each other, they use CICS facilities called MRO, Multiregion

Operation or ISC, Intersystem Communication. The decision to use either of these facilities may be based on whether the CICS systems are local (exist in the same CPU) or remote (exist in multiple CPUs). Many new concerns arise in multisystem failures, and debugging techniques change to accommodate them.

### 11.5.1  Function Shipping vs. Transaction Routing

Problem determination techniques differ based on the CICS facilities employed for inter/intra systems communication. In some configurations, regions are separated based on the resources that exist within them. In this situation, you may find one or more Terminal Owning Regions (TORs), Application Owning Regions (AORs) and File Owning Regions (FORs). These regions can have the ability to perform either function shipping or transaction routing. In function shipping, the regions share data. Function shipping provides the ability of one application program to access resources (such as data or temporary storage queues) that are owned by another CICS system. With transaction routing, regions share terminals. In this configuration, a terminal owned by one CICS system can execute a transaction in another CICS system. The transaction is routed to another region, where it executes and then returns to the originating region. Also, a combination of both function shipping and transaction routing is possible.

As you can see, this can pose new situations for problem determination. Terminals may not be defined to the region that actually executes the program. Files may be in a different region than the application. Applications may run in an entirely different processor than the user is physically connected to. Following are some operational and debugging techniques that can be used.

### 11.5.2  MRO/ISC Operation issues

Operation within a single CICS system is straightforward. All resources are self-contained. With MRO or ISC, this may not be the case. A user may log into a TOR, where terminals are owned, and inquire on resources in an AOR or FOR. A CICS-supplied facility is provided to allow you to direct requests to other CICS systems. The CRTE transaction is used for operator-directed requests. Via this facility, transactions can be routed into the CICS system of choice. Inquiries can be made into file states or terminal status in another region via the CEMT command in the region that contains the resource.

Users may also need to use the CEDF facility in the AOR that contains the application. The CRTE transaction can allow a programmer to perform online debugging in another CICS region. After establishing a session in the TOR, the CRTE facility can route the CEDF transaction into the AOR for diagnosis. Use of two-terminal mode in EDF is not supported, however, when both terminals are not connected to the same system.

Another change in this environment is the routing of system messages. Of course, each CICS system contains the resources for various classes of CICS messages. To investigate some problems, then, requires investigation into each system for activity within that system. Realize also that the message does not contain a unique CICS system identifier. Identification must be made not only of the message, but which CICS system produced the message. It is possible to use a common device, such as a printer, to route messages from several CICS systems. The installation must write a program, however, to process the messages and can insert a unique system identifier (such as the VTAM APPLID) into the text.

### 11.5.3  Abend Issues

Failures in an MRO or ISC environment also raise additional issues. The severity of the failure and recovery requirements of the installation must be considered during problem determination. Three categories of failures may be experienced:

1.  Task or transaction failure
2.  CICS system failure
3.  Session failure

In task failure, the application fails and produces a transaction dump within the CICS system where it executed. Normal dump processing can be done and the application analyzed for failure. Other CICS systems that are connected are notified of the failure, and the "partner" mirror transaction is abended. These other systems may experience abends such as ATNI (ISC) or AZI6 (MRO). If the mirror transaction abends first, notification is passed to the application, and the user application is abended. Debugging is complicated by these connections and the failure of them.

In a CICS system failure, when the region abends, the other systems are notified. Any applications that are executing that have sessions with the failing system are abended. Again, the ATNI and AZI6 abend codes are used to identify the failure as a result of intersystem communication. The abend codes of AZ** category are used for other intersystem communication problems that are not specifically caused from remote applications or system failure.

If the session fails and communication between the regions is broken, all local and remote applications using the session are abended. Again, the application has not caused the failure, but experiences the abend because the CICS systems are unable to communicate and are therefore unable to pass resources and requests.

This section has barely touched on the additional situations that may be experienced during intersystem communication. An in-depth discussion would be extensive. Be aware, however, of the issues that are raised in CICS systems that communicate with each other, and changes to your problem determination techniques. An entire manual is dedicated to this facility, the CICS Intercommunication Guide.

## 11.6    CICS SERVICE STRATEGIES

Most problems in the product after general availability are identified by IBM via contact with customers. Of course, all of us would like the product to ship error-free and never need to have maintenance applied. This is somewhat idealistic, and practically impossible. How many of our own programs (which we thoroughly test) are placed into use, and then experience problems later? No one can possibly test all conditions that could be experienced. In the case of CICS, testing of a specific function in one or more CICS regions could be performed. Would that be sufficient? What if the application ran in a MRO or ISC environment? What if the installation was running DB/2 or DL/1? Is the application running on an intelligent workstation, a VTAM terminal, or an asynchronous dial-up? CICS is such a dynamic system, capable of so many combinations of environments, it is unrealistic to expect the product ever to be error-free.

The service process, to many people, is an intimidating and confusing situation. In fact, the process is very straightforward when understood. Since some problems become product-related, we will define the service process, and how you can make it work for you. Believe me, the people on the other end of the phones are human beings, and honestly interested in solving your problem, too.

### 11.6.1    Terminology

The most intimidating part of the service process is understanding the terminology. Perhaps someday IBM will publish a document that explains all of this, but in the meantime, an understanding of some basics in CICS service will be covered.

**Level 1.** When a customer initially encounters a problem with CICS that he believes is related to the IBM code, a toll-free number is called and answered by a friendly person asking lots of questions. This initial contact records the account number, name, and the IBM component believed to be failing. If the customer responds "CICS," the call will be placed into a queue of people trained to respond to first-level CICS problems. Their primary responsibility is to translate the analysis of the problem into a search strategy, and search the IBM database of CICS problems with these same symptoms. Of course, the information provided to these people is critical to their ability to find a comparable failure. Be sure to give specific abend codes, CICS messages, and any detailed information. The amount of time it takes to resolve the problem may, and probably will, be a product of the quality of information recorded here.

There is also a facility that a customer can purchase from IBM that allows direct connection to the IBM database. Customers can then perform many of the searches themselves to find similar problems. This product contains the ability to order the maintenance and electronically receive the PTF. This could offer substantial time savings if the problem is critical and needs to be resolved immediately. IBM's Information Network has many facilities to allow the customer greater freedom in the service process.

If the problem matches the symptoms of another, perhaps one that has already been resolved, the customer can then apply specific maintenance to CICS. This maintenance may already be at the installation, in the form of a PUT tape, or may need to be shipped by IBM. It is hoped that the application of this fix will resolve the problem.

If the problem appears to be unique, therefore, not in the database of known CICS problems, Level 1 will 'queue' it to the next level of support. They may request that the customer perform some additional diagnostics, such as traces, so this information will be available when the next representative calls.

**Level 2.** These people work entirely in call-back mode. The Level 2 staff are currently located in Raleigh, N.C., for USA CICS support and are more highly trained technicians specializing in CICS problems. If Level 2 personnel call back, they are prepared to dive into the dump or whatever is necessary to resolve the problem. The customer should have all requested documentation available. Level 2 staff has access to the most detailed CICS internals to determine where the failure may be coming from. Realize, however, that a large percentage of the problems that CICS Level 2 analyzes can be traced back to an application, or an installation-inflicted failure. If these people determine that it may, indeed, be a failure in CICS code, they may request that documentation be shipped to them for further analysis. They may also recommend specific PTFs that correspond to the problem.

**Level 3.** Customers may never meet anyone from Level 3, especially since they are not even in the United States. These people are also called the change team, and are responsible for accepting the problems identified by Level 2 and actually implementing the fixes to the product. They produce the APARs to the CICS code to resolve failures identified after the product has shipped. Level 3 folks live in Eastleigh, England, close to the development folks in Hursley. (Whether they're in different places on purpose or by accident is not known.) They respond to the top-priority problems experienced by customers running the product.

**PTF.** The process of service is accomplished by an IBM product, SMP/E, a system maintenance product. Via SMP/E, you apply PTFs, program temporary fixes. These PTFs, it is hoped, will resolve the failure experienced in CICS. Since all IBM products are going to be OCO, customers cannot make changes to the source code and reassemble. PTFs allow the product to be maintained with only object code.

**APAR.** When a failure has been identified, the CICS change team constructs appropriate modifications to fix it. Before it is shipped out, the change must be tested with normal maintenance. During this testing, and before the change has been totally packaged for a PTF, it is still in APAR form. This maintenance can be applied, but it is merely in an early format within the service process.

**PUT.** The program update tape is shipped to all installations, and contains all maintenance for the installation's product profile. In other words, an installation receives a PUT from IBM on a regular basis, and would have PTFs for all products that are currently installed. Installations then apply these PTFs to keep the product current and avoid potential problems that have already been identified by other customers. There may be various schedules for putting on this maintenance, but IBM has a recommended PUT level for CICS. Check with service to find out what the recommended level is at any time.

**PUT Override.** This process was created by service to allow the installation to apply the most current maintenance available. Some maintenance may be held for some reason, such as actions that need to be taken, or documentation. There are informational entries in the service process that can more completely explain PUT override. The recommendation by IBM is to use PUT override to supplement your normal PUT processing. This will give you additional PTFs and APARs that will allow the maximum amount of maintenance to apply. This information is available in Information APARs in the RETAIN system.

**CBPDO and CBIPO.** The custom-built offerings allow customers to package their service, or installation, into one process. These services are designed to assist with product installation, and perhaps bypass the maintenance process altogether. Some installations order a new CBIPO on a scheduled basis and reinstall the product rather than applying service with PUT. Service techniques should be designed to give the installation the most stable and available system possible.

If customers have any questions or problems with the service process, they should notify the IBM account team. They are the contacts with any IBM product group and can assist in the process.

# Potential System Abends

In the previous chapter, we discussed many issues dealing with system support. Of course, system programmers spend a great deal of time attempting to avoid outages, and using whatever tools are available to maintain maximum availability. Too often, however, failures occur that impact the entire CICS region. These problems tend to be very highly visible to the organization. If a particular application has problems, it may impact one group of users or another. If an entire CICS system fails, every terminal connected to that system is affected, and all users notice. System programmers are usually torn from whatever they were doing and thrown into this crisis, since installations have a great deal to lose from down time. The worst time to develop debugging techniques is during a crisis. Even though many failures are different, a good, solid approach to problem determination is always the best course of action.

This chapter will cover several system failures, identify the most important items for these failures, and try to determine the causes. After analyzing several failures and the dumps produced, you will develop techniques that are common to most system problems. The first category of system problems covered are CICS wait or loop conditions. These situations do not always cause CICS to fail, but may produce an unusable system and force the system programmer to bring the region down. Another common system problem occurs during initialization; one of these failures will be analyzed for possible avoidance. Storage violations are probably the most dreaded CICS failures, so an entire chapter has been dedicated to them. These are only a small group of situations that you may experience in CICS, but understanding how to debug them will help in diagnosing other types.

## 12.1   CICS WAIT OR LOOP CONDITION

Whether CICS is in a wait or a loop, the results are usually the same. Transactions do not get dispatched, users start calling and saying their terminals are locked, everything grinds to a halt. One big difference between the two conditions is that a loop will probably also produce a call from operations. When CICS has a high dispatching priority in the system, which it should have, the loop will cause CICS to consume a large portion of the CPU. Of course, when it does, all other users and batch jobs are affected. If unable to stop the loop, you may have to cancel CICS to free up the resources.

### 12.1.1   Isolating the Condition

After the realization that CICS is having a problem, how can you isolate the problem as a wait or loop, and attempt recovery without an outage? One problem will be the inability to dispatch new tasks. If CICS can't dispatch new work, it will be impossible to execute a CEMT command to inquire about currently executing tasks. If your installation has a real-time monitor installed at the site, it may display all tasks and allow purging of the offending transaction. Products such as CICSPARS' and other non-IBM products can be very valuable in these situations. If the looping task can be purged, CICS may be able to recover and continue processing normally.

A wait condition is more difficult, since CICS may be waiting for a resource that cannot be provided. It may not be a single transaction; in fact, all transactions may be waiting for CICS to resume. These situations are usually not recoverable and

```
          ABEND CODE:  None, dump produced manually

          PROBABLE CAUSE:  Unknown, could be IBM code problem

          IMPORTANT DUMP ITEMS:    PRDMP - TASK SUMMARY
                                   PRDMP - USER TCA CONTENTS
                                   PRDMP - PROGRAM CHECK ABEND TRACE TABLE
                                   IPCS  - CSA EXECUTION STATUS CONTENTS
                                   IPCS  - ECAADDR CONTENTS
```

Figure 12-1    Significant items in a CICS wait state.

can only be aborted. In the process of recycling CICS, produce a dump of the region. This can be done either as a parameter of the OS CANCEL command, such as

```
CANCEL CICSPROD,DUMP
```

or with the OS DUMP command of the address space:

```
DUMP COMM=(text)
```

then

```
Rxx,JOBNAME=CICSPROD,...options,END
```

where xx is the reply identification returned by OS from the DUMP command. Reference MVS/XA System Commands for a full list of the options available in this facility. Once a dump of the address space is available, both PRDMP and IPCS can assist to analyze the conditions at the time of the wait or loop.

If the CICS dispatcher is unable to dispatch a task, it is usually caused by a wait condition that has not been satisfied. Many different types of waits can occur. Each one will be diagnosed differently, since it would be waiting for a different resource. For example, temporary storage waits could be caused by the lack of strings, buffers, I/O completion, or a number of other reasons. The storage block built for temporary storage management is DFHTSA. ECBs (event control blocks) are built and referenced here for temporary storage waits. If, then, a task is waiting for temporary storage strings, a wait is issued, and the address at DFHTSACA points to the ECB. A different field would be used in the DFHTSA control block for various temporary storage waits.

If a task is waiting for exclusive control of a VSAM file, the VSWA contains the address of the task that currently holds Dump control over the file. The chain VSWAOWND contains a list of all VSWAs waiting for control to be released. In VSAM file waits, therefore, the VSWA becomes the critical control block to investigate. The second example contains a deadlock caused by a VSAM exclusive control conflict and identifies the VSWA contents relevant to these wait conditions.

### 12.1.2    CICS Wait Condition — Example

CICS wait conditions can be caused by a number of different situations, but the initial approach to them can be similar. Figure 12-1 is a summary of the typical dump items relevant to a CICS wait. Of course, depending on the type of wait condition, other control block contents may need to be examined.

### 12.1.3    PRDMP — Task Summary

If there is no CICS monitor to identify the executing tasks at the time of the problem, the task summary in PRDMP will be the next best thing. Of course, this is after the fact, and the region probably had to be taken down, but at least the dump can be used to analyze the conditions. Figure 12-2 contains the task summary from the CICS wait.

The first significant item in the task summary is the identity of the current task. Since CICS is in a wait state, this could identify which task was in control. As shown, the current task (1) is not an application, but TCP (terminal control program). Obviously, TCP is unable to be dispatched for some reason. The other relevant task on the active chain is task number 23 (2), with a flag setting of 43C0 (3). This task is active, yet waiting for some I/O to complete. The other two tasks are CICS system tasks, journaling and DB/2. It appears, then, that TCP may be attempting to satisfy a request from task 00023, and CICS went into a wait. A further inspection of the contents of the related TCA will be necessary. Notice, however, that the task 00023

```
CICS21 DUMP                              MODULE IEAVTSDT DATE 08/09/88  TIME 14.33.37  PAGE 00000032

== SUMMARY OF TASKS ON THE ACTIVE CHAIN

DCAADDR TASK ID/ADDR  ECAADDR ECA FLAGS
01E000  00022/02F190  5D4970  80  8040   WAIT ON SYSTEM ECB
01E070  00023/02B190  248090  80  43C0   FILE I/O
01E1C0  JJJ/057190    66D7E8  80  8040   WAIT ON SYSTEM ECB
66AEE0  TCP/66B150            40  40     **** CURRENT TASK ****

== SUMMARY OF TASKS ON THE SUSPEND CHAIN

DCAADDR TASK ID/ADDR  ECAADDR ECA FLAGS
01E230  JJJ/028190            10  04     NON DISPATCHABLE
01E150  JJJ/02D190            10  04     NON DISPATCHABLE
01E0E0  JJJ/025190            10  04     NON DISPATCHABLE

== DCA-TCA ACTIVE CHAIN

 DCA 0001E000

  0000  81000070 00000000 00000000 0001E070  0066A714 0002F190 80400080 005D4970  *A.................X...1. ...)..*  0001E000
  0020  00000000 00000000 00000000 00000000  00000000 22008000 00000000 00000000  *..............................*  0001E020
  0040  00000000 00000000 00000000 00000000  00000000 00000000 0002F524 00000001  *.............................5..*  0001E040
  0060  00000000 00000000                                                         *........                      *     0001E060

 USERTCA 0002F190

  0000  0002F000 00000000 005D4954 0066AAD8  0002F5E8 005D4970 80400000 00818000  *..0......)....Q..5Y.)... ...A..*  0002F190
  0020  505F7606 00000000 00000001 0002F710  0002F5E8 405F7400 0002F580 00000000  *.¬.......7...5Y ¬...5.....*       0002F1B0
  0040  0002F000 480001E8 00000000 0002F710  005D4954 005D4970 505F7606 00023DF0  *..0....Y.......)..).. ¬....0*     0002F1D0
  0060  405F7818 0066CE28 00000000 0002F710  0002F5E8 405F7400 0002F580 000001C8  * ¬......7...5Y ¬...5...H*         0002F1F0
  0080  00000000 00000000 00000000 00000000  00000000 00000000 00000000 00000000  *..............................*  0002F210
  00A0  -        00DF LINES SAME AS ABOVE                                                                            0002F230
  00E0  00000000 00000000 24000000 00000000  00000000 00000000 00000000 00000000  *..............................*  0002F270

 SYSTCA 0002F000

  0000  8A040978 0002F000 0002F980 0002F980  8000022C 005D4BBC 0001E000 00000000  *..........0...9...9.....)......*  0002F000
  0020  00029190 00000000 00000000 00000000  00000000 00000000 00000000 00000000  *..J...........................*  0002F020
  0040  00000000 0002F290 00000000 00000000  00000000 00000000 00000000 00000000  *......2.......................*  0002F040
  0060  00000000 00000000 00000000 00000000  00000000 00000000 00000000 00000000  *..............................*  0002F060
  0080  FE02F7D0 00000000 FE02F570 FE02F978  0066CE28 0002F580 00000000 00000000  *..7.......5...9.....5.........*  0002F080
  00A0  00000000 00000000 00000000 00000000  C3E2E2E8 00000000 00000000 00000000  *................CSSY..........*  0002F0A0
  00C0  00000000 00000004 00000000 00000000  00000000 00000000 00000000 00000000  *..............................*  0002F0C0
  00E0  00000000 00000000 00000000 00000000  00000000 00000000 00000000 00000000  *..............................*  0002F0E0
  0100  00000000 00000000 00000000 00000000  00000000 00000000 00000000 00000000  *..............................*  0002F100
  0120  0C00010C 005D4BBC 00000000 0001E00C  00000000 00000000 00000000 00000000  *.....)........................*  0002F120
  0140  00000000 00000000 0002F2C0 0000025C  00000000 00000000 00000000 00000000  *......2....*..................*  0002F140
  0160  00000000 00000000 00000000 00000000  00000000 00000000 00000000 00000000  *..............................*  0002F160
  0180  00000000 00000000 00000000                                               *.............                 *     0002F180

 DCA 0001E070
```

Figure 12-2   CICS wait state: task summary.

shows an 'ECAADDR' of **248090** (4). This address will be more important later.

### 12.1.4   PRDMP — User TCA Contents

The user portion of the TCA contains information relevant to this task and its status. Some of the information has already been mapped out in the previous part of the report, the Task Summary. The summary showed the flags 43C0 for TCA **02B190**. The TCA user area, shown in Figure 12-3, at location +18, displays the TCATCDC, or Task Control Dispatch Indicator. As mapped in the summary, it contains 43C0 (1). The dispatch indicator for this task is 43, an I/O Event Wait. This task is dispatchable, but waiting for I/O to complete before it can be redispatched. It will resume when the event has occurred. CICS waits for an ECB (event control block) to be posted, meaning the I/O has completed. When the correct information has been returned, CICS can dispatch this task.

In the task summary was an ECAADDR of **248090** as the address CICS would reference for the ECB completion. The TCA user area, +14, should contain this address. At that offset into the TCA is TCATCEA, the Event Control Address. In the TCA at that address is **2248090** (2). Which is correct? Well, the contents of the TCA are correct — the task summary merely truncated the high-order position. Why would the task summary display only six characters of the ECAADDR? Why, of course, because in CICS/MVS 2.1 and older, CICS cannot dispatch any address running in 31-bit. All 24-bit addresses can be contained in the lower 3 bytes of an address, therefore the high-order byte need not be displayed.

Why then, does the TCA contain an address that CICS cannot use? And which address is correct, therefore containing the ECB? IPCS will be needed to reference these addresses, since they will not appear in the PRDMP report.

**PRDMP — Program Check Abend Trace Table.**  In the PC/Abend Trace Table are located either abends or program checks that have occurred to cause this wait. Figure 12-4 contains the entry from the PRDMP report. There are absolutely no entries in the table, so it can be assumed that no abends or

```
CICS21 DUMP                                          MODULE IEAVTSDT DATE 08/09/88  TIME 14.33.37  PAGE 00000033
        0000  81000070 00000000 00000000 0001E1C0  0001E000 0002B190 43C00143 C0248090  *A.........................*  0031E070
        0020  00000000 00000000 00000000 00000000  00000000 00008000 00613232 0002C120  *....................../....A.*  0001E090
        0040  00000000 00000000 00000000 00000000  00000000 00000000 0002B8C0 00000001  *.........................*  0001E0B0
        0060  0005E5A4 00000001                                                          *..VU....            *        0031E0D0

USERTCA 0002B190

        0000  0002B000 00000000 01023AF4 0066AAD8  0002B988 02248090 43C00100 C0B10000  *..............4...Q....H....../....*  0002B190
        0020  5060F666 00000060 02249F74 02249F74  0060F616 0060F5A0 00FDED70 00613232  * -6..-.........-6..-5....../..*  0032B1B0
        0040  00000004 00FDF464 00000003 00000002  02248090 0002C120 5060F666 0002C220  *.....4.........A. -6..B.*  0032B1D0
        0060  606116DE 00023A20 0000A0E0 0060F124  5060F7D8 006107D8 000001F4 000001FC  *-/............-1. -7Q./.Q...4..*  0032B1F0
        0080  8060E66C 00613232 0002C120 00454400  00000000 00000000 00000000 0002B528  *.-Wz./....A...........*  0002B210
        00A0  5044E038 00000000 0000000B 0045952C  00000470 0044E00A 0044F00A 0045300A  *.............N.......0....*  0002B230
        00C0  0045100A 0002B000 00022760 0066A670  00000000 01023AF4 00000000 00000000  *.........-...W.......4....*  0032B250
        00E0  00000000 00000000 24000000 00000000  00000000 00000000 00000000 00000000  *.........................*  0002B270

SYSTCA 0002B000

        0000  8A041118 0002C220 0002C430 0002C430  4400023C 0005FDF4 0001E070 00000000  *.......B...D...D....4....*  0002B000
        0020  0001E790 00023A20 00000000 00000000  00000000 0003B034 00000000 00000000  *..X..........................*  0002B020
        0040  00000000 0002B890 00000000 00000000  00000000 00202000 01000000 00000000  *.............................*  0002B040
        0060  00000000 00000000 80000000 00000000  00000000 00000000 00000000 00000000  *.............................*  0002B060
        0080  FE02BE90 00000000 FE02B910 FE02C118  0066CE28 0002B920 00000000 00000000  *.............A..............*  0002B080
        00A0  00023AF4 00000000 00000000 00000000  C6C9D3C5 00000000 12C00000 00000000  *...4........FILE.............*  0002B0A0
        00C0  00000000 00000000 00000000 00000000  00000000 00000000 9EF10846 1CA88400  *.................1...YD.*  0032B0C0
        00E0  00000000 0044E008 00000000 00000000  00000000 00000000 00000000 00000000  *.............................*  0002B0E0
        0100  00000000 0044E008 00200000 00000000  00000000 C9D5F2F5 C6D3C640 00000000  *...............IN25FLF ....*  0002B100
        0120  01000400 0005FE44 00067E04 00000000  01000300 0002B214 0003B034 00030000  *.........=.................*  0002B120
        0140  00000000 00000000 00000000 00000000  00000000 C94BD7E2 C9F1C3C9 C3D7F108  *........PSI.PSI1CICP1.*  0032B140
        0160  3310BDB1 00200000 00000000 00000000  00000000 00000000 00000000 00000000  *.............................*  0032B160
        0180  00000000 00000000 00000000 00000000  00000000 00000000 00000000 00000000  *.........................*  0002B180

DCA 0001E1C0

        0000  81000070 00000000 00000000 0066AEE0  0001E070 00057190 8040FF80 0066D7E8  *A......................PY*  0031E1C0
        0020  00000000 00000000 00000000 00000000  00000000 22008000 00000000 00000000  *.............................*  0031E1E0
        0040  00000000 00000000 00000000 00000000  00000000 00000000 000572C0 00000001  *.............................*  0001E200
        0060  0003638C 00000001                                                          *........            *        0001E220

USERTCA 00057190

        0000  00057000 00000000 00000000 0066AAD8  00057320 0066D7E8 8040FF00 00838000  *..........Q......PY....C..*  00057190
        0020  504D5108 00000000 00000000 0066D7E8  504CE3DE 00000000 504D502A 00000000  *(..........PY <T......(....*  00057180
        0040  00619A58 00000000 0066AAD8 0066D7E8  00057720 504D5108 00057720 00000000  */..........Q..PY......(....*  00057100
        0060  4061A17A 005E16AC 00000000 00057388  5061A162 00000000 00057320 00000000  */..:.;........H /.........*  00057170
        0080  004D5008 C4C6C8D1 C3C2E2D7 00000000  00000000 00000000 00000000 00000000  *.( .DFHJCBSP.............*  00057210
        00A0  004D5028 00000000 00000000 00000000  504CE3DE 00000000 00000000 00000000  *.(..........<T...........*  00057230
        00C0  00000000 00000000 00000000 00000000  00000000 00000000 00000000 00000000  *.............................*  00057250
        00E0  00000000 00000000 24000000 00000000  00057720 00000000 00000000 00000000  *.............................*  00057270

SYSTCA 00057000

        0000  8A040718 00057720 000577C0 000577C0  00D1D1D1 005D4BBC 0001E1C0 00000000  *.................JJJ.).........*  00057000
        0020  00023190 00000000 00000000 00000000  00000000 00036C24 00000000 00000000  *...................%.....*  00057020
        0040  00000000 00057290 00000000 00000000  00000000 00000000 00000000 00000000  *.............................*  00057040
        0060  00000000 00000000 00000000 00000000  00000000 00000000 00000000 00000000  *.............................*  00057060
```

Figure 12-3    CICS wait state: TCA user area.

program checks have occurred during the life of this region. It will be necessary to look elsewhere for this problem. This table may contain entries, especially in wait and loop situations, and therefore should be investigated.

**IPCS — CSA Execution Status Contents.** The CSA will be investigated fully for CSA execution status contents in the next failure, during initialization. Reference that section to see the actual offsets into the CSA that contain status information. Figure 12-5, however, is another Clist that 'checks' the CSA to locate specific fields, and provide descriptive results. The Clist indicates that CICS initialization has completed and CICS is in normal execution mode (1). This indicates that although CICS is in a wait condition, normal execution is possible. It will be necessary to look elsewhere for the reason for the wait.

**IPCS — ECAADDR Contents.** As previously noted, the address within the TCA and the address shown in the PRDMP differ for the ECAADDR. IPCS can

be used to analyze both of these addresses for their content, and determine which may actually be correct. Figure 12-6 contains an IPCS browse of address **00248090**. This portion of the dump appears to contain program code, or merely zeros. This does not appear to be the correct address. Figure 12-7 contains the browse of address **02248090**. The first byte in this address is **7F**. MVS/XA data areas, which are formatted in the MVS/XA Logic Manuals, contains the control block ECB. An ECB is 4 bytes, resides in the user's area, and is the result of a WAIT, POST, or EVENTS macro instruction.

From the MVS/XA documentation, we would find that a **7F** content of an ECB indicates

'Channel program has terminated without error'

This would indicate that the I/O is complete, since the channel program has terminated. On the other hand, the problem still exists with the address of this ECB. As previously noted, CICS is still unable to run above the line, and many 31-bit addresses are unavailable to the product.

```
CICS21 DUMP                                    MODULE IEAVTSDT DATE 08/09/88  TIME 14.33.37  PAGE 00000005

    0320  00000000 00000000                              *.......                          *    0066ADF8

== SYSTEM INITIALIZATION TABLE

 SIT 0066D858

    0000  E738E721 00000000 04C80268 00000000   0066DD40 00000000 000060E0 0066DD98  *X.X......H.......... .......-....Q*  0066D858
    0020  0066D818 00000000 04000000 00000000   00012C00 00177000 07D0001E 00000000  *..Q.............................*  0066D878
    0040  000F0800 0000A000 00001000 000003E8   000400C8 01F4FE00 999C0000 700C0000  *................Y...H.4..R.......*  0066D898
    0060  D8D70000 00000000 40404040 40404040   40404040 40E8F049 E740000F1 D5D54001  *QP...... ......... Y0.X .1NN .*    0066D8B8
    0080  D5D5E8D5 00E8D5D4 00D50100 00000000   00D5D640 40404040 D5D64040 404040D5  *NNYN.YNM.N.......NO    NO   NO  N*  0066D8D8
    00A0  D6404040 4040D5D6 40404040 40D5D640   40404040 D5D64040 404040D5 D6404040  *O   NO    NO    NO    NO    NO .*    0066D8F8
    00C0  40404040 40D5D6D6 4040000C 40404040   D5D64040 404040D5 D6404040 404040E2  * NO   NO   NO    NO    NO    .S*    0066D918
    00E0  E8E2D3C9 E2E34002 E7614040 40404002   C3614040 40404002 E3614040 40404002  *YSLIST .X/   .C/   .T/   .*        0066D938
    0100  D7614040 40404040 4000100C 20C640D5   D6E2E8E2 E8E2E8D5 D6D5D6C9 E2E2E2D5  *P/   ...F NOSYSYSYNONOISSSN*      0066D958
    0120  D6F15BD5 D6D5D6D5 D6E2E840 40404040   40404040 40404040 40404040 40404040  *O1$NONONOSY               *        0066D978
    0140  404040E2 5BE25B40 40404040 40404040   40404040 40404040 40404040 40404040  *   S$S$               *          0066D998
    0160  40404040 40404040 404040D5 D6F15BD5   D6D5D6D5 D6D5D6D5 D6404040 40404040  *          NO1$NONONONONO  *        0066D9B8
    0180  40404040 40D5D640 40404040 40D5D640   40404040 40404040 40404040 40404040  *     NO     NO          *          0066D9D8
    01A0  404040E8 404040E8 C5C50050 04000000   50500000 50500000 C1C1C3E2 C7D40000  *   YEE.....  .. ...AACSGM..*      0066D9F8
    01C0  000A020C 001C001C 001C001C 001C001C   001C001C 001C001C 0066DD80 E2E8E2C3  *..................... ....SYSC*  0066DA18
    01E0  035C0100 0023C000 40404040 40404040   40404040 40404040 40404040 40404040  *..*......                *          0066DA38
    0200  40404040 40404040 40404040 40404040   40404040 40404040 40404040 40404040  *                    *              0066DA58
    0220  -    031F LINES SAME AS ABOVE                                                                                      0066DA78
    0320  40404040 40404040 40404040 40404040   40404040 40404040 D761D740 40404040  *                   P/P     *        0066DB78
    0340  40404040 40404040 D761D540 40404040   40404040 40404040 40404040 40404040  *         P/N             *          0066DB98
    0360  40404040 40404040 D761F140 40404040   40404040 40404040 D761D340 40404040  *         P/1      P/L     *          0066DBB8
    0380  40404040 40404040 D761D740 40404040   40404040 40404040 40404040 40404040  *         P/P             *          0066DBD8
    03A0  -    043F LINES SAME AS ABOVE                                                                                      0066DBF8
    0440  40404040 40404040 40404040 40404040   40404040 40404040 00030003 00030003  *                   ........*        0066DC98
    0460  0000000A C4C6C8E9 C1E3C4E7 40404040   40404040 40404040 40404040 40404040  *....DFHZATDX             *          0066DCB8
    0480  40404040 40404040 40404040 D5D5D7E2   C9F1C3C9 C3D7D7E2 C9F1C3C9 C3D70000  *           NNPSI1CICPPSI1CICP..*    0066DCD8
    04A0  0000001E C1C4C6C8 C3D3E340 40000000   0000001E 0000001E C3E2C7D4 00000000  *....ADFHCLT  ..........CSGM....*    0066DCF8
    04C0  0000000C E3000000                                                          *....T...                          0066DD18
```

== ABEND SAVE AREA TRACE

| PC/ABEND TRACE 005D5268 |

```
    0000  D7D9D6C7 D9C1D440 C3C8C5C3 D261C1C2   C5D5C440 E3D9C1C3 C540E3C1 C2D3C57A  *PROGRAM CHECK/ABEND TRACE TABLE:*  005D5268
    0020  005D52A8 005D52A8 005D55A8 00000000   00000000 00000340 00000000 00000000  *.).Y.).Y.).Y............ .......*  005D5288
    0040  00000000 00000000 00000000 00000000   00000000 00000000 00000000 00000000  *................................*  005D52A8
    0060  -    033F LINES SAME AS ABOVE                                                                                      005D52C8
```

== CICS TRACE TABLE

 TRACE HEADER 005D8960

```
    0000  02200140 02200020 02207FE0 800003FF   004FB4AC 22E36E01 00000000 00000000  *... ......".......|...T>.........*  005D8960
```

```
  TIME OF DAY   ID REG 14  REQD TASK  FIELD A  FIELD B  CHARS  RESOURCE TRACE TYPE                              INTERVAL
 14:30:23.719360 CC 4049328E 0003 00024 06000000 0006E698 ......W.          CCP ENDBROWSE
 14:30:23.719392 F0 705ECF32 4004 00024 80000000 00024090 ....... .         KCP WAIT DCI=SINGLE                 00.000032
```

Figure 12-4   CICS wait state: PC/Abend trace table.

```
IPCS OUTPUT STREAM ------------------------------------------------- LINE 0 COLS 1 78
COMMAND ===>                                                  SCROLL ===> CSR
**************************** TOP OF DATA ****************************************
        THIS CICS DUMP IS OF THE SYSCICS  REGION
        TAKEN ON JULIAN DATE 88.222 AT 14.33.36
*************************************************

** PLTPI PHASE HAS COMPLETED
** | CICS IS IN EXECUTION | ①

** MAXIMUM NUMBER OF TASKS IS 020
** MAXIMUM ACTIVE TASK VALUE IS 000A
** MAXIMUM ACTIVE TASKS ACCUMULATED IS 0002
** NUMBER OF TIMES AT MAX TASKS IS 0000000
** CURRENT TASK ACCUMULATOR IS 001
** MAXIMUM NUMBER OF TASKS ACCUMULATED IS 002
** NUMBER OF TASKS CICS/VS HAS ORIGINATED IS 00027

** NUMBER OF TIMES STORAGE CUSHION HAS BEEN RELEASED IS 000
** NUMBER OF STORAGE REQUESTS QUEUED BECAUSE STORAGE
                               NOT AVAILABLE IS 000
** MAXIMUM NUMBER OF STORAGE REQUESTS QUEUED AT ANY ONE TIME
                       BECAUSE STORAGE NOT AVAILABLE IS 000
```

Figure 12-5   CICS wait state: CICS executions status.

```
ASID(X'002F') STORAGE   ------------------------------------------------------
COMMAND ===>                                                SCROLL ===> PAGE
00248090.   80AD3600  00000000  00000000  00000000   . ................ .
002480A0. TO 00248FFF. (X'00000F60' bytes)--All bytes contain X'00'
00249000. TO 0044CFFF. (X'00204000' bytes)--Storage not available
0044D000.   88001000  00000000  5CC4C6C8  C5D4C340   . h.......*DFHEMC .
0044D010.   405C44D0  28F0F2F1  F0C91702  0219E4D3   .  *.}.0210I....UL .
0044D020.   F2F6F2F8  F7401400  00000006  0C0C45E0   . 26287 .........\ .
0044D030.   8068D213  70542000  91802002  4780901E   . ..K.....j....... .
0044D040.   D2037068  30009102  20024780  903058F0   . K.....j........0 .
0044D050.   101CD207  706CF000  91082002  47809042   . ..K..%0.j....... .
0044D060.   58F01014  D2037074  F0009104  20024780   . .O..K...0.j..... .
0044D070.   905458F0  1018D203  7078F000  91202002   . ...0..K...0.j... .
0044D080.   47809086  D201C08A  5000D205  C0849EC8   . ....fK.{.&.K.{d.H .
0044D090.   9284C080  9200C081  58E0D0E8  05EE9501   . kd{.k.{a.\}Y..n. .
0044D0A0.   C0804780  80845860  C08C5060  707C18E1   . {.....d.-{.&-.@... .
0044D0B0.   4BE09ECE  D603E000  E0004770  93FAD208   . .\..O.\.\...l.K. .
0044D0C0.   70289ED6  91802002  478090B6  D2037028   . ...Oj.......K... .
0044D0D0.   300045E0  806C47F0  93FA47F0  930E9140   . ...\.%.01..01.j  .
```

Figure 12-6   CICS wait state: dump contents at **00248090**.

As it turns out, CICS passes control to VSAM (or more specifically DFP) to accomplish the data retrieval. VSAM returns the ECB completion when appropriate, and CICS regains control. In this problem, DFP posted an address to CICS that was invalid, and CICS was unable to continue. The wait resulted.

In defense of CICS, this was truly a DFP problem, and was resolved via maintenance to the appropriate DFP module. CICS problems tend to be extremely complex, since there are so many additional products and components that co-exist with CICS. Although not all wait or loop conditions are caused by internal IBM code, this should be consid-

```
ASID(X'002F') STORAGE   ------------------------------------------------------
COMMAND ===>                                                SCROLL ===> PAGE
02248090.   7F000000  00000000  00000000  00000000   . "............... .
022480A0.   0060E6EC  00000000  022480E4  0002B528   . .-W........U.... .
022480B0.   C0840000  00000000  00000000  00000004   . {d.............. .
022480C0. TO 022480CF. (X'00000010' bytes)--All bytes contain X'00'
022480D0.   00000000  73000040  00000000  02248088   . ............ .h .
022480E0.   0002C128  00000000  00000000  00000000   . ...A........... .
022480F0.   00000000  00000000  00000000  02249DFC   . ................ .
02248100. TO 0224810F. (X'00000010' bytes)--All bytes contain X'00'
02248110.   00000000  00000000  7F000000  02248F88   . .........".....h .
02248120. TO 0224887F. (X'00000760' bytes)--All bytes contain X'00'
02248880.   00000000  00000000  6148002C  00000000   . .........../...... .
02248890.   00000000  00000200  00005C00  E4E2C5D9   . ..........*.USER .
022488A0.   F0F10001  00000000  00000000  FFFFFFFF   . 01.............. .
022488B0.   FFFFFF00  00000000  43000054  02248910   . ................i. .
022488C0. TO 0224890F. (X'00000050' bytes)--All bytes contain X'00'
02248910.   42000064  00000000  00000000  00000000   . ................ .
02248920. TO 0224896F. (X'00000050' bytes)--All bytes contain X'00'
02248970.   00000000  00000000  600000C0  00010005   . .........-..{.... .
02248980.   00070000  002E0000  00000000  00000200   . ................ .
02248990.   000001F9  00000000  00000000  02248888   . ....9..........hh .
022489A0.   08000000  00000000  9EE748EC  D26B8B02   . .........X..K,... .
022489B0.   00010001  00000001  00000000  00000000   . ................ .
```

Figure 12-7   CICS wait state: dump contents at **02248090**.

ered during analysis of these conditions. As previously stated, every wait and loop can be a completely different condition. It may be necessary to reference other control blocks to debug those failures.

### 12.1.5   CICS Wait Condition From VSAM Exclusive Control Conflict

Figure 12-1 identifies the typical dump items relevant to a CICS wait condition. In VSAM conflicts, however, one additional item would need to be added to the list. The VSWA control block contains task storage built on behalf of VSAM file processing. A VSWA is another block of storage, very similar to the other types of task storage previously analyzed. VSWAs can be identified by an 8F storage type in the first byte. Previous storage was 8C-type, user storage created by the application. 8F storage is built by CICS when necessary to process VSAM file requests. VSWAs contain a great deal of information, but several fields in particular are extremely important for debugging. Listed below are the fields significant in VSAM exclusive control waits.

```
OFFSET    LENGTH    NAME       DESCRIPTION
  64        4       VSWAOWND   PTR TO VSWA
                               WAITING FOR ME
  68        4       VSWAOWNR   PTR TO VSWA
                               I'M WAITING FOR
  E4        4       VSWASV12   TCA OWNING THIS
                               VSWA
```

The contents of these fields will provide insight into the task that is waiting and the task that is causing the wait. The first step in debugging these problems is to reference the task summary, as the previous wait required.

**PRDMP — Task Summary.**   Figure 12-8 contains the task summary from this example. The task in a wait can be identified as task 00188 (1), with a flag setting of 8840 (2). The task is on the active chain, waiting to be dispatched, with a dispatch indicator of 88. This dispatch indicator is used when CICS is waiting for a system-level activity to complete. Also shown in the task summary, the task is waiting for a CICS-related ECB in File Control Program (3). This would indicate that the task is dispatchable, but must wait for some file control process to complete before continuing. No other tasks on the ac-

tive chain appear to be causing the problem, however, so further investigation must continue.

**PRDMP — User TCA Contents.**   The user portion of the TCA contains information relevant to the status of this task. The information located from the previous wait example could be used to determine task status and any other relevant information. Since this example has already been identified as a VSAM file conflict, the contents of the VSWA will be the most relevant.

**PRDMP — VSWA Contents.**   Figure 12-9 contains the portion of task-related storage built as a result of the VSAM request. Note that the task storage starting at location **000B41D0** is an 8F type (1), a VSWA. Since this control block contains the reason for the wait, the VSWA fields identified above need to be analyzed for content. At +64 into the VSWA would be the address of the VSWA waiting for this task to complete. This fullword contains **00000000** (1), signifying that no other request is waiting for this VSWA. The next fullword, however, contains **0004EBF0** (2). This address is a pointer to the VSWA causing the wait. How do you find the task that created this VSWA? One technique would be to utilize IPCS and locate this address. At +E4 into the VSWA would be the pointer to the TCA that created the storage. The PRDMP output can also be scanned to locate the block of storage at this address, and identify the TCA owning the VSWA.

Figure 12-10 contains another page of the PRDMP report, identifying the VSWA at **0004EBF0** (1). This VSWA is listed as task storage under task number 04D000. Referencing Figure 12-8 again, this task can be found on the suspend chain (4) in a terminal wait. If the TCA was investigated, it would show a CECI transaction executed by a user performing a read-for-update against a VSAM file. This created, of course, an exclusive lock against the record. Since CECI is a conversational transaction, this enqueue is retained until the CECI transaction releases the record. Any further requests by other tasks for this record will wait on the active chain, just as task 00188 is waiting.

This deadlock can be easily diagnosed in this example, since there are relatively few tasks on either the active or suspend chain. An active CICS region, however, could have many more tasks, and complicate the diagnostic process. The use of VSWA chaining, and investigation of the contents of the critical fields, can simplify the task. These fields

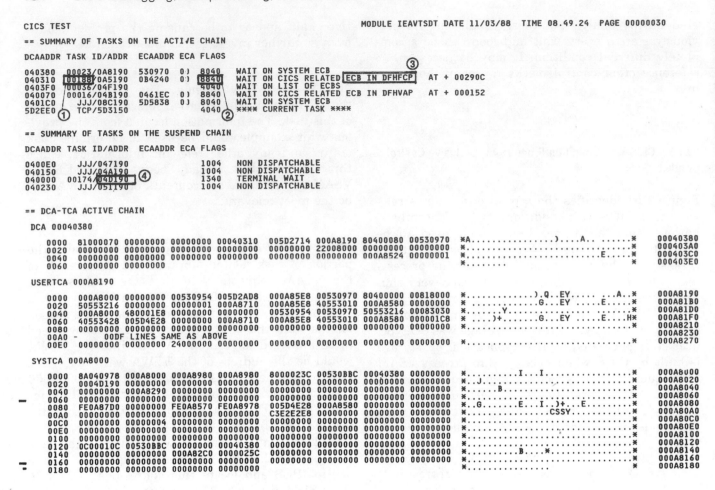

Figure 12-8   CICS wait state: task summary.

will always identify the VSWA that is causing the wait, and the owner of the VSWA.

## 12.2   FAILURE DURING INITIALIZATION

Many installations use a facility of CICS that allows programs to execute during initialization, and therefore create an environment or build specific data areas as soon as CICS is ready to begin dispatching applications. These programs can be placed into a table called the PLT (Program List Table), which is executed by CICS during one phase of its initialization. This can be very convenient; however, it can also produce some exposure for failure. It has been mentioned in previous chapters that these programs can cause outages, since if they produce program checks or otherwise fail, CICS initialization is affected. This example will look at one of these failures to analyze the cause,

and relevant dump items to allow bebugging of the problem in the shortest possible time.

### 12.2.1   Initialization SIT Options

Specify a suffix in the SIT if programs need to be executed at initialization. Since programs can be executed at both initialization and termination, use the SIT parameter PLTPI, specifying program initialization. The parameter PLTSD indicates the table containing programs to be executed at CICS termination. Use the table suffix, and place the program to be executed in the table. Of course, this table may soon become an online definition, since IBM is moving all table assemblies into RDO (Resource Definition Online).

Once created and assembled, any program in the table will be executed during CICS initialization. These programs are executed sequentially in the sequence that they appear in the table. Remember,

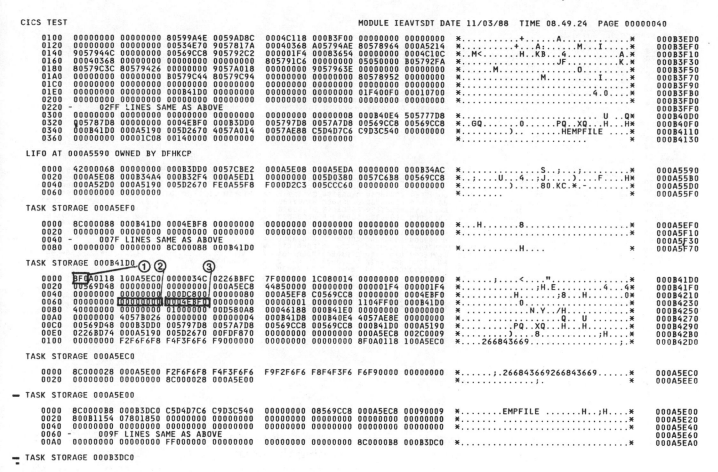

Figure 12-9   CICS wait state: task storage.

although CICS produces messages during initialization, unless the program takes overt action to produce messages, no messages are produced during startup. Some vendors send messages during their program execution to indicate successful processing. PLT programs that fail may not produce any information to document the failure or reason.

## 12.2.2  Failure During Initialization — An Example

If CICS fails during initialization, a message is usually written indicating a 601-type abend, and a dump is produced based on the DUMP options from the SIT. Figure 12-11 is a summary of the typical cause and dump items usually relevant for these failures.

**CSMT Messages.**  The first symptom of a failure during initialization is, of course, that the CICS region fails during startup, and if retried, will be continually unsuccessful. Of course, the first priority is

always to get the address space to successfully initialize. One of the hazards of application programs in PLT processing is the potential lack of control over changes in these programs. Many times, application programmers make changes and place the new copy into the production region. These changes may or may not be controlled and documented. If initialization fails due to these programs, the responsible parties may not have access to the changes that were made, or even know that changes have been made. For this reason, programs placed into the PLT should be controlled, perhaps more closely than other applications. These can affect the availability of the entire system. If the region fails to initialize, there may be messages in the CSMT log indicating the failure.

There may, however, be only normal messages, which suddenly stop, followed by a U601 abend. In many cases, there is no overt indication of the failing program. As previously mentioned, familiarization with the normal startup messages can identify normal processing. When a failure occurs, the last

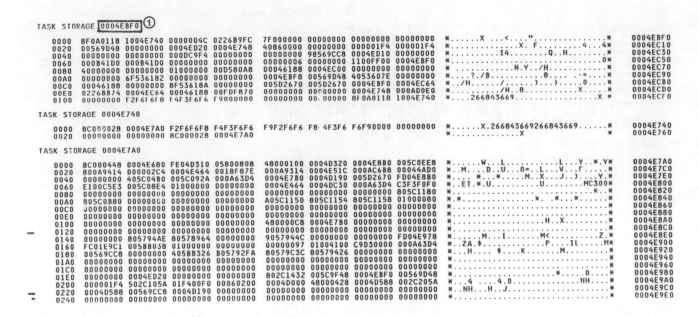

Figure 12-10   CICS wait state: task storage.

message displayed can identify the stage of initialization at the time of failure.

**PRDMP — Trace Table.** Since a dump is produced, one of the best indicators is the trace table of activity. This can show what was executing at the time of the failure, and possibly identify the failing module. Figure 12-12 shows the page of the dump containing the last trace entries. Notice that the trace ends without indicating any specific failure. The last several entries, however, indicate CICS's attempt at abend processing. The multiple entries by EIP show both ABEND ENTRY (1) and ABEND RESPONSE (2). Obviously, CICS was attempting to recover from a problem, but was unable to do so. Moving back in the trace to the previous page, Figure 12-13 shows the beginning of the problem. Notice the entry for the CICS load of the PLT program DFHPLTIS (1). The first module that the PLT at-

tempts to load via a LINK is COPMON (2). After locating the program entry, CICS acquires storage for the program, and is immediately intercepted with an attempt at HANDLE ABEND processing (3). This failure is unable to be resolved and results in the U601 abend in the dump.

**PRDMP — Task Summary.** Although the failing program has been identified, more information from the dump can be collected to assist in debugging the problem. Figure 12-14 contains the task summary from PRDMP output. It identifies the current task with a TCA user area address of **01F190** (1), but has no transaction identification other than III (2). Since the programs that execute during initialization are initiated by CICS, rather than being started from a transid, they are all identified by CICS initialization (III). The task summary validates the findings of failure during initialization,

```
ABEND CODE:  U601

PROBABLY CAUSE:  Program check in a PLT initialization program

IMPORTANT DUMP ITEMS:  PRDMP - TRACE TABLE

                       PRDMP - TASK SUMMARY

                       PRDMP - PROGRAM CHECK ABEND TRACE TABLE

                       IPCS  - PCABTTBL CLIST ANALYSIS

                       IPCS  - CSA INITIALIZATION STAGE CONTENTS

OTHER RELEVANT ITEMS:  CSMT MESSAGES FOR LAST SUCCESSFUL PROCESS
```

Figure 12-11   Significant items in an initialization failure.

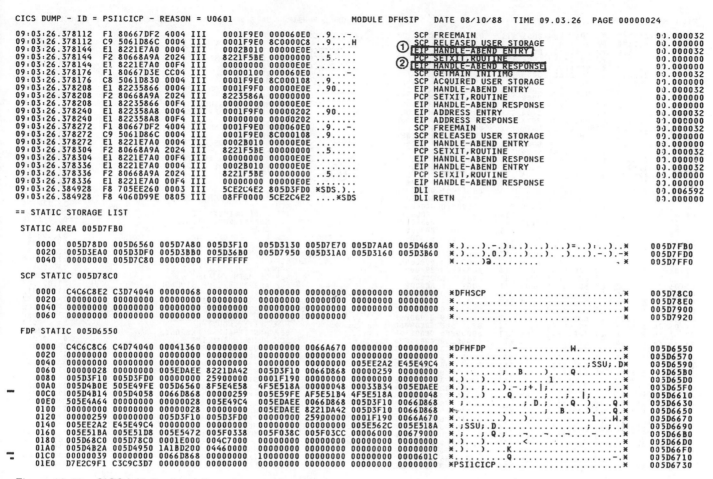

CICS DUMP - ID = PSI1CICP - REASON = U0601                          MODULE DFHSIP   DATE 08/10/88   TIME 09.03.26   PAGE 00000024

Figure 12-12   CICS initialization failure: trace table entries.

but gives no additional information concerning the specific program problem.

### PRDMP — Program Check Abend Trace Table.
This table contains entries detected by CICS during execution, and records both program checks and abends. The table is formatted by PRDMP and is usually found on the second page of the report, after the SIT. Figure 12-15 contains the PC/ABEND Trace Table from our dump. This table is cumulative and will contain entries for all program checks or abends, since the region has initialized up to a maximum of six entries. The first entry found in the table is past the headers of the control block, starting at offset +40. The first entry (1) recorded a PC (program check), the last two bytes is a counter, and contains a **0001** (2). The next four bytes contains the address of the TCA recording the program check. The contents, **0001F190** (3), matches the initialization task identifed in the task summary. The second entry in the PC/ABEND Trace Table begins at offset +C0 (4). This entry recorded an AB (abend), and contains the same ad-

dress in the second fullword, **0001F190**. These entries can be relevant to identify the type of program check, or abend, and trace the failure back to the task involved.

### IPCS — PCABTTBL CLIST Analysis.
The PC/ABEND Trace Table can contain additional information, but is not mapped out in the PRDMP report to make this information easily visible. A CLIST could be created to separate these entries and display them in a more readable manner. Figure 12-16 contains the output from an IPCS CLIST that displays each of the two entries. Notice that the CLIST also contains a counter to display the cumulative number of program checks and abends (1). The two table entries shown are in the reverse order of the contents of the control block. While the table in the dump is built as failures occur, it may be desirable to see the most current entry first, as the CLIST produces.

The second fullword in a PC/ABEND trace table contains an address to the TCA. It can be used to match the TCA in a task summary, or tasks that

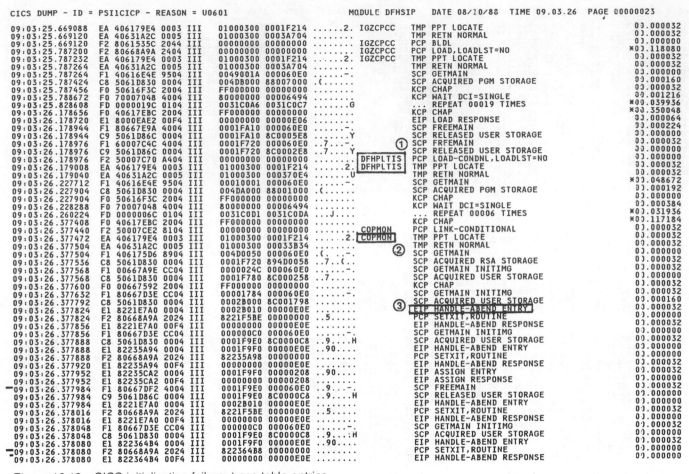

Figure 12-13    CICS initialization failure: trace table entries.

may need to be investigated. Other entries in the table may also be important, and all are mapped in Figure 12-17. Referencing these items, it is possible to locate contents of specific fields in the table. At +14 is the task identification (2), verifying the III initialization task displayed in the task summary. Starting at +30 are the registers (3), which may be of importance in some types of failures. At the end of the registers is the PSW (4), which may need to be used to determine the module executing at the time of the abend. By investigating the address 005EEA6C from the module map at the end of the dump, from Figure 12-18, this address is within the CICS module DFHSRP (1). CICS is obviously in System Recovery Program, attempting to avoid a failure. Especially significant in the PC/ABEND Trace Table is the interrupt information at +78 (5), or the next-to-last fullword of the table entry. This fullword can be used much like debugging program checks. The first two bytes contain the instruction length, the last two bytes are the interrupt code. In the first table entry is the interrupt code of "D."

The abend was within SRP, however, and is not the cause of the failure.

The second entry in the table is a program check. Notice the PSW entry at offset +70 (6), which contains an address 822216EE. This may not appear to be a legitimate address, but remember, some programs run above the line, in 31-bit mode. Their address can be well above values we are used to seeing. Using the module map from Figure 12-18, indeed several programs at the end of the map have extended addresses as starting locations. The module COPMON begins at address 0221DA42 (2). Since the high-order bit in the PSW address can be disregarded, it will be possible to calculate the off-set into this program by subtracting the two addresses. This would provide the location within the program of the failing instruction. Also identify the interrupt information from +78 in the table entry. The contents, 00060007, display an instruction length of 0006 and a program check 0007 (7). Chapter 4 contained techniques to determine the cause of the type 7 program check. Of course, program

```
CICS DUMP - ID = PSI1CICP - REASON = U0601          MODULE DFHSIP   DATE 08/10/88  TIME 09.03.26  PAGE 00000030

== SUMMARY OF TASKS ON THE ACTIVE CHAIN

DCAADDR TASK ID/ADDR  ECAADDR ECA FLAGS

01E000 ②[III/01F190]①             2000   **** CURRENT TASK ****
01E070 00016/029190  0241EC  00  8840   WAIT ON CICS RELATED ECB IN DFHVAP    AT + 000152
01E1C0 JJJ/058190  66D7F8  00  8040   WAIT ON SYSTEM ECB
66AEE0 TCP/66B150          4040   WAIT ON LIST OF ECBS

== SUMMARY OF TASKS ON THE SUSPEND CHAIN

DCAADDR TASK ID/ADDR  ECAADDR ECA FLAGS

01E230 JJJ/028190          1004   NON DISPATCHABLE
01E150 JJJ/02D190          1004   NON DISPATCHABLE
01E0E0 JJJ/025190          1004   NON DISPATCHABLE

== DCA-TCA ACTIVE CHAIN

 DCA 0001E000

  0000  81000070 00000000 00000000 0001E070  0066A714 0001F190 2000FF00 04006494  *A................X...1.......M*  0001E000
  0020  00000000 00000000 00000000 00000000  00000000 22008000 00000000 00000000  *.............................*  0001E020
  0040  00000000 00000000 00000000 00000000  C0000000 00000000 0001F2C0 00000001  *............................2...*  0001E040
  0060  00039ECC 00000002                                                         *........                     *  0001E060

 USERTCA 0001F190

  0000  0001F000 00000000 000060E0 0066AAD8  0001F320 00006494 2000FF00 04038018  *...0........;-...Q..3....M.......*  0001F190
  0020  00667592 0001F838 005D7AB8 0221D99C  006174B0 0066AAD8 005D7AA0 00618288  *...K..8..)..R../....Q.)..../BH*  0001F1B0
  0040  0001F000 8221DA42 006674CC 0066AAD8  005D3BBC 0001F780 4060D99E 4001F9E0  *...0.B.........Q.)...7. -R. .9.*  0001F1D0
  0060  80667DF2 00667CD8 0002B010 82235954  0001F038 0001F9E0 0001F9F0 0066A670  *...'2..әQ....B....0..9..90..W.*  0001F1F0
  0080  0802D990 00000000 D6D54040 C1E2D9C1  FF8D1000 005D4648 C3C14040 5CE2C4E2  *..R....ON  ASRA.....).CA *SDS*  0001F210
  00A0  80668A9A 80615880 0002D990 0002B078  0221FA6F 8221F878 0002B108 00618288  *..../....R......?B.8...../BH*  0001F230
  00C0  0000001C 0000000E 00668380 006152E8  00000000 0001F780 00000000 00000000  *........C../.Y....7........*  0001F250
  00E0  00000000 00000000 E5000000 0002B010  00000000 00000259 00000000 00000000  *.........V...................*  0001F270

 SYSTCA 0001F000

  0000  8A040718 0002B000 0001F9E0 0002C7A0  00C9C9C9 005D3BBC 0001E000 00000000  *.........9...G..III.).........*  0001F000
  0020  00025190 00000000 00000000 00000000  006693DA 00033B34 0001F720 0002B010  *................L.......7.....*  0001F020
  0040  0002B000 00000000 00000000 00000000  00000000 00000000 00282000 01030000  *.............................*  0001F040
  0060  00000000 00000000 00000000 00000000  00000000 00000000 00000000 0001F780  *............................7.*  0001F060
  0080  FE01F5B8 00000000 FE01F310 FE01F718  0066CE28 0001F320 00000000 00080007  *..5.......3...7......3.......*  0001F080
  00A0  00000000 00000004 00000000 00000000  C3E2E2E8 00000000 00000000 00000000  *.............CSSY...........*  0001F0A0
  00C0  00000000 00000000 00000000 00000000  00000000 00000000 9EF20119 AE01B100  *......................2.....*  0001F0C0
  00E0  00000000 8221D990 00000000 00000000  00000000 00000000 00000000 00000000  *....B.R.....................*  0001F0E0
  0100  00000000 8221DA42 32200200 00000000  00000000 00000000 00000000 00000000  *....B.......................*  0001F100
  0120  01040100 0001F228 0005F0F4 00000000  01000300 0001F214 00033B34 00000000  *......2..04........2........*  0001F120
  0140  00000000 00000000 00000000 FFFFFDA8  00000000 00000000 00000000 00000000  *...............Y............*  0001F140
  0160  00000000 00000000 00000000 00000000  00000000 00000000 00000000 00000000  *............................*  0001F160
  0180  04E2E8E2 C3404040 40000000 00000000                                       *.SYSC        .......         *  0001F180

 DCA 0001E070
```

Figure 12-14   CICS initialization failure: task summary.

checks, or ASRAs after initialization, are not diffi-cult to debug, but when the program check occurs at initialization, it certainly generates different re-sults.

**IPCS — CSA Initialization Stage Contents.** Within the CSA are many indicators that get updated con-stantly as CICS executes. If problems arise during initialization, some of these indicators can be inves-tigated to determine their contents. These can tell what stage of execution the system has successfully completed. This can give further information into the stage of initialization at time of failure. Figure 12-19 shows a display of the CSA during IPCS browse. The CSA is also produced within the PRDMP report, and can be referenced there if nec-essary. Locate the offsets within the CSA display, or create a CLIST that locates and lists specific en-tries. The items in the CSA that we may be inter-ested in are

```
+49   System Signal Indicator 2
      '10' PLTPI Phase has completed

+174  CICS Execution Status

      '01' CICS Initialization
      '02' CICS Execution
      '04' CICS Terminating
      '24' CICS Terminating Immediately

+175  CICS Execution Status 2
      '01' 1st Stage Initialization
      '02' 2nd Stage Initialization
      '03' 3rd Stage Initialization

+176  CICS Execution Status
      '01' CICS Initialization Complete
```

Use Figure 12-19 to browse in IPCS. From the PRDMP exit, the CSA starting address is shown as **0066A670**. Investigate the contents at location +49

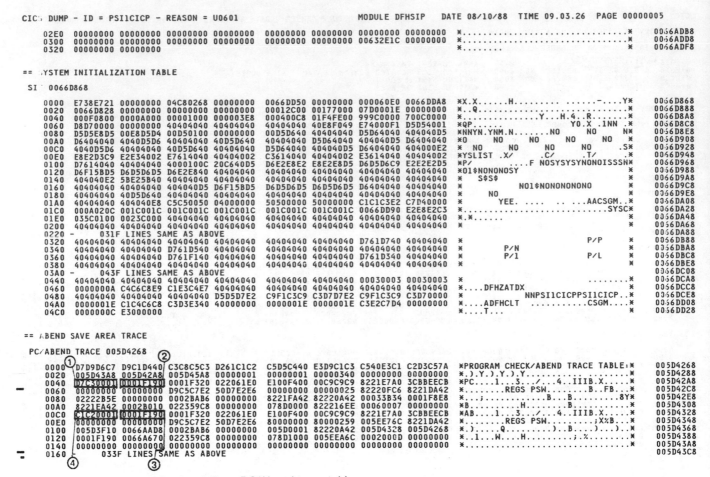

Figure 12-15    CICS initialization failure: PC/Abend trace table.

past that address. The location of that offset would be **0066A6B9**. This location in the CSA should indicate whether the PLTPI phase has completed. Since the byte at that location contains 00 (1), we know that the PLTPI has not completed processing. This verifies the premise that the failure occurred during execution of a program within the PLT. The CSA can also show in exactly which stage of execution CICS was at the time of the failure. Moving the IPCS browse to the CSA +174 will produce Figure 12-20. Displayed is a fullword containing 0104000 (1). Mapping out this information to the CSA contents previously described, CICS is in initialization, 01 at +174, in the third stage, 04 at +175, and has not completed this third stage, 00 at +176.

These CSA values may not seem particularly surprising, since previous investigation already identified the PLTPI module that is causing the failure. Many problems with CICS initialization are not this straightforward. It may be necessary to identify the status of CICS, in its exact execution status, especially if it is suspected that the problem may be with a CICS component. Of course, these offsets within the CSA may change with future releases. Reference the Data Areas manual for locations in the appropriate release of CICS.

In summary, it has been determined that the 601 abend was caused by a program check, type 007, and occurred in a module executing during PLT processing. In this example, the installation failed to provide a proper environment for a new vendor product. The product was therefore unable to initialize, and failed during execution of the PLT program. The best solution to this problem would be to take the program out of the PLT and recreate the problem via normal transaction processing to produce an ASRA dump. Follow the instructions in Chapter 4 to diagnose ASRA type abends.

```
IPCS OUTPUT STREAM ------------------------------------------------ LINE 0 COLS 1 78
COMMAND ===>                                                        SCROLL ===> CSR
***************************** TOP OF DATA *************************************
**** THERE HAVE BEEN 00000001 PROGRAM CHECK(S) ①
**** THERE HAVE BEEN 00000001 ABEND(S)


** PROGRAM CHECK/ABEND TRACE TABLE FOLLOWS
**           (MOST RECENT ENTRY FIRST)


STRTE
LIST 005D42A8. ASID(X'002E') POSITION(X'+0080') LENGTH(128) ENTRY(2) AREA
005D4328.                    C1C20001 0001F190 .          AB....1..
005D4330. 0001F320 022061E0 E100F400 00C9C9C9② ..3.../\..4..III.
005D4340. 8221E7A0 3CBBEECB 00000000 00000000 .b.X.............
005D4350. D9C5C7E2 50D7E2E6 80000000 80000259③ REGS&PSW.........
005D4360. 005EE76C 8221DA42 005D3F10 0066AAD8 ..;X%b....).....Q.
005D4370. 0002BAB6 00000000 005D0001 82220A42 .........)..b....
005D4380. 005D4328 005D4268 0001F190 0066A670 ..)...)....1...w..
005D4390. 022359C8 00000000 078D1000 005EEA6C④ ...H.........;.%.
005D43A0. 0002000D 00000000                   ........        .
          ⑤
STRTE


IPCS OUTPUT STREAM ------------------------------------------------ LINE 22 COLS 1 78
COMMAND ===>                                                       SCROLL ===> CSR
LIST 005D42A8. ASID(X'002E') LENGTH(128) ENTRY(1) AREA
005D42A8.                    D7C30001 0001F190 .          PC....1..
005D42B0. 0001F320 022061E0 E100F400 00C9C9C9 ...3.../\..4..III.
005D42C0. 8221E7A0 3CBBEECB 00000000 00000000 .b.X.............
005D42D0. D9C5C7E2 50D7E2E6 00000000 00000025 .REGS&PSW.........
005D42E0. 82220FC6 8221DA42 02222B5E 00000000 .b..Fb......;.....
005D42F0. 0002BAB6 00000000 8221FA42 82220A42 .........b...b....
005D4300. 00C33B34 0001F8E8 8221EA42 0002B010 .......8Yb........
005D4310. 022359C8 00000000 078D0000 822216EE⑥ ...H.........b....
005D4320. 00060007 00000000                   ........        .
*** TRACE ENTRY 6 IS UNUSED ***
          ⑦
*** TRACE ENTRY 5 IS UNUSED ***

*** TRACE ENTRY 4 IS UNUSED ***

*** TRACE ENTRY 3 IS UNUSED ***
```

Figure 12-16  CICS initialization failure: formatted PC/Abend trace table.

| Offset | Length | Contents |
|--------|--------|----------|
| 0 | 2 | ENTRY TYPE |
| 2 | 2 | PROGRAM CHECK OR ABEND NUMBER |
| 4 | 4 | TCA ADDRESS |
| 8 | 4 | CURRENT LIFO STACK ADDRESS |
| C | 4 | CURRENT TRACE ENTRY ADDRESS |
| 10 | 8 | TRACE ID and TASK ID |
| 18 | 8 | REGISTER 14 and TIME STAMP |
| 20 | 8 | RESERVED |
| 28 | 8 | CONSTANT 'REGS.PSW' |
| 30 | 128 | REGISTERS 0-15 |
| 70 | 8 | PSW |
| 78 | 4 | INTERRUPT INFORMATION |

Figure 12-17   CICS initialization failure: PC/ABEND trace table format.

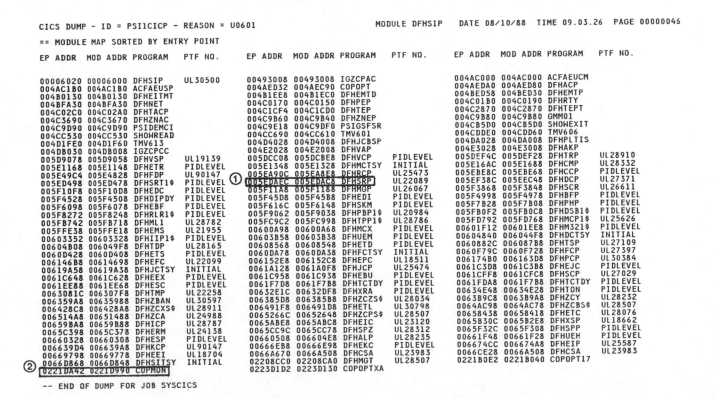

Figure 12-18   CICS initialization failure: module map.

```
***************************** END OF DATA *********************************


IPCS OUTPUT STREAM --------------------------------------------------- LINE 0 COLS 1 78
COMMAND ===>                                                          SCROLL ===> CSR
***************************** TOP OF DATA *********************************
```
┌─────┐
│ CSA │
└─────┘
┌──────────────┐                                          ┌───────────┐
│LIST 0066A670.│ ASID(X'002E')  LENGTH(512)               │ STRUCTURE │
└──────────────┘                                          └───────────┘
```
+00000000 0066A670. 00000000 00005FA8 000056C4 4060D99E .........y...D -R..
+00000010 0066A680. 005E16AC C0040000 005D4648 005EDCCC ..;..{....)...;...
+00000020 0066A690. 005D3130 0001F320 0066D868 0001F000 ..).....3...Q...0..
+00000030 0066A6A0. 48000230 905EDEEC 0001F388 5060D7BE ......;....3h&-P..
+00000040 0066A6B0. 25900000 004DA008 0000020C 0001F190 ......(.........1..
+00000050 0066A6C0. 0903263F 00000000 07D00100 00000000 ............}.....
+00000060 0066A6D0. 0031C0DD 00054600 00AE9538 00007F42 ...{......n..."..
+00000070 0066A6E0. 0000A000 00006000 00679000 0088223F ......-......h...
+00000080 0066A6F0. 0066C130 E0FFFFFE 0000001E 0066D868 ...A.\.........Q..
+00000090 0066A700. 00000000 00000000 0001D030 E738E721 ...........}.X.X..
+000000A0 0066A710. 00000000 0001E380 0001E230 0001E0E0 .......T...S...\\.
+000000B0 0066A720. 0001E000 0066AEE0 0066B150 C500FF00 ...\.....\...&E....
+000000C0 0066A730. 000A0000 00000468 0066AAD8 00C800C4 ..............Q.H.D.
+000000D0 0066A740. 00000000 00000000 00AE9538 00000000 ..........n......
+000000E0 0066A750. 406639D4 0061CFF8 006174B0 00659BA8 . ..M./.8./.....y.
+000000F0 0066A760. 005EF38C 0061FDA8 0060F79C 00604B08 ..;3../.y.-7..-...
+00000100 0066A770. 0060882C 00000000 005E16AC 805D4654 ..-h......;...)...
+00000110 0066A780. 00000000 0065F32C 01652BF0 005D7960 .......3....0.)'-.
```
                                    ①

Figure 12-19  CICS initialization failure: CSA contents.


```
ASID(X'002E') STORAGE --------------------------------------------------------
COMMAND ===>                  ①                          SCROLL ===> PAGE
0066A7E4.            ┌────────┐
           01040000 00000000 00000000 .. ............ .
```
```
0066A7F0.  00000000 00000000 00000000 000071F0 . ................0 .
0066A800.  00000000 00000000 00000000 0066A608 . ...............w. .
0066A810.  07FE58F0 D19C07FF 00954299 009544B1 . ...0J....n.r.n.. .
0066A820.  00177000 000C0000 E6D6D9D2 C1D9C5C1 . ........WORKAREA .
0066A830.  00000000 001C0000 000C000C 00016C00 . ...............%. .
0066A840.  00141D00 000C3200 00000000 00000000 . ................ .
0066A850.  01000000 000C0000 0C000C00 0C00000C . ................ .
0066A860.  00000C00 000C0000 0C00000C 00000C00 . ................ .
0066A870. TO 0066AADF. (X'00000270' bytes)--All bytes contain X'00'
0066AAE0.  005D3130 005F4998 005FD792 00000000 . .).....q..Pk.... .
0066AAF0.  0061A128 0061A1BC 005EDAEC 005ED498 . ./~../~...;...;Mq .
0066AB00.  00000000 00000000 00000000 00619A58 . ............./.. .
0066AB10. TO 0066AB1F. (X'00000010' bytes)--All bytes contain X'00'
0066AB20.  00000000 00000000 005E49C4 00000000 . ..........;.D.... .
0066AB30.  00000000 0066CD48 8066CD84 01F4F15B . ..........d.41$ .
0066AB40.  00000000 0000FE00 005F4528 0088223F . ..............h... .
0066AB50.  0060F4D8 0066A670 0066CE28 0061CB28 . .-4Q..w......./.. .
0066AB60.  005F11A8 82208CC0 00000000 00000000 . ...yb..{........ .
0066AB70. TO 0066AB7F. (X'00000010' bytes)--All bytes contain X'00'
0066AB80.  006674CC 00669798 00658438 006146B8 . ......pq..d../.. .
0066AB90.  00608568 0060D428 0061EE88 006152E8 . .-e..-M.../.h./.Y .
```

Figure 12-20  CICS initialization failure: dump contents at **0066A7E4**.

# 13

# Storage Violations

This chapter will cover failures to CICS that affect all applications within the system. These failures occur within CICS system resources or modules, and therefore cause the entire address space to fail. Total system availability is extremely important to many installations, and these outages cannot be tolerated. Many steps can be taken to avoid some of these problems, as will be shown in the discussion of several abends. Many installations have used facilities such as MRO/ISC to isolate applications that cause system failures, and XRF (extended recovery facility) to recover from the outages in the shortest possible time. The most deadly of all system failures is the storage violation, or storage overlay.

## 13.1 STORAGE VIOLATION ISSUES

Most system programmers will agree that storage violations are some of the most difficult failures to debug. These failures are also some of the most severe, since although created by an application, they impact the entire region and can cause a system outage. Why are storage violations so pervasive in CICS, and what can be done to determine the cause of the problem? Of course, avoidance is the best solution. If these failures can be avoided, the outages are not experienced. Time will be taken to discuss some simple techniques and philosophies that may assist in storage violation avoidance.

If the problem is not avoided, how can the failure be successfully analyzed? This chapter will look closely at storage management in CICS, and determine some specific conditions that produce storage violations. There are also some decisions that may need to be made concerning CICS storage manage-

ment. A SIT option specifies what type of processing CICS should invoke in case of storage violations. There are also some CICS tools that can assist in isolating a storage violation. These facilities may be valuable in problem determination of storage violations. Finally, a storage violation failure will be produced and analyzed for cause of the problem, and how it could have been avoided.

### 13.1.1 Storage Violation SIT Options

When CICS detects that a storage violation has occurred, it uses the SIT option SVD to identify whether CICS should attempt storage recovery, and, if so, what the maximum number of attempts should be. There are two philosophies concerning storage recovery. Some installations believe that recovery should not be attempted, and, if storage has been corrupted, that potential exposure to critical data cannot be tolerated. If, for example, a storage violation occurs, it could corrupt blocks of storage that contain critical data. If recovery is requested, and successful, CICS continues to process as if the violation never occurred. Data contained within those blocks of storage may now contain invalid, and incorrect, values. Transactions will continue to execute and assume the data is correct. The integrity of the data has been affected, and the installation may not detect the situation for long periods of time. For this reason, many installations choose to specify:

```
SVD=NO
```

in their SIT options. This parameter specifies that no storage recovery should be attempted by CICS.

At the first occurrence of a storage violation, CICS will fail with a 501 abend code and produce a storage violation dump. The dump is produced in accordance with the DUMP options specified in the SIT. This has guaranteed integrity of data, since CICS was not allowed to proceed, but has produced a system failure, and will require that the address space be recreated.

The opposing philosophy of storage management within CICS is to attempt recovery, and hope to avoid a system outage. If the SIT contains either of the following entries:

```
SVD=YES    or    SVD=nn
```

CICS will attempt to recover from the storage violation, and produce a dump as specified by the DUMP parameter option. After nn storage violations have occurred, recovery will be attempted, but no further dumps will be produced. By using this option, the installation can attempt to continue processing after a storage violation and possibly avoid a total system failure. The dump produced is available, and would assist in analysis of the violation. Of course, system failures can still happen, even if recovery is requested. If the storage corrupted happens to be a CICS management module, or some other critical area, CICS may not be able to continue processing. These storage violations cannot be assisted by recovery attempts, and an immediate system failure occurs. A typical message such as

```
DFH0601 - PROGRAM INTERRUPT OCCURRED WITH SYS-
TEM TASK KCP IN CONTROL
```

could be the result of a storage violation. This message is probably preceded by a

```
DFH0508 - A STORAGE VIOLATION HAS OCCURRED
```

The system task indicated in the first message identifies the CICS task that was in control at the time of the failure. Some installations choose to specify SVD=NO for their production CICS regions, and SVD=10 (for example) for test. In this way, storage violations caused during testing are recovered and allow testing to continue, yet recovery is not allowed in production systems.

### 13.1.2  Storage Chains

Task storage is chained off the task control block, the TCA. As displayed in several previous dumps, the TCA system area contains a pointer to the first piece of task storage. This first block of transaction storage, as found in Chapter 2, contains the TACB (task abend control block) and is built by CICS on behalf of the transaction. Additional pieces of storage are built by CICS as a result of a CICS command request, such as a HANDLE CONDITION, STARTBR, or user GETMAINS. Figure 13-1 shows a portion of a CICS trace and the steps that are taken to build these blocks of storage. Note that after control is passed to program MG004, CICS locates the program in the appropriate table (1), receives a normal return, and then requests SCP (storage control program) to GETMAIN storage (2). SCP then acquires user storage (3) to satisfy this request. In the trace entry from FIELD A and FIELD B, the type of storage built was 8C (4), which is user stoage, and the storage was built beginning at address **000AC000** (5). This block of storage was created by CICS to accommodate the program request, although the application itself did not perform the GETMAIN. If the contents of this storage were investigated, a block of data represented by Figure 13-2 would be found. Use this as an example of task storage, since all storage, whichever type is built, looks very similar.

In this example, the first fullword of storage at address **000AC000** is 8C0A3B58. The first four bytes of transaction storage always contain the following information:

Byte 1 — Class of storage
Bytes 3-4 — Length of this block of storage

The classes of storage identify the type of storage that was created. For example, type 8C indicates User Storage. The formatted dump isolates each block of storage and provides a title for the storage type. Since the example shown is actually unformatted, the class of storage is in the first byte of the block of storage. Type 8C is typical of user storage, since it is actually specific to this task, and not related to CICS system resources.

The next portion of this fullword is the length of this block of storage. Bytes 3-4 contain 3B58. If this hexadecimal value is translated to decimal, this block of user storage is 15,192 bytes. The character representation at the right of the unformatted dump displays a block of storage containing the Working Storage section of the program. Since CICS was preparing to execute the program after the transfer control (XCTL), Working Storage was loaded as a block of user storage on behalf of the task.

Storage control builds the block of storage, and in an attempt to control the limits of this storage, creates SAA chains (Storage Accounting Areas). The first fullword of storage contains the storage type

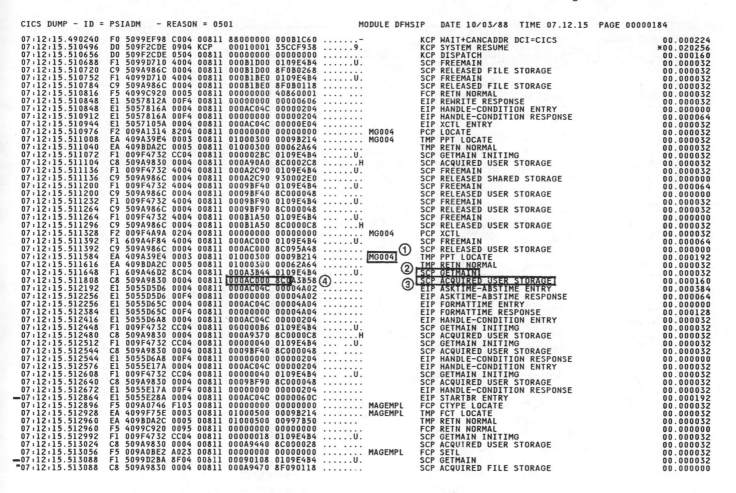

Figure 13-1    CICS storage violations: trace table entries.

and length. The second fullword in all transaction storage contains the pointer to the next portion of transaction storage "owned" by this task. As CICS builds storage on behalf of this task, it continues the chain. This chain not only contains forward pointers, but also backward pointers. In other words, all blocks of storage contain two fullwords of storage in the beginning and two fullwords at the end to complete the storage entry. Note in Figure 13-2 that the second fullword of information contains **000A90A0**. This address is the next piece of storage owned by this task. Within this block of storage, however, is also a backward pointer. At address **000AFB58** is the end of this block of storage. Figure 13-3 contains the portion of storage pointed to by the previous SAA. Notice that at the end of the storage are two fullwords, exactly as at the beginning of the storage (1). CICS uses this technique, called SAA chains, to insure that storage, once created, is intact when it is freed, or no longer needed. This chapter will show an example where this is not the case, where the forward or backward

SAA pointer is corrupted. Storage violations are the direct result of CICS's attempt to validate these Storage Accounting Areas; if the attempt is unsuccessful, a Storage Violation will result.

In this example, both the forward and backward pointers are intact and correct. This block of storage, when freed, will delete successfully. It is hoped that all of our storage frees this way, avoiding the failures from storage management.

How can a system programmer determine which chains in task storage are correct and complete, and which are not? It may be possible to utilize tools that are available, or to take the unformatted dump and chase the chains ourselves. Knowing that the TCA system area points to the first piece of storage in the chain, use that first address to locate the first SAA. The address at offset +4 into that block of storage points to the SAA in the second block of storage. Following these pointers, it is possible to locate every piece of task storage for this TCA. The last block of storage will contain an address pointing back to the TCA. Of course, IPCS

```
ASID(X'002E') STORAGE  --------------------------------------------------------
COMMAND ===>                                                   SCROLL ===> PAGE
000AC000.  8C0A3B58  000A90A0  00000000  00000000  . ................. .
000AC010.  0000002A  505676E0  A09A441A  9056771A  . .....&...\........ .
000AC020.  0056755A  505676C4  0055C0F0  005590F0  . ....!&..D..{0...0 .
000AC030.  0055B0F0  0055A0F0  00000000  005674F0  . ....0...0.......0 .
000AC040.  0055CBF0  0055C650  009A467C  E6D6D9D2  . ....0..F&...@WORK .
000AC050.  C9D5C740  E2E3D6D9  C1C7C540  C6D6D940  . ING STORAGE FOR   .
000AC060.  D4C7F0F0  F4404000  00000000  5C5C5C40  . MG004  .....***   .
000AC070.  C1E4C4C9  E360E2E3  C1D4D740  5C5C5C40  . AUDIT-STAMP ***   .
000AC080.  D7C7D47A  4040D4C7  F0F0F440  404040D7  . PGM:  MG004      P .
000AC090.  C7D4D97A  40C4D7C1  C4D7D4D9  40404040  . GMR: DPADPMR      .
000AC0A0.  40404040  40C4C1E3  C57A40F8  F861F0F8  .      DATE: 88/08 .
000AC0B0.  61F1F940  E3C9D4C5  7A40F1F1  7AF4F47A  . /19 TIME: 11:44: .
000AC0C0.  F5F040C1  D9C3C87A  40F0F0F0  F0F34040  . 50 ARCH: 00003   .
000AC0D0.  4040E4D7  D5D67A40  F0F0F0F0  F3404040  .   UPNO: 00003    .
000AC0E0.  40C4D3C1  7A4040F8  F861F0F8  61F1F940  . DLA:  88/08/19   .
000AC0F0.  D3C9C2D9  7A40D7E2  C9C1C44B  D3C9C2D9  . LIBR: PSIAD.LIBR .
000AC100.  C1D9D54B  E2D6E4D9  C3C54040  40404040  . ARN.SOURCE        .
000AC110.  TO 000AC11F. (X'00000010' bytes)--All bytes contain X'40', C' '
000AC120.  4040405C  5C5C40C1  E4C4C9E3  60E2E3C1  .    *** AUDIT-STA .
000AC130.  D4D7405C  5C5C0000  00000000  00000000  . MP ***.......... .
000AC140.  00000000  00000000  00000000  000000F0  . ...............0 .
000AC150.  F1000000  00000000  00000000  00000000  . 1................ .

ASID(X'002E') STORAGE  --------------------------------------------------------
COMMAND ===>                                                   SCROLL ===> PAGE
000AF9D0.  00564C10  00000000  00000000  00000000  . ...<............. .
000AF9E0.  TO 000AFA1F. (X'00000040' bytes)--All bytes contain X'00'
000AFA20.  00000000  00000000  00000000  00566F4A  . ..............?c .
000AFA30.  00000000  0055E3FA  00000000  0055DAAA  . .......T........ .
000AFA40.  00000000  0055E824  00000000  0055E876  . .......Y........Y. .
000AFA50.  00000000  00565CB2  00000000  0055EA02  . .......*........ .
000AFA60.  00000000  00566BCE  00000000  00566E76  . .......,........>. .
000AFA70.  00000000  0055E718  00000000  005617BC  . .......X........ .
000AFA80.  00000000  00564C16  00000000  00562BBE  . .......<........ .
000AFA90.  00000000  00564A6A  00000000  0055ECBC  . .......c|........ .
000AFAA0.  00000000  005658F4  00000000  0056145E  . .......4........; .
000AFAB0.  00000000  00565536  00000000  005670C4  . ................D .
000AFAC0.  00000000  00565AE2  00000000  00564C10  . .......!S......<. .
000AFAD0.  00000000  00565CAC  00000000  00566980  . .......*........ .
000AFAE0.  00000000  00566A54  00000000  0056697A  . .......|........: .
000AFAF0.  00000000  00566C68  00000000  005672F6  . .......%........6 .
000AFB00.  00000000  005673BA  00000000  00567480  . ................ .
000AFB10.  00000000  0056755A  00000000  000AF58C  . .......!......5. .
000AFB20.  000AF45C  000AEDF4  800AF42C  000ADE2C  . ..4*...4..4...... .
000AFB30.  800AF434  800AF3D4  000AF584  000AF584  . ..4...3M..5d..5d .
000AFB40.  800AF4FC  00000000  00000000  00000000  . ..4............. .
000AFB50.  00000000  00000000  8C0A3B58  000A90A0  . ................. .
                                      ①
```

Figure 13-2  CICS storage violations: dump contents at **000AC000**.

can be used to identify these addresses, until the last pointer references the TCA.

Figure 13-4 is an example of a CLIST that was written to automate this process. The CLIST identifies the transaction ID (1), the task ID (2), and then lists each block of transaction storage including storage type (3), length (4), and chain address (5). The storage type identifies the category of storage; the chain address is the address found at offset +4 into this SAA, the address to the next piece of stor-

age. The last entry's chain address is the pointer back to the TCA system area of this task.

These CLISTs can be invoked from within IPCS to map out any information within the unformatted dump. Many installations have written their own CLISTs, or used others from software exchanges such as SHARE. The CLIST produces in just a few seconds what could take much longer manually.

If a task completes and returns control to CICS, all storage created on behalf of this task is re-

```
ASID(X'002E') STORAGE  ----------------------------------------------------------
COMMAND ===>                                              SCROLL ===> PAGE
 000A90A0.  8C0002C8   000A9000   F1F9F2F1   F4F3F4F2   . ...H....19214342 .
 000A90B0.  F5F5F9F9   F9404040   40404040   40404040   . 55999            .
 000A90C0.  40404040   40404040   4040E800   005F4040   .            Y...   .
 000A90D0. TO 000A90EF. (X'00000020' bytes)--All bytes contain X'40', C' '
 000A90F0.  40404040   40404040   D5404040   40404040   .         N         .
 000A9100.  40404040   40404040   40404040   C6D3D6D9   .              FLOR .
 000A9110.  C9C4C140   D4C9D9D9   D6D94050   40D7D3C1   . IDA MIRROR & PLA .
 000A9120.  E3C5F6F1   F0F140D4   89998194   819940D7   . TE6101 Miramar P .
 000A9130.  92A6A840   40404040   F2F5F5F9   F9F940F3   . kwy      255999 3 .
 000A9140.  40F0F461   F0F161F8   F7404040   4040D489   . 04/01/87      Mi .
 000A9150.  99819481   99404040   40404040   404040C6   . ramar            F .
 000A9160.  D3F3F3F0   F2F3F0F0   F0F0F3F0   F5F9F6F2   . L330230000305962 .
 000A9170.  F7F5F5F0   40404040   4040C3C5   E640D340   . 7550      CEW L  .
 000A9180.  D5D5F1D5   D5D5D5D5   40D5D5F3   C1D5D540   . NN1NNNNN NN3ANN  .
 000A9190.  E8E8D5C2   F5F2D2C1   D9C5D540   E2D7C5D5   . YYNB52KAREN SPEN .
 000A91A0.  C3C54040   40404040   40404040   F9F9F9F9   . CE          9999 .
 000A91B0.  F9F9F9F9   F9F94040   40404000   00000CF2   . 999999     ....2 .
 000A91C0.  F5F5F9F9   F9404040   40404040   40404040   . 55999            .
 000A91D0. TO 000A91DF. (X'00000010' bytes)--All bytes contain X'40', C' '
 000A91E0.  404040D5   F0F4F0F1   F8F70000   0CF0F000   .    N040187...00. .
 000A91F0.  0C00000C   0000000C   0000000C   0000000C   . ................ .
 000A9200.  40000C00   000C000C   404040F0   F0F0F040   . ........    0000 .

ASID(X'002E') STORAGE  ----------------------------------------------------------
COMMAND ===>                                              SCROLL ===> PAGE
 000A9210.  00000CF0   F0F0F0F0   F040000C   000C0000   . ...000000 ...... .
 000A9220.  000C000C   0000000C   000C0000   000C000C   . ................ .
 000A9230.  0000000C   000C0000   000C000C   000C000C   . ................ .
 000A9240.  000C000C   000C000C   000C000C   000C000C   . ................ .
 000A9250.  000CF0F0   F040000C   40404040   E3C3C5D7   . ...000 ..    TCEP .
 000A9260.  D9F0F140   40D5D500   0C000000   0C40C3C5   . R01  NN...... CE .
 000A9270.  000C000C   000C000C   000C4000   00000C00   . ................ .
 000A9280.  00000CD5   F1F1F2F3   F3F8F6F5   F2F8F1F0   . ...N112338652810 .
 000A9290.  D5D54000   000CD5D5   D5D5F0F0   F0F0F0F0   . NN ...NNNN000000 .
 000A92A0.  00000CF8   F7F0F640   40000C40   40404040   . ...8706  ..      .
 000A92B0.  4040F0F0   F0F0F0F0   F1F0F0F3   F8F8F1F0   .   00000010038810 .
 000A92C0.  F0F3F8F8   C4C5C2D9   C140D340   E6C1D9C4   . 0388DEBRA L WARD .
 000A92D0.  40404040   40404040   4040F2F8   F0F140D5   .          2801 N .
 000A92E0.  40C540F2   F0F840E3   C5D9D9C1   C3C54040   . E 208 TERRACE   .
 000A92F0. TO 000A92FF. (X'00000010' bytes)--All bytes contain X'40', C' '
 000A9300.  40404040   4040D4C9   C1D4C940   40404040   .       MIAMI     .
 000A9310.  40404040   404040C6   D3F3F3F1   F8F0F0F0   .        FL3318000 .
 000A9320.  F0F04040   40404040   F3F0F5F9   F3F7F0F9   . 00      30593709 .
 000A9330.  F3F74040   40404000   07A55440   40404040   . 37      ..v.     .
 000A9340.  D6F0F0F0   F0F10000   5FC4C5C2   D9C1D3E6   . 000001...DEBRALW .
 000A9350.  C1D9C4C6   D3D6D9C9   C4C1D4C9   D9F1F9F2   . ARDFLORIDAMIR192 .
 000A9360.  F1F4F3F4   00000000   8C0002C8   000A9000   . 1434.......H.... .
```

Figure 13-3   CICS storage violations: CICS storage with SAA chains.

leased. At this time, the SAA chains are evaluated, and, it is hoped, all storage is freed so that it can be reused by another task. Figure 13-5 shows the entries from a CICS trace during this interval. As shown, the transaction completes and attempts to return control (1). At this time, a number of entries for storage are freed, all returning normal conditions from the request (2). The storage is then returned to CICS as free areas, and can be reused by new tasks as required. This example displays normal conditions when all storage is chained correctly. An example will be used soon where attempts to free this storage fail, and produce a storage violation. An important concept to realize at this point is that only when storage is released are the SAA chains evaluated. The performance penalties of checking every time may be prohibitive in a production environment. CICS attempts to free all storage and, if unsuccessful, produces a storage violation.

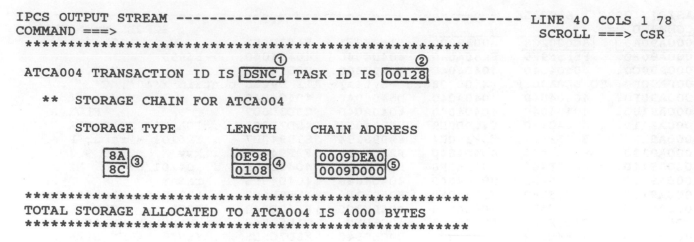

Figure 13-4   CICS storage violations: IPCS CLIST of task storage.

```
CICS DUMP - ID = PSIADM   - REASON = 0501                    MODULE DFHSIP   DATE 10/03/88  TIME 07.12.15  PAGE 00000177
07:12:14.264352  C9 509A986C 0004 00810 000B4080 8C0000C8 .. ....H           SCP RELEASED USER STORAGE         00.000000
07:12:14.264384  F2 009F4A9A 1004 00810 00000000 00000000 ........ MG003     PCP RETURN                       00.000032
07:12:14.264416  F1 609A4F84 4004 00810 000BCF20 0109E4B4 ......U.           SCP FREEMAIN                      00.000032
07:12:14.264448  C9 509A986C 0004 00810 000BCF20 8C0B5A48 ........           SCP RELEASED USER STORAGE         00.000032
07:12:14.264640  F0 409A384C 8004 00810 00000000 00000000 ........           KCP DETACH                       00.000192
07:12:14.264672  D8 409F0D50 0203 00810 02000000 0009C920 ......I.           SPP SYSTEM                       00.000032
07:12:14.264736  F5 609EB57A 1003 00810 100B8240 00000000 ........           FCP RELEASE                      00.000064
07:12:14.264832  F1 4099D710 4004 00810 000B8240 0109E4B4 ... ..U.           SCP FREEMAIN                      00.000096
07:12:14.264832  C9 509A986C 0004 00810 000B8240 8F0B0118 ........           SCP RELEASED FILE STORAGE        00.000000
07:12:14.264864  F5 4099C920 0005 00810 C5D4D7D4 E3D940E2 EMPMTR S           FCP RETN NORMAL                  00.000032
07:12:14.264928  FC 509E9C94 0B03 00810 03000000 0009E4B4 ......U.           ZCP ZISP ISC FREE                00.000064
07:12:14.264960  FC 409E41CE 0304 00810 00284880 0009E4B4 ......U.           ZCP ZDET DETACH                  00.000032
07:12:14.264960  FC 709DB7F8 1804 00810 005C4880 0009E4B4 .*....U.           ZCP ZSDS SEND                    00.000000
07:12:14.264992  FC 509DB8B8 1D04 00810 003B4880 0009E4B4 ......U.           ZCP ZSDR SEND RESPONSE           00.000000
07:12:14.265056  F0 609DD34E 0D04 00810 00040830 00000000 ........           KCP ATTACH HTA                   00.000064
07:12:14.265216  FC 409E4390 0B05 00810 03000000 0009E4B4 ......U.           ZCP RETN ZISP ISC FREE           00.000160
07:12:14.265248  D8 409EB9AA 0005 00810 00000000 00000000 ........           SPP RETN                         00.000032
07:12:14.265248  F0 509F0D5A 0304 00810 000BA490 00000000 ........           KCP DEQALL                       00.000000
07:12:14.265376  D0 509F1608 0704 00810 06180400 D4D4C7F1 ....MMG1    ①      KCP TERMINATE                    00.000128
07:12:14.266144  F1 409F0F26 4A04 KCP       000B2000 0000000          SCP FREEMAIN                      00.000768
07:12:14.266176  C9 509A986C 0004 KCP       000B4CB0 8F0B0218 ........        SCP RELEASED FILE STORAGE        00.000032
07:12:14.266208  C9 509A986C 0004 KCP       000B4000 8C000078 ........        SCP RELEASED USER STORAGE        00.000032
07:12:14.266240  C9 509A986C 0004 KCP       000B4C90 8C000018 ........        SCP RELEASED USER STORAGE        00.000032
07:12:14.266240  C9 509A986C 0004 KCP       000B4BD0 8C000058 ........        SCP RELEASED USER STORAGE        00.000000
07:12:14.266528  C9 509A986C 0004 KCP       000B8660 8C000028 ...-....        SCP RELEASED USER STORAGE        00.000288
07:12:14.266560  C9 509A986C 0004 KCP       000BC720 8C0000B8 ..G.....        SCP RELEASED USER STORAGE        00.000032
07:12:14.266816  C9 509A986C 0004 KCP       000BC4D0 8F0B0248 ..D.....        SCP RELEASED FILE STORAGE        00.000256
07:12:14.266848  C9 509A986C 0004 KCP       000B8210 8C000028 ........        SCP RELEASED USER STORAGE        00.000032
07:12:14.266880  C9 509A986C 0004 KCP       000B8570 9B000098 ...0....        SCP RELEASED JCA STORAGE         00.000032
07:12:14.266880  C9 509A986C 0004 KCP       000B81F0 8C000018 ........        SCP RELEASED USER STORAGE        00.000000
07:12:14.266944  C9 509A986C 0004 KCP       000BCE40 8F0B00D8 ... ...Q        SCP RELEASED FILE STORAGE        00.000064
07:12:14.267200  C9 509A986C 0004 KCP       000B8540 8C000028 ... ....   ②    SCP RELEASED USER STORAGE        00.000256
07:12:14.267200  C9 509A986C 0004 KCP       000B83E0 8C0000B8 ........        SCP RELEASED USER STORAGE        00.000000
07:12:14.267232  C9 509A986C 0004 KCP       000B83C0 8C000018 ........        SCP RELEASED USER STORAGE        00.000032
07:12:14.267264  C9 509A986C 0004 KCP       000B84C0 8F0B0078 ........        SCP RELEASED FILE STORAGE        00.000032
07:12:14.267264  C9 509A986C 0004 KCP       000B8360 8C000058 ...-....        SCP RELEASED USER STORAGE        00.000000
07:12:14.267296  C9 509A986C 0004 KCP       000B8190 8C000058 ........        SCP RELEASED USER STORAGE        00.000032
07:12:14.267296  C9 509A986C 0004 KCP       000B2FE0 8C000018 ........        SCP RELEASED USER STORAGE        00.000000
07:12:14.267328  C9 509A986C 0004 KCP       000B80D0 8C0000B8 ........        SCP RELEASED USER STORAGE        00.000032
07:12:14.267552  C9 509A986C 0004 KCP       000B2E30 8C000108 ........        SCP RELEASED USER STORAGE        00.000224
07:12:14.267584  C9 509A986C 0004 KCP       000B2000 8A040E28 ........        SCP RELEASED TCA STORAGE         00.000000
07:12:14.268320  D0 509F2CDE 0504 TCP       00000000 00000000 ........        KCP DISPATCH                     00.000736
07:12:14.268384  EE 709DD588 2214 TCP       005C4126 0109E4B4 .*....U. 010000EA  VIO SEND EB OIC DATA RQE1     00.000064
07:12:14.268384  EE 709DD588 0024 TCP       0694F5C2 11C57C13 ..5B.E.. 010000EA  VIO DATA                      00.000000
07:12:14.268416  FC 709DD84C 1204 TCP       00080001 1909E4B4 ......U.        ZCP ZFRE FREEMAIN                00.000032
07:12:14.268448  F1 609DDBF6 4104 TCP       000B0000 0109E4B4 ......U.        SCP FREEMAIN                     00.000032
07:12:14.268448  C9 509A986C 0004 TCP       000B0000 850B0A08 ........        SCP RELEASED TERMINAL STORAGE    00.000000
07:12:14.268576  FC 709DD84C 0304 TCP       00080001 0009E4B4 ......U.        ZCP ZDET DETACH                  00.000128
07:12:14.268608  FC 709DD84C 1204 TCP       00080001 0009E4B4 ......U.        ZCP ZFRE FREEMAIN                00.000032
07:12:14.268704  F0 409DE830 4004 TCP       40000000 00958D50 ........        KCP WAIT DCI=LIST                00.000096
07:12:14.469344  D0 509F2CDE 0904 KCP       40010001 35CCF80E .....8.         KCP SYSTEM RESUME                *00.200640
07:12:14.469472  D0 509F2CDE 0504 TCP       00000000 00000000 ........        KCP DISPATCH                     00.000128
07:12:14.469568  F0 409DE830 4004 TCP       40000000 00958D50 ........        KCP WAIT DCI=LIST                00.000096
07:12:14.926848  D0 509F2CDE 0904 KCP       40010001 35CCF83F .....8.         KCP SYSTEM RESUME                *00.457280
07:12:14.926912  F3 609F19A2 C003 KCP       00000000 00000000 ........        ICP ICE EXPIRY ANALYSIS          00.000064
07:12:14.926944  F0 609E66DA 0804 KCP       0009B190 0100808C ........        KCP RESUME                       00.000032
```

Figure 13-5   CICS storage violations: trace table entries of storage freed at task termination.

```
ABEND CODE:  U501

PROBABLE CAUSE:  Storage overlay of transaction or system storage

IMPORTANT DUMP ITEMS:   PRDMP - TRACE TABLE
                        PRDMP - TASK SUMMARY
                        PRDMP - TASK STORAGE
                        IPCS  - CURRENT TASK
                        IPCS  - CONTENTS OF TASK STORAGE
                        IPCS  - LISTING OF STORAGE CHAIN
OTHER RELEVANT ITEMS:   SYSLOG ENTRY FOR SDUMP
```

Figure 13-6   Significant items in a storage violation.

Unfortunately, when the corrupted storage is detected, the crime may have been committed long ago. Another problem that complicates these types of failures is detecting the actual offending task. At the time of the storage violation, the victim has been identified, but not the criminal.

### 13.1.3   Storage Violations — An Example

Previous sections have looked at trace table entries, storage chains, and actual contents of transaction storage when all goes well. Of course, this would be the preferable alternative. Unfortunately, conditions arise that produce irregular results and, in some situations, storage violations. Installations attempt to avoid these failures, but many times still experience them. Each incident will produce different causes and a variety of symptoms. One example will be analyzed, and an attempt will be made to isolate the critical items of storage violations. Previous chapters dealing with application failures identified abend codes, probable cause of the failure, and the important dump items. That same format will be used for storage violations.

Figure 13-6 is a summary of these items. Realize that in system failures, unlike transaction abends, it may be more difficult to pinpoint the specific cause. Most important are the items to reference within the dump, or other sources, to develop a technique for these types of failures. It will also be assumed, in system failures, that an unformatted SDUMP was requested. These dumps will allow the use PRDMP to format necessary information, and IPCS to reference additional storage within the dump.

**SYSLOG Entry for SDUMP.** The first symptom of a storage violation will be the creation of a dump; in this case, into a system dump dataset. If no storage recovery has been specified, the dump will be produced and CICS will abend. If storage recovery was requested, the dump will be produced and CICS will attempt to recover. In either case, an entry in the MVS system log will result. The item will display the abend code, time and date stamp, and other information relevant to the failure. It identifies the specific system dump that will be needed to process with PRDMP and IPCS for analysis. Now that storage violation has occurred, debugging will be required.

**PRDMP — Trace Table, Task Summary, and Task Storage.** As explained in Chapter 14, the IBM-supplied utility PRDMP can be utilized to format this unformatted dump. Submit the job as shown in Figure 14-6, using the system dump dataset identified in the previous step in the data definition. The resulting report will provide an abbreviated look at the contents of the dump. A few key items in this report are the most relevant for debugging storage violations. The first piece of this report used will be the trace table. Figure 13-7 shows the last page of the trace, with the corresponding storage violation. Note that directly preceding the violation was an entry to free user storage (1) by task 00811. The storage identified in the trace that was attempting to release was type 8C (2) at address **000A9370** (3). Obviously, CICS was unsuccessful with this request. CICS attempted to free the storage during the end of the transaction. Notice that the last CICS command was a RETURN to CICS (4). The next step is to attempt to find where this storage was created, and determine why it has been corrupted.

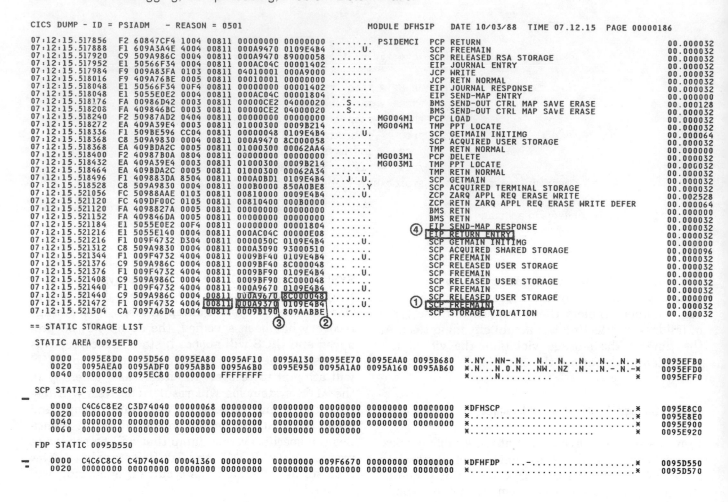

Figure 13-7   CICS storage violations: trace table entries at storage violation.

Moving back in the trace, as shown in Figure 13-8, the same task, 00811, executed a HANDLE CONDITION (1), and CICS created a block of user storage on behalf of this request. The storage GETMAINED was type 8C at address **000A9370** (2). Somewhere between this creation and the end of the task, this block of storage was overlayed and made the storage release fail. It may be possible to look through the trace; however, no additional entries can be found against this address. The trace has documented the creation of the storage and the failure of that storage to be freed. It will be necessary to look in other locations to attempt to detect the cause.

The Task Summary is represented by Figure 13-9, found on page 193 of the PRDMP report. The summary displays the active DCA chain; task 00811 is the current task. This further validates the task number found in the trace table. In this example, the task summary is of minimal significance, since the storage violation dump pertains

more to task storage than task status. It may, however, provide a visual look at other tasks that were executing at the time of the failure. In many cases, as previously mentioned, the storage violation identifies the victim. One of the other executing tasks may have actually caused the overlay.

A more significant item in the PRDMP report is the listing of task storage associated with each active task. Figure 13-10 contains the one page of a section titled "Task and User Related Storage." This is not the first page of the section, since it would start with the first TCA on the chain. As found in Figure 13-9, the TCA of notes appears second on the task summary. Move forward in this section to the second SYSTEM/USER TCA entry, found near the bottom of that page (1). Notice that the address of this TCA is the beginning of the TCA system area, **0009B000**. The address listed in the Task Summary from Figure 13-9 references the TCA user area, **0009B190**. Some people get confused because the report utilizes different ad-

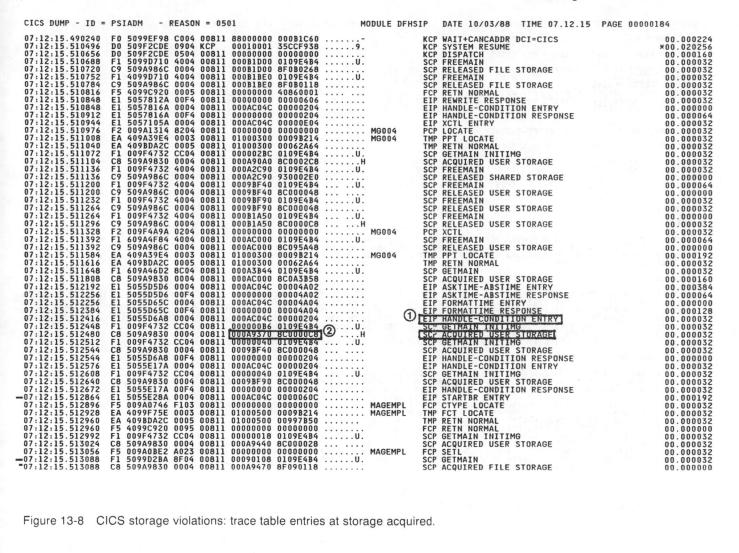

Figure 13-8   CICS storage violations: trace table entries at storage acquired.

dresses. Some items reference the address of the system area, some reference the user area.

The entries within this section of the report follow all blocks of storage chained off the TCA. Following the pages after the first entry is a page as represented by Figure 13-11. This page identifies that last correct task storage at address **000A9440** (1), and contains a pointer to the next one at **000A9370** (2). Immediately following this entry is the message:

```
DFH5055I  ZERO VALUE FOUND IN SAASAD
```

The PRDMP program detected a value in the SAA containing zeros. Of course, neither the storage type nor the address of the next SAA can be zeros, consequently the program terminated the chain. Unfortunately, the program does not produce the corrupted block of storage and does not display the extent of the problem. It does, however, provide

more information pertaining to the cause of the storage violation. It also validates the information from the trace table. The trace entry preceding the storage violation identified the storage unable to be released at address **000A9370**. This is the same address that was displayed in the pointer to the next task storage (2). To complete the analysis, it will be necessary to get into the unformatted dump with IPCS and view all related storage online.

**IPCS — Current Task, Task Storage, and Storage Chains.** With an unformatted SDUMP, IPCS can be used to browse any portion of the dump, or execute CLISTs to automate some of these functions. One of the mysteries still unsolved in the storage violation is the content of the task storage that was corrupted. Using the browse facility in IPCS, request the address and view the contents. Figure 13-12 contains the screen that would be displayed as a result of a browse request for **000A9370**. As pre-

```
CICS DUMP - ID = PSIADM   - REASON = 0501              MODULE DFHSIP   DATE 10/03/88  TIME 07.12.15  PAGE 00000193
== SUMMARY OF TASKS ON THE ACTIVE CHAIN

DCAADDR TASK ID/ADDR  ECAADDR ECA FLAGS

040310  00023/0A0190  95A970  00  8040   WAIT ON SYSTEM ECB
040000  00811/09B190          8800   **** CURRENT TASK ****
0402A0  00128/09D190          4040   WAIT ON LIST OF ECBS
040070  00017/04F190  09A73C  00  8840   WAIT ON CICS RELATED ECB IN DFHVAP   AT + 000152
0403F0  JJJ/070190    9F9828  00  8040   WAIT ON SYSTEM ECB
9F6EE0  TCP/9F7150            4040   WAIT ON LIST OF ECBS


== SUMMARY OF TASKS ON THE SUSPEND CHAIN

DCAADDR TASK ID/ADDR  ECAADDR ECA FLAGS

040380  JJJ/04D190            1004   NON DISPATCHABLE
040230  JJJ/079190            1004   NON DISPATCHABLE
0401C0  JJJ/04A190            1004   NON DISPATCHABLE
0400E0  JJJ/047190            1004   NON DISPATCHABLE


== DCA-TCA ACTIVE CHAIN

  DCA 00040310

      0000  81000070 00000000 00000000 00040000  009F6714 000A0190 80400080 0095A970  *A.....................NZ.*  00040310
      0020  00000000 00000000 00000000 00000000  00000000 22008000 00000000 00000000  *.........................*  00040330
      0040  00000000 00000000 00000000 00000000  00000000 00000000 000A07B4 00000001  *.........................*  00040350
      0060  00000000 00000000                                                          *........            *        00040370

  USERTCA 000A0190

      0000  000A0000 00000000 0095A954 009F6AD8  000A0878 0095A970 80090000 00818000  *.......NZ....Q.....NZ......A..*  000A0190
      0020  5097E436 00000000 00000001 000A09A0  000A0878 4097E230 000A0810 00000000  * PU..........PS.......*        000A01B0
      0040  000A0000 480001E8 00000000 00000000  0095A954 0095A970 009EFA56 0009A870  *.......Y.........NZ..NZ......Y.*  000A01D0
      0060  4097E648 009F8E28 00000000 000A09A0  000A0878 4097E230 000A0810 000001C8  * PW..........PS.......H*       000A01F0
      0080  00000000 00000000 00000000 00000000  00000000 00000000 00000000 00000000  *.........................*  000A0210
      00A0  -       00DF LINES SAME AS ABOVE                                                                        000A0230
      00E0  00000000 00000000 04000000 00000000  00000000 00000000 00000000 00000000  *.........................*  000A0270

  SYSTCA 000A0000

      0000  8A040C08 000A0000 000A0C10 000A0C10  8000023C 0095ABBC 00040310 00000000  *...................N.......*  000A0000
      0020  0007B190 00000000 00000000 00000000  00000000 00000000 00000000 00000000  *.........................*  000A0020
      0040  00000000 000A0520 00000000 00000000  00000000 00000000 00000000 00000000  *.........................*  000A0040
      0060  00000000 00000000 00000000 00000000  00000000 00000000 00000000 00000000  *.........................*  000A0060
      0080  FE0A0A60 00000000 FE0A0800 FE0A0C08  009F8E28 000A0810 00000000 00000000  *...-.....................*  000A0080
      00A0  00000000 00000000 00000000 00000000  C3E2E2E8 00000000 00000000 000A0290  *.................CSSY.......*  000A00A0
      00C0  00000000 00000004 00000000 00000000  00000000 00000000 00000000 00000000  *.........................*  000A00C0
      00E0  00000000 00000000 00000000 00000000  00000000 00000000 00000000 00000000  *.........................*  000A00E0
      0100  00000000 00000000 00000000 00000000  00000000 00000000 00000000 00000000  *.........................*  000A0100
      0120  0C00010C 0095ABBC 00000000 00040310  00000000 00000000 00000000 00000000  *.......N.................*  000A0120
      0140  00000000 00000000 000A0550 0000025C  00000000 00000000 00000000 00000000  *..........*..............*  000A0140
      0160  00000000 00000000 00000000 00000000  00000000 00000000 00000000 00000000  *.........................*  000A0160
      0180  00000000 00000000 00000000 00000000                                       *........            *        000A0180
```

Figure 13-9   CICS storage violations: task summary.

viously stated, the first eight bytes of a storage area contain the SAA. The first four bytes identify the storage type and length, and the next four bytes contain the pointer to the next block of storage. The first four bytes do not contain a storage type of length and, in fact, contain zeros (1). The second four bytes appear intact since they point to an apparently legitimate address, **000AC000**. The header SAA appears to have been corrupted, but only the first four bytes. Further investigate the severity of the overlay by attempting to find the trailing SAA, and determine if the end of the task storage has been affected. Further into this display is the trailing SAA (2). From this entry, it is obvious that the storage was built as an 8C type, with a length of C8. This same entry is displayed within the trace when the storage was built, in Figure 13-7 (2). There exists, therefore, an intact piece of user storage, except for the first four bytes.

Could the previous storage have extended its area and overlayed the first four bytes into this area? Browse back into the storage with IPCS and identify the previous addresses. Figure 13-13 contains the display of addresses directly preceding Figure 13-12. As displayed, another block of user storage exists beginning at address **000A9000**, with a length of 2C8 (1). In fact, the trailing SAA for this storage is intact, and directly precedes the four bytes of zeros (2). Since the trailing SAA has not been corrupted, it is unlikely that the program extended its storage area. It would have overlayed its own trailing SAA before it overlayed the header SAA of the next one. This browse of storage provided some valuable information concerning the contents of specific addresses. Again, investigation has found the victim and the results of the overlay.

Another facility available to utilize with IPCS are some CLISTs that either validate information already found or locate additional items. In some cases, the PRDMP task summary does not provide the identity of the current task, but merely lists all TCAs on the active and suspend chains. One CLIST

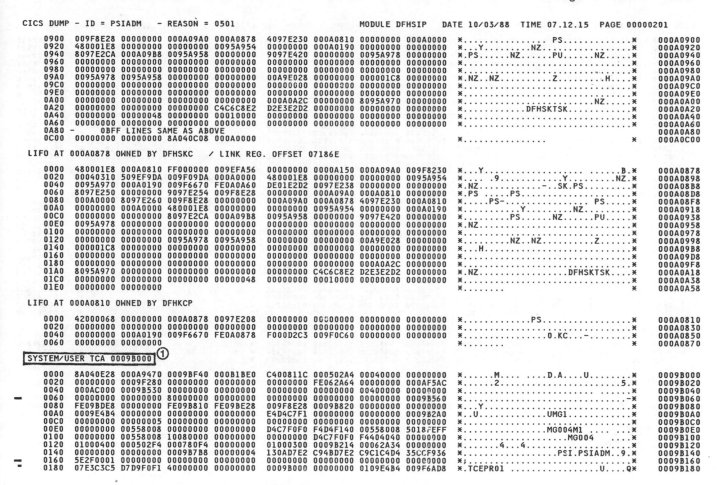

```
CICS DUMP - ID = PSIADM   - REASON = 0501                        MODULE DFHSIP   DATE 10/03/88  TIME 07.12.15  PAGE 00000201

   0900  009F8E28 00000000 000A09A0 000A0878   4097E230 000A0810 00000000 000A0000   *................PS.............*  000A0900
   0920  480001E8 00000000 00000000 0095A954   00000000 000A0190 00000000 00000000   *...Y.........NZ................*  000A0920
   0940  8097E2CA 000A09B8 0095A958 00000000   9097E420 00000000 0095A978 00000000   *.PS.......NZ.......PU.......NZ.*  000A0940
   0960  00000000 00000000 00000000 00000000   00000000 00000000 00000000 00000000   *..............................*  000A0960
   0980  00000000 00000000 00000000 00000000   00000000 00000000 00000000 00000000   *..............................*  000A0980
   09A0  0095A978 0095A958 00000000 00000000   00A9E028 00000000 000001C8 00000000   *.NZ..NZ.............Z......H...*  000A09A0
   09C0  00000000 00000000 00000000 00000000   00000000 00000000 00000000 00000000   *..............................*  000A09C0
   09E0  00000000 00000000 00000000 00000000   00000000 00000000 00000000 00000000   *..............................*  000A09E0
   0A00  00000000 00000000 00000000 00000000   000A0A2C 00000000 8095A970 00000000   *...................NZ...*  000A0A00
   0A20  00000000 00000000 00000000 C4C6C8E2   D2E3E2D2 00000000 00000000 00000000   *............DFHSKTSK...........*  000A0A20
   0A40  00000000 00000048 00000000 00010000   00000000 00000000 00000000 00000000   *..............................*  000A0A40
   0A60  00000000 00000000 00000000 00000000   00000000 00000000 00000000 00000000   *..............................*  000A0A60
   0A80  -     0BFF LINES SAME AS ABOVE                                                                                     000A0A80
   0C00  00000000 00000000 8A040C08 000A0000                                         *................      *  000A0C00

LIFO AT 000A0878 OWNED BY DFHSKC   / LINK REG. OFFSET 07186E

   0000  480001E8 000A0810 FF000000 009EFA56   00000000 0000A150 000A09A0 009F8230   *...Y..................B.*  000A0878
   0020  00040310 509EF9DA 009F09DA 000A0000   480001E8 00000000 00000000 0095A954   *....9............Y..........NZ.*  000A0898
   0040  0095A970 000A0190 009F6670 FE0A0A60   DE01E2D2 2097E238 00000000 00000000   *.NZ......-..SK.PS..........*  000A08B8
   0060  8097E250 00000000 9097E254 009F8E28   00000000 000A09A0 000A0810 00000000   *.PS.....PS...............PS....*  000A08D8
   0080  000A0000 8097E260 009F8E28 00000000   000A09A0 000A0878 4097E230 000A0810   *....PS-....Y............PS.....*  000A08F8
   00A0  00000000 000A0000 480001E8 00000000   00000000 0095A954 00000000 000A0190   *...........Y........NZ........*  000A0918
   00C0  00000000 00000000 8097E2CA 000A09B8   0095A958 00000000 9097E420 00000000   *...........PS......NZ......PU..*  000A0938
   00E0  0095A978 00000000 00000000 00000000   00000000 00000000 00000000 00000000   *.NZ...........................*  000A0958
   0100  00000000 00000000 00000000 00000000   00000000 00000000 00000000 00000000   *..............................*  000A0978
   0120  00000000 00000000 0095A978 0095A958   00000000 00000000 00A9E028 00000000   *..........NZ..NZ.........Z.....*  000A0998
   0140  000001C8 00000000 00000000 00000000   00000000 00000000 00000000 00000000   *...H..........................*  000A09B8
   0160  00000000 00000000 00000000 00000000   00000000 00000000 00000000 00000000   *..............................*  000A09D8
   0180  00000000 00000000 00000000 00000000   00000000 00000000 000A0A2C 00000000   *..............................*  000A09F8
   01A0  8095A970 00000000 00000000 00000000   00000000 C4C6C8E2 D2E3E2D2 00000000   *.NZ.................DFHSKTSK...*  000A0A18
   01C0  00000000 00000000 00000000 00000048   00000000 00010000 00000000 00000000   *..............................*  000A0A38
   01E0  00000000 00000000                                                           *........          *  000A0A58

LIFO AT 000A0810 OWNED BY DFHKCP

   0000  42000068 00000000 000A0878 0097E208   00000000 0000000C 00000000 00000000   *................PS............*  000A0810
   0020  00000000 00000000 00000000 00000000   00000000 00000000 00000000 00000000   *..............................*  000A0830
   0040  00000000 00000000 000A0190 009F6670   FE0A0878 F000D2C3 009F0C60 00000000   *................O.KC...-......*  000A0850
   0060  00000000 00000000                                                           *........          *  000A0870

┌─────────────────────────┐ ①
│ SYSTEM/USER TCA 0009B000 │
└─────────────────────────┘

   0000  8A040E28 000A9470 0009BF40 000B1BE0   C400811C 000502A4 00040000 00000000   *......M. ....D.A....U.......*  0009B000
   0020  00000000 0009F280 00000000 00000000   00000000 FE062A64 00000000 000AF5AC   *......2...................5.*  0009B020
   0040  000AC000 0009B530 00000000 00000000   00000000 00000000 00400000 00000000   *..........................*  0009B040
   0060  00000000 00000000 80000000 00000000   00000000 00000000 00000000 0009B560   *............................-*  0009B060
   0080  FE09BDE8 00000000 FE09B810 FE09BE28   009F8E28 0009B820 00000000 00000000   *...Y.......................*  0009B080
   00A0  0009E4B4 00000000 00000000 00000000   E4D4C7F1 00000000 00000000 0009B2A0   *..U..........UMG1...........*  0009B0A0
   00C0  00000000 00000000 00000005 00000000   00000000 00000000 00000000 00000000   *..........................*  0009B0C0
   00E0  00000000 00558008 00000000 00000000   D4C7F0F0 F4D4F140 00558008 5018FEFF   *............MG004M1 ........*  0009B0E0
   0100  00000000 00558008 10080000 00000000   00000000 D4C7F0F0 F4404040 00000000   *............MG004   ....*  0009B100
   0120  01000400 000502F4 000780F4 00000000   01000300 0009B214 00062A34 00000000   *.......4...4.................*  0009B120
   0140  00000000 00000000 0009B7B8 00000004   130AD7E2 C94BD7E2 C9C1C4D4 35CCF936   *................PSI.PSIADM..9.*  0009B140
   0160  5E2F0001 00000000 00000000 00000000   00000000 00000000 00000000 00000000   *;..........................*  0009B160
   0180  07E3C3C5 D7D9F0F1 40000000 00000000   0009B000 00000000 0109E4B4 009F6AD8   *.TCEPR01 ..............U....Q*  0009B180
```

Figure 13-10   CICS storage violations: TCA System/User area.

can locate this information from within the CSA and automatically display it within the IPCS session. Figure 13-14 contains the results of such a CLIST, and validates the task that PRDMP indicated as the currently active task.

Although PRDMP displays all "Task and User-Related Storage" in one section, it may be desirable to have just a quick look at task storage without seeing the actual contents of the data. These displays are extremely helpful, since they provide a snapshot of a situation, similar to the task summary in PRDMP. If, after reviewing the display summary, additional research is required, use IPCS to browse any contents of storage necessary. Figure 13-15 is the result of a CLIST that chases all storage chains for a particular task. This CLIST was used earlier in this chapter. The entries now contain the storage chain for the task being debugged. The transaction ID (1), and the task ID (2) have been previously identified in several sources. Note that one of the storage entries indicates a storage

type of 00 (3) with a length of 0000 (4), at chain address **000A9370** (5). This quick list of all storage created for task 00811 provides further information, since it continues the chain. Displayed are several items following the invalid entry; however, all seem to be intact. In fact, the last entry points back to the address of the TCA system area, **0009B000**. The mapping of all storage by the CLIST displays an entire storage chain, with only a single entry of four bytes corrupted. Of course, it is possible to have browsed the entire dump and followed the addresses manually. System programmers who have done this a couple of times quickly decide that automated commands certainly are a better way.

A number of entries have been analyzed within the dump, but none of them have proved conclusively which task caused the storage corruption. In fact, the storage could have been written over by CICS. Let's look at the facts. From the time that the storage was created until the storage violation occurred, no other task took control or was dis-

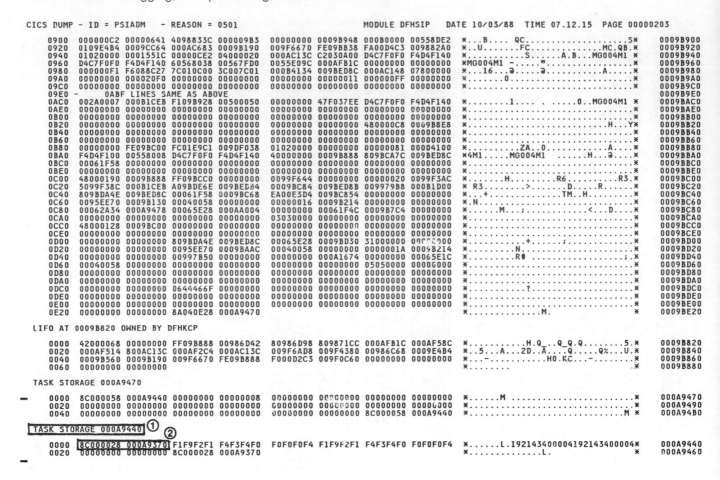

Figure 13-11    CICS storage violations: task storage.

Figure 13-12    CICS storage violations: dump contents at **000A9370**.

```
ASID(X'002E') STORAGE   ------------------------------------------------------
COMMAND ===>                                            SCROLL ===> PAGE
000A90A0.  8C0002C8   000A9000   F1F9F2F1   F4F3F4F2   . ...H....19214342 .
000A90B0.  F5F5F9F9   F9404040   40404040   40404040   . 55999            .
000A90C0.  40404040   40404040   4040E800   005F4040   .            Y...  .
000A90D0. TO 000A90EF. (X'00000020' bytes)--All bytes contain X'40', C' '
000A90F0.  40404040   40404040   D5404040   40404040   .        N         .
000A9100.  40404040   40404040   40404040   C6D3D6D9   .              FLOR .
000A9110.  C9C4C140   D4C9D9D9   D6D94050   40D7D3C1   . IDA MIRROR & PLA  .
000A9120.  E3C5F6F1   F0F140D4   89998194   819940D7   . TE6101 Miramar P  .
000A9130.  92A6A840   40404040   F2F5F5F9   F9F940F3   . kwy      255999 3 .
000A9140.  40F0F461   F0F161F8   F7404040   4040D489   . 04/01/87      Mi  .
000A9150.  99819481   99404040   40404040   404040C6   . ramar           F .
000A9160.  D3F3F3F0   F2F3F0F0   F0F0F3F0   F5F9F6F2   . L330230000305962  .
000A9170.  F7F5F5F0   40404040   4040C3C5   E640D340   . 7550       CEW L  .
000A9180.  D5D5F1D5   D5D5D5D5   40D5D5F3   C1D5D540   . NN1NNNNN NN3ANN    .
000A9190.  E8E8D5C2   F5F2D2C1   D9C5D540   E2D7C5D5   . YYNB52KAREN SPEN   .
000A91A0.  C3C54040   40404040   40404040   F9F9F9F9   . CE            9999 .
000A91B0.  F9F9F9F9   F9F94040   40404000   00000CF2   . 999999       ....2 .
000A91C0.  F5F5F9F9   F9404040   40404040   40404040   . 55999            .
000A91D0. TO 000A91DF. (X'00000010' bytes)--All bytes contain X'40', C' '
000A91E0.  404040D5   F0F4F0F1   F8F70000   0CF0F000   .    N040187...00.  .
000A91F0.  0C00000C   0000000C   0000000C   0000000C   . ...............   .
000A9200.  40000C00   000C000C   404040F0   F0F0F040   . .......    0000   .

ASID(X'002E') STORAGE   ------------------------------------------------------
COMMAND ===>                                            SCROLL ===> PAGE
000A9210.  00000CF0   F0F0F0F0   F040000C   000C0000   . ...000000 ......  .
000A9220.  000C000C   0000000C   000C0000   000C000C   . ...............   .
000A9230.  0000000C   000C0000   000C000C   000C000C   . ...............   .
000A9240.  000C000C   000C000C   000C000C   000C000C   . ...............   .
000A9250.  000CF0F0   F040000C   40404040   E3C3C5D7   . ..000 ..    TCEP  .
000A9260.  D9F0F140   40D5D500   0C000000   0C40C3C5   . R01 NN...... CE   .
000A9270.  000C000C   000C000C   000C4000   00000C00   . ...........  ...  .
000A9280.  00000CD5   F1F1F2F3   F3F8F6F5   F2F8F1F0   . ...N112338652810  .
000A9290.  D5D54000   000CD5D5   D5D5F0F0   F0F0F0F0   . NN ...NNNN000000   .
000A92A0.  00000CF8   F7F0F640   40000C40   40404040   . ...8706 ..        .
000A92B0.  4040F0F0   F0F0F0F0   F1F0F0F3   F8F8F1F0   .   00000010038810  .
000A92C0.  F0F3F8F8   C4C5C2D9   C140D340   E6C1D9C4   . 0388DEBRA L WARD  .
000A92D0.  40404040   40404040   4040F2F8   F0F140D5   .           2801 N  .
000A92E0.  40C540F2   F0F840E3   C5D9D9C1   C3C54040   . E 208 TERRACE     .
000A92F0. TO 000A92FF. (X'00000010' bytes)--All bytes contain X'40', C' '
000A9300.  40404040   4040D4C9   C1D4C940   40404040   .       MIAMI       .
000A9310.  40404040   404040C6   D3F3F3F1   F8F0F0F0   .        FL3318000   .
000A9320.  F0F04040   40404040   F3F0F5F9   F3F7F0F9   . 00       30593709  .
000A9330.  F3F74040   40404000   07A55440   40404040   . 37      ..v.      .
000A9340.  D6F0F0F0   F0F10000   5FC4C5C2   D9C1D3E6   . 000001...DEBRALW   .
000A9350.  C1D9C4C6   D3D6D9C9   C4C1D4C9   D9F1F9F2   . ARDFLORIDAMIR192   .
000A9360.  F1F4F3F4   00000000   8C0002C8   000A9000   . 1434.......H....   .
```

Figure 13-13   CICS storage violations: dump contents at **000A90A0**.

patched. Task 00811 was the only task executing, with CICS system code, of course. Nowhere in the trace did this task create storage that would have overlayed the address. Of course, CICS does many things behind the scenes, on behalf of the task. If no other task had access to this storage, it had to be the application or CICS that placed zeros into this SAA. If this storage violation was consistent, it could be possible to trace the process, and even turn on a storage trap. If this storage violation is not consistent, and may never reoccur, there would be no additional information to resolve the problem. The installation could, at this point, contact IBM with all the information discovered in the investigation. With the detailed description of the overlay and all supporting dump items, IBM may discover

```
------------------------ IPCS Subcommand Entry ------------------------
Enter a free-form IPCS subcommand or a CLIST invocation below:

===> |curtask|


-------------------- IPCS Subcommands and Abbreviations --------------------
ADDDSN,    AD    . DROPDUMP, DROPD  . INTEGER        . RENUM,    REN
ADDPROB,   AP    . DROPMAP,  DROPM  . IOSCHECK, IOSK . RUNCHAIN, RUNC
ANALYZE          . DROPSYM,  DROPS  . ISPEXEC        . SCAN
ASCBEXIT,  ASCBX . DSPL3270, DS     . LIST,     L    . SETDEF,   SETD
ASMCHECK,  ASMK  . END              . LISTDSN,  LD   . STACK
CBFORMAT,  CBF   . EQUATE,   EQU, EQ . LISTDUMP, LDMP . STATUS,   ST
CBSTAT           . EVALDEF          . LISTMAP,  LMAP . SUMMARY,  SUMM
CLOSE            . EVALDUMP         . LISTPROB, LP   . TCBEXIT,  TCBX
COMCHECK,  COMK  . EVALMAP          . LISTSYM,  LSYM . TRAPLIST
COMPARE,   COMP  . EVALSYM          . LISTUCB,  LISTU . TRAPOFF
COPYDDIR         . EVALUATE, EVAL   . MODDSN,   MD   . TRAPON
COPYDUMP         . FIND,     F      . MODPROB,  MP   . TSO
DELDSN,    DD    . FINDMOD,  FMOD   . NOTE,     N    . VERBEXIT, VERBX
DELPROB,   DP    . FINDUCB,  FINDU  . OPEN           . WHERE,    W
DIVDATA          . HELP,     H      . PROFILE,  PROF .


**** |ATCA005 IS THE CURRENTLY DISPATCHED TASK|
***
```

Figure 13-14   CICS storage violations: IPCS CLIST of current task.

another customer with a similar problem, and perhaps suggest maintenance already available to solve the problem. All storage violations are not resolvable, unfortunately.

### 13.1.4  Storage Violation Tools

There are some CICS-supplied transactions that may be of value when attempting to resolve storage violations. The transaction CSFE is the field engi-

```
IPCS OUTPUT STREAM --------------------------------------- LINE 51 COLS 1 78
COMMAND ===>                                                SCROLL ===> CSR
   ************************************************************
   TOTAL STORAGE ALLOCATED TO ATCA004 IS 4000 BYTES
   ************************************************************

ATCA005 TRANSACTION ID IS |UMG1,| TASK ID IS |00811|①②

   **  STORAGE CHAIN FOR ATCA005

       STORAGE TYPE      LENGTH      CHAIN ADDRESS

             8A          0E28        000A9470
             8C          0058        000A9440
             8C          0028        000A9370
            |00|③       |0000|④     |000AC000|
             |Error in Chain|
             8C          3B58        000A90A0
             8C          02C8        000A9000
             9B          0098        0009BFE0
             8C          0018        000B1B20
             8C          00B8        0009BE30
             8C          0108        0009B000
```

Figure 13-15   CICS storage violations: IPCS CLIST of task storage.

neering facility that can also be used by system programmers. This transaction can be used for debugging storage management problems, such as storage violations.

The CSFE DEBUG option can be activated to check both the FAQE (free area queue element) chains for CICS subpools and the user storage associated with the currently active task. If this facility is activated, it receives control before the CICS trace program returns control to the caller. If a storage violation is detected, a formatted dump is produced and the trap is deactivated. This debug option can detect storage problems at the time of failure, and trap all storage in a dump. Some storage violations can go undetected, and may only appear much later and be impossible to diagnose.

Of course, this facility is the most productive in the case of a consistent problem. When the trap is activated, CICS goes to a great deal of effort to evaluate the storage chains; this, of course, consumes resources. If this trap is activated for long periods of time and never traps the violation, it could impact CICS performance. It can, however, be a significant tool to assist in debugging storage violations. Refer to CICS Supplied Transactions, and CICS Problem Determination Guide for more information on this facility.

# CICS Dump Processing with DFHPDX

Previous chapters discussed formatted transaction dumps, formatted CICS region dumps, and unformatted CICS system dumps. Each type of dump has a purpose, and a place in the problem determination process. Unformatted dumps have been used very infrequently by many system programmers, mainly because there was no facility to take the unformatted contents and make any sense out of them. Some installations have written their own routines, or TSO command lists (CLISTs) to process the dump, to locate CICS control blocks and contents. IBM has provided a facility called IPCS to process unformatted dumps, but the product cannot format any CICS resources. There is now a facility in CICS to format both SDUMPs and SYSMDUMPs from a CICS release 1.7 and above. This chapter will explain how to use the facility, and how to interpret the output. Portions of the output from this facility have been used in several previous discussions of system failures. The output can be extremely valuable and save hours in analyzing problems.

## 14.1  CICSDATA

The command, or verb, in AMDPRDMP that requests CICS formatted output from an unformatted dump is CICSDATA. Before using this command in AMDPRDMP, two processes need to be completed. The first is to install the program, or exit, into a CICS loadlib for execution. The second is to make this command name known to AMDPRDMP.

The steps for each of these two processes is different, depending on the release of CICS and the release of MVS that the installation has installed.

## 14.2  INSTALLING DFHPDX INTO CICS/MVS 2.1

The instructions to install this facility can be found in the CICS/MVS Operations Guide for CICS/MVS 2.1. IBM incorporated this facility into CICS/MVS 2.1, so after installation of the product is complete, module DFHPDX will reside in the CICS loadlib. The only additional steps necessary are to define the verb, CICSDATA, to AMDPRDMP so that when executing the command it will correlate the program name to that command.

## 14.3  INSTALLING DFHPDX INTO CICS 1.7

IBM released the PRDMP facility after CICS 1.7 had been available for almost two years. In order to incorporate the function into the product, therefore, IBM shipped the facility as a PTF. The APAR PL18949 or maintenance from 8803 PUT level will apply the function into a CICS 1.7 system. All documentation to install the function, and utilize the product in a CICS 1.7 system is within the PTF cover letter. Since CICS manuals are not updated in CICS 1.7, any documentation change is made available via the service process (SMP apply of a PTF). The PTF adds the load module DFHPDX into the CICS load library for execution. For CICS 1.7 on an MVS/XA 2.2 system, follow the instructions in Section 14.4 to add the entry for AMDPRDMP processing. For CICS 1.7 on a prior release of MVS, follow the instructions detailed in Section 14.5. After the PTF for CICS 1.7 support has been installed and the AMDPRDMP facility has been changed, the facility is ready to execute. Follow the steps in Section 14.6 for utilization.

```
      EXIT EP(HASPBLKS) VERB(JES2)      /* JES2 analysis                */ 01850000
      EXIT EP(IATABPR)  VERB(JES3)      /* JES3 analysis          ƆP3C*/ 01900000
      EXIT EP(IEAVTREF) VERB(LOGDATA)   /* LOGREC formatter            */ 01950000
      EXIT EP(IEEMB817) VERB(MTRACE)    /* Master TRACE formatter      */ 02000000
      EXIT EP(IEAVNUCM) VERB(NUCMAP)    /* Nucleus mapping routine     */ 02050000
      EXIT EP(ISGDPDMP) VERB(Q)         /* Alias for QCBTRACE          */ 02100000
      EXIT EP(ISGDPDMP) VERB(QCBTRACE)  /* GRS ENQ formatter           */ 02150000
      EXIT EP(IARRDMP)  VERB(RSMDATA)   /* RSM analysis                */ 02200000
      EXIT EP(IRARMFMT) VERB(SRMDATA)   /* SRM analysis                */ 02250000
      EXIT EP(AMDSAFCM) VERB(SADMPMSG)  /* SADMP console message dump  */ 02300000
      EXIT EP(IEAVTFSD) VERB(SUMDUMP)   /* Summary dump formatter      */ 02350000
      EXIT EP(BLSQSUM1) VERB(SUMMARY)   /* Summary processor           */ 02400000
      EXIT EP(ASRSYMV)  VERB(SYMPTOM)   /* SYMREC symptom formatter    */ 02450000
      EXIT EP(ASRSYMV)  VERB(SYMPTOMS)  /* SYMREC symptom formatter    */ 02500000
      EXIT EP(IEDPRDMP) VERB(TCAMMAP) AMASK(X'00FFFFFF')   /* TCAM      */ 02550000
      EXIT EP(IEAVETFC) VERB(TRACE)     /* System TRACE formatter      */ 02600000
      EXIT EP(IKJVETSO) VERB(TSODATA)   /* TSO analysis           ƆD1A*/ 02637500
      EXIT EP(IGVSFMAN) VERB(VSMDATA)   /* VSM analysis                */ 02675000
      EXIT EP(ISTRAFD1) VERB(VTAMMAP) AMASK(X'00FFFFFF')   /* VTAM      */ 02712500
①     EXIT EP(DFHPDX) VERB(CICSDATA) /* CICS                          */ 02712600
/* ------------------------------------------------------------------- */ 02750000
/* TCB formatting exits--invoked in the order listed                   */ 02800000
/* ------------------------------------------------------------------- */ 02850000
                                                                           02900000
      EXIT EP(IECDAFMT) TCB            /* Data Management TCB exit     */ 02950000
      EXIT EP(IECIOFMT) TCB            /* IOS TCB exit                 */ 03000000
      EXIT EP(IEAVTFMT) TCB            /* RTM TCB exit                 */ 03050000
      EXIT EP(IEAVSSA1) TCB            /* Vector feature TCB exit      */ 03075000
/* ------------------------------------------------------------------- */ 03100000
/* CBSTAT exits--invoked in the order listed                           */ 03150000
/* ------------------------------------------------------------------- */ 03200000
                                                                           03250000
      EXIT EP(IEAVTRCA) CBSTAT(TCB)    /* RTM TCB status exit          */ 03300000
      EXIT EP(IEAVG701) CBSTAT(TCB)    /* COMMTASK TCB exit for WTORs  */ 03350000
      EXIT EP(IEAVTRCA) CBSTAT(ASCB)   /* RTM ASCB status exit         */ 03400000
      EXIT EP(IRARMCBS) CBSTAT(ASCB)   /* SRM ASCB status exit         */ 03450000
/* ------------------------------------------------------------------- */ 03500000
/* ANALYZE exits--invoked in the order listed                          */ 03550000
/* ------------------------------------------------------------------- */ 03600000
                                                                           03650000
      EXIT EP(IEAVESLX) ANALYZE        /* Supervisor lock analysis     */ 03700000
      EXIT EP(IOSVFMTH) ANALYZE        /* IOS I/O contention analysis  */ 03750000
      EXIT EP(ISGDCONT) ANALYZE        /* GRS ENQ contention analysis  */ 03800000
```

Figure 14-1    SYS1.PARMLIB member BLSCECT with CICSDATA verb.

## 14.4  INSTALLING CICSDATA INTO MVS/XA 2.2

This step applies to support for the PRDMP facility in MVS/XA 2.2. AMDPRDMP has a table called the Exit Control Table. This table must be modified to contain the CICS exit that will be invoked to format the dump. In MVS/XA 2.2, a new member was created in SYS1.PARMLIB. This member, BLSCECT, contains an entry for all AMDPRDMP control statements and IPCS verb exits. The member is created by the installation of MVS, and contains all verbs shipped and supported by the base product. It can be modified to add additional functions. Figure 14-1 contains a portion of this member. Notice that an item has been added to the end of the EXIT entries for the program DFHPDX (1). This entry defines the Exit Program (EP) DFHPDX to be invoked by the VERB CICSDATA. This is a very simple and clean way to add the function for

the exit. In older releases of MVS, the process becomes much more complicated. After installing DFHPDX into the CICS loadlib and updating the BLSCECT member in SYS1.PARMLIB, you are ready to invoke the program.

## 14.5  INSTALLING CICSDATA INTO MVS RELEASES PRIOR TO MVS/XA 2.2

In MVS releases 2.1.x, or prior to MVS 2.2, the verb exit table is in a SYS1.LINKLIB module called AMDPRECT. Since this module was created by MVS and no SYS1.PARMLIB member is available, you must modify the module with the proper information via a facility in MVS called SUPERZAP. This facility allows you to overlay the existing contents of a module with new values, and is docu-

```
//DUMPTJ JOB (,,9),SYS.PROG,MSGCLASS=X,CLASS=N,
// MSGLEVEL=(1,1)
//DUMPT    EXEC PGM=AMASPZAP                          00000040
//SYSPRINT DD SYSOUT=*                                00000050
//SYSLIB DD DSN=SYS1.LINKLIB,DISP=SHR
//SYSIN DD *                                          00000080
DUMPT AMDPRECT                                        00000081
```

Figure 14-2   Sample job to dump contents of AMDPRECT.

mented in MVS System Programming Library/Service Aids. The steps necessary would be as follows:

First, locate an empty slot in the table by running the DUMPT function of AMASPZAP. This step dumps, in hexadecimal format, the contents of the module that needs to be modified. Figure 14-2 shows a sample job to locate an empty slot in the table. Output similar to that in Figure 14-3 will be produced. This is a portion of the output of the DUMPT request. It displays the contents of AMDPRECT, from which you will need to locate an empty slot. Scanning through the output, you will see the first empty slot at location 0258 (1). These five fullwords contain the sequence necessary to reuse for the CICS exit. Insert both the command, or verb to use, plus the exit name for AMDPRDMP to execute. Remember how easy it was in MVS/XA 2.2, merely updating a parameter library? Well, instead, it is necessary to overlay the module with the hexadecimal representation of the same information. Not quite as easy, and definitely not clean. Figure 14-4 contains a sample job that would update the module with the information necessary. Identify the module name to ZAP, AMDPRECT (1). The next line is a VER, or verification statement to the program. Since it will be necessary to modify MVS operating system code, verification is first performed for the correct location.

The VER statement verifies that at offset 0258 into this module, the following contents already exist. If the VER statement does not match the actual contents within the module, the ZAP fails, and the modification does not take place. Assuming that the VER matches, the next line contains the REP, or replacement entries. In this example, we are replacing at location 0258 the hexadecimal entries contained in the five fullwords. The first two fullwords, C4C6C8D7,C4E74040, will insert the program name DFHPDX. The last two fullwords, C3C9C3E2,C4C1E3C1, will insert the command CICSDATA. As you can see, moving to MVS/XA 2.2 will provide a much easier facility to add entries into this table.

## 14.6   EXECUTING DFHPDX AGAINST CICS UNFORMATTED DUMPS

After following the appropriate instructions to install the program into a CICS load library and making the verb known to the AMDPRDMP facility

```
000160  C4E2 D5E6  C4D4 D740  C4E7 D9D9  D3D4 F5F0    0080 0000  C9D9 D3D4  4040 4040  4040 4040    *DSNWDMP DXRRLM50*
        CLC        XC         MVCK       MVZ                                MVZ   STH STH  STH STH    *....IRLM        *
000180  4040 4040  0000 0000  4040 4040  4040 4040    C1C4 E8C8  C4C6 D4E3  0400 0000  C4C1 C5C4    *     ....        *
        STH STH               STH STH    STH STH                      SPM                           *ADYHDFMT....DAED*
0001A0  C1E3 C140  C9C5 C5D4  C2F8 F1F7  0000 0000    D4E3 D9C1  C3C5 4040  C2D3 E2D8  E2E4 D4F1    *ATA IEEMB817....*
                              MVO                     NC   MVCK       STH                    NC     *MTRACE  BLSQSUM1*
0001C0  0000 0000  E2E4 D4D4  C1D9 E840  C1D4 C4E2    C1C6 C3D4  0000 0000  E2C1 C4D4  D7D4 E2C7    *....SUMMARY AMDS*
                        NC                                                             XC           *AFCM....SADMPMSG*
0001E0  C9C5 C4D7  D9C4 D4D7  0080 0000  E3C3 C1D4    D4C1 D740  C9C1 E3C1  C2D7 D940  0080 0000    *IEDPRDMP....TCAM*
                   MVCK NC                            NC   XC              MVCK                      *MAP IATABPR ....*
000200  D1C5 E2F3  4040 4040  C9C5 C1E5  E2E2 C1F1    8000 0000  4040 4040  4040 4040  C8C1 E2D7    *JES3    IEAVSSA1*
        MVN        STH STH                            SSM        STH STH    STH STH                  *....        HASP*
000220  C2D3 D2E2  0000 0000  D1C5 E2F2  4040 4040    C1E5 C6D9  C4C6 D4E3  0000 0000  C1E5 D4C4    *BLKS....JES2    *
        MVC                   MVN        STH STH                       NC                            *AVFRDFMT....AVMD*
000240  C1E3 C140  C9D2 D1E5  C5E3 E2D6  0000 0000    E3E2 D6C4  C1E3 C140  4040 4040  4040 4040    *ATA IKJVETSO....*
                        MVN                                 OC              STH STH    STH STH       *TSODATA         *
000260  0000 0000  4040 4040  4040 4040  4040 4040    4040 4040  0000 0000  4040 4040  4040 4040 ①  *....            *
                   STH STH    STH STH                 STH STH               STH STH    STH STH       *                *
000280  4040 4040  4040 4040  0000 0000  4040 4040    4040 4040  0000 0000                           *    ....        *
        STH STH    STH STH               STH STH      STH STH                                        *                *
```

**CCHHR- 0056000A06    RECORD LENGTH- 000000       MEMBER NAME  AMDPRECT

AMA113I COMPLETED DUMP REQUIREMENTS

AMA100I AMASPZAP PROCESSING COMPLETED

Figure 14-3   DUMPT output of AMDPRECT.

```
//ZAPJOB JOB (,,9),SYS.PROG,MSGCLASS=X,CLASS=N,
// MSGLEVEL=(1,1)
//ZAPCICS EXEC PGM=AMASPZAP                                              00000040
//SYSPRINT DD SYSOUT=*                                                   00000050
//SYSLIB DD DSN=SYS1.LINKLIB,DISP=SHR
//SYSIN DD *                                                             00000080
NAME AMDPRECT ①                                                         00000081
VER  0258 40404040,40404040,00000000,40404040,40404040                  00000085
REP  0258 C4C6C8D7,C4E74040,00000000,C3C9C3E2,C4C1E3C1                   00000087
```

Figure 14-4    Sample job to ZAP AMDPRECT with CICSDATA verb.

in MVS, using this product is as easy as running a batch job with the appropriate JCL. Of course, AMDPRDMP is fully documented in the IBM manual, Service Aids. However, since the MVS manual knows nothing about the additional verb, it will not contain instructions on how to execute the instructions. Figure 14-5 contains the CICSDATA command and the available parameters. The parameters merely request additional control blocks in the CICS dump. Utilize the parameter for the appropriate CICS data area, and it will appear in the output listing. If the command CICSDATA is used with no options, all available control blocks are reported. If analyzing a problem dealing with terminal failures, you may wish to request only the data areas relevant to that problem. Depending on the size of the region, and therefore the amount of storage that was dumped, the output from this job can be significant. Choose the output that will be most relevant to your problem. If you are diagnosing a difficult or unknown problem, you will probably decide to request everything. The amount of lines produced are still insignificant compared to printing the complete unformatted dump.

Figure 14-6 contains a sample job to invoke this facility. Of course, the JCL will vary based on the installations naming conventions. The most critical items in this job are the STEPLIB dataset containing the CICS module, and the dataset pointing to the unformatted dump (1). This dataset must be the SYS1.DUMP dataset or the SYSMDUMP dataset containing the unformatted dump. After executing this job, the output listing will contain the CICS data areas requested from the options. Following are several examples of the output created by this facility.

Figure 14-7 contains the first page of output from DFHPDX. Prior to this page in the listing will be several pages from AMDPRDMP; however, most of the contents pertain to the result of processing the

JOB = jobname/CURRENT

| | |
|---|---|
| PCT | PROGRAM CONTROL TABLE |
| PPT | PROCESSING PROGRAM TABLE |
| SCP | STORAGE CONTROL PROGRAM CHAINS |
| MCT | MONITOR CONTROL TABLE |
| DLI | DLI INTERFACE AND CONTROL BLOCKS |
| KCP | TASK SUMMARY, DISPATCHER QUEUES AND ENQ BLOCKS |
| TSP | TEMPORARY STORAGE QUEUES |
| ICE | INTERVAL CONTROL ELEMENTS |
| FCT | VSAM SUBTASK AND FILE CONTROL TABLE |
| TCT | TERMINAL CONTROL TABLE AND ENTRIES |
| MRO | MULTIPLE REGION OPERATION CONTROL BLOCKS |
| TDP | TRANSIENT DATA CONTROL BLOCKS |
| XRF | XRF CONTROL BLOCKS |

Figure 14-5    PRDMP control keywords.

```
//CICSDATA JOB (,,,9999),SYS-PROG,CLASS=N,MSGCLASS=X
//*                                                                     00000002
//* FOR PRINTING SYSMDUMPS AND SYS1.DUMPXX WITH CICS EXIT              00000003
//*                                                                     00000004
//PRINT     EXEC PGM=IKJEFT01,PARM=AMDPRDMP
//STEPLIB DD DSN=CICS210.LOAD,DISP=SHR
//SYSPRINT DD SYSOUT=*
//INDEX     DD SYSOUT=*                                                 00000008
//SYSUT1    DD SPACE=(CYL,(50,10)),UNIT=SYSDA
//SYSTSPRT DD DUMMY                                                     00000010
//SYSTSIN   DD DUMMY                                                    00000011
//SYSIN     DD *                                                        00000012
  CICSDATA KCP
  END                          (1)                                      00000170
//TAPE      DD DSN=SYS1.DUMP00,DISP=SHR
//                                                                      00000190
```

Figure 14-6 Sample job to execute CICS formatted dump program.

```
      (1)                                                        (2)                (3)
CICS TEST                                                 MODULE IEAVTSDT DATE 11/03/88  TIME 08.49.24  PAGE 00000004
-- FORMATTING CONTROL BLOCKS FOR JOB CICS21TS
 REGISTERS 0-15 00A93050

    0000   00000001 FFFF58C4 005D4230 005D2EE0  005CD948 005CE948 0052EDE8 00000001  *.......D.)...)...*R..*Z....Y....*   00A93050
    0020   0000A73C 0053D348 00000000 005877D8  005D4130 005D2670 00000000 80ABA130  *..X...L........Q.)...)..........*   00A93070

 DFHCSA 005D2670 (4)

    0000   00000000 00005F98 00031098 705CBA12  005D2FC0 00000000 FFFFFFFF 005D4230  *......¬Q...Q.*...)...........)..*   005D2670
    0020   FFFFFFFF 405CB9DA 005CC9DA 00000000  00000000 000B4000 0052EDE8 FFFFFFFF  *.... *...*I........... ....Y....*   005D2690
    0040   005877D8 00172000 0010020C 005D3150  0849239F 00040840 07D00100 00000000  *...Q.........).  ...... ........*   005D26B0
    0060   003077CC 00012C00 00ABA130 00006068  0000A000 00006000 005E1000 0088308F  *...............-.......-..;...H..*   005D26D0
    0080   005D4130 E8FFFFFE 0000001E 005D5888  000000D0 00000000 0003F030 E738E721  *.)..Y........).H...........0.X.X.*   005D26F0
    00A0   00000000 000402A0 000400E0 00040230  00040380 005D2EE0 005D3150 C500FF00  *.....................)...). E...*   005D2710
    00C0   000A0003 00000468 005D2AD8 00C800B0  00000000 00000000 00ABA130 00000000  *.........).Q.H..................*   005D2730
    00E0   405CB9D4 00584FF8 0057F4B0 005C1BA0  0054D30C 00587DA8 0057779C 005606F8  * *.M..|8..4..*.Y......'Y.......8*   005D2750
    0100   0056441C 00000000 0053D6AC 00531654  00000000 005C732C 015BABF0 00534960  *..........O..........*...$.0...-*   005D2770
    0120   00000000 00000000 005877D8 00569668  00560450 00446378 00063FF0 005D4C28  *...........Q..O... .......0.)<.*   005D2790
    0140   00000000 00531680 00000000 00000000  00000000 00530EA0 005D5838 00000000  *..........................).....*   005D27B0
    0160   00000000 00000000 00000000 5CCFBE60  0070FA1D 02000100 00000000 00000000  *............*..-................*   005D27D0
    0180   00000000 00000000 00000000 000071F0  00000000 00000000 00000000 005D2608  *...............0.............)..*   005D27F0
    01A0   07FE58F0 D19C07FF 00916766 00916892  00177000 000C0000 E6D6D9D2 C1D9C5C1  *...0J....J...J.K........WORKAREA*   005D2810
    01C0   00000000 001C0000 003C004C 00189C00  00492900 003B9700 00000000 00000000  *...........<.........P.........*   005D2830
    01E0   00000000 000C0000 0C000C00 0C00000C  00000C00 000C0000 0C00000C 00000C00  *................................*   005D2850
    0200   00000000 00000000 00000000 00000000  00000000 00000000 00000000 00000000  *................................*   005D2870
    0220 -       043F LINES SAME AS ABOVE                                                                                    005D2890
    0440   00000000 00000000 00000000 00000040  C100000C F1F16IF0 F361F8F8 001B6120  *............... A...11/03/88../.*   005D2AB0
    0460   0052D000 00000000                                                          *........                        *   005D2AD0

 CSAOPFL 005D2AD8 (5)

    0000   00000000 00000000 00530130 005505A8  005593A2 00000000 00582128 005821BC  *..............Y..LS............*   005D2AD8
    0020   00549AEC 00549498 00000000 00000000  00000000 00581A58 00000000 00000000  *......MQ........................*   005D2AF8
    0040   00000000 00000000 00000000 00000000  005409C4 00000000 00000000 005D4D48  *...................D.........)(.*   005D2B18
    0060   805D4D84 01F4F15B 00000000 0000FE00  00550138 0088308F 005774D8 005D2670  *.)(D.41$..............H.....Q.)..*   005D2B38
    0080   005D4E28 00584B28 0054D1A8 8220ACC0  00000000 00000000 00000000 00000000  *.)+.......JYB...................*   005D2B58
    00A0   00000000 00000000 005CF4CC 005D1798  005C0438 0057C6B8 00564158 00569018  *.........*4..).Q.*....F.........*   005D2B78
    00C0   00586E88 0057D2E8 005C2BE8 005CEEB8  005843D8 005C8328 0055BA48 0053D168  *..>H..KY.*.Y.*.....Q.*C.......J.*   005D2B98
    00E0   0054D0F8 005501E8 00551CA8 0055F768  00000000 00000000 005D2D80 005C4398  *...8...Y...Y..7..........)...*.Q*   005D2BB8
    0100   005B11F8 00584958 00584648 005B94A8  005B2C98 00000000 005BA66C 00000000  *.$.8.........$MY.$.Q.....$W%....*   005D2BD8
    0120   005AA8C8 005A39C8 005A05D8 00553E82  00554C72 0055DB22 0055C6A8 005585D2  *..YH...H...Q...B..<.......FY..EK*   005D2BF8
    0140   0055EF62 0055A162 00556D02 00553738  00557352 0054F478 0057E3FC 0000779C  *.........._..........4...T.....*   005D2C18
    0160   00536078 0059881C 00020BA8 005C330C  005C8508 00000000 00000000 005C9F48  *..-...H....Y.*...*E..........*..*   005D2C38
    0180   00538C08 005808A8 00000000 005C4C9C  00000000 00551D7C 00547E8C 0054690C  *.......Y.....*<........ə..=.....*   005D2C58
    01A0   0059D9A8 00000000 002CD008 00000000  00000000 0059CE48 00530E00 005D2E00  *..RY..........................)..*   005D2C78
    01C0   00534FB0 00078374 0000A000 0053D348  00000000 00531268 00000000 00040460  *..|...C.......L................-*   005D2C98
    01E0   00000000 00046188 000057B8 00000000  40000000 00000000 00000000 00000000  *....../H........ ...............*   005D2CB8
    0200   00000000 00000000 80C00000 0000A000  00453E68 C4D7C1C4 C3C9E200 00000000  *....................DPADCIS.....*   005D2CD8
    0220   0AD80AD7 00000000 00000000 00000000  00000000 00000000 00535DC0 00537000  *.Q.P..........................).....*   005D2CF8
    0240   9F5CCFB6 4C384400 9F041030 403AFC00  00000000 00000001 00006020 000A7420  *.*..<....... ............-.....*   005D2D18
    0260   00000001 80800000 00045008 40404040  8000DA98 00000000 00000000 00000000  *..........  .    ...Q...........*   005D2D38
    0280   00000000 00000000 00000000 00000000  00000000 00000000 00000000 00000000  *................................*   005D2D58
    02A0   00000000 00000000 0059CFB8 00000000  00000000 00000000 00000000 00000000  *................................*   005D2D78
    02C0   00000000 00000000 00000000 00000000  00000000 00000000 00000000 00000000  *................................*   005D2D98
    02E0   00000000 00000000 00000000 00000000  00000000 00000000 00000000 00000000  *................................*   005D2DB8
```

Figure 14-7 Formatted dump output: CSA and CSAOPFL.

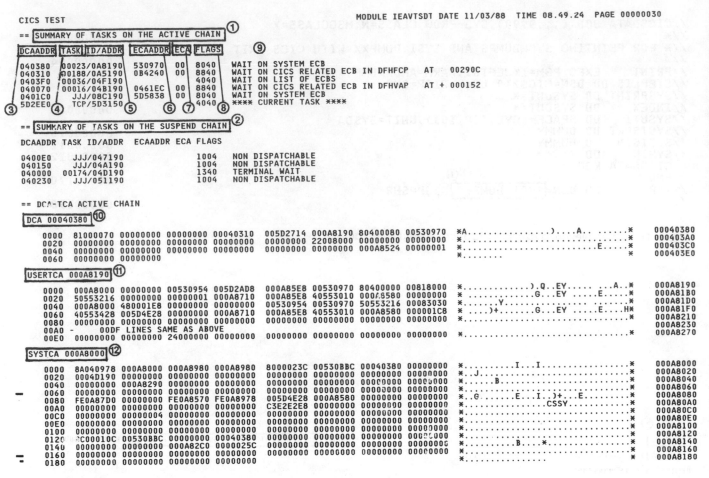

Figure 14-8   Formatted dump output: task summary and chains.

unformatted dump, and identity of the CPU hardware involved with the dump. Figure 14-7 contains the first page that would be relevant to CICS contents. Line one on every page will contain the following information:

1. Title of the dump, either keyed by the operator when requesting the dump, or the title from the SYS1.DUMP dataset.
2. Module in control at the time of the failure. The module IEAVTSDT is the MVS module invoked by dump control if the operator requested the dump from the console.
3. The time and date stamp logged at the time of the dump.

The first CICS control blocks listed are the CSA (4) and the CSA Optional Features List (5). These and other areas within the listing are identical to CICS data areas that could be requested by a formatted dump. Remember, however, that although the output is formatted, a complete dump of the entire ad-

dress space has been recorded. The areas displayed on this report are only a portion of the storage that is available within the unformatted dump.

Invocation of the CICSDATA verb will, by default, produce formatted output of the CSA, the CSA Optional Features List, the SIT, Abend Trace Table, Trace Table, Registers, and Static Storage. Using additional keywords will produce formatted control blocks corresponding to the keyword. For example, a request for KCP will also produce a task summary at the time of the dump and all active and suspend chains with corresponding user storage. The advantage of this facility, as opposed to a normal CICS formatted dump, is that requests can be made for portions of the dump that are relevant to the problem. Even a formatted dump of a normal CICS region can be a substantial amount of paper. This PRDMP facility provides selective format and review of control blocks, producing a much smaller report.

One of the most important pages within this formatted listing can be found far within the report.

Figure 14-8 contains a page that will be of incredible importance when diagnosing difficult failures. One of the critical pieces of information required in problem determination is the identity of the active and suspend chains. This information has been identified in previous chapters, and contains critical information pertaining to the failure. This example shows the "Summary of Tasks on the Active Chain" (1), as well as the suspend chain directly following (2).

Of course, IPCS can be used to locate pointers and chase these chains. Many systems programmers have done this themselves for years because no facility was available. This could, and has, taken hours to locate in a heavily loaded CICS region with many transactions active. This job can now be processed against an unformatted dump to provide a visual "look" at exactly what was happening in the region at the time of the failure.

The first summary identifies the active Dispatch Control Area (DCA) chain and some associated items (1). The items listed for you are:

3. The address of this DCA entry within the dump
4. The task number of the task, if available
5. The address of the TCA user area for this task
6. The address of the event control area for this task
7. The contents of the event control area status
8. The contents of the task control dispatch indicator
9. An interpretation of the above indicator

From these entries, tasks on both the active and suspend chain are available, with a small bit of information about each. This may appear insignificant, but can provide a wealth of information about the status of the region and currently executing tasks at the time of the failure.

Following these summaries is a complete listing of each DCA (10), the corresponding TCA User Area (11), and TCA System Area (12). The next several pages in the report will list the complete chains, both active and suspend. From these areas, it is possible to inspect contents of task control indicators to determine their potential relevance to the problem. This information, with minimal effort, can provide a quick snapshot of conditions and save enormous amounts of time in the problem determination process. Of course, if initial investigation proves to be inadequate, this information can supplement additional facilities. Since a full unformatted dump was recorded on DASD, IPCS can investi-

gate additional areas of the dump. The combination of DFHPDX to get a quick look at the problem and IPCS to investigate any other area of storage necessary, provide two powerful tools to debug many different types of problems.

## 14.7 INVOCATION OF VERBEXIT WITHIN IPCS

While the program DFHPDX was originally intended for batch processing, the facility can be executed from within an IPCS session. This may be desirable, since all functions for debugging are then available in one place, IPCS. In addition, MVS/ESA will require that all dump analysis be done with IPCS. The syntax to invoke the VERBEXIT may change with MVS/ESA, but the IPCS facility will be the focal point.

When DFHPDX is called by the VERBEXIT command in IPCS, this program must be available to the TSO session. Most CICS customers do not place the CICS load library in their TSO procedures. The module, then, must be placed into a library that is defined to the TSO procedure, or in a Linklist library. If the module cannot be located by the IPCS session, a message will be displayed indicating that the program cannot be found. The installation must place the CICS load library into the TSO procedure, or copy the module into an existing library. IEBCOPY can be used to move DFHPDX into the desired LOADLIB.

Remember, however, that moving DFHPDX into another library will require additional maintenance considerations. After updating CICS with SMP/E maintenance, this module may be enhanced or changed by one or more PTFs. SMP/E will update the module in the CICS libraries, but will not update that module in any other library. The new copy of DFHPDX will need to be moved into the alternate LOADLIB after applying maintenance. This step will need to be part of the SMP/E procedures when updating CICS.

After DFHPDX has been made available to the TSO session, the VERBEXIT command can be used within IPCS to execute the dump formatter. The syntax of this command is

```
VERBEXIT CICSDATA 'parm,parm...'
```

Execution of this facility with no parameters will utilize the defaults in the same way as a batch job. If a subset of the options is required, input the requested options into the parameter fields. In other words, if only a minimum of output is necessary, the following command can be used:

```
VERBEXIT CICSDATA 'KCP'
```

This will produce output of the CSA, trace table, task summary, and all task storage. Additional options can be chosen for portions of the dump required.

The result of this command will produce the report output into the IPCS session. The report will appear identical to the printed output produced by a batch job. It is possible, however, to remain within the IPCS session and scan the output. For example, the results of the previous command would display formatted control blocks, which could be inspected. The FIND command could be used to locate specific entries within the report. The IPCS session can scroll forward or backward through the report to locate necessary items.

If the IPCS session is using the standard message routing defaults, NOPRINT TERMINAL, the output is routed to the terminal. When the IPCS session terminates, the output is lost. If the information needs to be retained, the IPCS defaults can be changed to route the output to the print data set. IPCS allocates a file, IPCSPRNT to be used during the session. Some installations specify this file in the IPCS CLIST during invocation. Check the CLIST that invokes IPCS to determine the allocatiron. The routing can be modified with the IPCS commands OPEN and CLOSE to allocate the print output explicitly. If the IPCSPRNT allocation identifies the standard SYSOUT=A specification, any output routed to the print dataset will be released at session termination to this output print class.

You can, however, specify this output be routed to an IPCS browse dataset. If the following DD is placed into the IPCS CLIST, or specified in the IPCS OPEN command, output can be routed to a permanent file.

```
//IPCSPRNT DD DSN=IPCS.BROWSE,DISP=SHR
```

After this dataset is created, change the IPCS message definitions for the session with:

```
SETDEF PRINT NOTERMINAL
```

When the VERBEXIT command is used within IPCS, output will not be routed to the terminal, but rather to the IPCSPRNT allocated destination. If this is a permanently-defined dataset, the output can be browsed with ISPF. If routed to a SYSOUT, it can be printed for later review.

The dump formatting utility will continue to be a valuable tool in problem determination, and can be used in MVS/ESA within IPCS. The process is entirely supported in MVS/XA 2.2 and can be used with that release to gain experience with the function and syntax. Additional enhancements to both DFHPDX and IPCS will provide the tools necessary for debugging in future CICS offerings.

Since IPCS will continue to be enhanced, new function will provide even more reason to utilize this facility. Utilization with the existing version of MVS/XA will give customers the foundation to take advantage of these enhancements when available.

Since IPCS will continue to be enhanced, new functions will provide even more reason to utilize this facility. Utilization with the existing version of MVS/XA will give customers the foundation to take advantage of these enhancements when available.

# Acronym Glossary

**ABEND** — Abnormal End of a program, a software failure in the application.

**ACB** — Access Control Block, a VSAM control block built for processing the cluster.

**AID** — Attention Identifier, a field corresponding to a 3270 terminal function such as CLEAR, ENTER, etc.

**AMXT** — Active Maximum Tasks, specified in the SIT to limit the number of active tasks in the CICS system.

**AOR** — Application Owning Region, the address space containing the executing applications in a MRO or ISC environment.

**APPLID** — Application Identifier, the VTAM name for the application.

**APRM** — Application Programmer's Reference Manual for CICS programmers.

**BLL** — Base Locator for Linkage mechanism to address storage outside the working storage section of the application program.

**BMS** — Basic Mapping Support, the facility for screen manipulation within a CICS application program.

**CBIPO** — Custom Built Installation Process Offering, a technique to order MVS IBM products in an integrated package to reduce the number of installation tasks.

**CBPDO** — Custom Built Product Delivery Offering, a technique to order upgrades to MVS IBM products in an integrated package to facilitate the service process.

**CEMT** — The IBM CICS master terminal transaction to inquire, and change the status of most CICS resources.

**CLIST** — A TSO list of commands that can be executed as a single function, such as within an IPCS session; or, a condensed listing from a COBOL compiler output.

**COBOL** — Common Business Oriented Language, the industry-standard of programming languages in a business environment.

**CSA** — Common System Area, the main storage control area provided within CICS.

**DASD** — Direct Access Storage Device, on-line magnetic media storage such as 3350, 3370, 3380-type IBM devices.

**DCA** — Dispatch Control Area, created for each task and serves as a record of the dispatching priority and current status of the task.

**DCB** — Data Control Block, the MVS control block within which data pertinent to the current use of the data set is stored, such as record format, record length, etc.

**DCT** — Destination Control Table contains an entry for each transient data destination in CICS, whether intrapartition, extrapartition, indirect or remote.

**DD** — Data Definition, the JCL statement identifying the data definition name and the MVS dataset name.

**ECB** — Event Control Block, is used for communication among various components of programs after a request for WAIT, POST, or EVENTS macro instructions.

**EDF** — Execution Diagnostic Facility, the CICS facility to monitor a CICS application and diagnose problems within execution.

**EIB** — Execute Interface Block contains information of the transaction status during execution since it is built automatically via the command-level interface.

**EREP** — Environmental Record Editing and Printing Program reads error and other environmental records created by hardware and software components, and produces formatted reports. Software failures, such as DB/2 abends are recorded within this facility.

**FCT** — File Control Table, contains entries defining all files and other descriptive information about the file to CICS.

**FOR** — File Owning Region, the address space containing data to be referenced by applications executing in the MRO or ISC environment.

**GTF** — Generalized Trace Facility, can be invoked to monitor and create trace records of MVS facilities such as CICS, VTAM or DB/2.

**IPCS** — Interactive Problem Control System, the facility in MVS that provides online dignostics of software failures via unformatted dumps.

**IRLM** — IMS Resource Lock Manager, is used by both IMS and DB/2 to control access to data base resources.

**ISC** — Inter-System Communication, is used to enable CICS systems in separate mainframes to communicate with each other, or CICS systems in a single mainframe to communicate and share resources.

**JCL** — Job Control Language, the IBM MVS language for job control.

**JES** — Job Entry Subsystem, is used in MVS to control all peripherial devices such as readers and printers. JES manages the job as submitted for execution, and the output until purged.

**MRO** — Multi-Region Operation, is used to enable multiple CICS address spaces in a single mainframe to share resources. Typical MRO environments include a TOR, and multiple AORs and FORs.

**MVS/ESA** — Enterprise System Architecture, the most current version of MVS, starting with Version 3.1.

**MVS/XA** — MVS Extended Architecture, the first version of MVS to execute programs in 31-bit mode.

**NEP** — Node Error Program, used in CICS to control CICS-VTAM error handling and control processing at the time of the failure.

**OCO** — Object Code Only, IBM's direction to ship products in object code format without corresponding source code.

**PCT** — Program Control Table, contains control information for CICS to identify and initialize a transaction. This facility is currently replaced with the RDO TRANSACTION definition.

**PL/1** — Programming Language 1, an alternative programming language to COBOL that can be used in CICS for application development.

**PLT** — Program List Table, contains a list of programs that can be executed by CICS at startup or shutdown.

**PPT** — Processing Program Table, contains descriptions of programs and maps to be executed in CICS. This table has been replaced by the RDO PROGRAM and MAPSET definitions.

**PSW** — Program Status Word, contains execution status information pertaining to the instruction currently being executed by the operating system.

**PTF** — Program Temporary Fix, a change to an IBM product component, provides service capability after a product has shipped and been installed by the customer.

**PUT** — Product Update Tape, the facility IBM uses to provide scheduled service for installed products via PTFs.

**RCT** — Resource Control Table, used by CICS and DB/2 to identify DB/2 resources that will be used by CICS applications during execution.

**RDO** — Resource Definition Online, the recommended facility to define resources to CICS. As resources previously defined in tables are supported in RDO, table support will be removed. Eventually, all CICS resources will be defined via RDO.

**RSD** — Restart Dataset, the VSAM file built by CICS during COLD start, and continually referenced for resource definitions. This file becomes the critical source of information during emergency restart.

**SAA** — Storage Accounting Areas, the portion of CICS storage areas that chain that blocks of storage together and validate that the storage has not been corrupted.

**SBA** — Set Buffer Address, a control field in a data stream for proper mapping of data.

**SDSF** — System Display and Search Facility, the IBM product that provides information about jobs and resources within JES and allows the operator to control jobs, printers, queues and other system resources.

**SDUMP** — An unformatted dump produced by MVS as a result of the SDUMP macro, usually written to a SYS1.DUMPxx system dataset for later processing by IPCS.

**SF** — Start Field, a control field in a data stream to identify the start of a new field.

**SIT** — System Initialization Table, supplies the system initialization program with the information to initialize CICS with the selected options.

**SMP/E** — System Modification Program Extended, the IBM product that must be used to apply service to operating system components and products.

**SPOOL** — Simultaneous Peripheral Operations Online, the facility used by JES to manage multiple input and output resources in a multiprogramming environment.

**TACB** — Transaction Abend Control Block, the control block built by CICS whenever abend processing occurs and contains information such as the PSW and the registers at the time of the abend.

**TCA** — Task Control Area, a control block created by CICS for each task that is currently within CICS. A task may have a DCA, but until dispatched for the first time, may not have a TCA associated with it.

**TCP** — Terminal Control Program, the CICS management module performing all terminal functions, and usually the highest priority task.

**TCT** — Terminal Control Table, defines all network resources to CICS such as terminals, connections, sessions, etc. This facility has been replaced with corresponding definitions via the RDO facility.

**TCTTE** — Terminal Control Table Terminal Entry, the control block built for each individual device defined to CICS.

**TCTUA** — Terminal Control Table User Area, an extension to the TCT for user accessible (and modifiable) data.

**TIOA** — Terminal Input Output Area, storage built to manage input and outbound data streams during execution of an application.

**TOR** — Terminal Owning Region, the address space containing all terminal definitions in a MRO or ISC environment, therefore the CICS address space that processes logons and routes work to other regions.

**TWA** — Transaction Work Area, an optional area at the end of the TCA which provides the application with unique storage for the duration of the task.

**VSAM** — Virtual Storage Access Method, the access method recommended by CICS for most non-database file processing.

**VSWA** — VSAM Work Area, the control block built by CICS file control for VSAM dataset processing.

**VTAM** — Virtual Telecommunications Access Method, the access method recommended by IBM for network access and processing.

**XRF** — Extended Recovery Facility, used by MVS and CICS for recovery of systems after failures for maximum availability.

# 3270 Error Indicators and Codes (Partial Listing)

**PROG 401 —** 499 Program Checks

**401 —** Invalid command received: or SFE, MF, SA with invalid alias.

**402 —** An invalid (out of range) address was received following an SBA, RA, or EUA order; or an MF order addressed a nonfield attribute location.

**403 —** Data stream contains (1) data following a Rd, Rd Mod, or EAU command was received or (2) invalid parameter following an SFE, MF or SA order or (3) a GE or RA order was received with invalid parameters.

**404 —** The data stream ended before all required bytes on an SBA, RA, EUA, SF, SFE, MF or SA order were received.

**405 —** An invalid copy command was received.

**406 —** An invalid command sequence was received.

**407 —** A valid command or order that was received cannot be executed because: (1) SBA, Ra, or EUA order specifies an invalid address or (2) write data stream ends before all the required bytes of

SBA, RA, EUA, or SF order sequence are received or (3) write E/W, EWA with Start Print bit set in WCC is chained to the next command. The print operation is suppressed.

**413 —** The attempted function is not supported.

**431 —** Chaining error.

**432 —** Bracket error

**471 —** Extended data stream function cannot be executed.

**472 —** Improper command sequence from host caused a read structured field state error.

**475 —** WCC had the START PRINT bit set, but was not the last structured field.

**498 —** Negative response received.

**499 —** Exception request.

All above program checks are related to data stream errors, and should be diagnosed and debugged with instructions from Chapter 6, Typical Application Terminal ABENDS.

# Index